THE NEW
AMERICAN
COMMENTARY

An Exegetical and Theological
Exposition of Holy Scripture

THE NEW AMERICAN COMMENTARY

Volume
10

EZRA
NEHEMIAH
ESTHER

Mervin Breneman

BROADMAN
&HOLMAN
PUBLISHERS

© Copyright 1993 • Broadman & Holman Publishers
All rights reserved
4201-10
ISBN 0-8054-0110-5
Dewey Decimal Classification: 222
Printed in the United States of America

Editors' Preface

God's Word does not change. God's world, however, changes in every generation. These changes, in addition to new findings by scholars and a new variety of challenges to the gospel message, call for the church in each generation to interpret and apply God's Word for God's people. Thus, THE NEW AMERICAN COMMENTARY is introduced to bridge the twentieth and twenty-first centuries. This new series has been designed primarily to enable pastors, teachers, and students to read the Bible with clarity and proclaim it with power.

In one sense THE NEW AMERICAN COMMENTARY is not new, for it represents the continuation of a heritage rich in biblical and theological exposition. The title of this forty-volume set points to the continuity of this series with an important commentary project published at the end of the nineteenth century called AN AMERICAN COMMENTARY, edited by Alvah Hovey. The older series included, among other significant contributions, the outstanding volume on Matthew by John A. Broadus, from whom the publisher of the new series, Broadman Press, partly derives its name. The former series was authored and edited by scholars committed to the infallibility of Scripture, making it a solid foundation for the present project. In line with this heritage, all NAC authors affirm the divine inspiration, inerrancy, complete truthfulness, and full authority of the Bible. The perspective of the NAC is unapologetically confessional and rooted in the evangelical tradition.

Since a commentary is a fundamental tool for the expositor or teacher who seeks to interpret and apply Scripture in the church or classroom, the NAC focuses on communicating the theological structure and content of each biblical book. The writers seek to illuminate both the historical meaning and contemporary significance of Holy Scripture.

In its attempt to make a unique contribution to the Christian community, the NAC focuses on two concerns. First, the commentary emphasizes how each section of a book fits together so that the reader becomes aware of the theological unity of each book and of Scripture as a whole. The writers, however, remain aware of the Bible's inherently rich variety. Second, the NAC is produced with the conviction that the Bible primarily belongs to the church.

We believe that scholarship and the academy provide an indispensable foundation for biblical understanding and the service of Christ, but the editors and authors of this series have attempted to communicate the findings of their research in a manner that will build up the whole body of Christ. Thus, the commentary concentrates on theological exegesis, while providing practical, applicable exposition.

THE NEW AMERICAN COMMENTARY's theological focus enables the reader to see the parts as well as the whole of Scripture. The biblical books vary in content, context, literary type, and style. In addition to this rich variety, the editors and authors recognize that the doctrinal emphasis and use of the biblical books differs in various places, contexts, and cultures among God's people. These factors, as well as other concerns, have led the editors to give freedom to the writers to wrestle with the issues raised by the scholarly community surrounding each book and to determine the appropriate shape and length of the introductory materials. Moreover, each writer has developed the structure of the commentary in a way best suited for expounding the basic structure and the meaning of the biblical books for our day. Generally, discussions relating to contemporary scholarship and technical points of grammar and syntax appear in the footnotes and not in the text of the commentary. This format allows pastors and interested laypersons, scholars and teachers, and serious college and seminary students to profit from the commentary at various levels. This approach has been employed because we believe that all Christians have the privilege and responsibility to read and seek to understand the Bible for themselves.

Consistent with the desire to produce a readable, up-to-date commentary, the editors selected the *New International Version* as the standard translation for the commentary series. The selection was made primarily because of the NIV's faithfulness to the original languages and its beautiful and readable style. The authors, however, have been given the liberty to differ at places from the NIV as they develop their own translations from the Greek and Hebrew texts.

The NAC reflects the vision and leadership of those who provide oversight for Broadman Press, who in 1987 called for a new commentary series that would evidence a commitment to the inerrancy of Scripture and a faithfulness to the classic Christian tradition. While the commentary adopts an "American" name, it should be noted some writers represent countries outside the United States, giving the commentary an international perspective. The diverse group of writers includes scholars, teachers, and administrators from almost twenty different colleges and seminaries, as well as pastors, missionaries, and a layperson.

The editors and writers hope that THE NEW AMERICAN COMMENTARY will be helpful and instructive for pastors and teachers, scholars and students, for men and women in the churches who study and teach God's Word in various settings. We trust that for editors, authors, and readers alike, the commentary will be used to build up the church, encourage obedience, and bring renewal to God's people. Above all, we pray that the NAC will bring glory and honor to our Lord who has graciously redeemed us and faithfully revealed himself to us in his Holy Word.

SOLI DEO GLORIA
The Editors

Abbreviations

Bible Books

Gen	Isa	Luke
Exod	Jer	John
Lev	Lam	Acts
Num	Ezek	Rom
Deut	Dan	1,2 Cor
Josh	Hos	Gal
Judg	Joel	Eph
Ruth	Amos	Phil
1,2 Sam	Obad	Col
1,2 Kgs	Jonah	1,2 Thess
1,2 Chr	Mic	1,2 Tim
Ezra	Nah	Titus
Neh	Hab	Phlm
Esth	Zeph	Heb
Job	Hag	Jas
Ps (pl. Pss)	Zech	1,2, Pet
Prov	Mal	1,2,3 John
Eccl	Matt	Jude
Song	Mark	Rev

Commonly Used Sources

AB	Anchor Bible
ABD	*Anchor Bible Dictionary*
AEL	*Ancient Egyptian Literature,* M. Lichtheim
AJSL	*American Journal of Semitic Languages and Literatures*
AnBib	*Analecta Biblica*
ANET	*Ancient Near Eastern Texts,* ed. J. B. Pritchard
AOAT	Alter Orient und Altes Testament
AOTS	*Archaeology and Old Testament Study,* ed. D. W. Thomas
ATD	Das Alte Testament Deutsch
BASOR	*Bulletin of the American Schools of Oriental Research*
BDB	F. Brown, S. R. Driver, and C. A. Briggs, *Hebrew and English Lexicon of the Old Testament*

BHS	Biblia hebraica stuttgartensia
Bib	*Biblica*
BKAT	Biblischer Kommentar: Altes Testament
BSac	*Bibliotheca Sacra*
BSC	Bible Study Commentary
BT	*Bible Translator*
BurH	*Buried History*
BZAW	Beihefte zur ZAW
CAH	Cambridge Ancient History
CB	Cambridge Bible for Schools and Colleges
CBC	Cambridge Bible Commentary
CBQ	*Catholic Biblical Quarterly*
CHAL	Concise Hebrew and Aramic Lexicon, ed. W. L. Holladay
CTR	*Criswell Theological Review*
DOTT	*Documents from Old Testament Times,* ed. D. W. Thomas
EBC	Expositor's Bible Commentary
Ebib	*Etudes bibliques*
FB	Forschung zur Bibel
FOTL	Forms of Old Testament Literature
GKC	Gesenius' Hebrew Grammar, ed. E. Kautzsch, tr. A. E. Cowley
HAT	Handbuch zum Alten Testament
HDR	Harvard Dissertations in Religion
Her	Hermeneia
HKAT	Handkommentar zum Alten Testament
HSM	Harvard Semitic Monographs
HT	Helps for Translators
HUCA	*Hebrew Union College Annual*
IB	*Interpreter's Bible*
IBC	Interpretation: A Bible Commentary for Teaching and Preaching
ICC	International Critical Commentary
IDB	*Interpreter's Dictionary of the Bible,* ed. G. A. Buttrick et al.
IDBSup	IDB Supplementary Volume
IEJ	*Israel Exploration Journal*
IES	Israel Exploration Society
ISBE	*International Standard Bible Encyclopedia,* rev. ed. G. W. Bromiley
ITC	International Theological Commentary
JAOS	*Journal of the American Oriental Society*

JBL	*Journal of Biblical Literature*
JEA	*Journal of Egyptian Archaeology*
JNES	*Journal of Near Eastern Studies*
JSOR	*Journal of the Society for Oriental Research*
JSOT	*Journal for the Study of the Old Testament*
JSOTSup	JSOT—Supplement Series
JSS	*Journal of Semitic Studies*
JTS	*Journal of Theological Studies*
JTSNS	*Journal of Theological Studies, New Series*
KAT	Kommentar zum Alten Testament
KB	Koehler and W. Baumgartner, *Lexicon in Veteris Testamenti libros*
LCC	Library of Christian Classics
LLAVT	*Lexicon Linguae Aramaicae Veteris Testamenti*
NICOT	New International Commentary on the Old Testament
NJPS	New Jewish Publication Society Version
OTL	Old Testament Library
PCB	*Peake's Commentary on the Bible,* ed. M. Black and H. H. Rowley
POTT	*Peoples of Old Testament Times,* ed. D. J. Wiseman
RB	*Revue biblique*
RSR	Recherches de science religieuse
SBLDS	Society of Biblical Literature Dissertation Series
SBT	Studies in Biblical Theology
SR	Studies in Religion/Sciences religieuses
TDOT	*Theological Dictionary of the Old Testament,* ed. G. J. Botterweck and H. Ringgren
TJ	*Trinity Journal*
TOTC	Tyndale Old Testament Commentaries
TWAT	Theologisches Wörterbuch zum Alten Testament, ed. G. J. Botterweck and H. Ringgren
TynBul	*Tyndale Bulletin*
VT	*Vetus Testamentum*
WBC	Word Biblical Commentaries
WMANT	Wissenschaftliche Monographien zum Alten und Neuen Testament
ZAW	*Zeitschrift für die alttestamentliche Wissenschaft*

Contents

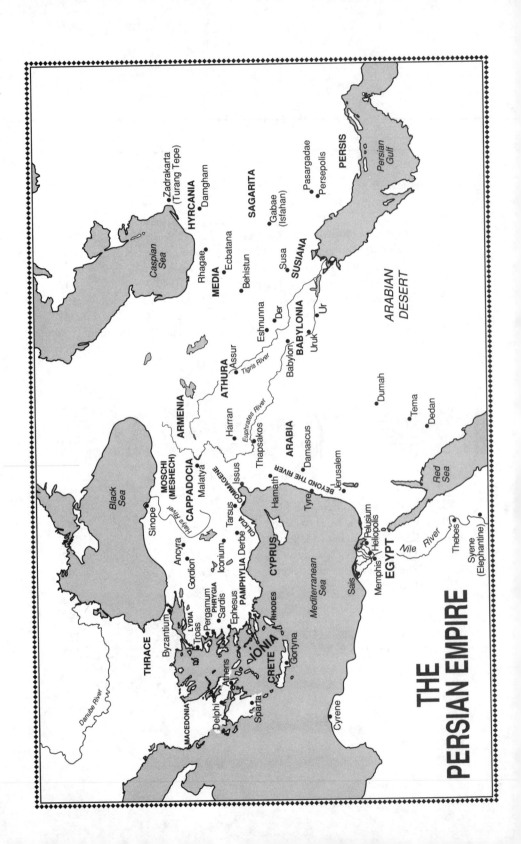

THE PERSIAN EMPIRE

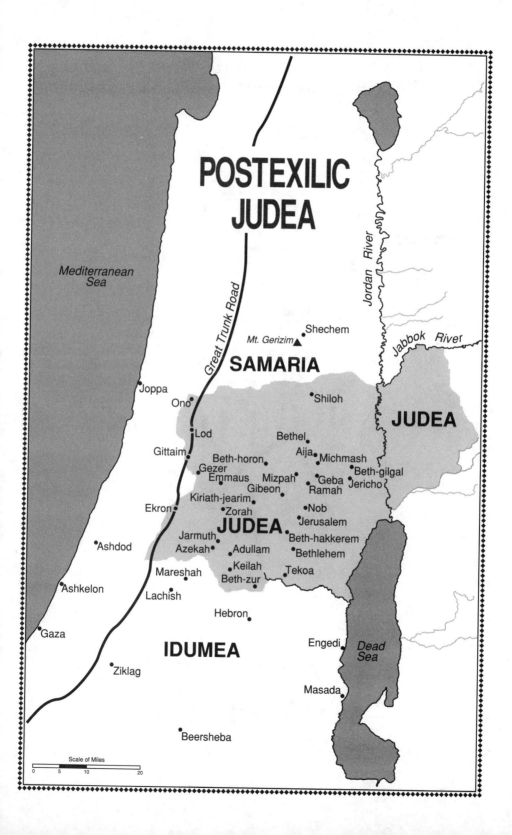

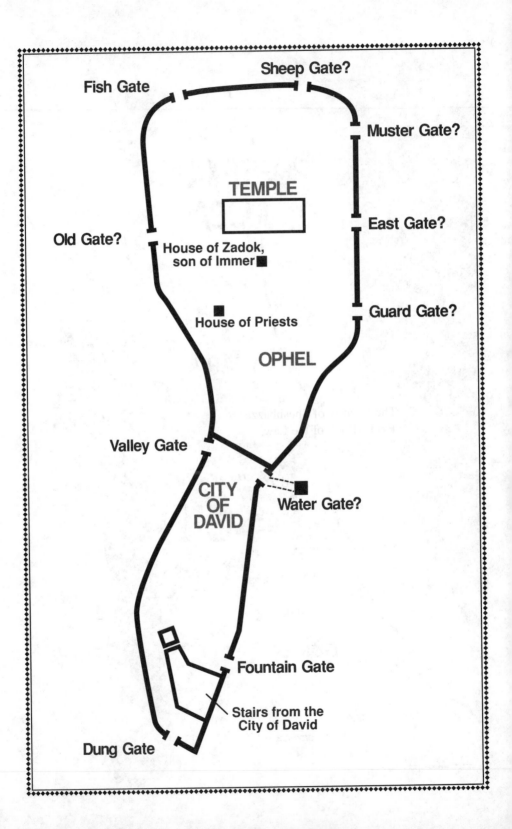

Ezra, Nehemiah

─────────── **INTRODUCTION** ───────────

1. The Historical Context—The Great Persian Empire

The Bible is the book of redemption. Its chief theme and purpose is God's great plan of salvation. But this plan of salvation is not some ethereal philosophy disconnected from daily life. Rather, it is developed within the history of humankind; and more specifically it centers on the history of one people, Israel. At the same time, Israel influenced other nations and was influenced by its historical context. Over half the Bible consists of historical narration; its authors emphasized God's acts in history. Therefore, to understand any book such as Ezra-Nehemiah (in the Hebrew Bible, they are one book, not two[1]), we must understand something of its historical context. The Bible teaches that the way God works with his people in one historical context, such as the Persian Empire, can help us understand his work in other contexts.

The Persian Empire replaced Babylon as the greatest power in the ancient Near East. All the events of Ezra-Nehemiah took place during the time of the Persian Empire. The Book of Kings describes the fall of Jerusalem to Nebuchadnezzar in 587 B.C. Jerusalem was destroyed, many of the Jews were killed, and most of the others were taken captive to Babylon. After Nebuchadnezzar's death in 562 B.C., the empire declined rapidly. Amel-marduk (the Evil-merodach who released Jehoiachin, 2 Kgs 25:27-30), Nebuchadnezzar's son, reigned for only two years; then his brother-in-law, Nergal-shar-usur, reigned for four years. He left a son whom rebels removed; and Nabonidus, of Aramean stock, became the last king (556–539). Nabonidus was not very popular in Babylon, especially among the priests of Marduk. He and his mother were devotees of the moon god, Sin, whose religious center was in Haran. Therefore he neglected the Babylonian religious ceremonies centered on the worship of Marduk. Nabonidus spent much of his time in the desert area southeast of Edom and left the affairs of Babylon in the hands of Belshazzar, as we see in Daniel.[2] The internal dissension resulting from Nabonidus's poor leadership made the empire ripe for conquest.

Both the Medes and the Persians were Aryan (Indo-European) tribes who moved south from the Urartian plateau from Russia. First they settled in the area of Lake Urmia (the northwestern part of Iran) but later migrated farther south. The Medes occupied the western part of Iran south of the Caspian Sea, while the Persians moved farther to the south-

---

[1] See the discussion under "Theories and Conclusions Regarding Composition."

[2] See the "Nabonidus Chronicle," No. 7 in the Babylonian Chronicle Series published most recently in A. K. Grayson, *Assyrian and Babylonian Chronicles* (Locust Valley, N.Y.: J. J. Augustin, 1975), 21-22, 104-11. A translation can also be found in *ANET*, 306. Also see A. L. Oppenheim, "The Babylonian Evidence of Achaemenian Rule in Mesopotamia," *The Cambridge History of Iran*, ed. H. Bailey (vol. 2, *The Median and Achaemenian Periods*, ed. I. Gershevitch [Cambridge: University Press, 1985], 537-45 for a discussion of the Chronicle.

east to part of Iran just north of the Persian Gulf.[3]

The Persian kings were called the "Achaemenids" after the founder of the dynasty, Achaemenes (700–675 B.C.), who was followed by Teispes (675–664). We have record of two branches of Teispes' family. One son, Cyrus I, ruled from 640 to 600 (?); and his son, Cambyses I, ruled from 600 to 559. Cambyses was the father of Cyrus I ("the Great"; 550–530 B.C.). After the reign of Cambyses II (530–522), Darius I ("the Great"; 522–486) took over the throne. But he was from the other branch of the Achaemenian family, through Teispes' other son, Ariaramnes (640–615?) and his son Arsames (590–550?), who was Darius's grandfather.[4]

The Achaemenid Family
Achaemenes
Teispses

Cyrus I (640–600)	Ariarmnes
Cambyses I (600–559)	Arsames
Cyrus I (550–530)	
Cambyses II (530–522)	Hystaspes
	Darius I (522–486)
	Xerxes I (486–465)
	Artaxerxes I (464–424)
	Darius II (423–404)
	Artaxerxes II (404–359)
	Artaxerxes III (359–338)

Until the time of Cyrus the Great, the Persians were vassals of the Medes. The Babylonian king Nabonidus rejoiced when Cyrus rebelled against Astyages and even helped him at first. By 550 Cyrus had defeated Astyages and taken over the whole Median Empire.[5] The nobles of both Media and Persia gave him their support and named him king of the Medes and Persians.

Babylon had reason to fear the growing empire to the north. Cyrus quickly marched across Upper Mesopotamia, conquering Armenia, Cappadocia, and Cilicia; then he attacked Croesus, king of Lydia, who was famous for his treasures of gold.[6] Cyrus defeated Croesus in 547, which allowed him to gain control over the Greek cities in Asia Minor. He then

---

[3] G. Widengren, "The Persians" in *Peoples of Old Testament Times*, ed. D. J. Wiseman (Oxford: Clarendon, 1973), 312-13.

[4] In the Behistun inscription, Darius says, "My father was Hystaspes, Hystaspes' father was Arsames; Arsames' father was Ariaramnes; Ariaramnes' father was Teispes; Teispes' father was Achaemenes" (E. Yamauchi, *Persia and the Bible* [Grand Rapids: Eerdmans, 1990], 70).

[5] J. Bright, *A History of Israel*, 3d ed. (Philadelphia: Westminster, 1981), 354.

[6] According to tradition, the first to invent coinage was the Lydian king Gyges (680–644). See Yamauchi, *Persia and the Bible*, 82, n. 82.

conquered more territory in the east into what is now Afghanistan; so the Persian Empire reached from there to the western shores of Asia Minor. It was only a matter of time before Cyrus would take over Babylon.

In 539 Cyrus ordered Gobryas, one of his officials, to attack the city. Babylon was quickly taken. Herodotus recounted a legend that the Persians were able to enter Babylon by diverting the Euphrates River, which ran through the city, into an artificial lake, thus lowering the water level enough for the soldiers to enter the city and take the Babylonians by surprise.[7] Daniel described how Belshazzar fell from power suddenly one night while he was banqueting. Xenophon corroborated this; he said the Persians attacked the city during a festival when "all Babylon was accustomed to drink and revel all night long."[8] Herodotus wrote: "The Babylonians themselves say that owing to the great size of the city the outskirts were captured without the people in the centre knowing anything about it; there was a festival going on, and even while the city was falling they continued to dance and enjoy themselves, until hard facts brought them to their senses."[9]

The famous Cyrus Cylinder is a clay barrel with a long inscription in cuneiform writing honoring Cyrus. It is mainly concerned with Cyrus's conquest of Babylon and apparently was written to influence public opinion in his favor and legitimize his rule over Babylon.[10] It is a long inscription that first tells of the misdeeds of Nabonidus and Belshazzar. Then Cyrus continues:

> Marduk . . . scanned and looked (through) all the countries, searching for a righteous ruler willing to lead him (i.e., Marduk) (in the annual procession). (Then) he pronounced the name of Cyrus (Ku-ra-as), king of Anshan, declared him . . . to be(come) the ruler of all the world.

Further on he spoke of Der and the region of the Gutians and said:

> I returned to (these) sacred cities on the other side of the Tigris [i.e., to the east], the sanctuaries of which have been ruins for a long time, the images which (used) to live therein and established for them permanent sanctuaries. I (also) gathered all their (former) inhabitants and returned (to them) their habitations. Furthermore, I resettled upon the command of Marduk, the great lord, all the gods of Sumer and Akkad whom Nabonidus has

---

[7] Herodotus 1.189-91. M. Mallowan ("Cyrus the Great [558–529 B.C.]" in *The Cambridge History of Iran* [Cambridge: University Press, 1985], 2.411-12) suggests that the Jews in Babylon may have aided the Persian entry.

[8] Xenophon, *Cyropaedia*, 7.5.15.

[9] 1.191

[10] See Yamauchi, *Persia and the Bible*, 88.

brought into Babylon (Su.an.na^{ki}) to the anger of the lord of the gods, unharmed, in their (former) chapels, the places which make them happy.[11]

Although the inscription does not refer to the restoration of foreign temples, Cyrus's decree recorded in Ezra 1:1-4 and the memorandum of it in Ezra 6:3-5 appear to reflect a general policy. He authorized funds to subsidize rebuilding the temple; but rather than an image, Cyrus returned to the Jerusalem temple the precious vessels Nebuchadnezzar had taken.[12]

The Persian Empire now included all of Babylon and Syria-Palestine. Although not mentioned in the Bible, Cyrus's son Cambyses (530–522) conquered Egypt in 525 B.C., making the Persian Empire greater than its predecessors.

Cambyses is considered to have been less benevolent than Cyrus; in fact, some considered him very much a tyrant. His conquest of Egypt was his greatest accomplishment. He also controlled the Libyans, west of Egypt, and even planned to take Carthage (the Phoenician colony that later fought with and almost conquered Rome); but the Phoenicians in his navy would not cooperate.[13] Cambyses also failed in a campaign to conquer Ethiopia.[14]

In 522 Cambyses received bad news from Persia: someone impersonating his brother Bardiya (Smerdis in Greek) had taken over the Persian government. Cambyses had earlier ordered his brother murdered so this would not happen. Cambyses hurried to return to Persia. But according to Herodotus, on his way through Syria, "as he was springing into the saddle, the cap fell off the sheath of his sword, exposing the blade, which pierced his thigh."[15] Whether the story is true (another is that he commit-

---

[11] *ANET*, 315-16.

[12] See the comments at Ezra 1. Cyrus's consistent policy was to restore foreign cult centers destroyed by the Babylonians and to grant dispersed peoples permission to return to their homelands. We have evidence of Persian support for the rebuilding of the Jewish temple at Elephantine (from the Elephantine texts), Cyrus's repairing of the Eanna temple at Uruk, and the Enunmah temple at Ur. Later, Cambyses authorized funds for the temple at Sais and the Amon temple at Hibis in Egypt. See Yamauchi, *Persia and the Bible*, 91; H. Jagersma, *A History of Israel in the Old Testament Period* [Philadelphia: Fortress, 1983], 193-94; Mallowan, "Cyrus the Great," 2.412-15. A. Kuhrt ("The Cyrus Cylinder and the Achaemenid Imperial Policy," *JSOT* 25 [1983]: 92-93) points to the text as an example of Cyrus's ability "to legitimize his conquest of Babylonia by manipulating local traditions. . . . He followed a policy similar to that of some earlier Assyrian rulers, whereby cities occupying a key-position in troublesome areas . . . had their privileges and/or exempt status reinstated and guaranteed by the central government."

[13] Yamauchi, *Persia and the Bible*, 110.

[14] Ibid., 115.

[15] Herodotus 3.64.

ted suicide), Cambyses evidently was wounded, gangrene set in, and three weeks later he died.[16]

Meanwhile at Susa the usurpers were killed by a group of seven conspirators. Finally Darius, one of the conspirators, was named king. This was Darius I ("the Great"; 522–486) from the other branch of the Achaemenian family mentioned earlier.[17] He endeavored to follow the policies of Cyrus in being benevolent to his subjects. Under him the Persian Empire reached its greatest power and most efficient organization.[18] Darius left many inscriptions telling about his exploits. The longest and most famous is the Behistun Inscription carved on a huge rock formation on the principal route that led from Mesopotamia to the Iranian plateau. The inscription was carved on a sheer cliff, 225 feet above the plain. It also includes reliefs of Darius, some officials, and some subjects. The texts cover an area twenty-three feet high and fifty-nine feet wide and are written in three languages: Elamite, Akkadian, and Old Persian. All three are written in syllabic signs of the cuneiform script. Darius also had the contents of the inscription distributed in different languages throughout his empire.[19]

During Darius I's reign, the construction of the temple in Jerusalem was resumed and completed (Ezra 5–6). As we will see in Ezra 4–5, the Jews' work on the temple had been halted because of the opposition of their neighbors. Cambyses apparently had supported the opposition. In Ezra 6 the Jews informed Darius that Cyrus himself had authorized the building of the temple. Darius searched the archives, found that it was true, so he again authorized the construction and commanded the opposition to cease. This was at nearly the same time that Darius planned to go to Egypt to settle unrest there. Merrill states that "no doubt [Darius's] itinerary through Palestine had something to do with the alacrity with which his wishes were implemented."[20]

At the same time, in 520 B.C., God raised up the prophets Haggai and Zechariah, who exhorted the people to renew the work on the temple.

---

[16] J. M. Cook, *The Persian Empire* (London: J. M. Dent & Sons, 1983), 50.

[17] On Darius's rise to power see R. N. Frye, *The History of Ancient Iran* (München: C. H. Beck'sche, 1984), 98-106.

[18] See R. Ghirshman, *Iran: From the Earliest Times to the Islamic Conquest* (Baltimore: Penguin, 1954), 144-45; Frye, *History*, 106-20.

[19] This is indicated by texts found in Babylon and in the Elephantine Jewish community in Egypt. See Yamauchi, *Persia and the Bible*, 133-34; Cook, *Persian Empire*, 67-69. This Behistun Inscription was the key that allowed modern scholars to decipher Akkadian writing. Their success was due largely to the perseverance and courage of H. Rawlinson, an Englishman, who at risk of his life copied the inscription from 1835 to 1847

The people responded, God removed the opposition, and the temple was dedicated in 515 (Ezra 6:16-18).

The other aspect of his activity interests us because it shows the Persian king's interest in using the laws of their subject peoples to maintain order in the empire. Diodorus says that Darius was ranked by the Egyptians as one of their great lawgivers.[21] The Demotic Papyrus 215 of the Bibliothèque Nationale of Paris quotes an order given by Darius in 519/518 B.C.: "Darius decrees that the wise men among the soldiers, the priests, and scribes assemble and write down all Egyptian laws having been in force until the year 44 of Amasis (526 B.C.)."[22] A similar interest on the part of Artaxerxes I for the laws of the Jews may help explain why he authorized Ezra to go to Jerusalem.[23]

During Darius's reign, the Greek settlements in Asia Minor rebelled against the Persian Empire. They were brought under control, but Darius then attempted to take the Greek mainland. He was defeated at the famous Battle of Marathon in 490 B.C.

Xerxes I (biblical Ahasuerus; 486–465) had served as viceroy over Babylon for twelve years under his father's rule. His great ambition as

---

[20] E. H. Merrill, *Kingdom of Priests: A History of Old Testament Israel* (Grand Rapids: Baker, 1987), 490. The decree to continue construction on the temple was given in 520; Darius marched to Egypt in 519. Two aspects of Darius's activities in Egypt are interesting to note. One was the construction of a canal from the Nile River to the Red Sea. Herodotus reported that Necho II (610–595 B.C.) had started the canal but did not complete it "in deference to an oracle, which warned him that his labor was all for the advantage of the 'barbarian.'" He said Darius later finished the canal. This is confirmed by four stelae found in this area of Egypt that tell of Darius's work on the canal. It was some fifty miles long and must have been 148 feet wide and ten feet deep (Yamauchi, *Persia and the Bible*, 153). Inscriptions from the Middle Kingdom of Egypt (2000–1786 B.C.) tell of a canal dug by the Egyptians between the Nile and the Red Sea. Its location has been indicated by recent satellite photos (W. H. Shea, "A Date for the Recently Discovered Eastern Canal of Egypt," *BASOR* 226 [1977]: 31-38).

[21] Diodorus 1.954.4.

[22] This text was written during the third century B.C. (Yamauchi, *Persia and the Bible*, 150; Cook, *Persian Empire*, 71-72).

[23] J. Blenkinsopp ("The Mission of Udjahorresnet and Those of Ezra and Nehemiah," *JBL* 106 [1987]: 409-21) argues on the basis of an autobiographical inscription by an Egyptian official named Udjahorresnet that Cambyses also conducted cultic reform in Egypt in accordance with local traditions. This included "expulsion of foreigners from the temple precincts; elimination of all ritual impurities; installation of legitimate cult personnel; reestablishment of traditional religious observances; provision of the necessary support from the Persian government." Udjahorresnet, a priest and scribe, may also have been involved in the codification of Egyptian law under Darius. He concluded his inscription with a prayer similar to that of Nehemiah (5:19; 13:14,22,31): "Remember all the useful things accomplished by the chief physician Udjahorresnet!"

king of Persia was to conquer Greece. After quelling revolts in Egypt and Babylon,[24] he began long and careful preparations for the Greek campaign, which began in the spring of 480 B.C. After initial successes, conquering the northern part of the Greek mainland and burning the acropolis in Athens, Xerxes' forces suffered a naval defeat at Salamis. A series of military blunders and defeats ended in their withdrawal from Greece.[25] The events of the Book of Esther took place during the reign of Xerxes I. Also the accusations against the inhabitants of Judah and Jerusalem mentioned in Ezra 4:6 may be related to the political events at the beginning of his reign when Xerxes put down revolts in Egypt.[26]

The Book of Esther portrays Xerxes as a powerful despot. Herodotus relates many details that also show his hasty decisions and indulgent character. The Book of Esther begins in his third year (483 B.C.). Xerxes had exhibited his wealth and power for six months (Esth 1:4). He had invited officials from all over his empire to come to Susa, perhaps to plan his expedition against Greece. Then he presented a sumptuous banquet for seven days (Esth 1:3,5). On this occasion his queen, Vashti, refused to obey his order to appear before him and was deposed.

Esther became queen in the seventh year of Xerxes (479 B.C.; cf. Esth 2:17). This was after Xerxes was defeated in his Greek campaign. Merrill suggests that the plot by palace officials to assassinate Xerxes, which Mordecai uncovered (Esth 2:19-23), may have been a result of Xerxes'

---

[24] The Babylonian Empire (except Elam) had become a Persian satrapy that included the lands west of the Euphrates called Abarnahara ("Beyond the River" or "Trans-Euphrates"). After the Babylonian revolt Babylon was joined to the satrapy of Assyria; and Abarnahara, including Palestine, Syria, Phoenicia, and Cyprus, became a separate satrapy whose capital is still unknown (A. L. Oppenheim, "The Babylonian Evidence of Achaemenian Rule in Mesopotamia" in *The Cambridge History of Iran,* ed. H. Bailey, vol. 2, *The Median and Achaemenian Periods,* ed. I. Gershevitch, [Cambridge: University Press, 1985], 564-67). Palestine included such provinces as Megiddo, Dor, Samaria, Judah, Ashdod, and Gaza (E. Stern, "The Province of Yehud: The Vision and the Reality," *The Jerusalem Cathedra: Studies in the History, Archaeology, Geography and Ethnology of the Land of Israel,* vol. 1, ed. L. I. Levine, 9-21 [Jerusalem/Detroit: Yad Izhak Ben-Zvi Institute/Wayne State University Press, 1981], 12; 1982:vii), though whether Judah was a separate province before the time of Nehemiah is uncertain.

[25] A. T. Olmstead, *History of the Persian Empire* (Chicago: University of Chicago Press, 1948), 253-61.

[26] Yamauchi suggests that there is also an allusion to Xerxes in Dan 11:2 if the first three kings can be interpreted as Cambyses, Gaumata, and Darius. In that case the "fourth" would be Xerxes. "Three more kings will appear in Persia, and then a fourth, who will be far richer than all the others. When he has gained power by his wealth, he will stir up everyone against the kingdom of Greece." Yamauchi, *Persia and the Bible,* 188.

humiliating defeat in his attempt to subdue the Greek mainland.[27]

Like the other Persian kings, Xerxes was a great builder. Frye suggests that "perhaps never since the ancient pharaohs of Egypt had so many workers labored on the construction and embellishment of royal structures."[28] Cyrus built a great palace complex at Pasargadae, the first Achaemenid capital, and Xerxes dedicated much of his energy to the massive constructions his father, Darius I, had begun in the new capital at Persepolis and the winter capital at Susa (in Elam, modern Khuzestan). According to Ghirshman, "Xerxes translated into stone his intoxication with the power he wielded."[29] One of the huge buildings Xerxes completed at Persepolis was the great audience hall, the Apadana, which covered an area almost four hundred feet square. The main hall was a square measuring nearly two hundred feet on each side. The hall and surrounding porticoes held seventy-two columns each sixty-two feet high. It is estimated that the Apadana could accommodate a crowd of ten thousand.[30]

Although Mordecai had saved Xerxes from one palace plot, his reign of twenty years was terminated by another such plot. Artabanus, the captain of his bodyguard, plotted to take over the throne and assassinated him in August of 465. Xerxes' oldest son was Darius, but he was murdered by his brother, Artaxerxes, at the encouragement of Artabanus.[31]

So Artaxerxes I (464–424) became the next king in the period of Ezra and Nehemiah's return to Jerusalem. In 460 Egypt revolted against the Persian satrap Achaemenes, who was the brother of Xerxes. The Athenian leader Pericles sent a large fleet of two hundred ships to help the Egyptians against the Persians. In 459 B.C. the Egyptians with Athenian help captured Memphis, the capital of Lower Egypt, but by 454 Egypt was again under weak Persian control.[32] The struggle continued until the Peace of Callias in 448 B.C. ended Greek interference in Egypt.[33] Although Megabyzus, the Satrap of Abarnahara, led the Persian forces that defeated the rebels in Egypt, some believe he led his own revolt against Persia in 448 B.C. The evidence for this, however, is questionable.[34]

---

[27] Merrill, *Kingdom of Priests*, 501.

[28] Frye, *History*, 125.

[29] Ghirshman, *Iran*, 172.

[30] Yamauchi, *Persia and the Bible*, 346.

[31] Frye, *History*, 127.

[32] Yamauchi, *Persia and the Bible*, 250.

[33] In the year 445 B.C. Herodotus, after his journeys through the Persian Empire, recited his history of the Persian wars in Athens (see Olmstead, *History*, 317).

[34] K. G. Hoglund, *Achaemenid Imperial Administration in Syria-Palestine and the Missions of Ezra and Nehemiah* (Atlanta: Scholars Press, 1992), 126-27.

All these events in the west must have influenced the attitude of Artaxerxes toward the reforms and building projects of Ezra (458 B.C.) and Nehemiah (445 B.C.). He was very interested in having a satisfied, secure, law-abiding, and peaceful Jewish community. Yamauchi notes that Ezra's commission (by Artaxerxes) "to administer the Law to his people . . . fits in perfectly with Persian policy."[35]

The last century of the Persian Empire until its fall to Alexander the Great in 331 B.C.—under Darius II (423–404), Artaxerxes II (404–359), Artaxerxes III (359–338), Arsas (338–336), and Darius III (336-331)—appears to have been characterized by revolts and economic decline. Increasing taxation and the greed of Achaemenid officials were factors in the growing impoverishment of the people. Interest rates on loans were 40 or 50 percent.[36] According to R. N. Frye, "The traditional explanation of the fall of the empire as the result of abuses of their positions by those in power, the decadence and corruption at court and among the aristocracy, combined with a fall in the standards of living of the common folk, can be further documented by Babylonian tablets."[37]

(1) The New Policy of the Persian Kings

Before Babylon fell to Cyrus in 539 B.C., many of the Babylonians looked upon Cyrus as a liberator. They were not happy with the way Nabonidus had neglected their religion. The Jews also looked with expectancy on the political change, for Cyrus adopted a new policy toward his subjected peoples.

The Assyrians had been very cruel. They had harshly suppressed the peoples they conquered; many times they had moved entire populations from one land to another and then replaced them with other conquered peoples. This was the case when they conquered the Northern Kingdom of Israel in 722 B.C.

The Babylonians, although somewhat less cruel, followed much the same policy. Thus when Jerusalem was destroyed in 587 B.C., many of the Jews were taken captive to Babylon. When the Persians took control, however, Cyrus encouraged the peoples he conquered to develop their own culture and continue their own religion. He and some of his successors even helped support the local priests in conquered nations. After conquering Babylon, he restored the place of Marduk as their principal

---

[35] Yamauchi, *Persia and the Bible*, 256.

[36] Frye, *History*, 129.

[37] Ibid., 130.

god and allowed captive peoples to return to their homelands.

(2) Organization and Policy of the Persian Empire

The "political organization" of the Persian Empire was different from that of Assyria and Babylon. It reached its greatest development during the reign of Darius I (522–486 B.C.). The whole empire was divided into twenty satrapies. Each one was governed by a Persian commissioner or satrap, usually from the Persian noble families. These satraps were virtual kings over their satrapies. They levied taxes and provided troops for the king. But Darius also instituted a system of controls. One was the placing of imperial troops under a royal officer directly responsible to the Persian king. Also royal inspectors, called by the Greeks "the king's eyes" and "the king's ears," could check on the satraps at any moment.[38] The satrapies were further divided into provinces, which were supervised by a governor, usually a descendant of the local nobility. Thus in Judah we read of Jews such as Zerubbabel and Nehemiah who served as governors.

In addition to paying attention to the organization of the empire, Darius I standardized the money and introduced uniform weights and measures. In his time industry and sea commerce flourished. He also opened a canal from the Red Sea to the Nile in Egypt.[39] By the time of Ezra and Nehemiah some of these conditions had changed. The wars with the Greeks and revolts in areas such as Babylon and Egypt demanded policy adjustments from time to time. Thus Judah had its own coinage. Archaeologists have found a large quantity of coins and seal impressions with *yehud* (Judah) inscribed on them. This indicates that Judah had a certain amount of autonomy.[40]

Palestine belonged to the satrapy "Beyond the River," which means the region west of the Euphrates. According to Herodotus this was the fifth satrapy. It included Syria, Phoenicia, and Palestine to the border of Egypt as well as Cyprus. This is the first time the term "Palestine" is

---

[38] Xenophon, *Cyropaedia* 8.2.10-12; Herodotus 1.114. See also Ghirshman, *Iran*, 144; Cook, *Persian Empire*, 84-85, 171-76.

[39] M. J. Dresden, "Persia," in *IDB* 3:743; also see comments on Darius I above.

[40] E. Stern ("The Archaeology of Persian Palestine," in *The Cambridge History of Judaism*, ed. W. D. Davies and L. Findelstein [Cambridge: University Press, 1984], 110-12) explains that although the Persian government reserved the privilege of minting gold coins, by the end of the fifth century silver coins could be minted in the various satrapies for use in local business. See also J. W. Betlyon, "The Provincial Government of Persian Period Judea and the Yehud Coins," *JBL* 105 (1986): 633-42; U. Rappaport, "The First Judean Coinage," *JJS* 1-17.

used to refer to the whole country; it had referred before only to the Philistine territory.[41]

(3) The Jews in the Exilic Period

THOSE EXILED TO BABYLON. The Babylonian siege of Jerusalem in 597 B.C. and the first deportation, which included the exile of King Jehoiachin, are generally considered the beginning of the Babylonian captivity (2 Kgs 24:10-17; Ezek 1:2; 33:21; 40:1). In 587 B.C. Jerusalem was decimated, and the final deportation of exiles was led to Babylon (2 Kgs 25:8-21). However, Israelite exiles were already in Mesopotamia. In Jewish tradition they are known as "The Ten Lost Tribes." When the northern tribes fell to Assyria in 722 B.C., many Israelites were taken captive. According to 2 Kgs 17:6; 18:11, they were taken to Halah, to Gozan on the Habor River, and to the towns of the Medes. Although most of the Jews who returned later to Palestine were from the tribes of Judah, Benjamin, and Levi, some descendants of the former northern tribes probably were among the returnees.[42]

The Babylonians usually settled their captives in different locations in Babylonia in order to provide labor and economic growth as well as for the purpose of strengthening their agriculture (Jer 29:5-7; 2 Kgs 18:32). They also were taken to administrative centers such as Calah, Nineveh, Babylon, Gozan, and Nippur. Psalm 137 mentions the rivers of Babylon. One important Jewish population center was Tel Aviv in the southern part of Babylon (Ezek 1:3; 3:15) on the River Kebar, a river-canal that passed by the large commercial city of Nippur. It was from Nippur that a group of tablets called the Murashu Texts were found that shed light on Jewish life in the exile.[43]

Although those captured in battle probably were taken to Babylon as slaves, and many of the exiles were poor, after their recovery from the emotional and physical distress of being uprooted (cf. Pss 74; 137) the situation of most Jews in Babylon appears to have been good (Jer 29:4-7; Ezek 8:1; Ezra 2:65-69). Only King Jehoiachin and his family, captured in 597 B.C., were confined; and they were released in 562 B.C. (2 Kgs

---

[41] Y. Aharoni, *The Land of the Bible* (Philadelphia: Westminster, 1979), 412.

[42] Some Hebrew names appear in the Assyrian Kannuy contracts about a century after 722. Kannuy may be the Canneh of Ezek 27:23, which was near Haran (see P. R. Ackroyd, *Exile and Restoration* [London: SCM Press, 1968], 43). These must have been descendants of the Jews exiled at the fall of Samaria in 722.

[43] M. D. Coogan, "Life in the Diaspora: Jews at Nippur in the Fifth Century B.C.," *BA* 37 (1974): 6-12.

25:27).[44] The rest of the Jews were free to settle in communities and to engage in normal agriculture or trade, as indicated by the business documents from the fifth century Murashu Texts.

This important corpus consists of seven hundred tablets dating from 454 to 404 B.C., that is, during the reigns of Artaxerxes I, Darius II, and Artaxerxes II. The Murashu family was not Jewish, but many of their clients were.[45] Yamauchi declares, in fact, that "among 2,500 individuals mentioned in the texts, about 70 (approximately 3 percent) can be identified as Jews . . . Jews were found in 28 of 200 settlements in the region of Nippur. . . . The Jews appear as contracting parties, agents, witnesses, collectors of taxes and royal officials. . . . Eleven of some two hundred officials in these texts were Jewish."[46] Y. Kaufmann explains that there is every indication that in general the Jewish population in exile in Babylon experienced "economic well-being, retention of rights, and the maintenance of a certain degree of autonomy."[47]

It should come as no surprise, then, considering conditions in Judah and Babylon, that when the Persians allowed the Jews to return under Sheshbazzar and Zerubbabel and again in the time of Ezra and Nehemiah, many preferred to remain in Mesopotamia. Ezra 8:15-20 shows that as late as Artaxerxes' reign there were colonies of priests, Levites, and singers.

INFLUENCES ON THE JEWISH CAPTIVES. During the captivity the Jews lived among a foreign population and labored in such occupations as agriculture, commerce, and administration. They naturally were influenced by their environment. The most important influence was the Aramaic language. During the captivity Aramaic became their principal spoken language. At some time, either during or after the captivity, they also adopted the square Aramaic script. Babylonian influence is seen in names such as Sheshbazzar and Zerubbabel.

The prophecies of Jeremiah and Ezekiel greatly influenced the Jewish captives in Babylon. Before the fall of Jerusalem few in Israel heeded

---

[44] Texts from the royal palace of Awel-Marduk (Evil-merodach) in Babylon indicate some food rations to King Jehoiachin and his five sons (*ANET*, 308).

[45] Occurring among the names of those who transacted business are the Jewish names Yahunatan, Tobyaw, Banayaw, and Zabadyaw. The Murashu Texts were found in the University of Pennsylvania excavations at Nippur in 1893.

[46] Yamauchi, *Persia and the Bible*, 243-44. Nippur was located about fifty-five miles southeast of Babylon and a hundred miles northwest of Ur, on a canal between the Euphrates and Tigris rivers.

[47] Y. Kaufmann, *History of the Religion of Israel,* vol. 4, *From the Babylonian Captivity to the End of Prophecy* (New York: KTAV, 1977), 5.

these prophecies; but when the predictions about Jerusalem's destruction came true, the Jews realized that Jeremiah and Ezekiel were truly prophets sent by God. Both Jeremiah and Ezekiel predicted the fall and destruction of Jerusalem as punishment for the Jews' unfaithfulness to God (Jer 1:11-19; 4:5-31; 25:1-14; Ezek 5:1-12; 12:1-16); but they also included messages of hope for the continued purpose of God for his people Israel (Jer 3:14-17; 23:3-8; 30:1–33:26; Ezek 34:11-16; 36:8-12). This included a return from captivity and the promise of the Messiah. Although Jeremiah's ministry appeared to be a complete failure during his lifetime, his messages became one of the principal reasons for the survival of the Jewish faith.

Ezekiel's preaching also influenced the Jews in Babylon. Three themes appear throughout his book: worship at the temple, the land of Israel, and the Lord's people (e.g., 46:3).[48] This influence took lasting root because these truths are also important in Ezra and Nehemiah. Ezekiel also emphasized the preservation of holiness; purity and justice are the essential marks of God's people. "All this is effected by divine action and by that alone. The new life is divinely given (cf. chaps. 36–37); the reordered land is made what it is by God; the new temple is his building."[49] These themes continue to be important as will be seen in Ezra and Nehemiah's concern for the holiness and separation of the exilic community.[50] The messages of both Jeremiah and Ezekiel kept alive the Jews' hope of returning to their own land.

THE JEWS WHO REMAINED IN THE LAND.   After carrying away captive the best of the Judahite population, the Babylonians did not bring other peoples into Judah as the Assyrians had done in the north after the fall of Samaria, thus creating a population vacuum in Judah. The extent of that vacuum is disputed among scholars. No doubt some of the Jews who fled to neighboring areas found their way back in a few years (cf. Jer 40:11-12). Ackroyd thinks a considerable number remained in the land. The poorer people whom the Babylonians did not take captive then

---

[48] Ackroyd, *Exile and Restoration*, 111.

[49] Ibid., 115.

[50] Much speculation has occurred about the development of Scripture during the exile in Babylon. Many theories take for granted that the Pentateuch developed during the exile from earlier traditions. For a review of contrary evidence, see D. R. Hildebrand, "A Summary of Recent Findings in Support of an Early Date for the So-Called Priestly Material of the Pentateuch," *JETS* 29 (1986): 129-38. Some think the synagogue or at least the custom of gathering together weekly to study Scripture had its origin during the exile. This is more likely than the speculation about the Pentateuch, but again there is no concrete evidence.

moved into leadership and occupied the land.[51] Nevertheless, the conditions in Judah were very poor. According to D. E. Gowan, "There does not exist sufficient evidence or probability of an active, creative group in the land during the exile, although the continuance of some form of Yahwism is not to be doubted."[52] The temple site was still considered holy and was visited by pilgrims who continued to make sacrifices on perhaps a rebuilt altar (Jer 41:4-8).

The remaining population must not have been very large. Although Ezra-Nehemiah indicates that some people did remain in the land,[53] even almost a century after the first return Jerusalem was still sparsely populated (Neh 7:4). In addition to those deported, thousands had certainly died either in battle or of starvation and disease; many were executed, and many had fled. Archaeological excavations indicate that Judah was sparsely populated in this period. S. Weinberg claims that archaeological surveys confirm the literary evidence. Except for the Negev and along the northern frontier, virtually all the fortified towns in Judah had been destroyed.[54]

THE JEWS IN EGYPT. Since the time of Joseph, Jews had frequently looked upon Egypt as a place of refuge (cf. 1 Kgs 11:17,40; Jer 24:8; 26:21), although they were repeatedly admonished by the prophets not to attempt to find security there (cf. 2 Kgs 18:21; Isa 20:5; 30:1-7; 31:1; 36:6; Jer 42:14–43:13). It is likely that some migrated there following the fall of the Northern Kingdom in 722 B.C. The inscriptions of Ashurbanipal show that Manasseh sent troops from Judah with the Assyrian army on its campaign to Egypt.[55] Some of these must have been placed by the Assyrians in Egyptian fortresses. The Bible tells of a group who left Judah for Egypt after the fall of Jerusalem, taking Jeremiah with them (2 Kgs 25:25-26; Jer 41:16-18). According to Jeremiah they became involved in syncretistic worship there (44:1-30).

---

[51] Ackroyd, *Exile and Restoration*, 26-28.

[52] D. E. Gowan, *Bridge between the Testaments: A Reappraisal of Judaism from the Exile to the Birth of Christianity*, 3d ed. (Allison Park, Pa.: Pickwick, 1986), 37.

[53] Aharoni (*Land of the Bible,* 355-56) notes that in Neh 11:25-35 the list contains quite a few towns in the Negev and Shephelah that were outside the limits of postexilic Judah. He thinks this indicates a permanent Judahite population that had avoided deportation and had remained in Judah. He also suggests that groups of Israelites also remained in other parts of the country such as Galilee because in the time of the Maccabees large numbers of Jews were there.

[54] S. Weinberg, "Postexilic Palestine: An Archaeological Report," *Proceedings of the Israel Academy of Science and Humanities* 4 (1971): 78-97.

[55] *ANET,* 294.

This is supported by the Elephantine papyri, our primary evidence of Jews in Egypt in the Persian period. This collection of fifth century B.C. papyri was from a Jewish military colony on the island of Elephantine (Egyptian *Yeb*) in the Nile. The site was a frontier outpost on Egypt's southern border occupied by Jewish mercenaries and their families. It was apparently founded sometime in the sixth century, perhaps soon after the destruction of Jerusalem. The papyri, consisting of legal documents and letters, date from the fifth century B.C. and reveal much about the political situation and about Jewish laws and customs there.[56]

THE JEWS WHO RETURNED. Ezra 1–2 describes the happy time in 538 B.C. when the first Jewish exiles were permitted to return to Judah. This was a day that was to have profound significance for the whole subsequent history of God's people. Nevertheless, the group that returned under Sheshbazzar was small. According to Ezra 2:64-65 the number of those returning was 49,897.[57] Later we know about five thousand returned with Ezra (Ezra 8:1-14), and other groups of Jews probably also arrived from Babylonia from time to time.

The province of Judah was small, some twenty-five hundred to three thousand square kilometers. In the north the border must have passed between Mizpah and Gibeon and on to the Jordan River north of Jericho. In the south the boundary can be traced along a line between Beth-zur and Hebron.[58] During the exile, the Edomites were driven gradually from their homeland by Nabatean Arabs. Consequently, they began taking over southern Judah, especially the hill country south of Beth-zur, so that those Jews returning from Babylon at the end of the sixth century held little but Jerusalem and its suburbs (see 1 Esdr 4:50).[59]

In Ezra-Nehemiah we read of neighboring politicians who were enemies of the Jews. Judah was surrounded by other provinces, all part of

---

[56] See B. Porten and J. C. Greenfield, *Jews of Elephantine and Arameans of Syene* (Jerusalem: Hebrew University, 1974); B. Porten, "Elephantine Papyri," *ABD* 2:445-55; P. R. Ackroyd, *Israel under Babylon and Persia* (London: Oxford University Press, 1970), 279-90; J. M. Miller and J. H. Hayes, *A History of Ancient Israel and Judah* (Philadelphia: Westminster, 1986), 435-36; *ANET*, 491-92.

[57] J. Bright (*A History of Israel*, 365), following Albright, estimates that by the time of Darius I the total population of Judah could not have been much more than twenty thousand. Others estimate around fifty thousand (see G. Widengren, "The Persian Period," in *Israelite and Judaean History*, eds. J. Hayes and M. Miller (London: SCM, 1977), 489-583. Bright thinks the population of fifty thousand was reached later, in the time of Nehemiah.

[58] Ibid., 522.

[59] See Ackroyd, *Exile and Restoration*, 20-31; L. C. Allen, *The Books of Joel, Obadiah, Jonah and Micah*, NICOT (Grand Rapids: Eerdmans, 1976), 131.

the fifth satrapy mentioned earlier. Samaria was the province on the north where Sanballat was governor.[60] Ammon-Gilead was the province on the east where Tobiah was governor. Arabia-Idumea was on the south where Geshem was governor. On the west was the province of Ashdod.

The tension between the Samaritan rulers and the Jews in Jerusalem has led to questions about the status of Judah as a province. The view argued by A. Alt in 1934 that the Babylonians placed Judah under the jurisdiction of Samaria has gained wide acceptance. He believed that Judah only became a province with its own governor in the time of Nehemiah. This explained why Nehemiah encountered such opposition from Sanballat, the governor of Samaria (Neh 2:19; 4:1-3,7-8; 6:1-9), since he was coming as governor to take over the administration of a new province of Judah.[61]

Ezra 2:63, however, mentions "the governor" of Judah, and both Sheshbazzar (Ezra 5:14) and Zerubbabel (Hag 1:1,14; 2:2,21) are called governor. Furthermore, Judah is called a *medînâ* (Ezra 2:1; Neh 1:3; 7:6), which some argue designates an independent administrative district.[62] Regarding the Samaritan opposition to Nehemiah, H. Tadmor has suggested that it resulted from jealousy that having a prominent court dignitary—a cupbearer—as governor would elevate the importance of Judah above that of Samaria.[63]

Some believe the issue of the political status of Judah has been settled by a collection of sixty-five bullae found in a jar near Jerusalem and two seals, probably found nearby.[64] The bullae were all made from twelve seals, some official, containing the name of the province Yehud (Judah). On various seals occur the names Elnathan, Yehoezer, and Ahzai, each designated "the governor." N. Avigad has dated the collection palaeo-

---

[60] There is a "Sanballat, governor of Samaria" mentioned in one of the letters found at Elephantine. See A. Cowley, *Aramaic Papyri of the Fifth Century B.C.* (Oxford: Clarendon Press, 1923), 108-22.

[61] See the helpful summary of his arguments and those of his followers as well as a convincing counterargument in Hogland, *Achaemenid Imperial Administration*, 69-86.

[62] G. Widengren, "The Persian Period," 510-11. S. McEvenue rejects this argument, however, and supports Alt's view in "The Political Structure in Judah from Cyrus to Nehemiah," *CBQ* 43 (1981): 353-64

[63] H. Tadmor, "Some Aspects of the History of Samaria during the Biblical Period," *The Jerusalem Cathedra*, vol. 3, ed. L. I. Levine (Jerusalem/Detroit: Yad Izhak Ben-Zvi Institute/Wayne State University Press, 1983), 8.

[64] S. Japhet, in "Sheshbazzar and Zerubbabel—Against the Background of the Historical and Religious Tendencies of Ezra-Nehemiah" (*ZAW* 94 (1982): 80), claims that "recently discovered epigraphic material proves that Judah was in fact a province." See also Aharoni, *Land of the Bible*, 414.

graphically to "the very late 6th century B.C.E.,"[65] although this date is disputed.[66] One of the seals, however, is inscribed "belonging to Shelomith, maidservant of Elnathan the governor." There is a strong likelihood that the woman to whom this seal belonged was in fact the daughter of Zerubbabel named in 1 Chr 3:19.[67] If so, this confirms Avigad's dating of the seals and the strong impression given in the Bible that Judah was a separate province under the Persians.

Little information is available about subsequent groups of Jews who returned to Judah. More must have come, for at the beginning of the Hellenistic period (331 B.C.) the Jewish community was well established. On the other hand, many Jews stayed in Babylon, and for centuries Babylon remained a center for Jewish studies. In the Hellenistic and Roman periods we also find colonies of Jews throughout the Mediterranean world.

2. The Relation of Ezra-Nehemiah to Chronicles

Many scholars think that the same author who wrote 1, 2 Chronicles also wrote Ezra-Nehemiah.[68] According to the Jewish tradition found in the Talmud (*Baba Bathra* 15a), Ezra was the author of both Ezra-Nehemiah and 1, 2 Chronicles. In modern times this view was followed by such authors as W. F. Albright,[69] J. Bright,[70] J. Myers,[71] and G. L. Archer, Jr.[72] Yamauchi, however, argues that the genealogies of Chronicles date its completion to about 400 B.C., which makes it unlikely that Ezra was the author if we assume he was at least forty years old when he returned to Jerusalem in 458 B.C.[73] The more commonly held view is

---

[65] N. Avigad, *Bullae and Seals from a Postexilic Judean Archive* (Jerusalem: The Institute of Archaeology of the Hebrew University, 1976), 35.

[66] Stern, "The Province of Yehud," 21.

[67] E. Meyers ("The Shelomith Seal and the Judean Restoration" *Eretz-Israel* 18 [1985]: 37) suggests that Elnathan, probably from a non-Davidic family, found it politically advantageous to marry Shelomith, of Zerubbabel's Davidic family, "to solidify his control over an office that was diminishing in fiscal power and which was being eclipsed by an ever-strengthening high priesthood."

[68] For a discussion of the unity of Ezra-Nehemiah, see below under "Theories and Conclusions Regarding Composition."

[69] Albright, "The Date and Personality of the Chronicler," *JBL* 40 (1921): 119-20.

[70] J. Bright, "The Date of Ezra's Mission to Jerusalem," in *Yehezkel Kaufmann Jubilee Volume,* ed. M. Haran (Jerusalem: Magnes, 1960), 81; cf. idem, *A History of Israel* [Philadelphia: Westminster, 1981), 398.

[71] Myers, *Ezra, Nehemiah*, xlviii.

[72] Archer, *A Survey of Old Testament Introduction* (Chicago: Moody, 1974), 405.

[73] E. A. Yamauchi, "Ezra-Nehemiah," EBC (Grand Rapids: Zondervan, 1988), 4.577.

that both works were produced by an anonymous person or group of persons called "the Chronicler." As Fensham notes, "This view is generally accepted today by conservative as well as critical scholars."[74] Of course, this view includes many divergent ideas about the influence of the Chronicler on the sources he used, such as the first-person Ezra Memoir and the Nehemiah Memoir (see discussion below under "Sources").

F. M. Cross developed a three stage theory of compilation. The first stage (Chr$_1$) was written by the Chronicler shortly after the foundation of the temple in 520 B.C. and consisted of 1 Chr 10 to 2 Chr 36 plus Ezra 1:1–3:13 (2 Chr 35–Ezra 3:13 being the *Vorlage* of 1 Esdr 1:1–5:65). The second stage (Chr$_2$) written by a disciple of the Chronicler in 450 shortly after Ezra's mission added Ezra 5:1–6:19 in Aramaic followed by the Ezra Narrative in chaps. 7–10. Finally, about 400 B.C. (Chr$_3$) the Nehemiah Memoir, having been composed and circulated independently (accounting for the repetition of Ezra 2 in Neh 7), was attached along with the genealogies of 1 Chr 1–9. This last stage omitted some material that exalted Zerubbabel and made Ezra and Nehemiah contemporaries by interlacing the two accounts.[75]

As T. Eskenazi explains, "The general consensus . . . has come apart in recent decades."[76] S. Japhet lists the four main arguments are used to maintain single authorship: (1) the repetition of the ending of Chronicles at the beginning of Ezra; (2) 1 Esdras continuing from 2 Chr 35 through Ezra; (3) "common vocabulary, syntactic phenomena and stylistic peculiarities"; and (4) "theological conceptions, expressed both in the material and its selection."[77] She then presents a thorough analysis of the third ar-

---

[74] F. C. Fensham, *The Books of Ezra and Nehemiah* (Grand Rapids: Eerdmans, 1982), 2. See also W. LaSor, D. Hubbard, and F. W. Bush, *Old Testament Survey* (Grand Rapids: Eerdmans, 1982), 647; D. J. A. Clines, *Ezra, Nehemiah, Esther,* NCB (Grand Rapids: Eerdmans, 1984), 9-10; A. E. Hill and J. Walton, *A Survey of the Old Testament* (Grand Rapids: Zondervan, 1991), 229. B. Childs mentions several characteristics of the Chronicler that also are found in Ezra-Nehemiah: (a) he selectively used source material; (b) he paraphrased earlier Scripture; (c) he arranged passages in typological patterns (e.g., Ezra 3:12; 6:22; Neh 8:17; 12:43); (d) he used prayer in paradigmatic fashion; (e) he used the prophecy-fulfillment "schema" (B. S. Childs, *Introduction to the Old Testament as Scripture* [Philadelphia: Fortress, 1979], 630-31).

[75] F. M. Cross, "A Reconstruction of the Judean Restoration," *JBL* 94 (1975): 11-14. Williamson has argued, on the other hand, the more likely view that Ezra 1–6 was composed after Ezra and Nehemiah memoirs were combined (see below under "Theories and Conclusions Regarding Composition").

[76] T. Eskenazi, *In an Age of Prose: A Literary Approach to Ezra-Nehemiah* (Atlanta: Scholars Press, 1988), 16. As S. Talmon notes, there has been a recent tendency not to view Ezra-Nehemiah as written by the same author as Chronicles.

[77] S. Japhet, "The Supposed Common Authorship of Chronicles and Ezra-Nehemia Investigated Anew," *VT* 18 (1968): 331-32.

gument and thirty-six significant linguistic and stylistic differences between the two works. Linguistic similarities, she explains, are to be expected if both writings come from the same general period of history. In conclusion Japhet states, "Our investigation . . . has proven that the books could not have been written or compiled by the same author."[78]

The issue, however, cannot be decided on the basis of linguistic evidence alone.[79] R. Braun has compared the ideology of Chronicles with that of Ezra-Nehemiah. Although there are certain themes found in both, he finds differences in the concept of retribution (clear in Chronicles but not in Ezra-Nehemiah), in the attitude toward Samaritans and foreigners (Chronicles is inclusive while Ezra-Nehemiah is exclusive), and in the strong emphasis in Chronicles on the Davidic monarchy.[80]

Regarding the repetition of Ezra 1:1-3 in 2 Chr 36:22-23, there are many explanations besides common authorship. Eskenazi believes the author of Chronicles included the verses from Ezra so that his work would end on a hopeful note.[81]

While recognizing that there is still room for discussion,[82] in this

---

[78] Ibid., 371.

[79] P. R. Ackroyd states that "the discussions of linguistic evidence for uniting or separating Chronicles and Ezra-Nehemiah have, on the whole, reached an inconclusive position" ("Chronicles-Ezra-Nehemiah: The Concept of Unity," *ZAW* 100 [1988]: 189-201). Eskenazi (*Age of Prose*, 20) and R. Braun ("Chronicles, Ezra, and Nehemiah: Theology and Literary History," *VTS* 30 [1979]: 53), while agreeing with Japhet's conclusions, do not think that linguistic studies alone are conclusive and attack the view of common authorship on other grounds. D. Talshir has attempted to show that Japhet's methodology was faulty (D. Talshir, "A Reinvestigation of the Linguistic Relationship between Chronicles and Ezra-Nehemiah," *VT* 38 [1988]: 165-93). M. A. Throntveit ("Linguistic Analysis and the Questions of Authorship in Chronicles, Ezra and Nehemiah," *VT* 38 [1982]: 215) says, "Perhaps the safest course would be to take seriously the *a priori* assumption of separate authorship and investigate both works individually from a theological point of view, leaving the question of authorship open until the intent and message of both are better understood." Japhet herself has pursued the matter further in *The Ideology of the Book of Chronicles and Its Place in Biblical Thought* (Frankfurt: Peter Lang, 1989).

[80] R. L. Braun, "Chronicles, Ezra, and Nehemiah: Theology and Literary History," in *Studies in the Historical Books of the Old Testament,* ed. J. A. Emerton, *VTSup* 30 (Leiden: Brill, 1979), 52-64. See also idem, "A Reconsideration of the Chronicler's Attitude toward the North," *JBL* 96 (1977): 59-62; J. D. Newsome, "Toward a New Understanding of the Chronicler and His Purposes," *JBL* 94 (1975): 201-17; H. G. M. Williamson, "The Chronicler's Purpose," *CBQ* 23 (1961): 436-42; idem, *Israel in the Books of Chronicles* (N.Y.: Cambridge University Press, 1977), 5-70; Eskenazi, *Age of Prose*, 22-33; S. Talmon, "Esra und Nehemia: Historiographie oder Theologie?" in *Ernten was man sät, Festschrift für Klaus Koch,* 329-56 (Neukirchen-Vluyn: Neukirchener, 1991).

[81] Eskenazi, *Age of Prose*, 18. See also Williamson, *1 and 2 Chronicles* (Grand Rapids: Eerdmans, 1982), 415; Japhet, "Supposed Common Authorship," 338-41.

commentary we will assume that the final author of Ezra-Nehemiah was not the Chronicler.

3. The Composition of Ezra-Nehemiah

(1) Sources

As in the case of Samuel, Kings, and Chronicles, the writer or writers of Ezra-Nehemiah evidently used a variety of sources. Kidner divides the sources into four categories: the memoirs of Ezra, the memoirs of Nehemiah, Jewish lists (such as genealogies, lists of towns and villages, etc.), and imperial decrees and correspondence.[83] Of course, the Ezra Memoirs and Nehemiah Memoirs also included various lists and genealogies.

THE FIRST SECTION OF THE BOOK. Ezra 1–6 contains the following sources: (1) the Edict of Cyrus (1:2-4); (2) an inventory of the articles brought for the temple (1:9-11); (3) a list of the captives who returned, almost identical with Neh 7 (2:1–3:1); (4) two letters of opposition summarized in 4:6-7; (5) a letter to Artaxerxes from Rehum and others (4:8-16); (6) Artaxerxes' reply (4:17-22); (7) a letter from Tattenai to Darius (5:6–17); and (8) Darius's reply including a memorandum of the Edict of Cyrus (6:3-12).

THE EZRA MEMOIRS. Chapters 7–10 of Ezra are usually considered to be based on memoirs written by Ezra (EM) sometime before the final compilation of the book. Some difficulties of changes from first to third person exist, but this is considered to be due to the editor's work. Many scholars also consider Neh 8–9 (and sometimes 10) part of the EM.[84] The EM include several sources: (1) a copy of Artaxerxes' letter to Ezra

---

[82] Some continue to hold to the unity of Ezra-Nehemiah-Chronicles. See P. R. Ackroyd, "The Chronicler as Exegete," *JSOT* 2 (1977): 2-32; idem, "The Historical Literature," in *The Hebrew Bible and Its Modern Interpreters*, ed. D. A. Knight and G. M. Tucker (Philadelphia/Chico: Fortress/Scholars, 1985), 305-11; Cross, "A Reconstruction of the Judean Restoration," 4-18; K.-F. Pohlmann, "Zur Frage von Korrespondenzen und Divergenzen zwischen den Chronikbüchern und dem Esra/Nehemia–Buch," in *Congress Volume: Leuven, 1989*, ed. J. A. Emerton, 314-30 (Leiden: Brill, 1991); J. Blenkinsopp, *Ezra-Nehemiah* (Philadelphia: Westminster, 1988), 41-54.

[83] D. Kidner, *Ezra and Nehemiah* (Downers Grove: InterVarsity, 1979), 134-35. See also R. W. Klein, "Ezra-Nehemiah, Books of," *ABD* 2.732-34.

[84] Some question the possibility of identifying the EM since there is little besides first person style to distinguish it from the rest of Ezra-Nehemiah. See Hogland, *Achaemenid Imperial Administration*, 46-47; U. Kellermann, *Nehemia: Quellen, Überlieferung und Geschichte* (Berlin: Alfred Töpelmann, 1967), 56-69.

(Ezra 7:12-26); (2) a list of the heads of families of the Jews who returned with Ezra (8:1-14); (3) an inventory of vessels and bowls (8:26-27); (4) Ezra's prayer (9:6-15); and (5) the list of those who had married foreign wives (10:18-44). If Neh 8–9 is part of the EM, we must include also (6) the reading of the Law (Neh 7:73b–8:18) and (7) a long prayer of confession (Neh 9:6-37). If chap. 10 is part of the EM (which is unlikely), it also includes (8) a list of those who signed the covenant agreement (Neh 10:1-28) and (9) the contents of the covenant (Neh 10:31-40). As K. Hogland has pointed out, "Comparison of the form and contents of these various documents with actual Achaemenid documents has given little cause to question the general authenticity of these citations in the narratives.[85]

THE NEHEMIAH MEMOIRS.   Another part of Ezra-Nehemiah is based on a first person document written by Nehemiah himself. It is called the Nehemiah Memoirs (NM) and is found in Neh 1–7 and in parts of chaps. 11–13. Several lists are used therein as sources: (1) the residents of Jerusalem (Neh 11:3-24), (2) villages occupied by Judah and Benjamin (Neh 11:25-36), and (3) priests and Levites (Neh 12:1-26).

S. Mowinckel argued that the NM had parallels with other ancient Near Eastern royal inscriptions that commemorate a king's achievements. Von Rad compared the NM with Egyptian inscriptions that speak of duties faithfully performed by Egyptian officials. Others have taken the "remember" sections and compared them to votive inscriptions in some Aramaic documents. Another view is that Nehemiah had to write a description of his accomplishments to justify himself to the Persian king.[86] U. Kellermann's view was that Nehemiah was appealing to God for vindication in response to a charge of some kind.[87]

Williamson suggests that the NM was written in two stages. The first stage may have been based on Nehemiah's report to Artaxerxes (in Aramaic). Then later, after the pledge of Neh 10 had been made, Nehemiah reworked the NM and added a number of short paragraphs (5:14-19; 13:4-14,15-22,23-31), which had to do with details or accomplishments in which due credit had not been given to him.[88]

---

[85] Hogland, *Achaemenid Imperial Administration*, 47.

[86] For a discussion of several attempts to analyze and explain the NM, see Williamson, *Ezra, Nehemiah*, xxiv-xxvi.

[87] His view is critiqued in J. A. Emerton, "Review of *Nehemia: Quellen, Überlieferung und Geschichte* by U. Kellermann," *JTS* n.s. 23 (1972): 173-77.

[88] Williamson, *Ezra-Nehemiah*, xxvi-xxvii. He notes that almost all the "remember" passages (5:19; 13:14,22,31, and two in negative form—6:14 and 13:29) are related to specific parts of the pledge in Neh 10.

At least some of these letters, documents, and lists constitute primary historical sources; some would have been from the Jewish archives in Jerusalem and some from the Persian archives. Some of the lists may have been drawn up by the author based on other lists. Many appear to be integral to the EM and NM rather than added by the final author.

(2) Theories and Conclusions Regarding Composition

There have been many theories regarding the process by which Ezra-Nehemiah was written. Some scholars have tried to rearrange the material to fit their reconstructions. Although literary criticism makes a valid contribution to interpretation, we must not base our interpretation on one particular reconstruction of the formation of the text. Source and redaction criticism may be of help, but the conclusions of those who do the redaction criticism are partly based on their own assumptions. As Ackroyd points out: "One scholar's hypothesis is another's flight of the imagination."[89] We can endeavor to discover whom God used and how he used his servants in writing Scripture, but we must do it in reverence to God's Word and in subjection to its authority as taught by Jesus and the apostles and affirmed throughout the Bible.

UNITY. Some scholars[90] have considered Ezra and Nehemiah to have been written as two separate books, authored by Ezra and Nehemiah, respectively. Certainly Ezra wrote much of the book that bears his name (at least the EM) as did Nehemiah (at least the NM). However, most scholars believe it more likely that Ezra-Nehemiah was compiled as one book by Ezra, Nehemiah, or someone else, using the memoirs along with other sources. Its unity is assumed by the Talmud, the Masoretes, probably the author of Ecclesiastes, the early LXX manuscripts, and the second century A.D. Christian canon of Melito of Sardis. A tradition of the division into two books was known by Origen in the third century and was strengthened by Jerome in the Latin Vulgate (fourth century). The earliest Hebrew manuscript to divide them is dated A.D. 1448.[91]

---

[89] P. R. Ackroyd, "Chronicles-Ezra-Nehemiah: The Concept of Unity," *ZAW* 100 (1988): 189-201.

[90] R. K. Harrison, *Introduction to the Old Testament* (Grand Rapids: Eerdmans, 1969), 1150; E. J. Young, *An Introduction to the Old Testament* (Grand Rapids: Eerdmans, 1964), 378, 386.

[91] S. Talmon, "Ezra and Nehemiah (Books and Men)," in *IDBSup*, 317-18. He does not rule out the possibility, however, that Ezra and Nehemiah may have existed separately before being combined, which, he says, could explain some of the problems of repetition and arrangement.

Certain stylistic features common to the whole work confirm the unity of Ezra-Nehemiah. One example is the use of summary notations to mark parenthetical material. A number of these summary notations or condensed summaries are found throughout the book. Talmon notes Ezra 4:4-5b, which defines 3:1–4:3 as a unit and looks ahead to 4:24 (and indicates that 4:6-23 is a parenthetical passage). Other examples are Ezra 6:13-14, which gives a precis of 5:1–6:12; Neh 12:26, which refers to 12:10-25; 12:47, which refers to 12:44-46; and 13:29b-31, which refers to issues treated in chaps. 10–13.[92] Another indication of unity is similar language used by Ezra ("the hand of the LORD my God was upon me" in Ezra 7:28) and Nehemiah ("the good hand of my God that was upon me" in Neh 2:8).[93] The reappearance of Ezra in Neh 8 and the parenthetical nature of Neh 8–10 (compare Neh 7:73 and 11:1) may also be taken as confirming the unity of Ezra-Nehemiah.

ARRANGEMENT. One's conclusion regarding the relation of Neh 8–10 to the EM becomes a key part of one's theory of composition of the whole book. According to Widengren, many scholars assume that the material now in Neh 8–10 was originally part of Ezra 7–10 and was moved "to associate Ezra and Nehemiah with one another in a common activity."[94] Others prefer to keep the chronological order of the chapters as they appear in our text. In either case, many questions remain. If Ezra was in Jerusalem the whole time (thirteen years between the events of Ezra 10 and Neh 8), why does Nehemiah not mention him before? Or if Neh 8–10 belongs with Ezra, why is Nehemiah mentioned in Neh 8:9?

A number of recent studies have challenged the so-called "general consensus" that Neh 8–10 belongs with Ezra 7–10. Myers thinks the author composed Neh 8–9 from Ezra material, though chap. 10 seems out of place, belonging with Neh 13.[95] Williamson, after making a careful redaction-critical analysis, concludes that Neh 8 was originally part of

---

[92] See S. Talmon, "Ezra and Nehemiah," *IDBS,* 322. Talmon carefully explains the use of summary notations to indicate certain sections somewhat as we would use parentheses. The example in Ezra 4:4-5 is noted both by Williamson and Talmon. It is seen as a "summary notation" to indicate the juxtaposition of events from the reigns of Cyrus (Ezra 3:1-6) and Darius (Ezra 3:7ff.).

[93] Hogland, *Achaemenid Imperial Administration*, 47. See also Ezra 7:6,9; 8:18,22,31; Neh 2:18.

[94] Widengren, "The Persian Period," 491-92. LaSor, et al., (*Old Testament Survey*, 646) also considers Neh 7:73b–10:39 as the second half of the EM, intentionally placed out of chronological order. They understand Ezra 7:1–10:44 to have been the first part of EM, Neh 1:1–7:73a as the first part of NM, then 7:73b–10:39 as the second part of EM, and 11:1–13:31 as the second part of NM.

[95] Myers, *Ezra, Nehemiah*, 152.

the EM and fits chronologically between Ezra 8 and 9. Although some of Neh 9 is from the EM, it includes a psalm of praise that existed before or was composed separately. Also, it cannot be placed before Ezra 9–10. Nehemiah 10 was not part of the EM nor of the NM but was originally an independent document. Perhaps it came from the temple archives. Chronologically, Williamson thinks it follows Neh 13.[96]

Fensham, while accepting the view that Neh 8–10 was composed from the memoirs of Ezra, does not think the chapters are misplaced.[97] Kidner, on the other hand, does not consider these chapters to have ever been part of the Ezra material. He accepts the present order and position as correct. The thirteen-year gap between Ezra's arrival in Jerusalem and this reading of the law is no problem because Ezra would have been busy teaching the law all that time. There may even have been other public readings, but that does not diminish the importance of this special occasion of revival.[98] R. K. Harrison, however, does not think Ezra was necessarily in Jerusalem the whole time. His position as "Secretary of State for Jewish Affairs" in the Persian Empire may have necessitated his return to Babylon after a period of about two years in Jerusalem. He may have returned then with Nehemiah and helped in the reforms, possibly leaving again after the rebuilding was complete in 445/6 B.C.[99]

CONCLUSION. To what conclusion can we arrive? We must admit that the narrative of Neh 7:73a is apparently resumed in 11:1; this favors the conclusion that chaps. 8–10 are parenthetical. Also the style of at least chap. 8 (and probably most of chap. 9) appears to coincide with that of the EM. This is one reason to conclude that although the Book of Ne-

---

[96] Any discussion of this complicated issue must take into consideration Williamson's careful analysis (*Ezra, Nehemiah,* 275-86). He postulates that these three chapters, Neh 8–10, had independent origins and were put together by the editor who combined the Ezra and Nehemiah material. The editor/author's purpose was to show the importance of the law for the renewal of the covenant. Thus he completed the pattern of reading the law (chap. 8), including antecedent history (chap. 9) and the actual covenant renewal (chap. 10). The editor used "repetitive resumption" to show that the narrative of 7:73a continues in 11:1. However, recognizing Williamson's careful work does not necessarily imply accepting all of his conclusions. We agree that the author was relying on a separate source for Neh 10 but consider that Neh 9 was at least based on the EM. Furthermore, even if there were as many stages as he proposes, they need not have been separated by long periods of time. K. Hogland claims that Williamson's view fails for lack of evidence. He prefers Eskenazi's view that whether or not the book's author employed memoirs of Ezra or Nehemiah, the shifts between first and third person in the book are literary devices and cannot serve as clear indications of sources. See Hogland, *Achaemenid Imperial Administration,* 46-47; Eskenazi, *Age of Prose,* 127-35.

[97] Fensham, *Ezra and Nehemiah,* 215.

hemiah is made up largely of Nehemiah's own writing (NM), the final work probably depends on another author.

If the final author was Ezra, he could have taken part of his own memoirs and included it with other material in this section. That would explain why there are so many different opinions about which parts of the material are from the EM. So we conclude that the author inserted Neh 8–10 into the NM. But if Ezra was the final author, it makes little difference whether it was a part of his prior composition (EM) or was written for this context.

Furthermore, if Neh 8–10 was included in the EM, that does not necessarily imply that these chapters are out of place chronologically. The description of the revival in Neh 8 could have been part of the EM even though it occurred after the completion of the walls.[100] Fensham's view is a reasonable one (similar to Harrison; see above), that Ezra arrived in 458, promoted his reforms, then returned to Susa. Later, sometime during Nehemiah's twelve-year governorship, he returned to Jerusalem and supported Nehemiah's reforms. That was when the episode of Neh 8 took place. That the ministries of Ezra and Nehemiah overlapped is taken for granted by the author of Ezra-Nehemiah. We conclude, therefore, that regardless of how the account was given in the original memoirs of Ezra and Nehemiah, these chapters in the present work are not a later interpolation but describe the events as they occurred.

The evident theological purpose of the author also points to the same conclusion. B. Childs has pointed out that the book consists of four main

---

[98] Kidner, *Ezra and Nehemiah*, 150-52. The possibility of a series of readings of the law or even of a different way of looking at the chronological relationship between Ezra and Nehemiah cannot be ruled out. L.McFall ("Was Nehemiah Contemporary with Ezra in 458 B.C.?" *WTJ* 53, no. 2 [1991]: 263-93) thinks that Nehemiah was using a dynastic method of reckoning when he spoke of the twentieth year of Artaxerxes in Neh 5:14; 13:6. That is, Nehemiah was counting the twentieth year of the dynasty, beginning with Xerxes, which was 485. So Nehemiah went to Jerusalem as governor in 465; his twelve-year term as governor ended in 454. The whole episode of the rebuilding of the wall occurred during his second visit to Jerusalem in 445. Thus Ezra and Nehemiah were both in Jerusalem in 458. McFall uses a number of arguments and thinks this way of reckoning solves many of the difficulties in regard to the reading of the law in Neh 8. Although the proposal reminds us that we should not be too arrogant concerning any theory of chronological relationships, we should have more confirmation (from other documents) to accept such a "dynastic reading" of Nehemiah's calculations. Also the theory poses additional problems about the lack of mention of Nehemiah and Ezra together on other occasions. The suggestions offered by Pablovsky and by Fensham (see note below) are more acceptable.

[99] Harrison, *Introduction*, 1148-49.

[100] Pablovsky similarly proposed that Ezra went to Jerusalem with royal authority at Nehemiah's request and was a "prime mover" in his reforms (Myers, *Ezra, Nehemiah*, xlviii).

parts; the first three lead up to the last one, which emphasizes the reordering of community life. Thus the author deliberately placed Neh 8 (the reading of the law) in this last section thereby showing Ezra and Nehemiah in the work of reshaping the community.[101] Childs notes that the reading of the law in Neh 8 is firmly anchored to the twentieth year of Artaxerxes by the larger context in which it is set. In regard to the relation of Ezra and Nehemiah, Childs says: "The initial work of Ezra (7–10) as well as the building of the wall by Nehemiah (Neh 1–6) receive their significance only in the light of the religious reordering of the community of faith in Neh 8–12. The explicit intent of the author is to describe this event as one shared by both Ezra and Nehemiah."[102] The purpose of the reading of the law was not to reform Israel; rather it was the reformed people who were ready to hear the reading of the Law. Childs concludes: "The attempt to shift the reading of the law to Ezra 8 derives from a typical Protestant misunderstanding of Old Testament law. Far from being a legalistic system which seeks to dictate religious behavior by rules, the tradition assigned the law a liturgical function which had been reserved for the restored and forgiven community."[103]

It appears, then, that the process of composition involved, first, the writing of the memoirs of Ezra and Nehemiah (perhaps in stages as Williamson argues) and the other source documents contemporary with the events. This would have occurred before the end of Artaxerxes I's reign in 424 B.C. The memoirs were then combined (perhaps by Ezra), adding other material from the temple archives.[104] Finally, someone, whether Ezra (the most likely possibility), Nehemiah, or another recognized teacher of Israel "whose heart God had moved," added Ezra 1–6 and shaped the whole work into a historical-theological document that would edify and stabilize the new restored community as the people of God.[105]

If the final author was Ezra, we can assume that Ezra-Nehemiah was written around 420 B.C. or shortly before.[106] But even if the final author was one of Ezra's disciples or someone else, we could conclude that the book was written before 400 B.C. since there is no person or event mentioned in Ezra-Nehemiah that requires a later date.[107]

---

[101] The four sections are: Ezra 1–6, the release under Cyrus and the construction of the temple; Ezra 7–10, Ezra's arrival and his reforms; Neh 1–6, the building of the walls; and Neh 7–13, the reordering of the community's life (Childs, *Introduction to the Old Testament*, 632-33).

[102] Ibid., 635.

[103] Ibid., 636.

[104] Williamson suggests this could have taken place around 400 B.C., but it could have occurred anytime after the events of Neh 10–13.

4. Historical Questions

(1) The Chronology of Ezra and Nehemiah

If we take Ezra-Nehemiah as it stands, it appears that Ezra arrived in Jerusalem in 458 B.C., the seventh year of King Artaxerxes (Ezra 7:7-8), and Nehemiah arrived thirteen years later in 445 B.C., the twentieth year of Artaxerxes (Neh 2:1). However, while the traditional date of Nehemiah's arrival has generally been maintained, during the past century many scholars have argued that dating Ezra's arrival after Nehemiah's makes more sense of the historical data. Several apparent historical anomalies have been noted that lead to this conclusion. For example, if Ezra came to Jerusalem to teach the Lord's Law in Israel (Ezra 7:10), why did he wait thirteen years for a public reading of the Law (Neh 8)? And in view of Ezra's reforms (Ezra 9–10), why did Nehemiah find the situation so deteriorated only a few years later (Neh 1:3; 5:1-5; 13:1-31)?[108] The traditional date for Ezra's coming to Jerusalem is based on understanding Ezra 7:7-8 as referring to Artaxerxes I (464–424 B.C.). Some have argued that the king referred to is Artaxerxes II (404–359 B.C.), thus dat-

---

[105] Williamson suggests that this may have occurred around 300 B.C. (ibid., xxxv-xxxvi). He admits that this is a theory. However, any theory includes certain assumptions supplied by its author. In fact, the assumptions he makes here—that the author found the NM and EM already combined and that one of the author's purposes was to argue against the Samaritan schism and the building of the Samaritan temple (Williamson, *Ezra, Nehemiah*, xxxvi, 400)—determine many of his conclusions about the process and date of composition. We can agree that Ezra 1–6 probably was the last part of Ezra-Nehemiah to be written. It was composed after the combination of the Ezra and Nehemiah material. As we later note, however, there need not be much time between the combining of the EM and NM and the composition of Ezra 1–6. In fact, the final author may have done it himself before writing Ezra 1–6. We would also suggest that Williamson's second stage of composition—the combining of the NM, EM, and some other materials—could have been part of the final author's work.

[106] Harrison (*Introduction*, 1150) thinks Ezra and Nehemiah were basically in their present form by 440 or 430 B.C.

[107] LaSor, et al., *Old Testament Survey*, 647. Myers gives a list of reasons why the Chronicler (whom he assumes wrote both Chronicles and Ezra-Nehemiah) must not be placed later than 400 B.C. He mentions that both the postexilic list of the Davidic family and the lists of priests and Levites in Neh 12 terminate before 400 (*Ezra, Nehemiah*, lxvi-ii). Bright (*History of Israel*, 398-99) and LaSor use the same arguments. LaSor notes that the Septuagint continues the list of 1 Chr 3 to include four additional generations. If Ezra-Nehemiah were written later, it would also include additional generations. Myers also notes that the name of Bigvai, who was governor of Judah in 408 B.C. (known from the Elephantine documents), is not mentioned in Ezra-Nehemiah (*Ezra, Nehemiah*, lxix-lxx).

[108] Bright, *History of Israel*, 393.

ing Ezra's arrival in 398 B.C., allowing no overlap between Nehemiah's ministry and that of Ezra.[109] Following W. F. Albright,[110] J. Bright has advocated a third view emending "the seventh year" in Ezra 7:7-8 to read "the thirty-seventh year" of Artaxerxes I, which was 428 B.C. This allows some overlap of the ministries of Ezra and Nehemiah but avoids a long interval between Ezra's arrival and his reading of the Law.[111]

Recent work on Ezra-Nehemiah, however, tends to prefer the traditional order and Ezra's arrival in Jerusalem in 458 B.C. Fensham says, "Although admittedly certain problems remain with the traditional view, it is by far the more satisfactory solution because the text as transmitted is kept intact and the sequence of the different chapters is accepted as a reliable guide to the chronology."[112] This is the most reasonable. The following gives the main objections to the traditional date together with a brief answer to each.[113]

1. There is almost no indication that Ezra and Nehemiah worked together. They only appear together in two texts, Ezra 8:9 and Neh 12:36, assumed by many to be textual additions.[114] However, those dating Ezra's return in 398 B.C. must prove that the editor of the book mistakenly put Ezra and Nehemiah together or intentionally altered the facts. Also we must remember that both the EM and NM were concerned with each one's own work. It was not necessary to mention the other. Haggai

---

[109] See H. H. Rowley, "The Chronological Order of Ezra and Nehemiah," in *The Servant of the Lord* (London: Lutterworth, 1965), 135-68.

[110] Albright, *The Biblical Period from Abraham to Ezra* (New York: Harper & Row, 1963), 45-55, 62-65.

[111] Bright, *History of Israel*, 391-402. He reconstructs the text's chronological order as Ezra 7–8 (Ezra's arrival), Neh 8 (reading the Law), Ezra 9–10 (Ezra's reforms), Neh 9–10 (confession and covenant). However, since there is no textual support for his emendation, there is little reason to accept it. See the critique by J. A. Emerton, "Did Ezra Go to Jerusalem in 428 B.C.?" *JTS* 17 (1966): 1-19.

[112] Fensham, *Ezra and Nehemiah*, 9. Williamson (*Ezra, Nehemiah*, xliv) also accepts the earlier date for Ezra. D. J. A. Clines (*Ezra, Nehemiah, Esther*, NCB [Grand Rapids: Eerdmans, 1984], 23) and Blenkinsopp (*Ezra-Nehemiah*, 144) seem undecided but prefer the traditional date. Kidner, after a lengthy discussion of the different arguments, notes that the proponents of alternates to the biblical order really claim nothing stronger than probability for their suggested reconstructions. He concludes that "if that is the case, the narrative that we already have must surely take precedence over the narratives that we do not have" (Kidner, *Ezra and Nehemiah*, 158). LaSor, et al., (*Old Testament Survey*, 651) says, "No tangible evidence necessitates dating Ezra after Nehemiah."

[113] Kidner gives detailed answers to each of the arguments (*Ezra and Nehemiah*, 146-58), and Williamson also has a lengthy discussion (*Ezra, Nehemiah*, xxxix-xliv). See also Bright, *A History of Israel*, 392-403.

[114] Widengren, 504-5; Myers, *Ezra, Nehemiah*, xxxvi.

and Zechariah both preached to the small Judahite community in 520, but neither book mentions the other prophet. LaSor says, "None of the facts presented nor the problems alleged present either compelling reasons for doubting the contemporaneity of Ezra and Nehemiah or valid objections to the order clearly presupposed by the biblical text."[115]

2. According to some scholars, it seems odd, almost absurd, to think that thirteen years passed after Ezra's initial arrival in Jerusalem before he had the public reading of the Law described in Neh 8. Also 1 Esdras places Neh 8 with Ezra 8, on which basis it is argued that the public reading of the Law must have taken place early in Ezra's ministry. In response the thirteen-year period between Ezra's arrival and his reading the law presents many details about which we do not know. This may not have been the first time the people met to read the Law. In fact, as Kidner points out, "the sensitivity of the people to Ezra's consequent distress, and their extraordinary readiness to make amends, all clearly imply a recent and powerful campaign of education in the law."[116] Moreover, as mentioned above, the law was not read so much for the purpose of bringing a reform; that was already begun earlier by Ezra's prayer and confession. Rather, the law was read as part of the liturgical celebration by the revived community.[117] This episode must have occurred more toward the end of Ezra's ministry than at the beginning as is often assumed.

3. Nehemiah's attacks on divorce would imply that Ezra's work had not yet been done. If Ezra's reforms were successful, Nehemiah should not have had to impose the same reforms. However, it is reasonable that Ezra could have produced a radical change but that a number of unresolved cases remained. Besides, any reform will have its opponents and after time will lose impetus. "Those who argue that Ezra was no 'second Moses' if his people relapsed into old ways must have forgotten the story of the original Moses."[118] A relapse is especially likely if Ezra had to return to Babylon as Harrison and Fensham have suggested.[119] In addition, the personalities of Ezra and Nehemiah were very different, and also Nehemiah was dealing with isolated cases. The main problem had been

---

[115] LaSor, et al., *Old Testament Survey*, 651. See also Hogland, *Achaemenid Imperial Administration*, 43-44; E. A. Yamauchi, "The Reverse Order of Ezra/Nehemiah Reconsidered," *Themelios* 5 (1980): 7-13.

[116] Kidner, *Ezra and Nehemiah*, 152.

[117] Childs, *Introduction to the Old Testament*, 636.

[118] Kidner, *Ezra and Nehemiah*, 153.

[119] This suggestion (mentioned above) remains hypothetical, however, since there is no explicit mention of Ezra's return in the text.

adequately taken care of under Ezra's reform, but Nehemiah seemed to be responsible for bringing coherence and unity to the restoration.

4. The identity of the high priest is another factor. Eliashib was high priest in the time of Nehemiah (Neh 13:28). Yet Ezra 10:6 says that Ezra spent the night in the chamber of Johanan, son of Eliashib, whom some assume to have been high priest at that time. Johanan may even have been the grandson of Eliashib (taking the Jonathan of Neh 12:11 as identical with Johanan of v. 22). According to the Elephantine Papyri, a Johanan was high priest in Jerusalem in 401 B.C. This would place Ezra later than the period of Nehemiah. But this argument, based on the identity of the high priests, rests on two assumptions: (a) that Johanan was high priest in the time of Ezra and (b) that Johanan was Eliashib's grandson. The first is not stated but assumed because Ezra stayed in his chamber. The second requires the emendation of the text in Neh 12:11 and the assumption that in Ezra 10:6 and Neh 12:23 we should read "grandson" instead of "son." This is possible but not very probable in this context. Again, we simply do not have enough information. Even those who use this argument "regard it as more than probable but less than proven."[120] F. M. Cross proposed a different solution, maintaining the date of 458 for Ezra. He argued that there were several Johanans and Eliashibs who were high priests during the Persian Empire. According to his reconstruction of the genealogies, a Johanan I would have been high priest in the time of Ezra and Eliashib II in the time of Nehemiah. Both names were repeated later in the succeeding generations.[121]

---

[120] Kidner, *Ezra and Nehemiah*, 155.

[121] This would explain the Johanan of the Elephantine Papyri (Cross, "A Reconstruction of the Judean Restoration," 4-18). G. Widengren ("The Persian Period," 507-9) thinks that Cross's theory is based on too many assumptions. But certainly it indicates we should not reject the facts of the biblical text in favor of other assumptions. Also it is important to remember that Cross's reconstruction owes much to his study of the Samaria Papyri and Bullae found at Wadi Daliyeh in 1962 and 1963. In a cave some nine miles north of Jericho and nearly fifteen hundred feet above the Jordan were found twenty papyri of legal and administrative documents and one hundred and twenty-eight clay seal impressions (bullae). These seals, plus signet rings and coins, date the text to ca. 375–335 B.C. Cross finds it significant that these texts indicate the existence of another Sanballat at the beginning of the fourth century. Based on that evidence he can postulate that there may have been a Sanballat III reflected in Josephus's story. Thus the historical difficulties that had been caused by the discrepancies between Josephus's story (and the Elephantine Papyri) and the details of Ezra-Nehemiah can be cleared up (F. M. Cross, "Papyri of the Fourth Century B.C. from Dâliyeh," in *New Directions in Biblical Archaeology* [Garden City: Doubleday, 1969], 45-69). See also the discussion of various theories in Williamson, *Ezra, Nehemiah*, 151-53.

5. In Ezra 9:9 "a wall of protection in Judah and Jerusalem" is mentioned. Thus, Nehemiah must have already constructed the walls before Ezra arrived. This is possible, but the phrase in Ezra's prayer probably is to be taken figuratively of spiritual protection (see Ps 80:12), especially in view of the phrase "in Judah"[122] and the figurative "tent peg" (NIV "firm place") in the previous verse. Furthermore, the term for "wall" (*gādēr*) refers to a vineyard wall rather than a city wall, suggesting the figure of Israel as God's vineyard which he had appointed the Persians to protect.[123]

Other arguments sometimes used against the early date of Ezra are likewise not convincing. The argument that conditions in the Persian Empire were more favorable later is not precise. In fact, some argue that because of the disturbances in Egypt a little earlier, Artaxerxes I supported Ezra so he would have a friendly people in Judah. Hogland has noted that Ezra's return in 458 B.C. would have been two years after the Egyptian victory over the Persians at Papremis and just "as the imperial court was assembling a great expeditionary force to counteract the Greek intrusion into the Egyptian revolt."[124] This was a strategic time to send Ezra and Nehemiah to "create a web of economic and social relationships that would tie the community more completely into the imperial system."[125] To accomplish this it was necessary and customary for Ezra first to carry out a legal reform to serve as the basis for the restructuring of the community, especially by clarifying the community's membership.[126] Thus, "the traditional view makes the most sense of the relationship between Ezra's reforms and those of Nehemiah. . . . Ezra's juridical role makes more sense as an action that preceded the more directly administrative role of Nehemiah."[127]

We conclude, then, that it is much better to take the biblical text as it stands and maintain the traditional dating of 458 B.C. for Ezra and 445 B.C. for Nehemiah.

---

[122] Clines, *Ezra, Nehemiah, Esther,* 124.

[123] Blenkinsopp, *Ezra-Nehemiah*, 184.

[124] Hogland, *Achaemenid Imperial Administration*, 226. He also argues (202-5, 243) that Persia's interest in Palestine at this time is most clearly demonstrated by the sudden appearance there of a series of fortresses distinctive to the mid-fifth century.

[125] Ibid., 244.

[126] Ibid., 207, 234-44.

[127] Ibid., 44.

(2) The Identity of Sheshbazzar

The relation between Sheshbazzar and Zerubbabel is not clear. In Ezra 3:8 we read that Zerubbabel and others began the work of building the house of God, and in Hag 1:1 he is called governor of Judah. In Ezra 5:14, however, Sheshbazzar is called governor; and v. 16 says, "This Sheshbazzar came and laid the foundations of the house of God in Jerusalem." Some suggest that Sheshbazzar and Zerubbabel were the same person. However, it is preferable to consider them two distinct persons. Fensham mentions two possible ways to see their relationship: (1) Sheshbazzar was governor at the beginning, then Zerubbabel became governor and completed the temple; or (2) Sheshbazzar was responsible to the Persian government, officially regarded "by the outside world" as the temple builder, though Zerubbabel really built it.[128]

The most logical conclusion and the one that best explains the biblical data is that Sheshbazzar was the leader and governor when the first group of captives came (Ezra 1:8; 5:14).[129] He disappears from our view quickly, and his nephew Zerubbabel, who accompanied Sheshbazzar to Judah and led in the building project, continued as governor (Ezra 3:2; Neh 12:1; Hag 1:1).[130]

(3) Ezra's Book of the Law

Many scholars have tried to discern exactly what was included in Ezra's Book of the Law of Moses (Neh 8:1). There are essentially four different proposals:[131] (1) it was the whole Pentateuch, perhaps in its final stages of development, either existing previously or presented by Ezra as a new work on that occasion; (2) it was only the Priestly Code that had been edited in Babylon, including most of the laws of Exodus, Leviticus, and Numbers; (3) it was legal material from various sources, most of which eventually was included in the Pentateuch; or (4) it was some form of Deuteronomy.[132] At this point Kidner notes, "Where historical scepticism reaches the end of its road, we can either draw back to one of the intermediate positions that we have noticed or take the alterna-

---

[128] Fensham, *Ezra and Nehemiah*, 49.

[129] Some argue that he was the Shenazzar who was a son of King Jehoiachin mentioned in 1 Chr 3:17-18 and thus a Davidic descendant (called "prince of Judah" in Ezra 1:8). See Clines, *Ezra, Nehemiah, Esther*, 41.

[130] See Aharoni, *Land of the Bible*, 414.

[131] Kidner, *Ezra and Nehemiah*, 158-64.

[132] This is the view of Kellermann, who accepts very little Ezra-Nehemiah material as historically reliable (Williamson, *Ezra, Nehemiah*, xxxvii).

tive path of accepting the account at its face value."[133]

The latter path is the wisest. The author takes for granted that this Book of the Law of Moses was known by the exiles and had existed for a long time. Whereas Widengren claims that identifying it "with the whole Pentateuch or the 'Pentateuch in penultimate form' is an impossible hypothesis,"[134] Kidner shows that this assumption, dependent on the whole process of modern literary criticism of the Pentateuch, is really "the end-product of a naturalistic approach which in my view cannot fail to distort the Pentateuch (or any other scripture), since it conscientiously rules out of its initial reckoning the one thing that sets these writings apart from all others: the direct and all-pervading activity of God in the making of them."[135] There is nothing in Ezra-Nehemiah that would argue against believing that Ezra had the whole Pentateuch. In fact, as Myers points out, stipulations from all parts of the Pentateuch are found in Ezra-Nehemiah.[136]

Other factors would support the same conclusion. Certainly the Samaritans would not have so wholeheartedly accepted the Pentateuch if it had been a work recently presented by Ezra.[137] It is significant that the Samaritans accepted only the Pentateuch as authoritative, not the Prophets and the Writings. When Ezra read from the Book of the Law of Moses, the people took it as authoritative. The fact that Ezra had the whole Pentateuch does not imply that he read all of it on this occasion. There must have been a long-standing tradition behind its reading, for there is no evidence that they had to be convinced of its authority.

---

[133] Kidner, *Ezra and Nehemiah*, 162.

[134] Widengren, "The Persian Period," 536.

[135] Kidner, *Ezra and Nehemiah*, 164.

[136] *Ezra, Nehemiah*, lxii. Kidner includes examples of material from Neh 9–13 that presupposes narrative and legal material from each of the five books of Moses (*Ezra and Nehemiah*, 164). See also Blenkinsopp, *Ezra-Nehemiah*, 153-55. He concludes by rejecting an identification with the Pentateuch but acknowledges Ezra-Nehemiah's familiarity with material from Exodus, Leviticus, Numbers, and Deuteronomy. On the antiquity of Leviticus see R. K. Harrison, *Leviticus: An Introduction and Commentary*, TOTC (Downers Grove: InterVarsity, 1980), 22-25; G. J. Wenham, *The Book of Leviticus*, NICOT (Grand Rapids: Eerdmans, 1979), 8-13.

[137] One of the conclusions of B. K. Waltke's study of the Samaritan Pentateuch ("The Samaritan Pentateuch and the Text of the Old Testament," in *New Perspectives on the Old Testament*, ed. J. B. Payne [Waco: Word, 1970], 235) was that "the Pentateuch must be older than the fifth century. If the scribal scholars of the second Jewish commonwealth found it necessary to modernize the Pentateuch to make it intelligible to the people (cf. Neh. 8) in the fifth century, then obviously the original Pentateuch antedates this period by many years."

(4) Relation to the Apocryphal Book of 1 Esdras

Occasionally in the commentary, reference will be made to the book of 1 Esdras. In the Septuagint our books of Ezra and Nehemiah were joined in one book and designated as "Esdras B." Another book known as "Esdras A" is the same book as that designated 3 Esdras in the Vulgate Bible or 1 Esdras in the Apocrypha.[138] The book includes the material found in 2 Chr 35–36, almost all of Ezra with an additional section (3:1–5:6) and the addition of Neh 7:38–8:12, which speaks of Ezra.

Since 1 Esdras is quite similar to our Book of Ezra, there has been much discussion about its origin. It could be based on another Hebrew text of Ezra-Nehemiah or ultimately derived from the Hebrew text of Ezra-Nehemiah, perhaps through another Greek version. Josephus used 1 Esdras instead of Ezra-Nehemiah for his information concerning this period in Jewish history.

The book contains some historical inconsistencies. One primary problem is its inconsistent chronology. It proceeds from the reign of Cyrus to that of Artaxerxes, then goes back to the time of Darius, and finally back to Artaxerxes again. The additional story of the three soldiers (3:1–5:6) and their debate about who or what is the strongest also introduces self-contradictory material. Zerubbabel wins the debate, and Darius rewards him by sending him to rebuild the temple in Jerusalem. However, in 6:23 Darius does not know that Zerubbabel has authority. The story itself probably had a Persian origin. Eskenazi has argued that 1 Esdras is a compilation from the canonical books of Chronicles and Ezra-Nehemiah whose purpose was to glorify Zerubbabel and to encourage restoration under a Davidic descendant.[139] Comparing Ezra-

---

[138] As in *The New English Bible, with the Apocrypha,* Oxford Study Edition (New York: Oxford University Press, 1972). The book known as 4 Esdras in the Vulgate is a Latin pseudepigraph, an apocalyptic writing. It is now included in some editions as 2 Esdras. The relation of the different names for these books can be shown in the following table:

LXX	Vulgate	English
1 Esdras	3 Esdras	1 Esdras (Apocryphal book)
2 Esdras B	1 Esdras	Ezra
3 Esdras G	2 Esdras	Nehemiah
	4 Esdras	2 Esdras (Apocryphal book)

[139] Eskenazi, *Age of Prose,* 155-74. See also idem, "The Chronicler and the Composition of 1 Esdras," *CBQ* 48 (1986): 39-61; Williamson, *Israel in the Books of Chronicles,* 21-36.

Nehemiah with 1 Esdras is interesting, but certainly 1 Esdras cannot be used to correct Ezra-Nehemiah.

5. The Theology of Ezra-Nehemiah

(1) Purposes of the Book

Since the author seems to have used the EM and NM, the question arises about the purpose of each of these writings. The reasons may be somewhat different for the two memoirs; for example, the NM may constitute, at least in part, Nehemiah's report to the Persian king. When we try to determine the comprehensive motives for the book, however, we find that the EM and NM are quite in accord with the purposes of the final author.

(2) The Continuity of God's Plan and People

One of the chief objectives of Ezra-Nehemiah was to show the Jews that they constituted the continuation of the preexilic Jewish community, the Israelite community that God had chosen.[140] Thus, in this community they were to see a continuation of God's redemptive activity. This continuity is emphasized by allusions to the exodus in recounting postexilic parallels. The returnees experienced a new exodus. As soon as the new temple, which took the place of the preexilic temple, was completed, they celebrated the Passover (Ezra 6:19-22). Later, after reading the Law, they celebrated the Feast of Tabernacles (Neh 8). These feasts celebrate God's great saving acts in the exodus.

God's recurrent action in Israel's history proved to the postexilic community that they represented the continuation of God's redemptive plan. God's providential care is repeatedly emphasized. It was God who was responsible for the decree of Cyrus (Ezra 1:1, "The LORD moved the heart of Cyrus"). He also secured the permission for construction to continue (Ezra 5:5, "The eye of their God was watching over the elders of the Jews"; 6:14, "They finished building the temple according to the command of the God of Israel"; and 6:22, "The LORD had filled them with joy by changing the attitude of the king of Assyria") and for Ezra and his group to come to Jerusalem (Ezra 7:27, "The God of our fathers,

---

[140] Eskenazi (*Age of Prose,* 41) has noted the structural and thematic importance of the lists of persons that impress upon the reader that "the real subject of the book is the people—named and unnamed, famous or forgotten—whose presence is memorialized with almost tiresome specificity."

who has put it into the king's heart to bring honor to the house of the
LORD"). He even protected them on the way (Ezra 8:22, "The gracious
hand of our God is on everyone who looks to him"). It was God who secured Nehemiah's appointment as governor (Neh 2:8, "Because the gracious hand of my God was upon me, the king granted my requests") and
guided in all the details of the construction of the wall (Neh 4:14, "Remember the Lord, who is great and awesome," and 4:20, "Our God will
fight for us!"). God frustrated the plans of the Jews' enemies and preserved this community. Just as we find throughout the prophetic books
and the whole Bible, the author of Ezra-Nehemiah interpreted history in
terms of God's actions.

In fact, the author emphasized that God can use even foreign rulers to
fulfill his purposes for the Jewish community. This is noted in the Edict
of Cyrus (Ezra 1; 6), in Artaxerxes' letter to Ezra (7:11-27), and in many
details of Nehemiah's assignment (Neh 1–6). God's sovereignty encom-
passes the entire world, all nations, to assure the continuation of his redemptive plan through the Jewish people.

This continuation of the people of God also meant the continuation of
the covenant. This little community of returned Jewish exiles was receiving the blessings of God's covenant with Abraham and with Israel at Sinai. The prayers of Ezra 9:6-15; Neh 1:5-11; and Neh 9:5-37 demonstrate
their deep consciousness of the covenant. "You are the LORD God, who
chose Abram . . . and you made a covenant with him. . . . You have kept
your promise" (Neh 9:7-8). Ezra and Nehemiah recognized and confessed that the people broke the covenant and for that reason suffered the
captivity. But they appealed to God's covenant mercy and promises for
the reestablishment of the covenant community.

In fact, this new situation under foreign rule meant that the Jewish
people became again more strictly a covenant community and not a nation as in the monarchy. The community's identity did not now depend
on its political institutions and identity as a nation but on its special covenant relation to God. In God's providence this was a step in the preparation for the New Testament transition to the church under the new
covenant in which all believers are one in Christ and where physical, ethnic, political, and geographic distinctions are overcome.[141]

(3) Separation

The emphasis on continuity with the covenant people of God led to a

---

[141] LaSor, et al., *Old Testament Survey,* 657.

strong emphasis on separation from any form of defilement or syncretism with the surrounding people. The postexilic community was a tiny island in a great sea of peoples and religious traditions. It was important that the covenant community remain pure in doctrine, customs, and ethical norms. Ezra's and Nehemiah's actions may seem harsh, but the Book of Ezra-Nehemiah should show us how important it was in God's plan that this covenant community continue. As Merrill has written, "Against the backdrop of the Exile, a judgment that had taken place precisely because the covenant nation had abandoned this principle of exclusivity, it is most evident why Ezra-Nehemiah gives evidence of such interest in the purity of the postexile remnant."[142] Through this community God brought to the whole world his revelation in the Scriptures and his redemption in Christ.

This was a crucial point in the history of the Jewish people. Unchecked assimilation would have meant the end of the community. Some blame Ezra and Nehemiah for the "legalism gone to seed" that we find in the Jewish community in the time of Jesus.[143] It is true that later, especially after the life-and-death conflict with Hellenism in the Maccabean period, some of these emphases were exaggerated. Some of the Jews accepted Hellenism and virtually abandoned their Jewish faith, "but it was such conservative and exclusivistic groups as the Hasidim that preserved Judaism and led the way toward Christianity."[144]

(4) Scripture

Ezra-Nehemiah affirms the centrality of the Law (the Torah, or the first five books of the OT) of God in the life of the community. Though it has become popular to say that Ezra introduced the Pentateuch to the community, this is nowhere stated in the book. The people already knew that the law of Moses was authoritative. Ezra was not presenting a new book recently finished; he was recalling the people to the law of God which they had neglected.

The situation as seen in the Book of Malachi is similar to that of Ezra-Nehemiah. Malachi may have preached slightly before Ezra's time

---

[142] E. H. Merrill, "A Theology of Ezra-Nehemiah and Esther," in *A Biblical Theology of the Old Testament,* ed. R. B. Zuck (Chicago: Moody, 1991), 194.

[143] But "the real error lay with those who perpetuated these measures and attitudes long after they were needed, thus producing that prejudice against Gentiles which the New Testament exposes and which the early Church had difficulty in overcoming" (LaSor, et al., *Old Testament Survey,* 656).

[144] R. A. Bowman, "Ezra—Nehemiah," *IB,* vol. 3 (Nashville: Abingdon, 1954), 566.

in Jerusalem. That situation of ethical laxity and neglect did not prevail because the law did not exist but because the priests had failed to teach it (Mal 2:6-9; 3:7; 4:4). As in the Protestant Reformation, the Bible's impact on people's lives awaited only its availability, not its existence.

Ezra-Nehemiah teaches that Scripture reveals God's will. The revival started with those who "trembled at the words of the God of Israel" (Ezra 9:4; 10:3). Ezra's prayer in Ezra 9 and that of the people in Neh 9 both show a profound understanding of God and his ways as revealed in the Pentateuch. The Book of Ezra-Nehemiah calls the people back to the centrality of God's revelation in "the Law of Moses, which the LORD, the God of Israel, had given" (Ezra 7:6). It constantly says the people acted "in accordance with what is written" (Ezra 3:2-4; 6:18; Neh 8:14-15). More than anywhere else in Scripture, these books show the power of God at work through written texts.[145] As Artaxerxes wrote to Ezra (7:25), the Bible is "the wisdom of your God, which you possess [lit., which is in your hand]."

(5) Worship

The religious or worship experience of the people is also central in Ezra-Nehemiah. When the first group of exiles returned from Babylon, they first built an altar to sacrifice to God; only afterwards did they build the temple. Still later they built the walls. This priority is correct; worship and a correct relation to God must be at the center of our personal lives and the believing community.

This emphasis on worship is visible throughout the book in the details about sacrifices, the priests and Levites, and the singers. Several important religious celebrations are described (Ezra 3:10-13; 6:16-22; Neh 12:27-43). The daily sacrifices were accompanied with songs and thanksgiving (Neh 11:17,23; 12:8-9). The temple staff and organization were important (Neh 11:15-24).

The temple was vital to the Jewish community, for it was a symbol of God's presence and a reminder that they were to be "a kingdom of priests and a holy nation" (Exod 19:6). "The community without worship," Merrill has observed, "could serve no effective function."[146] One of the purposes of the book is to show how God led and provided for the

---

[145] Eskenazi (*Age of Prose,* 58; see also 41-42, 110-11) observed, "The repetition of "as it is written" in Ezra 3:4 [and 3:2b] stresses the theme of compliance with the definitive written documents and the fulfillment of the written word in the life of the community."

[146] Merrill, "A Theology of Ezra-Nehemiah and Esther," 196.

rebuilding of the temple and the city as God's dwelling place.[147] When
the temple was completed, the people celebrated with a large dedication
service, where they "offered a hundred bulls, two hundred rams, four
hundred male lambs and, as a sin offering for all Israel twelve male
goats" (Ezra 6:17). Soon afterward they celebrated the Passover. Then
when the city wall was complete another great celebration was held (Neh
12:27–13:3).

The need to protect the purity of their worship was one of the motives
for the Jews' emphasis on separation. The Jews seem to have been cured
of idolatry by this time, but they were concerned to protect their worship
from surrogate forms of their own religion. As we reflect on God's work
in history, we can thank him that this community of believing, worshiping Jews was preserved.[148]

(6) Prayer

The importance of prayer is taken for granted throughout Ezra-
Nehemiah. Particularly Ezra's extensive prayer in Ezra 9 and that of the
people in Neh 9 show their belief that God hears and answers prayer.
They praised God, confessed sins, depended on God's promises, and
made requests.

Furthermore, the work of Ezra and Nehemiah was bathed in prayer.
Before starting out on the journey to Jerusalem, Ezra proclaimed a fast
"so that we might humble ourselves before our God and ask him for a
safe journey" (Ezra 8:21). Nehemiah fasted and prayed "for some days"
(Neh 1:4) before attempting to ask the king's permission to return to
Jerusalem. Nehemiah constantly mentions short prayers that he made in
moments of crisis (e.g., Neh 2:4-5). He presents us with an admirable example of combining prayer with action. Several times he asked God to
"remember" him (Neh 5:19; 13:14,22,31). The whole book can teach us a
great deal about trusting God in prayer.

(7) History

Ezra-Nehemiah consists mostly of narration; therefore we can call it
historiography. In fact, over half of both the Old and New Testaments

---

[147] See Eskenazi, *Age of Prose,* 53-57, for an argument that the temple and the city together constitute the house of God in Ezra-Nehemiah.

[148] Fensham says: "It is amazing that such a small, poor group of people could have
become the foundation for the development of one of the largest religions of modern
times, Christianity" (*Ezra and Nehemiah*, 19).

consists of narration. So our understanding of history and of a biblical view of history is vital for a proper understanding of these books.

We live in a time when people are conscious that history has molded our culture and our society. We are aware of the fact that today's decisions determine tomorrow's history. One's way of looking at history determines one's worldview. What one believes about God, about creation, and about humanity determines one's way of looking at history. Is there a supreme being who intervenes in history? in the affairs of nations, of peoples, of individuals? Does God control history? Is the human being merely a highly developed animal or a special creation made in God's image? Is everything determined so that our decisions will not really make any difference? Will God right all wrongs? Does punishment await those who disobey God? Is there a glorious future for those who love God? Can we be sure of the final victory? Do present decisions determine that future?

Most modern philosophies of history were influenced by the Bible; however, many ideas that originated in Judeo-Christian circles have become grossly distorted and antibiblical in perspective. We cannot insist that all Christians must have exactly the same historical perspective. However, a Christian's way of looking at history, including biblical history, should take seriously the Bible's own perspective. In other words, our philosophy of history must be coherent with scriptural teaching concerning history. One of the chief causes for scepticism about the historicity of some of the material in Ezra-Nehemiah (and other biblical books) is that some scholars try to force on the biblical narrative historical perspectives (philosophies of history) that clash with the Bible's own view of history. One's presuppositions about the supernatural, about God's intervention in historical happenings, and about the possibility of miracles and the possibility that God can reveal his will to human beings are crucial in the interpretation of biblical narrative.

The narrative of Ezra-Nehemiah does not pretend to be "objective" history, but is rather history with a passion.[149] It was written for a purpose, as we have seen. The author wanted to teach certain truths to readers of the work. Ezra-Nehemiah is theological history—history presented with a theological interpretation and purpose. Since the author wrote under God's inspiration, this theological interpretation is trustworthy and

---

[149] We may question whether such a thing exists. Any history is written from some point of view. Even daily newspaper reports about current historical happenings are not completely objective. A journalist decides what news is important, and the story is influenced by the writer and editor.

authoritative for God's people.

The author of Ezra-Nehemiah did not pretend to give us a complete record of all that happened in the postexilic community. Rather, he carefully chose the material in order to show God's providence, the continuity of the covenant community, the importance of keeping separate from pagan nations, and the need to obey God's law.

We usually think of Deuteronomy and the Former Prophets (Joshua, Judges, Samuel, Kings) as the part of the Old Testament most occupied with a conscious presentation of a view of history. This view of history includes the following postulates or premises: (1) God is sovereign; (2) humanity was created in God's image; (3) God created the universe (it did not evolve under its own innate powers); (4) a biblical view of history involves a biblical understanding of metaphysics; (5) humanity has become alienated from God; (6) there is a divine plan of salvation; (7) God made a covenant with his people; (8) God makes promises and fulfills them; (9) historical events demonstrate that God fulfills his promises; (10) not everything that happens is according to God's desires (in the universe are enemies of God and malignant forces); (11) the nature of God's action in a given moment is related to humankind's response; and (12) the proclamation of God's Word is the most effective power in history.[150] While this is based on the historical books mentioned, the same view of history is seen throughout the whole Bible.

Ezra-Nehemiah may not enunciate all these premises to the extent that we find them in Samuel and Kings; but if we examine the book closely, we will see that the author took for granted the same view of history. God is sovereign; it was God who put Cyrus in power and moved him to let the Jews return to their land. God moved Darius to give the order to complete the temple. All of Ezra-Nehemiah reflects the idea that God is the driving force behind the events that led to the restoration of the Jewish community.

The Books of Deuteronomy, Kings, and Chronicles show that disobedience brought God's punishment and led to the Babylonian captivity. Ezra-Nehemiah makes the same point. The people suffered the exile because of their sins (e.g., Ezra 9:7); now they must cleanse themselves and put away foreign wives, or they will again be punished (9:14). God's favor and kindness, however, cannot be earned by obedience but are the results of his mercy and grace (Ezra 9:8-9,13; Neh 9:17-25,28,31).

Ezra-Nehemiah shows that God is faithful in keeping his promises. In

---

[150] From M. Breneman, "La visión de la historia en el Antiguo Testamento," published by the Kairos Community in Buenos Aires, Argentina.

fact, the first sentence of the book places its entire account in the context of promise-fulfillment: "In order to fulfill the word of the Lord spoken by Jeremiah, the Lord moved the heart of Cyrus" (Ezra 1:1). Although the prophets are not mentioned frequently in Ezra-Nehemiah, the author certainly was familiar with their message and saw the return from exile as the restoration promised in Isaiah and Jeremiah. The influence of Jer 31 can be seen in Ezra 7–9 as the author used similar themes and vocabulary in combining the teaching on repentance and God's salvation.[151] He sees the return from Babylon to Jerusalem as the new exodus prophesied by Isaiah and Jeremiah. It was at least a partial fulfillment of prophetic expectations.

Ezra's prayer in Ezra 9 also takes up the remnant theology of Isaiah and Jeremiah. In 9:14 he says, "Shall we again break your commands and intermarry with the peoples who commit such detestable practices? Would you not be angry enough with us to destroy us, leaving us no remnant or survivor?" The word "remnant" (šĕ'ērît) is the same as in Jer 31:7. But in the next verse ("We are left this day as a remnant") he used pĕlêṭâ for "remnant." This is the word used for "remnant" in Isa 10:20-21 and 37:31-32. The passage also includes other parallels with Isa 10.[152] Ezra recognized that the people were still guilty of disobedience. The presence of this remnant is a partial fulfillment of prophecy, but in view of the prophetic promises the people's continuing sinfulness means there must be greater fulfillment in the future. The prayer in Neh 9 also recognizes that the situation under Persia was not the glorious future promised in the prophets: "But see, we are slaves today, slaves in the land you gave our forefathers so they could eat its fruit and the other good things it produces. Because of our sins, its abundant harvest goes to the kings you have placed over us. They rule over our bodies and our cattle as they please. We are in great distress" (vv. 36-37).[153]

In his prayer Ezra used a number of motifs from Jeremiah and Isaiah "in ways that are both overlapping and complementary, in order to express the belief that the exiles' situation is a stage on the way to an ulti-

---

[151] J. G. McConville, "Ezra-Nehemiah and the Fulfillment of Prophecy," *VT* 36 (1986): 216.

[152] Ibid., 220.

[153] McConville challenges the popular view that sees no eschatological hope in Ezra-Nehemiah. He notes K. Koch's article "Ezra and the Origins of Judaism," *JSS* 19 (1974): 173-97, in which Koch shows that the author of Ezra-Nehemiah saw the exilic community as a partial fulfillment of the promises in the Pentateuch, but he looked forward to a greater future fulfillment. He points out that "Torah for Ezra was essentially not law but promise" (McConville, "Fulfillment of Prophecy," 206).

mate fulfillment of prophecy."[154] Ezra-Nehemiah teaches the same view of history and of God's intervention in history that the prophets had. It does not quote the prophets but does show evidence that the postexilic community saw itself as a God-preserved remnant through which God would continue to fulfill his promises.

6. The Significance of Ezra

According to Ezra 7:10, "Ezra had devoted himself to the study and observance of the Law of the Lord, and to teaching its decrees and laws in Israel." But he is not even mentioned in 2 Maccabees, although Nehemiah was honored (2 Macc 1:18-36). Likewise, Ezra is not among the list of Israel's heroes in Ecclesiasticus (Sirach), although Nehemiah was included (49:11-13).[155] In the Talmud, however, Ezra was considered the founder of the Great Assembly (*Megilla* 18b). The great rabbis considered him the founder of the postexilic scribal and rabbinic activity. Among many talmudic references to his work, most significantly he is credited with reestablishing the law in Israel after it had been forgotten (*Sukkah* 20a). Another text says that Ezra and the Torah were more important than the reconstruction of the temple (*Megilla* 16b).[156] According to 2 Esdras, Ezra was the only prophet left after the Babylonian destruction of Jerusalem (12:42). A second Moses, he rewrote the Scriptures in forty days (14:19-48); like Elijah, he would be taken up to heaven (8:19; 14:9). Josephus also praised Ezra and said he lived to a ripe old age and died in Jerusalem *(Ant.,* 120-58).[157]

The Book of Ezra-Nehemiah presents Ezra as a strong personality. He did not emphasize the law as an end in itself; rather, he was convinced that the covenant community needed to return to God by taking seriously his revelation and applying it to every aspect of life. Ezra's prayer of confession (Ezra 9) demonstrates his genuine concern for the spiritual life of the people. He realized, "as perhaps no one else had since Moses

---

[154] Ibid., 222.

[155] Blenkinsopp, *Ezra-Nehemiah,* 55-56, explains the omissions as deliberate. Second Maccabees is a pro-Hasmonean document that viewed Nehemiah as a role model. Identified with Zerubbabel, he was understood to be "the real founder of the Second Commonwealth, the forerunner of those who had to repeat the task after the lapse of more than three and a half centuries." Ecclesiasticus, he says, anticipates this ideology, preferring Nehemiah's "political realism" to "Ezra's single-minded theocratic ideal" and stricter marriage policy.

[156] Myers, *Ezra, Nehemiah,* lxxii-lxxiii. See also Blenkinsopp, *Ezra-Nehemiah,* 57-59.

[157] Myers, *Ezra, Nehemiah,* lxxii.

and the prophets, that man cannot live by bread alone, only by and through the words that proceed from the mouth of God."[158]

7. The Significance of Nehemiah

Nehemiah was a genuine leader, an excellent administrator, and a man of prayer. He exhibited many principles of sound administrative practice. Nehemiah's singlemindedness of purpose, attention to detail, willingness to delegate authority, dedication to service, and dependence on God were combined in a man who can simply be labeled as a servant of God.

Although neglected by the author of 1 Esdras, Nehemiah is praised in Sir 49:13 and 2 Macc 1:18-36.[159] Josephus also presented a positive picture of Nehemiah (*Ant.,* 159-83). Certainly Nehemiah's work in establishing the Jerusalem community, defending it against its neighbors and against syncretism, has left its mark on history. Because this community persevered, our Old Testament was completed and preserved. Because the Jewish people continued as instruments in God's redemptive plan, the Savior came and fulfilled God's great plan of salvation.

OUTLINE OF EZRA-NEHEMIAH

---

[158] Ibid., lxxiv.

[159] Blenkinsopp, *Ezra-Nehemiah,* 57, explains that the intent of 1 Esdras "appears to be to elevate Zerubbabel and Ezra as the founding fathers at the expense of Nehemiah. And in that case it could be plausibly read as countering the kind of pro-Hasmonean propaganda represented by the letter [2 Macc 1:10b-2:18]."

      (1) Spiritual Preparation (8:21-23)
      (2) Administrative Preparation (8:24-30)
   8. The Journey (8:31-32)
   9. The Temple Donations Delivered (8:33-34)
 10. Worship and Sacrifices (8:35-36)
IV. Keeping the Covenant: The Problem of Intermarriage (9:1–10:44)
   1. Ezra's Humility and Consternation (9:1-5)
   2. Ezra's Prayer of Confession (9:6-15)
      (1) Confession of Sin (9:6-7)
      (2) Recognition of God's Goodness (9:8-9)
      (3) Recognition of Disobedience (9:10-12)
      (4) Plea for God's Mercy (9:13-15)
   3. The Covenant to Change (10:1-6)
   4. The Assembly of the People (10:7-11)
   5. Positive, Orderly Response (10:12-17)
   6. Those Guilty of Intermarriage (10:18-44)
V. Restoring Jerusalem: Nehemiah Builds the Walls (1:1–7:73a)
   1. News from Jerusalem (1:1-3)
   2. Nehemiah's Concern and Prayer (1:4-11)
      (1) Confession of Sin (1:4-7)
      (2) Plea for God's Help (1:8-11)
   3. Nehemiah's Mission and Commission (2:1-10)
      (1) Nehemiah's Sadness (2:1-2)
      (2) Nehemiah's Request (2:3-5)
      (3) The Requests Granted (2:6-8)
      (4) Action and Opposition (2:9-10)
   4. Nehemiah Surveys the Walls (2:11-20)
      (1) The Secret Inspection by Night (2:11-16)
      (2) Nehemiah Presents the Challenge (2:17-18)
      (3) Opposition by Ridicule (2:19-20)
   5. Building for Unity: The Community Rebuilds the Wall (3:1-32)
      (1) Repairing the Northern and Western Walls (3:1-15)
      (2) The Construction of the Eastern Wall (3:16-32)
   6. Opposition to Building the Wall (4:1-23)
      (1) Opposition by Ridicule (4:1-6)
      (2) Opposition by Plot (4:7-9)
      (3) Internal Opposition: Discouragement and Fear (4:10-15)
      (4) Diligence and Readiness in the Work (4:16-23)
   7. Oppression within the Community (5:1-19)
      (1) Extortion by the Rich (5:1-5)

I. PROPHECY FULFILLED: FIRST RETURN FROM EXILE
   (1:1–2:70)
   1. The Providence of God: The Decree of Cyrus (1:1-4)
      (1) Introduction (1:1)
      (2) The Proclamation of Freedom (1:2-4)
   2. Moved by God to Return (1:5-11)
   3. The Restoration of the Community: List of Returnees (2:1-70)
      (1) The Leaders (2:1-2a)
      (2) Names of Clans (2:2b-20)
      (3) Geographical Names (2:21-35)
      (4) The Priests (2:36-39)
      (5) The Levites (2:40-42)
      (6) The Temple Servants (2:43-54)
      (7) Descendants of Solomon's Servants (2:55-58)
      (8) Others (2:59-63)
      (9) The Totals and Contributions for the Temple (2:64-69)
      (10) Settlement in the Villages (2:70)

————————**I. PROPHECY FULFILLED: FIRST RETURN**————————
FROM EXILE (1:1–2:70)

The first six chapters of Ezra describe the first return (or returns) from exile and the reconstruction of the temple. Ezra does not appear on the scene until chap. 7, some eighty years after the events of the first chapter and fifty-eight years after the completion of the temple (chap. 6).

Although the small Jewish community faced many problems, we must commend them for putting first things first. In emphasizing worship, they built the altar and then the temple. Their efforts to rebuild the temple, however, were stalled by opposition. After nearly two decades, in 520 B.C., God used the prophets Haggai and Zechariah to stir up the people by stimulating them to *faith,* to overcome the opposition, and to *action,* to finish the temple.

According to Dan 1:1, some Jews had been deported to Babylon in 605 B.C. In 597 others had been exiled, among them Ezekiel. Jerusalem had been destroyed in 587 B.C., and many more of the Jews had been carried to Babylon. It was a hard time for the Jews to maintain their faith. Both Jeremiah and Ezekiel had explained that these calamities came upon them as punishment for disobedience and because they had not returned to God. Their messages called the people to repentance and warned them of God's severe judgment by death and exile. But they also had prophesied a message of hope, the promise of a return to their own land. God used these prophecies to keep Israel's faith alive during these years.

Although many Jews in Babylon were comfortably settled and had little desire to return to Judah, others prayed for and desired to return. They longed to worship God together and offer sacrifices in their own temple according to their own law and traditions. So the first chapters of Ezra tell the story of a second exodus, one of the most important events in Jewish history and thus in the history of God's redemptive plan.

1. The Providence of God: The Decree of Cyrus (1:1-4)

(1) Introduction (1:1)

¹In the first year of Cyrus king of Persia, in order to fulfill the word of the LORD spoken by Jeremiah, the LORD moved the heart of Cyrus king of Persia to make a proclamation throughout his realm and to put it in writing:

1:1 Typical of biblical history, the author explained events in terms of the divine will. Neutral "objective" history free from "prejudices" and "presuppositions" does not exist. A person's view of history, which is part of one's whole worldview, is important. It is formed, at least partly, by one's theological convictions. It affects how one understands historical events and determines how one understands biblical events. Ezra helps us form a biblical view of history; at the same time, a biblical view of history enables us to understand Ezra. We have here, then, a theological interpretation of events.

The author of Ezra-Nehemiah presented his material in a chronological framework. The author was concerned about history but did not pretend to give a complete history of postexilic times. Rather, he chose events that were significant in the reestablishment, continuity, and reorganization of the covenant community. This whole section (Ezra 1–6) emphasizes God's sovereignty and his providence; God works in history to fulfill his will. God has preserved the covenant community; he has brought the Jews back to their land; he has even used the rulers of other nations to fulfill his purposes.

Cyrus's decision did not just happen. At a specific time, 538 B.C.,[1] the Lord caused Cyrus to act in a way that fulfilled specific prophecies. Jeremiah (25:11-12; 29:10) had predicted that the Babylonian captivity would last for seventy years and then God would fulfill his "gracious promise to bring [them] back to this place."[2] The Hebrew word used in Ezra 1:1 suggests that the author was also familiar with Jer 51:1,11 and the remarkable prophecies of Isa 41:2,25; 44:28; 45:1,13.[3]

As noted in the Introduction, the author of Ezra-Nehemiah understood this as a fulfillment of prophecy, but not necessarily a complete fulfillment. Judah was not completely restored (Jer 29:14; 30:18-21), the Jews did not have their own king (Jer 30:8-9), the palace was not rebuilt (Jer 30:18), and Israel did not rule over other nations (Isa 45:14; 49:22-23).[4]

The "proclamation" is the famous "Edict of Cyrus." A secular historian would not have seen God's hand in this. The Cyrus Cylinder, a clay barrel inscription found in Hormuzd Rassam's excavations at Babylon (1879–82), shows that this king made similar proclamations concerning other people's gods.[5] But our author saw here the providence of God, a theme that is prominent throughout the book. The author of Ezra-Nehemiah, with his biblical view of history, challenges us also to believe that God works within a specific time frame, that he has a plan, that he keeps his word, and that his prophecies will be fulfilled. God *does* influ-

---

[1] Cyrus entered Babylon in October of 539, so this decree would have been given in 538 B.C.

[2] The present passage does not mention the seventy years, but the parallel in 2 Chr 36:20 does. Some commentators point out that from the fall of Jerusalem (587) until the first return (538) would not have been long enough to fulfill the prophecy of seventy years. If we calculate until the completion of the temple (516), it would be almost exactly seventy years. But as Fensham points out (*The Books of Ezra and Nehemiah* [Grand Rapids: Eerdmans, 1982], 43), Jer 29:10 refers to Babylonian rule and could also be calculated from the fall of Nineveh (612) or the accession of Nebuchadnezzar (605). In any case, Ezra 1:1 shows that God remembered his promise and fulfilled it.

[3] The Hebrew word used here, הֵעִיר ("moved"), means "stir up." H. G. M. Williamson (*Ezra, Nehemiah* [Waco: Word, 1985], 9-10) suggests that the author had these passages in mind since the same Hebrew word is used in Jer 51 and Isa 41, and he also had in mind passages that point to the more specific prophecy of Isa 44:28; 45:1,13. Notice how explicit it is Isa 45:13: "I will raise up Cyrus in my righteousness. . . . He will rebuild my city and set my exiles free."

[4] See J. G. McConville, "Ezra-Nehemiah and the Fulfillment of Prophecy," *VT* 36 (1986): 205-24; F. C. Holmgren, *Ezra and Nehemiah* (Grand Rapids: Eerdmans, 1987), 7.

[5] *ANET,* 315-16. Cyrus tells how Marduk chose him to be ruler of all the world and how he delivered Babylon into his hands. Then he tells how he sent back their former inhabitants to certain cities and also returned their gods (images) to their sanctuaries. See Introduction.

ence people to accomplish his will. J. G. McConville explains that "behind this opening verse . . . lies the affirmation that all the might of the ancient world was in subjection to God, and put at the disposal of his people for their salvation."[6]

The last phrase, "and to put it in writing," is significant; for in the ancient Near East important matters were put in writing. Thousands of clay tablets containing laws, receipts, decrees, and covenants give evidence of this. Later in Ezra (chap. 6) we will see why the written document again became significant for the Jewish community.

The word "writing" is a somewhat technical term used of writings or inscriptions designated for the public eye. The Edict of Cyrus was announced orally and also displayed publicly in writing.

(2) The Proclamation of Freedom (1:2-4)

2 "This is what Cyrus king of Persia says:
"'The LORD, the God of heaven, has given me all the kingdoms of the earth and he has appointed me to build a temple for him at Jerusalem in Judah. 3Anyone of his people among you—may his God be with him, and let him go up to Jerusalem in Judah and build the temple of the LORD, the God of Israel, the God who is in Jerusalem. 4And the people of any place where survivors may now be living are to provide him with silver and gold, with goods and livestock, and with freewill offerings for the temple of God in Jerusalem.'"

1:2 This is the Edict of Cyrus or the Cyrus Decree. The decree sounds as though Cyrus were a true believer in the God of Israel. But other inscriptions[7] indicate that Cyrus followed a consistent policy of honoring the religions and customs of his different subject peoples.

In Ezra 6:3-5 we find an Aramaic version of the decree to rebuild the

---

[6] J. G. McConville, *Ezra, Nehemiah, and Esther* (Philadelphia: Westminster, 1985), 7.

[7] Williamson (*Ezra, Nehemiah*, 11-12) notes several examples. R. de Vaux (*The Bible and the Ancient Near East* [N.Y.: Doubleday, 1971], 65-67) cites a number of texts that show Cyrus's support of the religious customs of different cities in Mesopotamia. A rather long inscription from Babylon, the Cyrus Cylinder, also says: "Marduk, the great lord, a protector of his people, beheld with pleasure his good deeds and his upright heart and therefore ordered him to march against his city Babylon" (p. 65). Also at Uruk the sanctuary of Ishtar was repaired soon after Nabonidus's reign. Bricks from the paved floor show it was Cyrus's work: "Cyrus, king of the lands, who loves the Esagila and the Ezida, son of Cambyses, the mighty king, I" (p. 68). In the restored wall of a temple in Ur, a brick was inscribed with the following: "Cyrus, king of all, king of Anshan, son of Cambyses, king of Anshan, the great gods have delivered all the lands into my hand; the land I have made to dwell in a peaceful habitation" (p. 69).

temple. It is often said to be the same decree, but there are some differences. In 6:3-5 only the rebuilding of the temple is referred to, not the return. Also it includes the return of the vessels. Ezra 1:2-4 and 6:3-5 could be shorter versions of a longer decree. E. Bickerman says they are two independent records concerning the same case. Ezra 6:3-5, he says, is a memorandum or record of the decree. "It is an instruction for the royal treasury concerned with the expenses for building anew the temple in Jerusalem."[8] It was a document stored in Ecbatana, where Cyrus stayed in the summer of his first year. What we have in Ezra 1 is the "royal proclamation" announced throughout the kingdom. "Thus there were (at least) two orders of Cyrus relevant to the return from captivity; a royal proclamation addressed to the Jews and published by the heralds everywhere in many languages, including Hebrew (Ezra 1), and on the other hand, a *Memorandum* to the royal treasurer, in Aramaic, which was not made public at this time."[9]

The decree shows familiarity with biblical terms and themes.[10] Some suggest that the author was giving a free rendering of the decree; however, Cyrus more likely conferred with the Jews in making the proclamation[11] because in other decrees he used the language of the people involved.

1:3 Certainly God's providence is evident here. "Let him go up" should be understood as permission, even encouragement to go, but not a command. The Jews were free to decide. A major theme of the book is introduced as their purpose for going: to "build the temple of the LORD, the God of Israel."

1:4 Verse 4 is somewhat ambiguous about whether "survivors" refers to the Jews or to all the people in these areas. It likely refers primarily to the Jews who decided to stay in Babylon, but it may also include other neighbors.[12] Notice that those who went had to *decide* to go. This decision would result in insecurity, hardship, and suffering as the returnees started a new, precarious community. But they had a purpose: they were concerned that the faith of their community continue. Their faith, decision, and action were of great importance in the continuation of

---

[8] E. Bickerman, "The Edict of Cyrus in Ezra 1," *JBL* 65 (1946): 251.

[9] Ibid., 253.

[10] "The God of Heaven" occurs frequently in the Elephantine Papyri (Fensham, *Ezra and Nehemiah*), 43.

[11] This probably was in response to a petition by the Jews. Williamson (*Ezra and Nehemiah*) notes one clear example from the Elephantine Papyri when the Jews there asked for authorization to rebuild their temple. The other is the Xanthos trilingual inscription.

[12] See comments on v. 6.

God's plan of redemption, both in providing the Scriptures and in preparing the way for the Redeemer.

The "survivors," or the ones who remained,[13] were encouraged to provide goods, gifts, and offerings for those who returned to Jerusalem. God's work is best accomplished with the freewill offerings[14] of those who worship him.

2. Moved by God to Return (1:5-11)

[5]Then the family heads of Judah and Benjamin, and the priests and Levites—everyone whose heart God had moved—prepared to go up and build the house of the LORD in Jerusalem. [6]All their neighbors assisted them with articles of silver and gold, with goods and livestock, and with valuable gifts, in addition to all the freewill offerings. [7]Moreover, King Cyrus brought out the articles belonging to the temple of the LORD, which Nebuchadnezzar had carried away from Jerusalem and had placed in the temple of his god. [8]Cyrus king of Persia had them brought by Mithredath the treasurer, who counted them out to Sheshbazzar the prince of Judah.

[9]This was the inventory:

gold dishes	30
silver dishes	1,000
silver pans	29
[10]gold bowls	30
matching silver bowls	410
other articles	1,000

[11]In all, there were 5,400 articles of gold and of silver. Sheshbazzar brought all these along when the exiles came up from Babylon to Jerusalem.

1:5 The ones who responded to Cyrus's decree and began preparations to return to Jerusalem were those "whose heart God had moved." God sovereignly uses his own people as well as foreign rulers (v. 1) to accomplish his will. Their purpose in going to Jerusalem also was God-centered; they went to build the house of the Lord. The author made clear that the return from the exile was God's work; God took the initiative,

---

[13] The Heb., הַנִּשְׁאָר, is better understood as "those who remained." These were not survivors of the destruction of Jerusalem but ones who remained in Babylonia and did not go up to Jerusalem.

[14] The somewhat technical priestly term הַנְּדָבָה ("freewill offering") also indicates the Jewish influence on the language of the decree.

and the people responded.

The author emphasized the rebuilding of the temple and the vessels that belonged in it. From the beginning he made clear that he considered the restoration and rebuilding of the worshiping community as the most significant event in this history. Here is a parallel with the exodus. The large section of the Book of Exodus dedicated to the construction of the tabernacle and the establishment of worship (chaps. 25–40) is often given little attention by the modern reader. Perhaps Ezra-Nehemiah is often neglected because it deals with the same theme. However, "It must not be overlooked that revelatory events only continue to be revelatory through the formation of some kind of community structure which 'remembers' the event and reflects on its implications for life."[15] Religious traditions and "institutionalization" may sometimes become obstacles to true faith if they become the objects of faith, but they are also necessary to the survival of faith and faithfulness to God's word.[16]

"Family heads" (v. 5; lit. "the heads of the fathers"[17]) refers to the extended family, the normal sociological division of the people. The community of families made the important decisions. The Jews who returned to Jerusalem returned by family units. The biblical pattern emphasized the family unit as the basis of society. Modern tendencies to revoke this only lead to sociological confusion.

The author of Ezra-Nehemiah was careful to emphasize the continuity of the postexilic community with the preexilic Judean community. He included everyone under four genealogical headings: Judah, Benjamin, priests, and Levites. We do not hear of a return of the exiles from the Northern Kingdom, Israel. Thus in Jewish legend they are spoken of as the ten lost tribes. However, the author of Chronicles noted that some from the northern tribes went to live in Judah after the division of the kingdom (2 Chr 11:16) and even included some from Ephraim and Manasseh among those who resettled after the Babylonian captivity. Thus some descendants from other tribes were among those who returned from captivity (see 1 Chr 9:3).[18]

Behind the decision to go was God's work in the heart.[19] God raises up leaders and gives them responsibility, and God works in others to re-

---

[15] Holmgren, *Ezra & Nehemiah*, 12.

[16] Ibid.

[17] רָאשֵׁי הָאָבוֹת is common in the Persian period and corresponds to מִשְׁפָּחָה in the preexilic period (Williamson, *Ezra, Nehemiah,* 15).

[18] See D. Kidner, *Ezra and Nehemiah,* TOTC (Downers Grove: InterVarsity, 1979), 34.

[19] The author used the same word הֵעִיר that he used in v. 1, "The LORD *moved* the heart of Cyrus."

spond and participate in his work. Revivals are a result of God's work in the whole community and in each individual.

God's work requires decision and faith, but it also calls for planning and preparation and demands a specific goal. The establishment of the Jewish community in their land was important; but here the immediate, realizable goal was the construction of the temple. We can imagine the intense discussion in the villages where Jews lived, the difficulty of making such a momentous decision, and the packing of clothes and household essentials. No doubt those who were leaving had to sell or give away some of their possessions.

1:6 "All their neighbors assisted them" does not seem to have in mind primarily their Jewish neighbors, as was the case in the decree (v. 4). Throughout the book the author included motifs of the exodus. Here he remembered how the Israelites borrowed goods from their neighbors when they left Egypt[20] and later gave abundant freewill offerings for the tabernacle. The people gave or "loaned" to the Israelites so much that Exod 12:36 says they "plundered" the Egyptians. This aspect of the exodus is also remembered in Israel's poetry: "He brought out Israel, laden with silver and gold" (Ps 105:37). As has been true throughout history, God moves people to provide for his work.

1:7 The fact that "King Cyrus brought out the articles" is significant. When a king captured a nation, he would take that nation's gods (images) and cult objects to his own capital. This symbolized the victory of his gods over the gods of the subject peoples. So in addition to their great value as beautiful and costly objects, they symbolized religious values. In 587 Nebuchadnezzar had carried these objects to Babylon.[21] Cyrus's decision to return the objects used in Israelite worship (of course there were no images of God) shows his seriousness in respecting his subjects' religion and customs. The memorandum of Cyrus's decree in Ezra 6:5 specifically mentions that these objects were to be returned to the temple in Jerusalem.

1:8 Both the name "Mithredath" and his title "treasurer"[22] are Persian words, confirming the book's Persian context. "Sheshbazzar" was a Jew with a Babylonian name.[23] Although he disappeared from the scene, he led the first group of returnees.[24] The articles were handled seriously

---

[20] Note a similar emphasis in Exod 3:21-22; 11:2; 12:35-36; Ps 105:37. Also see the second exodus theme in Isa 43:14-16.

[21] See 2 Kgs 24:13; 25:13-16; 2 Chr 36:10,18; Jer 52:17-19; Dan 1:2.

[22] Hebrew הַגִּזְבָּר from Persian *ganzabara* (Fensham, *Ezra and Nehemiah*, 46).

[23] Probably *šamaš-abla-uṣur*, "The sun god protects the father" (Williamson, *Ezra, Nehemiah*, 5; Fensham, *Ezra and Nehemiah*, 46).

and carefully: the treasurer "counted them out" to Sheshbazzar.

1:9-10 The author apparently had a copy of the memorandum or inventory list of the objects, but it is not clear to us what each article represents. Ibn Ezra, the Jewish commentator, said the "gold dishes" were the vessels used to collect the blood of the slaughtered lambs.[25] The translation of the word for "silver pans" is uncertain; some have related it to a Hebrew word used for the knife used in the ritual slaughter of animals.[26]

1:11 The total of "5,400 articles" is not the same as the sum of those listed. Several explanations have been suggested. Perhaps the list in vv. 9-10 refers only to the most important vessels. Or the author, in using the inventory list, may have copied only an exemplary part of the list but included the total.

Throughout chap. 1 the author's purpose was clearly to show the small postexilic Jewish community their legitimate continuity with the preexilic community and with God's plan of redemption. Therefore he used motifs from the exodus; he emphasized God's providence; he mentioned Judah, Benjamin, priests, and Levites; and he explained that even the former articles from the temple had been returned.[27] How thrilling this climax must have been to his readers, "when the exiles came up from Babylon to Jerusalem" (v. 11). In light of subsequent history God's continuing work in that community, which culminated in providing the Messiah and the promised salvation, demonstrates that this was one of the most important events in history.

3. The Restoration of the Community: List of Returnees (2:1-70)

The modern reader usually skips or skims this chapter. Why was this long list of names included? What value did it have for its first readers? What value does it have for us? Again, the author and his readers were concerned about the continuity of this community with the preexilic Jewish nation. It was important to show that this community, though small and weak, continued God's plan for Israel. They were his covenant people and thus inherited the promises concerning the future. For this it was important that members of the community, valued as individuals by God, be sure of their genealogy. The author was concerned to preserve the pu-

---

[24] See Introduction.

[25] J. J. Slotki, *Daniel, Ezra and Nehemiah,* Soncino Books of the Bible (London: Soncino, 1951), 114.

[26] Ibid.

[27] See P. R. Ackroyd, "The Temple Vessels—A Continuity Theme," *VTS* 23 (1972): 166-81.

rity of the Jewish community.

This same list, with some variations, appears again in Neh 7:6-73 (and 1 Esdr 5:4-46). Either one is a copy of the other, or both are copied from the same original. If the author already had the substance of the book (Ezra 7 to Neh 13) before writing Ezra 1–6, he must have taken this list from that composition.[28] But that still does not tell us how the list originated or when. The list seems to be a composite of different lists. Some names are listed by ancestral families and others by geographical location. A number of factors point to a much earlier date than Nehemiah. Williamson appears to be correct in his conclusion that most parts of the list already existed by the time the real work of building the temple began and that it reflects more than one return; perhaps groups of exiles returned at various times during the reigns of Cyrus and Cambyses.[29]

What was the purpose of making this list or the lists from which it is derived? Several suggestions have been offered. According to Alt the list was to legitimize land rights after the return from exile. Galling argued it was written to distinguish the true Israelites from the Samaritans and to show, on the occasion of Tattenai's request in Ezra 5:3-4, those authorized by Cyrus to return to Judah and rebuild the temple.[30] Or, as Brueggemann has written: "The genealogies are a guarantee that Israel is not adrift in a vacuum of this present generation but has security and credentials. And as long as Israel can name names, utter their precious sounds, it has a belonging place which no hostile empire can deny."[31]

---

[28] Williamson (*Ezra, Nehemiah*, 29-30) notes several reasons in the lists themselves that indicate the priority of the list in Neh 7. It is evident that one of these was copied from the other, rather than both from another list, since the similarities include the introduction and closing comments. Most commentators agree that Ezra 2 is a copy of Neh 7: (1) In Neh 7:73 the seventh month and the related comments correspond to the continuation of the narrative in 8:1; such is not the case in Ezra 3:1. (2) Ezra 2:68-69 appears to be a summary of Neh 7:70-72. To these reasons Williamson adds two more: (3) Although Ezra 2:68-69 is a summary, it adds a few words that fit the context in Ezra 2. (4) The revision in Ezra 2:70 in relation to Neh 7:73 points to the same conclusion (see the discussion in the Introduction).

[29] Ibid., 31. There are several reasons for dating the component parts early: (1) The mention of Babylonian towns of origin in Ezra 2:59 indicates a time shortly after their return. (2) In Ezra 2:61 the descendants of Hakkoz are excluded from the officiating priests, but later in Ezra 8:33 (see Neh 3:4,21) and in 1 Chr 24:10 they are included. (3) Whereas in Ezra 2:62 there was no priest administering Urim and Thummim, from 520 B.C. onward there was a high priest. (4) Other details such as the status of the priests' helpers and the use of the gold drachma (probably before the daric of Darius) indicate its early origin.

[30] K. Galling, "The 'gola-list' according to Ezra 2//Nehemiah 7" *JBL* 70 (1951): 149-58. See also Clines, *Ezra, Nehemiah, Esther*, 44.

[31] W. Brueggemann, *The Land* (Philadelphia: Fortress, 1977), 145-46.

Whatever the list's purpose, these individuals were honored as being the first to return (Neh 7:5), showing their faith in the promises of God and especially the value they placed on the land God had promised to Abraham. In its present context the list is more related to chap. 3 than to chap. 1; in fact, it prepares us for the great work of rebuilding in the succeeding chapters. The list in Neh 7 serves the opposite function of signaling the conclusion of the rebuilding of temple (Ezra 1–6), community (Ezra 7–10), and city (Neh 1–6).[32]

(1) The Leaders (2:1-2a)

[1]**Now these are the people of the province who came up from the captivity of the exiles, whom Nebuchadnezzar king of Babylon had taken captive to Babylon (they returned to Jerusalem and Judah, each to his own town, [2]in company with Zerubbabel, Jeshua, Nehemiah, Seraiah, Reelaiah, Mordecai, Bilshan, Mispar, Bigvai, Rehum and Baanah):**

2:1 To God each individual and family is significant. Thus the group of returnees is not simply lumped together, but valuable space in Scripture is given to otherwise unknown families and individuals. The group of exiles was not large, but it was vital to God's plan. Before describing the rebuilding of the temple (chaps. 3–6), the author listed the principal families of the community, the heroes of this drama. Through them God's purposes in Israel were continued.

They returned to Jerusalem and Judah. The word "province" here probably refers to Judah rather than Babylon. As previously noted, this summary list probably includes different groups that returned from Babylon to Judah at different times. This helps to explain Sheshbazzar as the leader in chap. 1 and Zerubbabel's being mentioned here.[33] We do not know what happened to Sheshbazzar or how soon Zerubbabel became the governor.

"Each to his own town" again emphasizes the continuing link with the preexilic covenant community through the family territorial inheritance. It was important for the postexilic community to reaffirm its roots in the preexilic covenant community based on the Mosaic legislation.

---

[32] T. C. Eskenazi, *In An Age of Prose* (Atlanta: Scholars Press, 1988), 37.

[33] See the Introduction for the identity of the two men. Ezra 3:2 says Zerubbabel was the son of Shealtiel, King Jehoiachin's eldest son. But 1 Chr 3:19 lists him as son of Pedaiah, another son of Jehoiachin. Thus there may have been a levirate marriage (Deut 25:5-10; Ruth 4:10) between Pedaiah and the widow of Shealtiel. So Zerubbabel would still have been considered the heir of Shealtiel. See J. B. Payne, "1 Chronicles," *EBC* 4:339.

2:2a Several other names in the list of leaders sound familiar, but these names were quite common. "Jeshua" was the high priest, called "Joshua" in Haggai and Zechariah.[34] "Nehemiah," however, was not the Nehemiah who came to Jerusalem in 445 B.C.; and this was almost certainly not the Mordecai from the Book of Esther. "Seraiah" was also the name of Ezra's father (7:1). "Bigvai" (also in v. 14) is a Persian name that also occurs in the Elephantine Papyri as the governor of Judah following Nehemiah.[35]

Some differences exist between this list of eleven and the twelve of Neh 7. The name Nahamani (Neh 7:7) may have been lost here in the process of copying.[36] The number twelve again emphasizes the continuity of the postexilic community with the real Israel (cf. 6:17).

(2) Names of Clans (2:2b-20)

The list of the men of the people of Israel:

[3]the descendants of Parosh	2,172
[4]of Shephati	372
[5]of Arah	775
[6]of Pahath-Moab (through the line of Jeshua and Joab)	2,812
[7]of Elam	1,254
[8]of Zattu	945
[9]of Zaccai	760
[10]of Bani	642
[11]of Bebai	623
[12]of Azgad	1,222
[13]of Adonikam	666
[14]of Bigvai	2,056
[15]of Adin	454
[16]of Ater (through Hezekiah)	98
[17]of Bezai	323
[18]of Jorah	112
[19]of Hashum	223
[20]of Gibbar	95

---

[34] According to Hag 1:1 he was the son of Jehozadak, the high priest. Thus he was the grandson of Seraiah, the last high priest in office before the exile (2 Kgs 25:18; 1 Chr 6:15).

[35] Clines, *Ezra, Nehemiah, Esther*, 49.

[36] S. Japhet, "People and Land in the Restoration Period," in *Das Land Israel im biblischer Zeit*, ed. N. Kamp and G. Strecker (Göttingen: Vandenhoeck und Ruprecht, 1983), 112. T. Eskenazi (*Age of Prose*, 50) suggests another possibility is that the list here assumes Sheshbazzar as the twelfth name (from 1:8).

2:2b-20 The term "Israel" (v. 2) is used to describe those listed here. The Bible usually designates by this term either the entire nation of twelve tribes descended from the patriarchs or, later, the Northern Kingdom, which fell to the Assyrians. Its use here is another indication that this group is viewed as the heir to the biblical covenants and the recipients of God's continued faithfulness to his people. As McConville wrote, "In a political world in which Israel as a power is no more than a memory, God is awakening something infinitely more significant, because it is spiritual."[37]

Finding one's name on a list is frequently satisfying and encouraging; it gives assurance that arrangements have been made—that one is expected, valued, and privileged. Such was surely the case with these numbered here among the people God was welcoming back to the land of promise, a land that represented God's commitment to redeem the earth from sin and judgment and to establish a divine and eternal kingdom of righteousness.

The names in this list are nearly identical to those of Neh 7, but more variation occurs in the numbers. This no doubt is due to the notorious difficulty in copying Hebrew numbers.[38]

Several of these names occur elsewhere. Eleven of the names also occur in Ezra 8 as persons accompanying Ezra to Jerusalem. Fourteen are listed as signing the agreement of separation in Neh 10. Since the name "Pahath-moab" (v. 6) literally means "governor of Moab," he may have been a governor of part of Moab during the united monarchy (cf. 1 Chr 4:22). "Elam" (v. 7) may have been the same man mentioned in 1 Chr 8:24. S. Moscati published a stamp with *zk'*, "Zaccai" (v. 9).[39] "Agzad" (v. 12) appears in the Aramaic Papyri from Elephantine in Egypt.[40] Nehemiah's list has "Gibeon" instead of "Gibbar" in v. 20, suggesting that the section on place names may start with v. 20 rather than v. 21.

(3) Geographical Names (2:21-35)

[21]the men of Bethlehem	123
[22]of Netophah	56
[23]of Anathoth	128
[24]of Azmaveth	42

---

[37] McConville, *Ezra, Nehemiah, and Esther*, 16.

[38] Blenkinsopp, *Ezra-Nehemiah*, 85-86; H. L. Allrick, "The Lists of Zerubbabel (Nehemiah 7 and Ezra 2) and the Hebrew Numerical Notation," *BASOR* 136 (1954): 21-27.

[39] Fensham, *Ezra and Nehemiah*, 51.

[40] Ibid.

[25]of Kiriath Jearim, Kephirah and Beeroth	743
[26]of Ramah and Geba	621
[27]of Micmash	122
[28]of Bethel and Ai	223
[29]of Nebo	52
[30]of Magbish	156
[31]of the other Elam	1,254
[32]of Harim	320
[33]of Lod, Hadid and Ono	725
[34]of Jericho	345
[35]of Senaah	3,630

2:21-35 It is not clear why some of the returnees are mentioned by families and some by geographical names. Williamson suggests that the latter were the poorer people who did not have land in their name.[41] Another suggestion is that vv. 2b-20 list those who could trace their lineage to a known Jewish ancestor, while those in vv. 21-35 could only identify themselves by their former city or property (Williamson rejects this in view of vv. 59-63). These geographical names appear to represent the places where these families had lived before the exile rather than the towns where they settled after the exile.[42] Some of the verses (in Hebrew) begin with "the men of," and some begin with "the sons of,"[43] but the terms appear to be synonymous. Many of these places can be identified.[44] Most of the locations are in Benjamite territory; only Netophah and Bethlehem are south of Jerusalem.

Again the author emphasized the continuity of God's covenant people.

---

[41] Williamson, *Ezra, Nehemiah,* 34. Reference is made to the poor of the land in 2 Kgs 25:12, people who were not deported when Jerusalem fell. However, here the people evidently were returnees from exile. Either these were different people or the poor mentioned in 2 Kgs 25 were later taken to Babylon.

[42] Ibid.

[43] The NIV translation does not show this. Verses 22-23,27-28 begin with "the men of"; all the others from v. 21 to v. 35 begin with "the sons of."

[44] Netophah is south of Jerusalem on the road to Bethlehem. Anathoth, northeast of Jerusalem, was the home of Jeremiah. Azmaveth may be El Hizneh, north of Anathoth. Kiriath Jearim lies nine miles northwest of Jerusalem; Kephira is north of that, and Beeroth is twelve miles north of Jerusalem. Ramah was the home of Samuel and was six miles north of Jerusalem. Geba was a priestly town eight miles north of Jerusalem; Micmash lies just north of that. Bethel is twelve miles north of Jerusalem, and Ai is one and a half miles east of that. Nebo is not the Nebo of Moab. Lod, Hadid, and Ono are farther from Jerusalem, near the coast in the area of Joppa. Senaah sometimes has been identified with Magdalsenna, some five miles north of Jericho; but this identification is not certain. In addition the number of men listed seems very large. Some suspect it is a textual error.

The material is presented to show God's providence in reestablishing the covenant community, in reordering its religious life (Neh 8–10), and in revitalizing its cultural heritage (Neh 11–13). Thus the identification of the families and their place of origin was important for the self-identity of the people. They needed to recognize their roots in the preexilic Israelite community as reassurance that they were the continuation of God's redemptive plan, that God would not forsake them.

We can be glad that they did continue as God's covenant community and that they continued to be used in God's redemptive plan. Through this community and their descendants we have the Scriptures, and through this community Jesus Christ came into the world. Even though the community was practically unnoticed in the world at that time, they constituted the center of God's redemptive plan.

Sometimes Christians suffer from a "minority complex," thinking they are of little significance in present history. But the New Testament makes clear that the church, made up of true believers in Jesus Christ, is the center of God's attention and the chief means of fulfilling his mission in the world.[45] We need to remember our heritage from generations of believers who have preceded us and understand the influence our decisions will have for the future.

(4) The Priests (2:36-39)

36 The priests:

the descendants of Jedaiah (through the family of Jeshua)	**973**
37of Immer	**1,052**
38of Pashhur	**1,247**
39of Harim	**1,017**

2:36-39 Having listed the "laymen" first, the author moved to the temple ministers in vv. 36-58. The priests constituted about 10 percent of the returnees. David had organized the priests into twenty-four family groups (1 Chr 24), but only four of the twenty-four are represented here. These are also the only four priestly families listed several generations later when Ezra returned (Ezra 10:18-22).[46] By New Testament times,

---

[45] See, for example, Matt 16:18; Eph 1:22-23; 3:10,21; 1 Tim 3:15.

[46] Jedaiah, Immer, and Harim are also named in 1 Chr 24. Additional priestly families (from 1 Chr 24) of Jehoiarib and Jakin are listed in 1 Chr 9:10 as returning from exile. In addition, Neh 10:2-8 lists as signers of the agreement Malkijah, Abijah, Mijamin, Maaziah, and Bilgai (Bilgah?), all names of priestly families in 1 Chr 24. Sheconiah is another name from 1 Chr 24 listed in Neh 12:3 as returning with Zerubbabel.

however, they were again organized into a system of twenty-four courses with the ancient Davidic names (*Tosephta* 2.1.216). The names, especially the mention of Jeshua the high priest, show the linkage of the returnees with the preexilic community.

(5) The Levites (2:40-42)

40 **The Levites:**

> **the descendants of Jeshua and Kadmiel**
> **(through the line of Hodaviah)**   **74**

41The singers:

> **the descendants of Asaph**   **128**

42The gatekeepers of the temple:

> **the descendants of Shallum, Ater,**
> **Talmon, Akkub, Hatita and Shobai**   **139**

2:40-42 The Levites were members of the tribe of Levi who were not also descendants of Aaron. There was a small number of Levites in relation to priests.[47] Later, Ezra could get only thirty-eight to go with

---

[47] There is a tendency today to assume that all this development of the priestly and levitical hierarchy was a postexilic phenomenon and the Chronicler read it back into Israel's earlier history. Kidner, however (*Ezra and Nehemiah,* 40), noted that the tithe law in Num 18:21,26 takes for granted a much larger number of Levites than priests. The law gave the tithes to the Levites, who were to give a tenth to the priests. This is an indication that these laws were not made at this time, or they would have reflected a smaller number of Levites. Y. Kaufmann says: "Nothing proves more clearly how mistaken is the view that in postexilic times, the Torah book was still being added to and revised. . . . The founders of postexilic Judaism were not the composers, but merely the collectors of the Torah literature. They did not alter anything of what they found written, much less add to it" (Y. Kaufmann, *The Religion of Israel* [Allen & Unwin, 1961], 193). It is possible that the priestly hierarchy received new emphasis after the exile, but certainly we must accept the tradition that David had organized the priests, Levites, singers, and helpers as Chronicles says. It is not unreasonable that David would organize singers for cultic service in his time. The Ugaritic materials show that singing was important in Canaanite cultic practices (Fensham, *Ezra and Nehemiah,* 53); in fact, the Ugaritic material suggests that many of Israel's poetic and musical forms were strongly influenced by the Canaanite environment. Modern skepticism about the cultic development in the early monarchy rests on no new evidence but rather on philosophical and ideological tendencies. Note Brueggemann's comments about the "subjectivity" of "the critical guild" ("Jeremiah: Intense Criticism/Thin Interpretation," *Int* 42 [1988]: 275).

him to Jerusalem (Ezra 8:15-20). This may have been because Levites would have no inheritance to return to since their inheritance was the Lord (Josh 13:33; 14:3-4; 18:7; 21:1-42). Although it originally was a curse (Gen 34:25-31; 49:5-7), God had turned their landlessness into a blessing (Exod 32:25-28; Num 18:20; Deut 33:8-11), but it may have been difficult for many of them to accept this point of view.

The descendants of Jeshua and Kadmiel in v. 40 evidently were those designated especially to assist the priests (cf. Ezek 44:10-14). Nehemiah 11–12 puts the singers and Levites together. According to 1 Chr 15:16-24, David had organized the singers into twenty-four groups to correspond to the twenty-four groups of priests. The work of the gatekeepers and their organization by Samuel and David is described in 1 Chr 9:17-29.

(6) The Temple Servants (2:43-54)

⁴³ The temple servants:

the descendants of Ziha, Hasupha, Tabbaoth,

⁴⁴Keros, Siaha, Padon,
⁴⁵Lebanah, Hagabah, Akkub,
⁴⁶Hagab, Shalmai, Hanan,
⁴⁷Giddel, Gahar, Reaiah,
⁴⁸Rezin, Nekoda, Gazzam,
⁴⁹Uzza, Paseah, Besai,
⁵⁰Asnah, Meunim, Nephussim,
⁵¹Bakbuk, Hakupha, Harhur,
⁵²Bazluth, Mehida, Harsha,
⁵³Barkos, Sisera, Temah,
⁵⁴Neziah and Hatipha

2:43-54 The term translated "temple servants" (*nĕtînîm*) literally means "the given" or "the dedicated ones." Ezra 8:20 says they were given to assist the Levites to perform the more mundane temple duties. They may have originated as circumcised foreigners conquered by David (cf. Exod 12:48; Num 15:14-16), although the term is found elsewhere only in Ezekiel and Chronicles. The many foreign names in the present list confirm that the group probably consisted of individuals of non-Israelite descent. According to Num 31:30-47, some war captives were given to serve the Levites.[48]

Jewish rabbinic tradition identified the temple servants with the Gibeonites whom Joshua had assigned to be "woodcutters and water carriers for the community and for the altar of the LORD" (Josh 9:27). The group may well have included descendants of the Gibeonites along with others.[49] Along with the priests and Levites, they were exempt from taxes (Ezra 7:24). They were also among those who signed the agreement in Neh 10 (v. 28).[50]

(7) Descendants of Solomon's Servants (2:55-58)

55 The descendants of the servants of Solomon:

**the descendants of Sotai, Hassophereth, Peruda,
56Jaala, Darkon, Giddel, 57Shephatiah, Hattil, Pokereth-Hazzebaim and Ami**

**58The temple servants and the descendants of the servants of
Solomon**   **392**

2:55-58 This group is closely related to the temple servants, since both groups are included here in one total. There were only 392 persons for all these forty-five families or clans, or an average of fewer than nine per clan. Many scholars think Solomon's servants were from the native population whom Solomon used for work on the temple.[51] The names "Hassophereth" ("the scribe") and "Pokereth-Hazzebaim" ("the gazelle keeper") could be names of guilds and suggest that these servants, while similar to the temple servants, were involved in more secular tasks.[52] Ezra 7:24, however, appears to call the same group "other workers at this house of God."

(8) Others (2:59-63)

59The following came up from the towns of Tel Melah, Tel Harsha, Kerub, Addon and Immer, but they could not show that their families were descended from Israel:

60 The descendants of Delaiah, Tobiah and Nekoda   **652**

61 And from among the priests:

---

[48] Ezek 44:6-9 indicates that Israel was not always careful about using foreigners as temple servants who were genuinely converted. They even may have allowed foreigners to serve as priests (see R. H. Alexander, "Ezekiel," in *EBC*, 6:975-76).

[49] See Josh 11:19-20; 21:17; 1 Kgs 3:4-5; 1 Chr 12:4; 21:29; 2 Chr 1:5; Neh 3:7; 7:25.

[50] Williamson, *Ezra, Nehemiah,* 35-36.

[51] Slotki, *Daniel, Ezra and Nehemiah,* 122.

[52] Kidner, *Ezra and Nehemiah,* 41.

The descendants of Hobaiah, Hakkoz and Barzillai (a man who had married a daughter of Barzillai the Gileadite and was called by that name).

[62]These searched for their family records, but they could not find them and so were excluded from the priesthood as unclean. [63]The governor ordered them not to eat any of the most sacred food until there was a priest ministering with the Urim and Thummim.

2:59-63 Both Ezra-Nehemiah and Chronicles emphasize genealogical lists. Formerly each family's tract of land guaranteed continuity, but during the exile they had to depend on genealogical records. The context indicates that the names listed here as origins are Babylonian towns from which the exiles came. Apparently some had lost their family records or allowed them to lapse during the exile. Some may have been proselytes, that is, converts. Other passages indicate that Jewish families normally maintained family registers (Neh 7:5; 1 Chr 7:5). Local officials also kept records (1 Chr 5:17; 9:22). These families were not sent back to Babylon but apparently were eventually accepted in the community. Temporarily at least, they probably were given the status of circumcised foreigners.

In addition to emphasizing the continuity of the people of God, Ezra-Nehemiah also stresses the physical as well as spiritual purity of the Jewish community, which was important at this point in history. Later this led to an attitude of spiritual pride (John 8; Rom 9:6). Therefore the New Testament condemns reliance on one's physical ancestry for acceptance with God (e.g., Phil 3:3-8). Often an emphasis that is important at one time may be wrongly emphasized and become a stumbling block at a later time. Ezra-Nehemiah challenges us to avoid having current decisions or emphases become institutionalized to the point of hindering God's will in the future.

A principle that continued into the New Testament was that spiritual leadership carries higher qualifications and demands than membership in the community of faith. From the time of Moses (Num 16:40), descent from Aaron was an essential qualification for priesthood. So to avoid defilement or the Lord's displeasure, these priests were excluded.

A man named Barzillai (Ezra 2:61) helped David when he fled from Absalom (2 Sam 17:27; 19:32). It is interesting that the priest who married his daughter took his name. Some have suggested he took that family name so he could inherit property. The fact that priests did not inherit land (Num 18:20) may have meant his exclusion from priestly work.[53]

---

[53] Kidner, *Ezra and Nehemiah*, 42.

The descendants of Hakkoz at least probably were reinstated later if Meremoth, the priest of Ezra 8:33, is the same as the Meremoth of Neh 3:4,21.

The word for governor in Ezra 2:63 (*tiršāta³*) is a Persian word used again in Neh 7:65,70; 8:9; and 10:1. Here it most likely refers to Sheshbazzar. The Urim and Thummim were sacred lots used to know the will of God (1 Sam 14:37-42; Num 27:21). According to Exod 28:30 they were small objects, perhaps pebbles or precious stones, which the high priest carried in his garments. Few details are given about how they were used. Passages such as 1 Sam 23:9-12 and 30:7-8 indicate that the question asked required a yes or no answer; thus the priest would use Urim and Thummim to obtain an indication of God's will.[54] The phrase "until there was a priest ministering" could refer to the unavailability of the Urim and Thummim or the absence of a priest qualified to use them. If it refers to a high priest, this part of the list must have been written originally before 520 B.C. when Joshua was high priest (Hag 1:1).

(9) The Totals and Contributions for the Temple (2:64-69)

[64]**The whole company numbered 42,360, **[65]**besides their 7,337 menservants and maidservants; and they also had 200 men and women singers. **[66]**They had 736 horses, 245 mules, **[67]**435 camels and 6,720 donkeys.**

[68]**When they arrived at the house of the LORD in Jerusalem, some of the heads of the families gave freewill offerings toward the rebuilding of the house of God on its site. **[69]**According to their ability they gave to the treasury for this work 61,000 drachmas of gold, 5,000 minas of silver and 100 priestly garments.**

2:64-67   The numbers in the lists add up to 29,818, but the "whole company" here is 42,360. Nehemiah 7 and 1 Esdras (5:41) have the same total of 42,360, although the totals of the other numbers add up to 31,089 in Neh 7 and 30,143 in 1 Esdras. So we can assume that the 42,360 is correct. The question is, What happened to the other numbers? The dif-

---

[54] Thus the Urim and Thummim were a form of casting lots. A further hint of their use can be gained from the text of 1 Sam 14:41 reconstructed from the Septuagint: "If this guilt is in me or in Jonathan my son, give Urim, and if it is in thy people Israel, give Thummim." Some have suggested that "the Urim and Thummim were two flat objects; one side of each was called Urim, from אָרַר 'to curse,' and when both displayed this side the answer was negative; the other side was Thummim, from תָּמַם, 'to be perfect,' and a complete Thummim meant 'yes'; one Urim and one Thummim meant 'no reply'" (*NBD*, 1306). The Urim and Thummim are not mentioned between the early monarchy and postexilic times, perhaps because God made his will known through the prophets.

ferences between Ezra, Nehemiah, and 1 Esdras can be explained by
copyist errors; but the larger total is not explained. Some suggest that it
includes the women;[55] others suggest that it includes families from tribes
other than Judah and Benjamin that were not in these lists.[56] More likely
is the suggestion that since this is a composite list, some families simply
were omitted; but the overall total remains correct.

The quantity of "servants, singers, horses and donkeys" tells us something about the economic condition of the people. So many "menservants
and maidservants" indicate wealthy people in the group. Also the
wealthy utilized horses, whereas poorer people used donkeys. As we
would expect, there were many more donkeys than horses. Some years
later when the prophet Haggai prophesied (520 B.C.), the economic situation had worsened considerably; the community was suffering from
poverty.[57]

2:68-69 God's work is usually accomplished through the freewill offerings of the common people (cf. 1:4,6; Exod 25:2-9; 35:21-29). McConville has noted, however, that "there may be a hint of the disappointing
performance that is to come in the notice that only *some* of the heads of
families gave willingly."[58]

Some differences are found between this list and Neh 7; here the numbers are rounded off, another indication that the list in Neh 7 was written
earlier.

(10) Settlement in the Villages (2:70)

**[70]The priests, the Levites, the singers, the gatekeepers and the temple ser-
vants settled in their own towns, along with some of the other people, and
the rest of the Israelites settled in their towns.**

2:70 While those connected with the temple settled in Jerusalem,
other families and groups settled in towns around Jerusalem, many of

---

[55] This would be a surprisingly small number of women if that is the case.

[56] The above list, however, calls all "men of the people of Israel"; there would hardly
have been that many from the former northern tribes, although we know from 1 Chr 9:3
that some from northern tribes were included in the postexilic community. See Kidner,
Ezra and Nehemiah, 43.

[57] Haggai says that because they neglected God's house, they suffered crop failures
(1:7-11).

[58] McConville, *Ezra, Nehemiah, and Esther*, 17. Clines, on the other hand, rejects this
interpretation as "unbelievable." He interprets these verses in terms of Neh 7:70-72, where
it seems that there were two different categories of gifts (*Ezra, Nehemiah, Esther*, 61).

them in the towns where their families lived before the exile.[59] As in Joshua's day after the conquest, the people "had rest" (Josh 11:23). The story was not quite that simple, however, as the following chapters indicate. What mattered to the author at this point was that a large group of exiles whom God had disciplined for disobedience now responded to the good news of deliverance and restoration and set their hope on God's promises.

This entire chapter serves as a prelude to the great event of building the temple and reestablishing worship as prescribed in the law of Moses. Although modern Western culture places considerably less emphasis on genealogy, it was very important to the community restored in Judah. God had founded Israel as an ethnic as well as a spiritual entity. The renewal of God's plan of redemption depended on the reestablishment of that entity on the land God had given them. It was a great blessing for those who returned to be part of what God was doing. Their jubilation is expressed in Ps 126:2—"Our mouths were filled with laughter, our tongues with songs of joy."

---

[59] "Jerusalem" occurs in the LXX version and also in 1 Esdr 5:46. See Clines, *Ezra, Nehemiah, Esther,* 62. Williamson (*Ezra, Nehemiah,* 271-73) thinks a comparison with Neh 7:73 indicates a complex development of the passage. See the explanation at Neh 7:73.

II. RESTORING WORSHIP: CONSTRUCTION OF THE TEMPLE
(3:1–6:22)
1. The Foundation of Worship: Preparation and Beginning
(3:1–4:5)
(1) The Altar and Sacrifices (3:1-6)
(2) Materials for the Temple (3:7)
(3) Beginning to Build (3:8-9)
(4) Praise to God (3:10-13)
(5) Rejection of Help from Enemies (4:1-3)
(6) Persistent Opposition (4:4-5)
2. Examples of Opposition (4:6-24)
(1) In the Reign of Xerxes (4:6)
(2) The Letter to Artaxerxes (4:7-16)
(3) The Reply of Artaxerxes (4:17-22)
(4) The Effects of Opposition (4:23-24)
3. Prophecy Fulfilled: The Temple Built (5:1–6:22)
(1) A New Beginning (5:1-2)
(2) Building Activity Investigated (5:3-5)
(3) The Report Sent to Darius (5:6-17)
(4) The Edict of Cyrus Discovered (6:1-12)
(5) The Completion of the Temple (6:13-15)
(6) The Temple Dedicated (6:16-18)
(7) The Passover Celebrated (6:19-22)

II. RESTORING WORSHIP: CONSTRUCTION OF THE TEMPLE (3:1–6:22)

1. The Foundation of Worship: Preparation and Beginning (3:1–4:5)

Lacking a reference to a specific year, 3:1-7 gives the impression that these events followed immediately after chaps. 1–2 and occurred in the first year of the return. Thus in "the seventh month," or about six months after the exiles' arrival in Jerusalem, they built the altar. Then another seven months later (3:8) they laid the foundations of the temple. Many have argued, however, that this seems to leave a short time for "the Israelites" to have settled in their towns (3:1) and a short time for the logs to be ordered and brought from Lebanon (3:7). Furthermore, Sheshbazzar was the leader in chaps. 1–2, and here Zerubbabel and Jeshua are leaders, under whom the foundation of the temple was laid (3:10). In Ezra 5:16, however, the document the Jews sent to Darius says, "Sheshbazzar came and laid the foundations."

Some have assumed that the author confused Zerubbabel and Sheshbazzar. Others have argued that they were the same person (see Introduction). A more likely explanation is that Zerubbabel was a subordinate leader under Sheshbazzar.[1] Alt, Galling, and others have disregarded the date given in 3:8 ("the second month of the second year," 537 B.C.) when the text says Zerubbabel and Jeshua began to build. They dated the beginning of construction in the time of Haggai and Zechariah, around 520 B.C.

S. Talmon, in a literary analysis of Ezra and Nehemiah, points out some stylistic techniques of the author that help us understand his process of compilation and mark out the component parts. He explains that 3:1–4:3 as a general summary of the founding of the second temple. The summary is theologically oriented, emphasizing praise and continuity with the former temple. The author used elements from both the time of Cyrus and the time of Darius. Since his purpose was theological, he was not primarily concerned with chronology.[2] A literary approach is helpful, although it does not allow us to disregard the chronological references in the text.

The events of 3:1-6, the construction of the altar and the beginning of worship, probably occurred in 538 B.C. Verse 1 reads literally, "Then the seventh month came and the sons of Israel were in towns." This would not necessarily have required a long period of time. Although the building materials were ordered then (3:7), they were not all necessary for laying the foundations and may have taken several months to acquire. It is difficult to determine how much building occurred in the second year (3:8). If work on the foundation was not completed in that year, however, it probably was finished soon after (3:10), followed by the celebration recounted in 3:10-13. Then construction stopped until 520 B.C.

---

[1] J. Myers suggests that Sheshbazzar may have been an elderly man in 538, perhaps fifty-five or sixty; and he may have been more of a figurehead with Zerubbabel in charge of affairs (*Ezra and Nehemiah*, AB [Garden City: Doubleday, 1965], 28).

[2] S. Talmon, "Ezra and Nehemiah," *IDBSup* (Nashville: Abingdon, 1976), 322. Talmon explains that Ezra 4:4-5 is a recapitulating remark that defines 3:1–4:3 as a unit and ties it to what follows in chaps. 5–6.

(1) The Altar and Sacrifices (3:1-6)

[1]When the seventh month came and the Israelites had settled in their towns, the people assembled as one man in Jerusalem. [2]Then Jeshua son of Jozadak and his fellow priests and Zerubbabel son of Shealtiel and his associates began to build the altar of the God of Israel to sacrifice burnt offerings on it, in accordance with what is written in the Law of Moses the man of God. [3]Despite their fear of the peoples around them, they built the altar on its foundation and sacrificed burnt offerings on it to the LORD, both the morning and evening sacrifices. [4]Then in accordance with what is written, they celebrated the Feast of Tabernacles with the required number of burnt offerings prescribed for each day. [5]After that, they presented the regular burnt offerings, the New Moon sacrifices and the sacrifices for all the appointed sacred feasts of the LORD, as well as those brought as freewill offerings to the LORD. [6]On the first day of the seventh month they began to offer burnt offerings to the LORD, though the foundation of the LORD's temple had not yet been laid.

3:1 The words and construction of "when the seventh month came" are similar to Neh 7:73b–8:1a. It has been suggested that if the list of Ezra 2 depends on that of Neh 7, the wording may have been influenced by that of Nehemiah. The similarity could also be coincidental, however. Clines has suggested that the returnees may have timed their journey so they could be in Jerusalem for the seventh month, the most important month in the liturgical calendar (Num 29; Lev 23).[3]

The "seventh month" was Tishri (Sept.-Oct.). On the first day (v. 6) they would have celebrated the New Year and Feast of Trumpets (Lev 23:23-25); on the tenth day was the Day of Atonement (although this is not mentioned here, perhaps because there was not yet a sanctuary; see Lev 16). From the fifteenth until the twenty-first they celebrated the Feast of Tabernacles. This feast was a time of great rejoicing, consequently an appropriate focus in the author's narrative. It was also in the seventh month at Tabernacles that Solomon had gathered the people together to dedicate the first temple (1 Kgs 8:2).

The people assembled "as one man," demonstrating a strong sense of community. They had a common bond of faith in God and a common purpose to worship and obey him. Even in times when it is difficult or dangerous to assemble, God is honored and his work is accomplished when his people unite to worship and obey him. As God's people have discovered repeatedly, united worship is a necessary means of dealing with difficult or dangerous situations.

---

[3] D. J. A. Clines, *Ezra, Nehemiah, Esther*, NCB (Grand Rapids: Eerdmans, 1984), 64.

3:2 While Ezra-Nehemiah does not emphasize the role of leaders, it acknowledges that leadership is important. In the construction of the temple, two major leaders stand out, Jeshua and Zerubbabel. The fellow priests and associates of Zerubbabel also are mentioned. In Christian circles at times no one is willing to lead, perhaps because of a lack of commitment or because of an overemphasis on "humility." At other times Christian leaders become too powerful and use their positions for self-aggrandizement. God resists the proud and gives grace to the humble, but people should not let false humility keep them from accepting leadership. Being able to lead is a gift; people should not reject the "prestige" and confidence that others put in them as leaders if God can use that for his glory (1 Tim 3:1). Certainly leaders must maintain a humble attitude and must delegate responsibilities to others, as is evident with Jeshua and Zerubbabel and is exemplified in Nehemiah.

Many times the hardest part of a project is getting started. Someone must take the initiative. In accordance with historical precedent, the returned exiles began by building the altar. David had built an altar here before there was a temple (2 Sam 24:25). Furthermore, they followed the instructions of the law of Moses. Thus they built the altar with field stones, not with dressed stones (Exod 20:25; Deut 27:6). Ezra 4:2 and Jer 41:5 indicate there may have been an altar there previously. In ancient times sacred spots continued to be used for sacrifice even after their temples or altars were destroyed.[4] If the people of the land (Jews not taken into captivity and some others) had some kind of an altar here or were using the place for sacrifice, we can understand why they were offended when their help was refused (4:2). Even if there were some kind of altar there before, the exiles probably would have considered it defiled and would have rebuilt it to be sure it was "in accordance with what was written."[5] If the people of the land and the Samaritans were using an altar there, it would represent a form of syncretism. One of the principal concerns of Ezra-Nehemiah is to avoid syncretism. The returned exiles wanted to begin correctly; they were careful to worship God according to his revelation in Scripture.

"The Law of Moses" was considered authoritative. Some modern scholars speculate that the Pentateuch came into being in the postexilic period (see Introduction). They assume that parts of it were carried back from Babylon and later consolidated. However, the normal interpretation

---

[4] F. C. Fensham, *The Books of Ezra and Nehemiah*, NICOT (Grand Rapids: Eerdmans, 1982), 59.

[5] Clines, *Ezra, Nehemiah, Esther*, 65.

of the text would indicate that the Pentateuch had this authority before
the time of Ezra. There is also no reason to doubt that it was the whole
Pentateuch.[6] Moses is called the "man of God" in a number of passages
(Deut 33:1; Josh 14:6; 1 Chr 23:14; 2 Chr 30:16). Later this term refers
to other prophets: Samuel (1 Sam 9:6), Elijah (1 Kgs 17:18), and Elisha
(2 Kgs 4:7).

3:3 The Hebrew for "despite" can also be translated "because of";[7]
but however it is understood, it is clear that the Israelites were afraid.
Courage is not lack of fear; it is the will to act in spite of fear. They recognized, if only partially, that their power consisted not in armies but in
the knowledge and service of God.[8] The Jewish community determined
to worship God according to the ancient specifications, and the emphasis
on continuity persisted. They built the altar "on its foundation," which no
doubt means on its exact preexilic location. In the Old Testament, building an altar was a significant act. In the life of the patriarchs it marked a
new dedication to God or a new experience of God's presence and leading (Gen 12:7; 13:4; 22:9; 26:25; 33:20; 35:1,7; Exod 17:5). "Burnt offerings" also emphasized dedication, consecration, and commitment; in
the burnt offerings the whole animal was burned as a symbol of total
consecration to God. The returned exiles offered "both the morning and
evening sacrifices" as the Pentateuch specified (Num 28:2,4). Thus the
sacrificial system was reinstituted on a daily basis.

In "the peoples around them" we have the plural form of an often-
discussed phrase, "the people of the land."[9] In earlier times it referred to

---

[6] Stipulations from all parts of the Pentateuch are found in Ezra-Nehemiah. See Myers,
Ezra, Nehemiah, lxvii, for examples.

[7] The subordinate clause of v. 3 could be literally rendered "because (כִּי) in (בְּ) fear
upon (עַל) them from (מִן) the peoples of the lands." Fensham (*Ezra and Nehemiah,* 59)
says כִּי "must be taken as causal," and he understands בְּ to mean "out of" but translates
them together "in spite of," evidently because of the context. According to Blenkinsopp
(*Ezra-Nehemiah,* 94) the MT is "impossible." He deletes בְּ as an error and translates "for
they lived in fear of the local inhabitants," explaining that "as at the time of David, the
building of an altar and offering sacrifice had the purpose of warding off danger to the
community" (pp. 97-98). His understanding is certainly possible and has the advantage of
taking כִּי in its more common causal sense, although it is also found with a concessive
idea, "even though" (e.g., Gen 8:21). Another possibility is that it was the peoples of the
lands who were afraid of the returnees, an allusion to the response of Israel's enemies in
the days of Moses and Joshua (Exod 15:16; Josh 2:9; 5:1).

[8] J. G. McConville, *Ezra, Nehemiah, and Esther* (Philadelphia: Westminster, 1985), 6.

[9] Here it is הָאֲרָצוֹת מֵעַמֵּי. The expression הָאָרֶץ עַם in later times referred to the
poor people of the land (Hag 2:4). See S. Talmon, "The Judaean ʿam haʾareṣ in Historical
Perspective," in *King, Cult and Calendar in Ancient Israel: Collected Studies* (Jerusalem:
Magnes Press, 1986), 68-78.

the landowning families who made up the ruling class. But here it evidently refers to the surrounding peoples (e.g., Ashdod, Samaria, Ammon, Moab, Edom), persons of foreign descent (including part Jews) living in Judah, and to Jews in the land who had not maintained their faith without compromise. Some were people established there by the Assyrians (4:2). Ezra-Nehemiah shows a growing animosity between these people and the Jewish community returned from exile. Therefore we have in these books an example of a believing community living in a hostile environment.

3:4 The Feast of Tabernacles was one of the three most important religious celebrations in the Jewish religious calendar. The pilgrim festivals, when all the men of Israel were to come to Jerusalem, were Passover in the spring, Pentecost (Weeks or Harvest) in the summer, and Tabernacles or Ingathering in the fall (Exod 23:14-17; Deut 16:16). In Num 29:12-38 is an extensive list of sacrifices to be offered each of the seven days of Tabernacles. Again, these returned exiles kept the feast "in accordance with what is written," emphasizing the authority of the Pentateuch (Exod 23:16; 34:22; Lev 23:33-36,39-43; and Deut 16:13-15). During the Feast of Tabernacles the people lived for seven days in tents or booths to remind them of God's protection of their ancestors in the wilderness, his continuing providential care, and their dependence on him. As J. G. McConville has written: "It is far more difficult to hear the message of fragility of life and the fact of dependence upon God for each succeeding breath amid the settled affluence and long life-expectancy that so many in the modern western world enjoy. Yet all our securities are ultimately illusory. Any attempt to peel them away, whether by temporary abstention from some of the good things of life, or whether by deliberate exposure to and sharing of the hard realities experienced by the poor and disadvantaged, can only be salutary."[10] Having just returned from exile in Babylon, this festival would have had special significance. It was also at the festival of Tabernacles that Ezra was to read the Law to the people (Neh 8:14-18).

3:5 Leviticus 23 specifies the different feasts. The community of Jews who returned from exile was careful to set up and continue (not just a momentary impulse) its worship according to Scripture.[11] The heart

---

[10] McConville, *Ezra, Nehemiah, and Esther,* 20-21.

[11] Given the emphasis on keeping all the feasts, it seems strange that no mention is made of the Sabbath. First Esdras 5:52 adds "and the sacrifices of the sabbaths." On the basis of this addition, Myers adds it here (*Ezra, Nehemiah,* 25). This addition is not necessary, however, to the interpretation of the text. Because v. 6 says burnt offerings had already begun on the first of the month, Fensham translates וְאַחֲרֵיכֵן "and besides" rather than "after that."

that loves God desires to worship him in a way that pleases him. The people even "brought . . . freewill offerings to the LORD." The true worshiper is not miserly with God.

3:6 The point of v. 6 is that even though the sacrificial system had been reinstituted, there remained much to be done. For almost four hundred years Israel had connected worship necessarily with the temple. In fact, they had come to rely more on the temple than on the Lord (Jer 7). Now that the temple had been destroyed and they had discovered God's presence even in exile, they could worship God even without a temple.

(2) Materials for the Temple (3:7)

7Then they gave money to the masons and carpenters, and gave food and drink and oil to the people of Sidon and Tyre, so that they would bring cedar logs by sea from Lebanon to Joppa, as authorized by Cyrus king of Persia.

3:7 When Solomon built the first temple, he hired the Phoenicians of Tyre with wheat, barley, olive oil, and wine (2 Chr 2:10,15) to send "cedar, pine, and algum logs from Lebanon" to Joppa (2 Chr 2:8,16). Even the way of describing these arrangements is reminiscent of 2 Chr 2:8-15 and 1 Kgs 5:11,18 (cf. also the prophetic passage in Isa 60:10-14).

Even though the Jewish community was small and relatively poor, the people set high standards of workmanship in doing God's work. They chose capable, talented masons and carpenters; they sent for the best grade wood from Lebanon. Not only did the legitimacy of their endeavors derive from historical precedent; they also had official approval, "as authorized by Cyrus."[12]

(3) Beginning to Build (3:8-9)

8In the second month of the second year after their arrival at the house of God in Jerusalem, Zerubbabel son of Shealtiel, Jeshua son of Jozadak and the rest of their brothers (the priests and the Levites and all who had returned from the captivity to Jerusalem) began the work, appointing Levites twenty years of age and older to supervise the building of the house of the

---

[12] Hebrew רִשְׁיוֹן, "grant" or "permission," appears only here in the Hebrew Bible, but it is quite common in rabbinic Hebrew (J. J. Slotki, *Daniel, Ezra, and Nehemiah*, The Soncino Books of the Bible [London: Soncino, 1951], 127). If 4:4-5 is a recapitulating note, indicating that this section may include events from the "reign of Cyrus . . . and down to the reign of Darius," the author may have been combining elements here of a first attempt at building, sometime after 538, and then of the recommencement and actual building in 520–516. Williamson dates the events of 3:7–4:3 to the time of Darius.

LORD. [9]Jeshua and his sons and brothers and Kadmiel and his sons (descendants of Hodaviah) and the sons of Henadad and their sons and brothers—all Levites—joined together in supervising those working on the house of God.

3:8 Solomon also began building his temple in the second month (1 Kgs 6:1). This was the month after Passover, or April-May in our calendar, the beginning of the dry season. Therefore it was the ideal time to start building. However, little more than repairing the foundation was done until the time of Haggai and Zechariah, 520–516 B.C. (5:2).

Zerubbabel and Jeshua were prominent in the prophecies of Haggai and Zechariah (Jeshua is Joshua there). In fact, the prophecies concerning Zerubbabel (Hag 2:23; Zech 4:6-10) may have led many to believe that he was the expected (messianic) king mentioned by several prophets.[13] After Zerubbabel dropped out of the picture,[14] Jeshua, the high priest, became the major leader of the people.

These verses stress unity, cooperation, and enthusiasm for the project. Although Zerubbabel and Jeshua were the principal leaders, they delegated the supervising to the Levites. Ezra-Nehemiah is an excellent sourcebook for administrative principles. The leaders knew how to make decisions, but they also delegated authority to others. The work was done in an orderly and efficient manner.

The age of service for priests and Levites varied according to the period and the need. In Num 4 the age of service was from thirty to fifty. In Num 8:24-25 those from twenty-five to fifty could minister in the tabernacle. In 1 Chr 23:3 the qualifying age was thirty, but in v. 27 it was changed to twenty. It is also twenty in 2 Chr 31:17.

3:9 The Levites were the supervisors and were directed by their leading families. They all "joined together in supervising those working." The term "those working" also can refer to officials;[15] this is an example of admirable leadership, commendable organization, and excellent cooperation. The names of the leading families of Levites are taken from the list in 2:40. "Henadad" appears also in Neh 10:9.

(4) Praise to God (3:10-13)

[10]When the builders laid the foundation of the temple of the LORD, the priests in their vestments and with trumpets, and the Levites (the sons of

---

[13] Zerubbabel may be considered a prototype of the coming Messiah, but the prophecies of Haggai and Zechariah looked forward to a more complete future fulfillment.

[14] Ironically, Zerubbabel is not mentioned again after Ezra 5:2.

[15] D. Kidner, *Ezra and Nehemiah,* TOTC (Downers Grove: InterVarsity, 1979), 47.

Asaph) with cymbals, took their places to praise the LORD, as prescribed by David king of Israel. [11]With praise and thanksgiving they sang to the LORD:

"He is good;

his love to Israel endures forever."

And all the people gave a great shout of praise to the LORD, because the foundation of the house of the LORD was laid. [12]But many of the older priests and Levites and family heads, who had seen the former temple, wept aloud when they saw the foundation of this temple being laid, while many others shouted for joy. [13]No one could distinguish the sound of the shouts of joy from the sound of weeping, because the people made so much noise. And the sound was heard far away.

These verses again show the theological interests of the author. He put worship at the center of community life and emphasized God's goodness and love. He also stressed continuity with the preexilic worship practices, emphasizing the importance of the priests and the sons of Asaph, whom David had assigned to worship with musical instruments (1 Chr 16:5; 25:1). The author even quotes from a psalm (Ps 100:5) frequently used earlier (1 Chr 16:34; 2 Chr 5:13). Jeremiah 33:11 had prophesied that after Jerusalem was destroyed in this same place this psalm would again be sung with gladness, joy, and thank offerings. Though there was not yet a temple, God was enthroned upon the praises of Israel.

3:11 They worshiped God and sang "with praise and thanksgiving." The word translated "sang" is literally "answered," probably referring to antiphonal choral singing as David had organized. Here there is a conscious effort to restore the elements of worship that David had instituted.

Nevertheless, as McConville has written, "The worship of Israel was no dull affair, nor any model for dry formality in Christian worship today."[16] As on other occasions when the people shouted in praise to God (e.g., Josh 6:16-20; 1 Sam 4:5-6; 2 Sam 6:15; 2 Chr 15:14), the great shout indicates that the people expressed their emotions in their praise to God, for they praised him with all their hearts. Their shouts of praise were fitting for this historic moment as the Jews saw the restored temple beginning to become a reality. Their hearts were full of praise to God, even though the construction had just begun. True faith praises God even before the answer has materialized. Although Abraham had to wait many years for the realization of God's seemingly impossible promise, "he did not waver through unbelief regarding the promise of God, but was

---

[16] McConville, *Ezra, Nehemiah, Esther*, 22.

strengthened in his faith and gave glory to God" (Rom 4:20-21).

3:12-13 The author has given us a touching account of the scene and of the emotional climax. Present on the occasion were people of all ages—children, youth, adults, and those in old age. As is usually the case, their perspective and their emotions varied. The older priests, Levites, and family heads, who remembered Solomon's temple, wept because this temple would be much simpler than the former one.[17] Others shouted for joy because their desire and longing of many years was being fulfilled. Thus joy was mixed with sadness, as their enthusiasm was mixed with fear (3:3), suggesting that as wonderful as the experience of God's grace is, there is yet more to come. Nevertheless, God was glorified, and "the sound was heard far away." Other people who were not of their community knew that something was happening. The celebration made an impact on the whole vicinity.

(5) Rejection of Help from Enemies (4:1-3)

1When the enemies of Judah and Benjamin heard that the exiles were building a temple for the LORD, the God of Israel, 2they came to Zerubbabel and to the heads of the families and said, "Let us help you build because, like you, we seek your God and have been sacrificing to him since the time of Esarhaddon king of Assyria, who brought us here."

3But Zerubbabel, Jeshua and the rest of the heads of the families of Israel answered, "You have no part with us in building a temple to our God. We alone will build it for the LORD, the God of Israel, as King Cyrus, the king of Persia, commanded us."

4:1-3 "The enemies" (v. 1) encountered by the Jews were the same as "the peoples around them" referred to in 3:3; 4:4; and elsewhere (9:1-2,11; 10:2,11; Neh 9:24,30; 10:31-32). Many were from Samaria, descendants of those brought by the Assyrians from elsewhere in their empire (v. 2; cf. 4:10; Neh 4:2). We know that Sargon II of Assyria repopulated Israel, the Northern Kingdom, with people from other conquered nations after the fall of Samaria in 722 B.C. The Bible gives no record of Esarhaddon (king of Assyria, 681–669 B.C.) having done the same (unless

---

[17] See Hag 2:3; Zech 4:10; Eccl 4:10; Phil 3:13-14. Compare, however, Ezra 6:3 with 1 Kgs 6:2. We do not know the dimensions of Zerubbabel's temple, and the text does not specify why the old men wept. There evidently was something inferior about the new construction. J. G. McConville ("Ezra-Nehemiah and the Fulfillment of Prophecy," *VT* 36 [1986]: 210) believes that the mingling of joy and sorrow "seems to have been deliberately presented thus to suggest once again a situation that is good as far as it goes, but might be better."

the sixty-five years of Isa 7:8 refers to it), but it is by no means unlikely. He did transport populations from one place to another; so he may have moved some to Syria-Palestine. A further resettlement by Ashurbanipal (669–633) is mentioned in 4:10.

The author considered this incident crucial and instructive for maintaining the purity of the covenant community. This attitude of exclusiveness displayed by the Jews ("You have no part with us") is troublesome to our modern society, where perhaps the highest virtue is the willingness to accept and cooperate with persons whose beliefs and practices differ from one's own. If we are tempted to think that Zerubbabel and the other leaders were sinfully separatistic or mistaken in their evaluation of those who offered their assistance, we must observe that these outsiders are identified as "enemies." Their motives were clearly subversive.[18] These neighbors claimed to worship the same God as the Jews. However, though they acknowledged him by name, they also worshiped other gods. As 2 Kgs 17:33 points out, this mixed population (including some Jews) "worshiped the LORD, but they also served their own gods in accordance with the customs of the nations from which they had been brought." The exilic or postexilic author of Kings also says: "To this day they persist in their former practices. They neither worship the LORD nor adhere to the decrees and ordinances." In God's sight such "syncretism" is not real worship but is sin and rebellion and would have proved fatal to the spiritual life of the new community.

They did not have the same convictions; they did not submit to the authority of God's Word; they were not dedicated to the one true God. "Such, then, is the uncompromising verdict of Scripture on the claim *we worship your God as you do,* when it is put forward as a multifaith proposition."[19] If one set of religious convictions is true, an opposing set must be false. The clear logic of this simple proposition has been obscured by modern muddled thinking. The danger of syncretism is ever present. We can be thankful that God used the Jews' decision to maintain the integrity of the Jewish community and continue his plan of redemption. Through this community all the world has received the Bible and God's offer of eternal salvation through the Lord Jesus Christ. The

---

[18] Blenkinsopp (*Ezra-Nehemiah,* 107) explains: "The leaders in the province of Samaria may well have seen the emergence of a new, aggressive presence in Judah, and one which enjoyed the favor of the imperial government, as threatening. . . . An offer to share the labor, and presumably also the expense, of rebuilding the sanctuary would have been taken to entail, and would in fact have entailed, a share in controlling the temple itself with all that implied."

[19] Kidner, *Ezra and Nehemiah,* 49.

church is continually faced with the similar challenge of keeping the
message true and pure.

Of course, the Jews' decision did not remove the opposition. In fact,
the animosity seems to have grown. From this point to the end of Nehemiah they had to function in a hostile environment. In spite of that opposition, however, the covenant community was established as a
worshiping community to serve the living God.

(6) Persistent Opposition (4:4-5)

**4Then the peoples around them set out to discourage the people of Judah
and make them afraid to go on building. 5They hired counselors to work
against them and frustrate their plans during the entire reign of Cyrus king
of Persia and down to the reign of Darius king of Persia.**

4:4-5 Again, these verses pick up the theme of opposition from 3:3
and introduce the following section where the matter is elaborated. Furthermore, the mention of Darius in v. 5 looks ahead to 4:24, thus marking
the intervening verses as an excursus. The author actually only took up
the opposition to the building of the temple again in chaps. 5–6, which
refer to events in the reign of Darius I (522–486). The rest of chap. 4
(note v. 16) refers to later opposition, not to temple building but to the
building of the walls under the reigns of Xerxes[20] (486–465) and Artaxerxes I (464–423). However, the author included it to stress his theme of
persistent opposition.[21]

"The peoples around them" (v. 4) were no doubt the same as those of
3:3, referred to as "enemies" in 4:1. "Set out to discourage" is literally
"relaxing the hands" or "making weak the hands" to disable by causing
despair. The same phrase is used in Jer 38:4 to refer to a continuing process of discouragement.[22] The "counselors" may have been Persian officials bribed to obstruct the builders in every possible way.[23] Verse 5
shows that there was a continuing plan to discourage and frustrate the
work of building the temple. The author summarized what he had just
written by including all the time from the reign of Cyrus (to 530),

---

[20] Hebrew אֲחַשְׁוֵרוֹשׁ is *Khshayarsha* in Persian and *Xerxes* in Greek. This was the son
of Darius I, the same King Xerxes of whom we read in the Book of Esther. Nothing more
is said about opposition to the Jews during his reign.

[21] The Hebrew verbs in v. 4 translated "discourage" and "make afraid" are participles,
stressing the persistence of opposition.

[22] Slotki, *Daniel, Ezra, and Nehemiah*, 131. This phrase is found in the Lachish Ostracon (VI); cf. *ANET*, 322. See also 2 Sam 4:1; Isa 13:7; Jer 6:24.

[23] Blenkinsopp, *Ezra-Nehemiah*, 108.

through that of Cambyses (530–522), down to the reign of Darius I (522–486).

2. Examples of Opposition (4:6-24)

(1) In the Reign of Xerxes (4:6)

⁶At the beginning of the reign of Xerxes, they lodged an accusation against the people of Judah and Jerusalem.

4:6 Both vv. 5 and 24 of this chapter are from the reign of Darius (522–486), in whose reign the temple was finished. The material between v. 5 and v. 24 is from later times (see comments on 4:4-5). Therefore the first question that confronts the reader of this passage is chronological: Why is Cambyses (530–522) not mentioned, and why were events from the reigns of Xerxes (486–465) and Artaxerxes (464–423) included here if the author was referring to the opposition to the building of the temple, completed in 516?

Many theories have been set forth to explain the difficulty. Josephus rearranged the account placing Cambyses before Xerxes and substituting Xerxes for Artaxerxes.[24] The author's interest here, however, was more thematic than chronological. Verse 16 shows his awareness that this account of opposition in vv. 6-23 had to do with the walls and not the temple. But why did he bring it in here? The author had just shown how the Jews rejected an offer of help from the neighboring people and how these people harassed them. Here he demonstrated that the decision to reject their help was justified; they were enemies, and subsequent history demonstrates how much they hated the Jews and worked against them. As D. Kidner explains: "Without this foretaste of history to reveal the full seriousness of the opposition, we would not properly appreciate the achievements recorded in the next two chapters (5 and 6) nor the dangers hidden in the mixed marriages which Ezra would set himself to stamp out (chaps. 7–10)."[25]

The author used information from documents that he had at his disposal to show the persistence of this opposition even after the temple was finished. We may assume that failure to mention Cambyses only meant

---

[24] He also has both Ezra and Nehemiah in the reign of Xerxes. First Esdras has only Artaxerxes followed by Darius (2:12–4:63). Blenkinsopp and many others doubt the historical value of 1 Esdras and Josephus at this point. See L. L. Grabbe, "Josephus and the Reconstruction of the Judean Restoration," *JBL* 106 (1987): 231-46.

[25] Kidner, *Ezra and Nehemiah*, 48.

that he had no sources for that period.

The theme of opposition to God's people is prominent throughout the Bible. The Pharaoh of the exodus tried to destroy God's chosen people. Later, when Pharaoh Merneptah (1220 B.C.) on his stele told of a military victory over Israel, he said Israel was destroyed, never to rise again.[26] We could also mention the Amalekites (Exod 17:8-16), the Edomites (Ezek 25:12; 35:15; 36:5; Joel 3:19; Amos 1:11; Obadiah), the Philistines (1 Sam 4), and others. Throughout history many others have tried to destroy the people of God—both the Jews as God's chosen people and Christians as the people of God in the new covenant. As Jesus was persecuted, so many of his followers have been persecuted and put to death (cf. John 15:18-25). "In fact," said Paul, "everyone who wants to live a godly life in Jesus Christ will be persecuted" (1 Tim 3:12). In our supposedly "enlightened" world there are many thousands of Christian martyrs each year. Ezra reminds us that we live in a fallen world and participate in a struggle; there are enemies who try to hinder God's plan. Whenever God initiates a spiritual work, there will be opposition. But God is sovereign and faithful; his enemies will not prevail. Even a small, seemingly defenseless community of his people can count on his guidance, protection, and power.

(2) The Letter to Artaxerxes (4:7-16)

[7]**And in the days of Artaxerxes king of Persia, Bishlam, Mithredath, Tabeel and the rest of his associates wrote a letter to Artaxerxes. The letter was written in Aramaic script and in the Aramaic language.**

[8]**Rehum the commanding officer and Shimshai the secretary wrote a letter against Jerusalem to Artaxerxes the king as follows:**

[9]**Rehum the commanding officer and Shimshai the secretary, together with the rest of their associates—the judges and officials over the men from Tripolis, Persia, Erech and Babylon, the Elamites of Susa,** [10]**and the other people whom the great and honorable Ashurbanipal deported and settled in the city of Samaria and elsewhere in Trans-Euphrates.**

[11]**(This is a copy of the letter they sent him.)**

To King Artaxerxes,

From your servants, the men of Trans-Euphrates:

[12]**The king should know that the Jews who came up to us from you have gone to Jerusalem and are rebuilding that rebellious and wicked city. They**

---

[26] *ANET,* 378.

are restoring the walls and repairing the foundations.
¹³Furthermore, the king should know that if this city is built and its walls are restored, no more taxes, tribute or duty will be paid, and the royal revenues will suffer. ¹⁴Now since we are under obligation to the palace and it is not proper for us to see the king dishonored, we are sending this message to inform the king, ¹⁵so that a search may be made in the archives of your predecessors. In these records you will find that this city is a rebellious city, troublesome to kings and provinces, a place of rebellion from ancient times. That is why this city was destroyed. ¹⁶We inform the king that if this city is built and its walls are restored, you will be left with nothing in Trans-Euphrates.

4:7 Artaxerxes, who became king by murdering his older brother, ruled from 464 to 423 B.C.; this included the time of Ezra and Nehemiah. A major concern of the first half of his reign was the Egyptian revolt that began in 460 and was supported by the Greeks, who continued to fight the Persians until the Peace of Callias in 448 (see Introduction). This was a major challenge to Persian control in the eastern Mediterranean and would have caused Artaxerxes to listen seriously to such charges of sedition as he was receiving from Samaria.[27]

"Bishlam" is correctly rendered here as a proper name, although some think it is a phrase meaning literally "in peace" (an Aramaism related to Hebrew *šālôm*). Blenkinsopp translates, "Tabeel . . . *in accord with* Mithredath."[28]

The end of v. 7 is literally "and he wrote the letter written in Aramaic and translated[29] in Aramaic." The alternate translation in the NIV margin is "written in Aramaic and translated." This could mean that while the letter had been written in Aramaic, the author's copy had been translated into Hebrew.[30] Since the actual letter is not given, however, it more likely would mean that although the letter had been written in Aramaic it was translated into Persian when it was read to the king.[31] The final word "Aramaic" may not be part of the clause but indicates that the following

---

[27] See K. G. Hoglund, *Achaemenid Imperial Administration in Syra-Palestine and the Missions of Ezra and Nehemiah* (Atlanta: Scholars Press, 1992), 163.

[28] Blenkinsopp, *Ezra-Nehemiah*, 109-10. Williamson (*Ezra, Nehemiah,* 54) argues it is likely a proper name.

[29] This is a participle of a verb תרגם, a loanword from Akkadian, from which comes the word *targum*.

[30] Williamson, *Ezra, Nehemiah,* 61.

[31] Blenkinsopp, *Ezra-Nehemiah*, 112. This was normal Persian practice and is reflected in 4:18. See J. Naveh, "Hebrew and Aramaic in the Persian Period," in *The Cambridge History of Judaism*, vol. 1, *Introduction: The Persian Period*, ed. W. D. Davies and L. Finkelstein (Cambridge: University Press, 1984), 116.

section (4:8–6:18) is in Aramaic. If the NIV translation is correct, the author's point may be that his source was written not only in the Aramaic script but also in the Aramaic language. It is commonly thought that during the exile Hebrew began to be written in Aramaic script rather than in the traditional Hebrew script.[32] If that is true, this verse may reflect that practice.

4:8-11 From here through 6:18 the text is in Aramaic. Aramaic became the *lingua franca* of the Assyrian Empire in the eighth century and grew in importance through the Neo-Babylonian and Persian Empires. No doubt the author's documents, the letters and replies, were written in Aramaic. Since the Jews became bilingual (Hebrew and Aramaic) during the exile, to avoid changing back and forth between languages he also put his comments in Aramaic.

These verses serve as the introduction to the letter quoted in vv. 12-16. In v. 8 the author explained that this was a letter of accusation from the officials in Samaria[33] against the Jews ("against Jerusalem") who were attempting to rebuild Jerusalem. Verses 9-10 probably came from the official summary of the letter found on the outside of the papyrus scroll.

Ashurbanipal was king of Assyria from 669 to 633. We have no record of his settling other people in Israel, though it was the custom of the Assyrian kings to do so. We know that Ashurbanipal suppressed a rebellion in Babylon in 648, conquered Elam in 642 and Susa in 641, and later led his armies to the west.[34] So we have no reason to doubt that he settled people from the east in Palestine.

Rehum and the others probably emphasized the eastern origin of the people to enhance their claim to be loyal to the king and separated from any kind of rebellion of the local indigenous people such as the Jews. Mention of the satrapy Trans-Euphrates ("Beyond the River") that in-

---

[32] Naveh doubts that the change took place before the end of the Persian period. The earliest clear evidence consists of third-century biblical manuscripts from Qumran written in Aramaic script ("Hebrew and Aramaic," 128). Whenever the change took place, it had an important impact on scribal work, the standardizing of the text, and even the collection of the canon. Changing the script would soon make the old manuscripts unreadable to the new generation. Only what was considered important would be preserved and recopied in the new script. While most Qumran manuscripts were written in the square script, the tetragrammaton, the name of God, is written in the old cursive script.

[33] Contrary to the translation "commanding officer," Rehum was not a military officer. The term would be better rendered "chancellor" (Blenkinsopp, *Ezra-Nehemiah,* 112; Williamson, *Ezra-Nehemiah,* 54).

[34] Williamson, *Ezra, Nehemiah,* 62.

cluded Palestine is more rhetoric serving to enhance the writers' position and credibility.

4:12 No doubt Jews moved from Mesopotamia to Jerusalem at different times; but if we understand "from you" to refer specifically to Artaxerxes, this refers to building activity following Ezra's return, whether or not encouraged by him. Since Nehemiah had a specific mandate in 445 B.C. to rebuild the city, it could not refer to him. In Neh 1:3 Nehemiah received news that in Jerusalem the wall was broken down and the gates were burned. That may have been the wall started here, and its destruction may have been the direct result of Artaxerxes' reply (vv. 18-22). The whole letter is inflammatory, however, and a gross exaggeration and cannot be used to determine Jewish activity other than the fact that some building was underway (v. 23).

4:13 Three different words for taxes are used. Based on their Babylonian parallels they refer to a monetary tax, payment in kind (oil, grain, etc.), and a kind of duty tax.[35] After the costly campaigns against the Greeks, the empire could not afford to lose any revenue. The opposition played on the fears of the king that he might lose revenues and even the whole western province (v. 16). The early years of Artaxerxes' reign had been difficult, and there were a number of rebellions in the west; so even though these dangers are exaggerated in the letter, they would arouse concern in the king, causing him to take notice and act.

4:14-15 "We are under obligation to the palace" is literally, "We have eaten the salt of the palace." Salt was often used to seal covenants; thus it implies loyalty (cf. Lev 2:13; Num 18:19; 2 Chr 13:5). "Eating the salt of" came to be an idiomatic expression for "being in the service of" or "receiving a salary from." Our word "salary" is derived from Latin *salarium*, "salt money."[36] A pretense of loyalty and concern for the king's honor is used with no mention of the true motives of personal gain.

The Persian kings considered themselves the successors of the Babylonian kings, who are referred to here as "your predecessors." The officials here knew that records were kept from former administrations. In fact, in the ancient world all peoples where writing was known kept royal chronicles. There is some irony in the statement, "That is why this city was destroyed." While that was the Babylonian motivation, the real reason was the judgment of God (2 Chr 36:15-19). The author was certainly aware that the plans of God supercede human intentions (1:1; 5:12).

---

[35] Myers, *Ezra, Nehemiah,* 34, 150,
[36] Slotki, *Daniel, Ezra and Nehemiah,* 135.

4:16 "You will be left with nothing in Trans-Euphrates." Although the Jews had often been rebellious under the Assyrian and Babylonian kings, certainly this little band of Jews would not pose a serious threat to Artaxerxes. However, because of prior troubles in the west (Syria-Palestine and Egypt), Artaxerxes would have been sensitive to any signs of unrest.

(3) The Reply of Artaxerxes (4:17-22)

[17]The king sent this reply:

To Rehum the commanding officer, Shimshai the secretary and the rest of their associates living in Samaria and elsewhere in Trans-Euphrates:

Greetings.

[18]The letter you sent us has been read and translated in my presence. [19]I issued an order and a search was made, and it was found that this city has a long history of revolt against kings and has been a place of rebellion and sedition. [20]Jerusalem has had powerful kings ruling over the whole of Trans-Euphrates, and taxes, tribute and duty were paid to them. [21]Now issue an order to these men to stop work, so that this city will not be rebuilt until I so order. [22]Be careful not to neglect this matter. Why let this threat grow, to the detriment of the royal interests?

This raises the question of contradictory orders; how could the same king later send Nehemiah to build the walls? Certainly he felt pressures from different sides and could change his opinion when presented with additional information. In fact, in v. 21 he left open this possibility, "until I so order." Without that providential addition, Nehemiah indeed would have had a difficult time gaining the king's approval for his plans (cf. Dan 6:8,12,15; Esth 1:19; 8:8). The situation that moved Nehemiah to pray and act (Neh 1–2) may have been the result of the events mentioned here.

4:17-18 The author no doubt had a copy of the letters before him, for the form and expressions follow exactly what we know of official royal letters of this time. The reply also shows the surprising efficiency of administrative communication in the Persian Empire. Letters could travel between Samaria and the Persian court in about a week.

The letter probably was translated by the scribe as he read it to the king. The word *mĕpāraš*, rendered "translated" here, is from a verb that can also mean "to separate" or "to distinguish" and is sometimes translated adverbially as "plainly" or "clearly."[37] Williamson, however, translates "verbatim," explaining that the term has "some such meaning as 'piece by piece,' . . . i.e., 'in full,' not just in summary."[38]

4:19 "A long history of revolt" could refer to Hezekiah's revolt against Sennacherib about 700 B.C. and the participation of later kings in revolts against the Babylonians.

4:20-22 The sentence begins, "Powerful kings were over Jerusalem." The phrase is ambiguous and can be taken as powerful kings of Jerusalem, such as David and Solomon, who ruled a large area; or it could refer to other powerful kings who ruled over Jerusalem and received taxes from Jerusalem. There is more irony at the end of Artaxerxes' reply when he ordered the Samarian officials not to neglect the very thing they wanted to do in the first place.[39]

(4) The Effects of Opposition (4:23-24)

[23]As soon as the copy of the letter of King Artaxerxes was read to Rehum and Shimshai the secretary and their associates, they went immediately to the Jews in Jerusalem and compelled them by force to stop.
[24]Thus the work on the house of God in Jerusalem came to a standstill until the second year of the reign of Darius king of Persia.

4:23 Israel's enemies lost no time in complying with the decree of Artaxerxes. Both Josephus and 1 Esdr 2:30 say they went to Jerusalem with horses and troops. If some work had been done, they may have destroyed it at this time. This could have been the situation reported to Nehemiah in Neh 1:3, "The wall of Jerusalem is broken down, and its gates have been burned with fire."[40]

4:24 The author so skillfully crafted his account that v. 24 appears to logically follow v. 23. The connection, however, is with v. 5. As noted earlier, vv. 6-23 are a parenthesis to show the real attitude of those who

---

[37] KJV and Blenkinsopp, *Ezra-Nehemiah*, 109,115. Blenkinsopp understands "clearly" to refer to the process of translation.

[38] Williamson (*Ezra, Nehemiah*, 53,56). See also Vogt, *Lexicon*, 140.

[39] I. Jerusalmi (*The Aramaic Sections of Ezra and Daniel*, 2d ed. [Cincinnati: Hebrew Union College-Jewish Institute of Religion, 1978], 12) argues that לְמָה is a negative telic particle and should be translated "lest" instead of "why."

[40] Myers, *Ezra and Nehemiah*, 39. Nehemiah arrived in Jerusalem in 445 B.C. Therefore some commentators think this entire episode was related to a rebellion of Megabyzus (satrap of Trans-Euphrates) in 448 B.C., although some doubt this rebellion (see Introduction). Williamson (*Ezra, Nehemiah*, 63) thinks it is significant that the letter of Artaxerxes was written by a chancellor and his associates rather than the satrap. This could support the theory that Megabyzus was in rebellion at this time. Another theory would link the episode with an earlier rebellion in Egypt.

offered help in v. 2 and to show the continuity of the opposition to the Jews even after the period of temple construction. The surrounding peoples obstructed the rebuilding of the temple, and later they would obstruct the rebuilding of the city.

Darius I (522–486) took over the Persian Empire after the civil war following the death of Cambyses (see Introduction). As often happens in such times of uncertainty, the empire was threatened with dissolution. There were revolts in every direction. But by Darius's second year (520 B.C.), he had put down the rebellions and stabilized the empire (except for trouble in Egypt in 518–519). Under his rule the Persian Empire reached its greatest power and splendor.[41]

3. Prophecy Fulfilled: The Temple Built (5:1–6:22)

(1) A New Beginning (5:1-2)

¹Now Haggai the prophet and Zechariah the prophet, a descendant of Iddo, prophesied to the Jews in Judah and Jerusalem in the name of the God of Israel, who was over them. ²Then Zerubbabel son of Shealtiel and Jeshua son of Jozadak set to work to rebuild the house of God in Jerusalem. And the prophets of God were with them, helping them.

Work on the temple had been stopped for a long time. After sixteen years a new beginning was needed. "Like every spiritual advance, from Abraham's to the missionary expansion in Acts, this venture began with a word from the Lord."[42] For this God used two prophets, Haggai and Zechariah, whose messages of rebuke, exhortation, encouragement, and assurance were desperately needed by the restored community. Their mission was to bring about spiritual renewal and to motivate the people to restore the proper worship of the Lord.

5:1 The messages recorded in the Book of Haggai were delivered between August and December 520 B.C. Temple construction was resumed in September. Zechariah's messages began in October, and his last dated message was delivered in February 519.

"In the name of the God of Israel," Haggai reprimanded the people for neglecting God's house, the temple. The people had used the opposition as an excuse and turned their attention to their own houses. They had given in to their fear (3:3) and discouragement (4:4-5) and had concerned themselves with trying to meet their own physical needs. The spiritual

---

[41] See the Introduction. Also see Fensham, *Ezra and Nehemiah,* 77-78.

[42] Kidner, *Ezra and Nehemiah,* 53.

needs of the community and the work God had called them to had been set aside. But as McConville has written, "There is always an effective answer to discouragement in the bold proclamation of the word of God."[43]

"Who was over them" is grammatically ambiguous. It can mean that God was over the prophets or that he was over the Jews. Both were under God's lordship, so it can apply to both; it would seem best to apply the phrase to the Jews because the whole community was subject to God's will.

5:2 "Zerubbabel and Jeshua" are the same two men mentioned in 4:4 and many times in Haggai and Zechariah. Zerubbabel was the son of Shealtiel, who was the oldest son of King Jehoiachin. King Jehoiachin was still considered the legitimate king of Judah even after he was carried captive to Babylon. In Hag 2:2 Jeshua is called the high priest. Although God used prophets to motivate and encourage the people (6:14; perhaps they even helped in the construction), he also used others to organize and coordinate the work.

Haggai and Zechariah show that Zerubbabel was an important leader as "governor of Judah" (Hag 1:1). So it seems strange that Zerubbabel disappears from the narrative in Ezra. He is not even mentioned in Ezra's description of the completion of the temple. A number of theories have been proposed to explain his disappearance, but the biblical text gives no indication of what happened.[44]

(2) Building Activity Investigated (5:3-5)

[3]At that time Tattenai, governor of Trans-Euphrates, and Shethar-Bozenai and their associates went to them and asked, "Who authorized you to rebuild this temple and restore this structure?" [4]They also asked, "What are the names of the men constructing this building?" [5]But the eye of their God was watching over the elders of the Jews, and they were not stopped until a report could go to Darius and his written reply be received.

---

[43] McConville, *Ezra, Nehemiah, and Esther,* 32.

[44] Some have conjectured that Zerubbabel was involved in a rebellion and thus was removed by the Persians. It is suggested that Zechariah's words (Zech 4; 6:12), which attached messianic significance to Zerubbabel's ministry, could have encouraged such a rebellion. It is, however, only conjecture; the text gives no such indication. Neither did Haggai and Zechariah speak against the Persian government. Zerubbabel may simply have died before the temple was completed (Fensham, *Ezra and Nehemiah,* 78-79). T. C. Eskenazi (*In an Age of Prose* [Atlanta: Scholars Press, 1988], 48-53) argues that his absence from the narrative results from the author's focus on the people as a whole rather than on the leaders. See also S. Japhet, "Sheshbazzar and Zerubbabel," *ZAW* 94 (1982): 66-98.

5:3 Documents from the first and third years of Darius mention Ushtanni as satrap of Babylon and Abarnahara (Trans-Euphrates).[45] Commentators formerly thought that Tattenai was the same man. Apparently, however, Tattenai was governor of Abarnahara, the western half of the satrapy. A cuneiform text names him as governor of Abarnahara in 502 B.C. He probably ruled from Damascus, and Ushtanni ruled from Babylon.[46] The word "governor" (*paḥat*) is used rather broadly and can refer to an assistant of the satrap.[47] "Shethar-Bozenai" probably was Tattenai's secretary.

The first two years of Darius's reign were stormy ones due to numerous revolts. So it is natural that the authorities of this western province should have inspected such new building activity as the Jews were doing. Their questions were logical; Tattenai and his men were simply fulfilling their duty as government officials. Their awareness of this new building activity, however, may have resulted from a report from the Samarian officials.

The Aramaic for "restore this structure" is difficult to translate, largely because the exact meaning of the key word *'uššarnā'* is not known. An alternate translation is "to complete [the preparation of] this material."[48] It is not clear what stage the building had reached; but since Tattenai took time to write to Darius and wait for a reply without stopping the work, it probably was still in its early stages.

5:4 "They also asked" follows the LXX rendering, which the context demands.[49]

5:5 "The eye of God" refers to God's watchful providence. Kings had their spies, which the Persians called the King's Eye or the King's Ear. But "God's people could take assurance in their conviction that God's intelligence system is not only more efficient than any king's espionage network but is omniscient" (cf. 2 Chr 16:9; Pss 33:18-19; 34:15; Zech 4:10).[50] Ezra-Nehemiah constantly reiterates God's providence in

---

[45] Slotki, *Daniel, Ezra and Nehemiah*, 139.

[46] Blenkinsopp, *Ezra-Nehemiah*, 120.

[47] A. T. Olmstead, "Tattenai, Governor of Across the River," *JNES* 3 (1944): 46.

[48] Williamson (*Ezra, Nehemiah*, 67, 70) points out that in other Aramaic documents the word refers to materials used in building walls or boats, most likely wood or timber. Others translate "roofing," "timber," "supplies," "furnishings," or even "wall."

[49] The MT אֲמַרְנָא לְהֹם מַן־אֱנוּן שְׁמָהָת גֻּבְרַיָּא ("we told them the names of the men") does not make sense in context. The first person verb אֲמַרְנָא may be a textual corruption influenced by v. 9; or perhaps the author was following so closely his copy of the letter that he failed to change the phrase from first person to third person.

[50] E. A. Yamauchi, "Ezra-Nehemiah," EBC (Grand Rapids: Zondervan, 1988), 4:629.

the life of his people. The reestablishment of the covenant community was the result of a continuing series of God's providential acts.

The whole transaction of sending this report to Darius, searching for the records, and sending back a reply would have taken four or five months. Tattenai could easily have stopped the work, but the author saw here God's intervention. God so guided Tattenai's attitude that he allowed the Jews to continue the construction until he could check with King Darius. In order to fulfill his purpose, God used and coordinated the preaching of the prophets, the work of the leaders, the determination of the whole community, and the decisions of "pagan" government officials.

The Jews continued the work even though there was a possibility the king would stop the project and thus nullify all their efforts. This persistence and perseverance indicates the people's faith that God would continue to keep the door open for continuing the work. It also shows the influence of the prophets Haggai and Zechariah.

(3) The Report Sent to Darius (5:6-17)

[6]This is a copy of the letter that Tattenai, governor of Trans-Euphrates, and Shethar-Bozenai and their associates, the officials of Trans-Euphrates, sent to King Darius. [7]The report they sent him read as follows:

To King Darius:

Cordial greetings.

[8]The king should know that we went to the district of Judah, to the temple of the great God. The people are building it with large stones and placing the timbers in the walls. The work is being carried on with diligence and is making rapid progress under their direction. [9]We questioned the elders and asked them, "Who authorized you to rebuild this temple and restore this structure?" [10]We also asked them their names, so that we could write down the names of their leaders for your information. [11]This is the answer they gave us:

"We are the servants of the God of heaven and earth, and we are rebuilding the temple that was built many years ago, one that a great king of Israel built and finished. [12]But because our fathers angered the God of heaven, he handed them over to Nebuchadnezzar the Chaldean, king of Babylon, who destroyed this temple and deported the people to Babylon.

[13]"However, in the first year of Cyrus king of Babylon, King Cyrus issued a decree to rebuild this house of God. [14]He even removed from the temple of Babylon the gold and silver articles of the house of God, which Nebuchadnezzar had taken from the temple in Jerusalem and brought to the temple in

Babylon.

"Then King Cyrus gave them to a man named Sheshbazzar, whom he had appointed governor, [15]and he told him, 'Take these articles and go and deposit them in the temple in Jerusalem. And rebuild the house of God on its site.' [16]So this Sheshbazzar came and laid the foundations of the house of God in Jerusalem. From that day to the present it has been under construction but is not yet finished.'"

[17]Now if it pleases the king, let a search be made in the royal archives of Babylon to see if King Cyrus did in fact issue a decree to rebuild this house of God in Jerusalem. Then let the king send us his decision in this matter.

5:6   D. J. Clines explains the term translated here "officials" as "imperial troubleshooters, armed with powers of punishment."[51]

5:7   "Report" here is the same word translated "reply" in 4:17. The report is well organized and official. It presents (1) an account of the inspection of the work; (2) the questions asked the Jews; (3) a lengthy account of the Jews' answer; and (4) a request that King Darius check the records concerning Cyrus's decree and that he, Darius, decide the matter.

5:8   That these Persian officials should say "the great God" may seem strange. But the Persians liked to use the religious language of their subject peoples. The phrase can also be translated "the great house of God."

"Large stones" is another phrase sometimes translated differently, such as "smooth" or "polished."[52] It is true that the second temple did have large stones in its foundation.[53] At least the seriousness of the construction aroused the Persian officials' suspicion.

Different suggestions have been made about the "timbers" that were used here. Some suggest that the setting of the rafters was involved.[54] Others think "timbers" had to do with paneling or supports for the roof. The first temple had three courses of stones and one of timbers (1 Kgs 6:36), and the ratio here was the same (Ezra 6:4). This may have been precaution against earthquake damage.

5:9-10   The questions asked were legitimate. Apparently the Jews were courteous and answered correctly. No doubt their integrity had something to do with Tattenai's positive attitude. As subjects of the Persian Empire the Jews had certain rights. They displayed common sense in taking advantage of their citizenship.[55]

---

[51] Clines, *Ezra, Nehemiah, Esther,* 85-86. See also Myers, *Ezra. Nehemiah,* 42.

[52] Williamson, *Ezra, Nehemiah,* 70.

[53] Note the large stones at the bottom of the Wailing Wall in Jerusalem.

[54] Myers, *Ezra. Nehemiah,* 43.

5:11 The Jews gave a good testimony. They did not hide their allegiance to God. Here the Jews saw themselves as continuing something that was done nearly five hundred years before by King Solomon.

5:12 The returned exiles saw the relation between history and theology. What their ancestors did determined their history. The Christian faith is tied to the fact that God made promises and fulfilled them in history, exemplified by Jesus, who actually came, died, and rose again. Although God is sovereign, decisions we make *do* affect history. History is a dialogue between God and humankind.

The people knew their history and theology and could express them to these Persian officials. Normally in the ancient Near East if one nation subjugated another, that nation's god or gods were considered the more powerful.[56] But the great prophets of Israel had warned God's people that if they did not turn back to God, Jerusalem would be destroyed and they would be carried into captivity. At the time they did not believe the warnings, but later they recognized that Jeremiah and Ezekiel were of God. God used the messages of those prophets to preserve the faith of Israel during the exile. Now the Jews, understanding the theological reasons for their calamity, did not hesitate to tell their neighbors why they had suffered that exile. Today the church needs to understand why we believe what we believe and why we do what we do. The whole church, all believers in Jesus Christ, must theologize, not just the experts in theology.

5:13 Usually Cyrus is called the king of Persia. However, several cuneiform inscriptions support the use of "king of Babylon." One such inscription found on a clay barrel says: "I am Cyrus, king of the world, great king, legitimate king, king of Babylon, king of Sumer and Akkad."[57] It was, of course, during his first year not as king of Persia but as king of Babylon that he issued the decree.

"King Cyrus issued a decree" was the Jews' most important argument. They had legal backing, and Cyrus was still honored as the great founder of the Persian Empire. In fact, Darius consciously tried to follow the policies Cyrus had used.

5:14 As noted earlier, the "gold and silver articles of the house of God" were considered important when a king conquered a nation. In oth-

---

[55] Under God's providence, Tattenai and King Darius recognized these citizenship "rights." Cf. Rom 13:6-7.

[56] There were exceptions. In the Moabite Stone inscription King Mesha said his people became subject to Israel because their god was angered with them.

[57] *ANET,* 316.

er nations these objects would have included their idols.

Here "Sheshbazzar" is called governor. From 1 Chr 3:18 we know that Sheshbazzar was the fourth son of King Jehoiachin. Although some have tried to make Sheshbazzar and Zerubbabel the same person, as Myers says, "There can be no doubt as to the substantial historicity of both."[58] Apparently Sheshbazzar's time as governor did not continue long, for this verse appears to speak of him as someone in the past; and in Ezra 3:2 Zerubbabel already was the leader.[59]

5:15 The two commands might seem to be contradictory: "Deposit them in the temple," and "rebuild the house of God." The first command anticipates the second one. It was understood that the temple had to be built first.

The phrase "on its site" is significant. In ancient times it was considered important to rebuild the temple in the same place as the former one. Thus archaeologists nearly always find in excavations of successive layers of occupation that after a destruction, the new temple was built exactly over the old site.

5:16 Part of the confusion about Sheshbazzar and Zerubbabel is due to the fact that Ezra 3:10 speaks of laying the foundation under Zerubbabel's supervision. Some think the author was confused; that is doubtful. It is possible that Sheshbazzar did not complete the foundation, or because of the years that had passed, Zerubbabel's men had to relay the foundations. Some explain the difference by noting that Sheshbazzar is credited with the work in a Persian context here, whereas it is in a Jewish context in 3:10 that Zerubbabel is credited. This suggests the possibility that Sheshbazzar, to whom the temple articles were entrusted (1:11), may have been a Persian leader.[60]

That first beginning was 536 B.C.; the present was 520 B.C. Apparently there had been sporadic attempts to continue the building, but it took the preaching of Haggai and Zechariah to mobilize the people to take seriously the challenge.

5:17 The request of Tattenai and his men to "let a search be made" was logical. The archives of the Babylonian Empire would have been stored in Babylon, but one would expect those of Cyrus to be in Susa, his capital. In the next chapter we see they were actually found in Ecbatana,

---

[58] Myers, *Ezra. Nehemiah,* 45.

[59] See comments on 3:2.

[60] McConville (*Ezra, Nehemiah, and Esther,* 11) believes he "was probably a Babylonian governor whom Cyrus left in office, and who was in due course, perhaps on his death, succeeded by Zerubbabel."

Cyrus's summer capital. Apparently the Jews did not possess a copy of Cyrus's decree or they would have shown it to Tattenai.

(4) The Edict of Cyrus Discovered (6:1-12)

[1]King Darius then issued an order, and they searched in the archives stored in the treasury at Babylon. [2]A scroll was found in the citadel of Ecbatana in the province of Media, and this was written on it:

Memorandum:

[3]In the first year of King Cyrus, the king issued a decree concerning the temple of God in Jerusalem:

Let the temple be rebuilt as a place to present sacrifices, and let its foundations be laid. It is to be ninety feet high and ninety feet wide, [4]with three courses of large stones and one of timbers. The costs are to be paid by the royal treasury. [5]Also, the gold and silver articles of the house of God, which Nebuchadnezzar took from the temple in Jerusalem and brought to Babylon, are to be returned to their places in the temple in Jerusalem; they are to be deposited in the house of God.

[6]Now then, Tattenai, governor of Trans-Euphrates, and Shethar-Bozenai and you, their fellow officials of that province, stay away from there. [7]Do not interfere with the work on this temple of God. Let the governor of the Jews and the Jewish elders rebuild this house of God on its site.

[8]Moreover, I hereby decree what you are to do for these elders of the Jews in the construction of this house of God:

The expenses of these men are to be fully paid out of the royal treasury, from the revenues of Trans-Euphrates, so that the work will not stop. [9]Whatever is needed—young bulls, rams, male lambs for burnt offerings to the God of heaven, and wheat, salt, wine and oil, as requested by the priests in Jerusalem—must be given them daily without fail, [10]so that they may offer sacrifices pleasing to the God of heaven and pray for the well-being of the king and his sons.

[11]Furthermore, I decree that if anyone changes this edict, a beam is to be pulled from his house and he is to be lifted up and impaled on it. And for this crime his house is to be made a pile of rubble. [12]May God, who has caused his Name to dwell there, overthrow any king or people who lifts a hand to change this decree or to destroy this temple in Jerusalem.

I Darius have decreed it. Let it be carried out with diligence.

6:1 King Darius took notice of Tattenai's letter and did as Tattenai had suggested. No doubt the rebellions, especially in the west, during his first years made Darius sensitive to these details. Also, like Cyrus, Darius was concerned that his subject peoples be content. Search was first made in Babylon since that was the capital of the satrapy. It may seem strange that they should look for such a decree in the "treasury." However, archaeologists noted that at Persepolis rooms used for storing archives were linked to the treasury.[61]

6:2 Because thousands of clay tablets have been found in Mesopotamia, we generally assume that writing in Mesopotamia was done on tablets. However, even Assyro-Babylonian scribes sometimes used parchment (leather) or papyrus as well as clay. Diodorus writes of the "royal parchments" on which the Persians kept their records.[62] Had this record been written in Persian, it probably would have been on a clay tablet, but it was written in Aramaic.

The decree was finally found in Ecbatana instead of Babylon. The Persians used Ecbatana as their summer palace because of its comfortable climate due to its high elevation. Cyrus lived in Babylon during the winter, in Susa in the spring, and in Ecbatana in the summer. He resided in Ecbatana the first summer as king of Babylon.

We have seen another version of this edict in Ezra 1, but with a number of differences.[63] In Ezra 1 the decree was in a form that could have been announced to the people. Here the "memorandum" or "record" is most likely a quote of Cyrus's decree or part of it, an instruction for the royal treasury concerned with the expenses for building the temple in Jerusalem.[64] It may have been a longer document, but only matters that had to do with Tattenai's letter were copied here.[65]

6:3 The king took seriously the details of worship. Sacrifices were an important part of the cult in the religions of the Persian Empire as

---

[61] Williamson, *Ezra, Nehemiah,* 80.

[62] R. de Vaux, *The Bible and the Ancient Near East* (Garden City: Doubleday, 1971), 90.

[63] For an excellent discussion of the decree, see E. J. Bickerman, "The Edict of Cyrus in Ezra 1," in *Studies in Jewish and Christian History* (Leiden: Brill, 1976), 72-108.

[64] See comments on Ezra 1:3-5. In Egyptian Aramaic זכֿן (the Aramaic word used here is דְּכְרוֹנָה) is used for extracts of decrees without including details. But the annals of the Persian kings are sometimes referred to as בְּסְפַר־דָּכְרָנַיָּא (Ezra 4:15) or סֵפֶר הַזִּכְרֹנוֹת (Esth 6:1); therefore we must have here an actual quotation of the text of the decree (de Vaux, *The Bible and the Ancient Near East*, 93).

[65] A similar memorandum was found at Elephantine sent by the governors of Judah and Samaria: "Memorandum (*zkrn*) from Bigvai and Delaiah: Let it be an instruction to you in Egypt to say to Arsames about the house of the altar of the God of heaven which was built a long time ago, before Cambyses, in the fortress of Jeb, and which Waidrang, that reprobate, destroyed in the fourteenth year of king Darius (II): that it be rebuilt on its (original) site as it was before, in order that cereal offering and incense be offered on this altar, as was done previously" (Blenkinsopp, *Ezra-Nehemiah,* 124).

well as among the Jews. Of course the sacrifices had different meanings in other religions. Many times it was thought that the gods needed food; frequently the worshiper tried to manipulate his god by giving him sacrifices. In Israel sacrifice was for forgiveness of sins and for worshiping God.

Regarding the foundations, some would translate "preserved" or "retained" instead of "laid," since work on the foundations had already been done (3:10; 5:16).[66] The decree of Cyrus put emphasis on building the temple on the same site as the former temple. However, the next sentence, "ninety feet high and ninety feet wide," seems to contradict this. According to 1 Kgs 6:2, Solomon's temple was ninety feet (sixty cubits) long, thirty feet wide (twenty cubits), and forty-five feet high (thirty cubits). Apparently there has been textual confusion here. The length was inadvertently missed; the scribe's eye went back to the first sixty (cubits), and he repeated it instead of the original twenty (as in 1 Kgs 6:2).

6:4 "Three courses of large stones and one of timbers" are the same proportions as in Solomon's temple (1 Kgs 6:36), but there they refer to the inner court. Some think the wood refers to the inner paneling on the wall.[67]

Some commentators have doubted the veracity of the edict because it contains so many minute details of distinctively Jewish customs and because they think Cyrus would not have gone so far as to provide funds to help build the temple. However, it is possible that a Jewish scribe advised Cyrus on drawing up this decree. Also Cyrus was concerned that this temple take the place of the temple destroyed by Nebuchadnezzar. It was simply a replacement, not something new. We have other documents from the reigns of Cyrus, Cambyses, and Darius that prove these kings gave similar support for the restoration of the cults of their subjected peoples in regions as widely separated as Babylon, Turkey, and Egypt.[68]

6:5 It is remarkable that "the gold and silver articles of the house of God" agrees so well with what the Jews told Tattenai in 5:14-15; it certainly lends credence to the integrity of their report. Again we notice the importance these kings put on the "cult objects" contained in temples. Jeremiah had prophesied that these things would be taken to Babylon and later returned to Jerusalem (Jer 27:21-22).

6:6 The transition is not very smooth; the author finished quoting the edict of Cyrus and then gave a summary of the letter Darius sent to

---

[66] United Bible Societies, *Preliminary and Interim Report on the Hebrew Old Testament Text Project* (Stuttgart, 1976), 505. Also Williamson, *Ezra, Nehemiah,* 71.

[67] See Fensham, *Ezra and Nehemiah,* 88.

Tattenai. "Stay away from there" sounds rather brusque; but it is a technical, legal term that means the accusation was rejected.[69] So, as the next verse explains, Tattenai and his men were not allowed to interfere with the work. Darius endorsed the decree of Cyrus and used his own authority to help carry it out.[70]

6:7   There is a special emphasis on the fact that this was God's temple and it was being built on "its site," on the same place it was originally located. One significant difference, however, between this temple and the earlier one was that there would be no ark of the covenant in the most holy place symbolizing the presence of God.[71] It would be awaiting, in a sense, the Lord of the temple, the messianic "messenger of the covenant" to make his presence known there (Mal 3:1; cf. Matt 21:12-17; John 7:14).

The term "governor" indicates that the Jews had some freedom for self-government within the province, for they had a governor. Also we would suppose that the governor here was Zerubbabel. However, it seems strange that he is not mentioned. In fact, he is not mentioned again in the whole Book of Ezra.[72]

6:8   The Jews naturally would have been anxious after Tattenai's visit. But what could have been reason for discouragement and defeat turned out to be an advantage. As the hymnwriter William Cowper wrote, "The clouds ye so much dread are big with mercy." Certainly God "is able to do immeasurably more than all we ask or imagine" (Eph 3:20).

6:9   Darius was concerned that the cult be practiced correctly, so he

---

[68] De Vaux, *The Bible and the Ancient Near East*, 92-93. De Vaux notes that Cyrus also returned the religious statues stored in Babylon to their distinctive sanctuaries in different parts of Mesopotamia. Also Darius II wrote a letter supporting the Feast of Unleavened Bread at Elephantine. Other ordinances of Cambyses and Darius I "fixed in detail the constitution of the temples and the priests of Egypt." Darius also restored a temple of Ptah and rebuilt the sanctuary of the Oasis of El-Khargah in Egypt. This was done by funds allocated by the Persian king. Also, "The discovery of bricks bearing the stamp of Cyrus in the Persian repairs to the Eanna (temple) at Uruk and to the Enunmah at Ur proved beyond any doubt that they were state undertakings supported by public funds." De Vaux says, "To sum up then, there is no valid objection whatsoever against the two edicts. Indeed they contain certain indications of authenticity" (pp. 92-93). See also A. R. Millard, "A Decree of a Persian Governor," *BurH* (1974): 88.

[69] F. Rundgren, "Über einen juristischen Terminus bei Esra 6:6," *ZAW* 70 (1958): 213.

[70] Williamson says that Darius was in many ways "a much truer successor of Cyrus than was Cambyses" (Williamson, *Ezra, Nehemiah,* 81).

[71] The absence of the ark is declared in the Mishna (*Yoma* 5.2) and implied in 1 Macc 1:21-24; 4:47-49.

[72] See note on 5:2.

made provision for sacrificial animals. The same would be true of the religious practices of other people subject to Darius. In fact, the Persepolis treasury documents show concern for details of worship and sacrifice. Various documents indicate that Cyrus, Cambyses, and Darius all showed concern for their subject peoples.[73] However, the attention to details such as "wheat, salt, wine and oil" surprises us. This again may show the help of a Jewish scribe in preparing the letter. According to the Pentateuch, wheat was used in a special grain offering (Lev 2:1-3) and sometimes as a substitute for an animal in the sin offering (Lev 5:11-13).

"Salt" was added especially to the grain offering, but it was also to be added to all the offerings (Lev 2:13). "The salt of the covenant" is a phrase that appears several times (Lev 2:13; Num 18:19; 2 Chr 13:5; Mark 9:49), salt being a symbol of covenant relationship. *Wine* was used in the drink offering (Exod 29:40; Lev 23:13), which accompanied other offerings. *Oil* was used in the continual burnt offering, in the grain offering (Lev 2:4,15), and in anointing the priest (Exod 29:21).

These items were to be provided daily, for worship was to be practiced every day. Precisely the products that were considered staple foods— grain, oil, and wine along with animals—were to be offered to God. Under the new covenant we rejoice because in Christ all these offerings were fulfilled for us. Real worship consists of daily dedicating ourselves to the Lord (Rom 12:1-2).

6:10 The king took seriously religious matters. He wanted all his peoples to pray to their gods in behalf of him and his sons.[74] This tactic also won the favor of his subject peoples. The New Testament tells us to pray for our political leaders (cf. Rom 13:1-7; 1 Tim 2:1-2).

6:11 The translation "he is to be lifted up and impaled" is uncertain, but a severe penalty is clearly prescribed. It was common for ancient covenants to include curses against those who broke the covenant. Also Assyrian, Aramaic, and Persian decrees and laws often included harsh threats of punishment for those who disobeyed.[75] The further punishment, "His house is to be made a pile of rubble," finds parallels in Dan 2:5; 3:29.

6:12 This verse contains an additional curse. The phrase "caused his Name to dwell there" reflects an understanding of biblical theology (cf.

---

[73] See comments and note on Ezra 6:4; also Williamson, *Ezra, Nehemiah*, 82.

[74] There is a similar request in the inscription on the Cyrus Cylinder (*ANET*, 316): "May all the gods whom I have resettled in their sacred cities ask daily Bel and Nebo for a long life for me and may they recommend me (to him)."

[75] See Myers, *Ezra. Nehemiah*, 52, for examples.

Deut 12:5), a strong indication that a Jewish scribe helped Darius prepare this decree. Darius was in fact speaking almost prophetically. As Daniel prophesied, God would do this very thing, destroying the king and kingdom that would oppose him and his people and then would establish an everlasting kingdom of righteousness (Dan 7:23-27).

(5) The Completion of the Temple (6:13-15)

¹³Then, because of the decree King Darius had sent, Tattenai, governor of Trans-Euphrates, and Shethar-Bozenai and their associates carried it out with diligence. ¹⁴So the elders of the Jews continued to build and prosper under the preaching of Haggai the prophet and Zechariah, a descendant of Iddo. They finished building the temple according to the command of the God of Israel and the decrees of Cyrus, Darius and Artaxerxes, kings of Persia. ¹⁵The temple was completed on the third day of the month Adar, in the sixth year of the reign of King Darius.

6:13 This victory of God's people clearly displays the providence of God at work through these pagan potentates. God in his providence works everything together to fulfill his plan. He used the prophets Haggai and Zechariah to inspire the people to work; he used the kings' decrees to open doors and provide the means. The author displayed the holy enthusiasm all Christians should share when they realize they are part of God's plan to fulfill his kingdom.

6:14 The "command" (*ta'am*) of God and the "decrees" (*tĕ'ēm*) of the Persian kings are translated from the same word in Aramaic. The Massoretes, however, distinguished between them by using different vowels. The most powerful word on earth at that time was the decree of a Persian king, but silently and mysteriously the king was being directed by an even more powerful divine word. God uses the decisions of kings and rulers to accomplish his commands.

The inclusion of Artaxerxes here causes problems, for he was king nearly a century later. A number of solutions have been offered. The author wrote this after the walls were built in the time of Artaxerxes I. Just as he included the opposition under Artaxerxes (chap. 4), here he included his support for the Jews, although this support had to do with the building of the walls instead of the temple.[76] Verse 14 makes clear that building ("the temple" is not in the Aramaic text) would continue with divine direction and Persian support through the time of Artaxerxes. T.

---

[76] There is a tradition that some temple construction occurred during his time. Artaxerxes did at least make provisions for the temple (7:16-17).

Eskenazi understands 6:14 as the key verse of Ezra-Nehemiah. The point, she says, is that temple (Ezra 1:7–6:22), community (7:1–10:44), and city (Neh 1:1–7:5) were all built according to the one command of God working through the decree (singular in Aramaic) of the king (also singular).[77]

6:15 "The temple was completed." What a note of triumph! The work was taken up in earnest under Haggai and Zechariah's preaching on September 21, 520 B.C. It was finished on March 12, 515 B.C.,[78] nearly four and a half years later. This was seventy-two years after the destruction of the temple in 587; therefore it corresponds closely with the seventy years of captivity Jeremiah prophesied (Jer 25:12-14; 29:10; see Zech 1:12-17).[79]

(6) The Temple Dedicated (6:16-18)

[16]Then the people of Israel—the priests, the Levites and the rest of the exiles—celebrated the dedication of the house of God with joy. [17]For the dedication of this house of God they offered a hundred bulls, two hundred rams, four hundred male lambs and, as a sin offering for all Israel, twelve male goats, one for each of the tribes of Israel. [18]And they installed the priests in their divisions and the Levites in their groups for the service of God at Jerusalem, according to what is written in the Book of Moses.

6:16-17 The whole community had worked together to build the temple. They had seen God's hand of protection and provision. So now they celebrated. Celebrations have always been vital for the people of God. They are occasions of fellowship, of worship, of glorifying God. They bind the community together and enable everyone to understand the purpose and history of the community. The term translated "dedication" is ḥănukkâ, the name of the Jewish holiday that celebrates a similar rededication of the temple after its defilement by the Seleucid King Antiochus IV (1 Macc 4:52-59; John 10:22).

"This house of God" in v. 17 perhaps intends to compare this dedication with Solomon's dedication of the first temple (1 Kgs 8). There the number of animals sacrificed was much greater: "twenty-two thousand

---

[77] Eskenazi, *Age of Prose,* 38-42.

[78] First Esdras 7:5 says the twenty-third day of Adar which would be April 1, 515. Some prefer this because it was a Friday instead of a Sabbath as the third of Adar would have been (Myers, *Ezra. Nehemiah,* 50).

[79] Different ways of calculating the seventy years have been used. No doubt the figure "seventy years" was intended as a round number; it is not necessary to find an exact seventy years in order to recognize the fulfillment of the prophecy.

cattle and a hundred and twenty thousand sheep and goats" (1 Kgs 8:63). These were fellowship offerings in which the fat and certain parts were burned and the meat was eaten by the people. So we can assume that the dedication service involved a huge feast in which all participated. The returned exiles formed a much smaller group, but the sacrifice of "a hundred bulls, two hundred rams, four hundred male lambs" was a large undertaking.

The people also offered twelve male goats as a sin offering "for all Israel . . . one for each of the tribes of Israel." Again, we have the emphasis on continuity with the historic community of Israel. Even though most of the returnees were from the tribes of Judah, Benjamin, and Levi, all the tribes were represented in the sacrifice. They were the people of God, the heirs of his covenants (cf. Rom 9:4-5).

6:18 The organization of the priests and Levites was reinstated as it was practiced before the exile. The different divisions and their duties are given in detail in 1 Chr 23–27. Chronicles mentions David's work of reorganizing the priests and Levites, but here the author emphasized the authority of "the Book of Moses."

The statement "according to what is written in the Book of Moses" is one indication that the author of Ezra was not the same as that of Chronicles, for the chronicler emphasized the organizing of priests and Levites as David's work. In the Pentateuch, Exod 29:1-46 and Lev 8:1-36 speak of the dedication of the priests; the appointment of the Levites is seen in Num 3:5-9 and 8:5-22. The author took for granted an ancient tradition that the people had known a lifetime before the coming of Ezra. So the Book of Moses must have been known before the time of Ezra.

Here the Aramaic section ends; v. 19 continues in Hebrew.

(7) The Passover Celebrated (6:19-22)

19On the fourteenth day of the first month, the exiles celebrated the Passover. **20**The priests and Levites had purified themselves and were all ceremonially clean. The Levites slaughtered the Passover lamb for all the exiles, for their brothers the priests and for themselves. **21**So the Israelites who had returned from the exile ate it, together with all who had separated themselves from the unclean practices of their Gentile neighbors in order to seek the LORD, the God of Israel. **22**For seven days they celebrated with joy the Feast of Unleavened Bread, because the LORD had filled them with joy by changing the attitude of the king of Assyria, so that he assisted them in the work on the house of God, the God of Israel.

6:19 The fourteenth day of the first month was the day stipulated in the Pentateuch to celebrate the Passover (Exod 12:6). In 515 B.C. it would have been April 21 (according to our calendar). About three weeks after the dedication of the temple the people gathered for another joyous celebration.

The Passover with the following Feast of Unleavened Bread was one of three pilgrim feasts (along with Tabernacles and Pentecost, according to Exod 23:14-17; see comments on 3:4). It commemorated Israel's deliverance from Egyptian bondage and was continued from the time of the exodus throughout the history of the Jews. It is important in the New Testament, for it prefigured redemption by Christ's death (1 Cor 5:7). Although Passover must have been kept yearly throughout Israel's history, celebrations of the Passover are only recorded when related to some important event in the national life of Israel (Num 9:5; Josh 5:10; 2 Kgs 23:21; 2 Chr 30; 35).[80] The Passovers celebrated in 2 Chr 30 under Hezekiah and in 2 Chr 35 under Josiah were part of revival movements in Judah with emphasis on uniting the people. Even those Israelites who remained in the area of the Northern Kingdom after its fall to Assyria were included. Here the author must have had these historical events in mind when he wrote of this Passover.

6:20 "The priests and Levites had purified themselves" by means of a ritual washing with water (Exod 29:4; Num 8:7). The author of Chronicles emphasized the need for this purification. In fact, Hezekiah's great Passover celebration was delayed a month because there were not enough ceremonially pure priests (2 Chr 30:2-3).

The Hebrew reads "they slaughtered," but the rest of the verse implies that "they" were the Levites. In the Pentateuch this is not specified as the duty of the Levites; Exod 12:6 indicates that each family killed its Passover lamb, and Deut 16:2 does not mention the Levites. The Levites apparently performed this service regularly in the second temple period.

6:21 This verse shows that there were Jews living in Judah other than the ones who returned from the exile. Apparently many had been assimilated with non-Jewish people who also lived there. The religious fervor of the returned exiles served to call these Jews back to the religious and ethical norms of the Torah, the books of Moses. Ezra and Nehemiah may give the impression that the returned exiles were very exclusive, but at least they accepted the other Jews (who had not been in Babylon) when they made a definite decision to follow God according to the Torah traditions.

This decision involved two basic determinations, one negative and the

---

[80] Slotki, *Daniel, Ezra and Nehemiah*, 148.

other positive—similar to those a Christian must make today. First, they "separated themselves from the unclean practices of their Gentile neighbors." In order to follow Christ, we must reject an immoral life-style. The biblical faith is an ethical faith. God is holy and demands that his children be holy. The other decision is a positive one: "To seek the Lord." This means turning to him, seeking communion with him, seeking to do his will. Time after time the prophets condemned the people and announced God's judgment because the people did not seek the Lord (Isa 9:13; 31:1; Hos 7:10; Zeph 1:6; Jer 10:21).

6:22 "The Feast of Unleavened Bread" was really a separate feast that started the day after the Passover (Lev 23:6) and lasted for seven days (15th to the 21st of the first month); but the two were so united in practice that they virtually constituted one (Exod 12:15).

Again there is emphasis on the joy accompanying their celebration (cf. v. 16). Throughout the Bible joy is a characteristic of the believing community as well as the individual believer. In the Old Testament thirteen different Hebrew roots (twenty-seven different words) are used to express joy in worshiping God.[81] The most frequent root is *śāmaḥ*, the one used here. Many motives are given for rejoicing, such as a wise son (Prov 10:1), God's word (Jer 15:16), and the feasts (Neh 2:43); but the chief reason is God himself (Ps 9:2). Joy comes from the deep consciousness of God's presence, as indicated here, in relation to God's actions (Ps 92:4). Later in this same community Nehemiah said, "The joy of the LORD is your strength" (Neh 8:10).

Some think the designation "king of Assyria" is a mistake. The author, however, must have been thinking in terms of a continuation of virtually the same empire from the time of the Assyrians through that of the Persians.[82] The Babylonians, then the Persians, subjugated the territorial empire of the Assyrians. Herodotus (1.178), for example, referred to Babylon as the capital of Assyria. The author may have used the term to allude to the era of Gentile oppression of Israel that had begun under the Assyrians. Nehemiah spoke of "hardship . . . from the days of the kings of Assyria until today" (Neh 9:32). Although Gentile domination was not over (cf. Neh 9:36-37), God had given Israel a brief period of favor in the eyes of their foreign rulers. He had directed the king's decision, and the people understood that this was God's working. Just as God could use the godless Assyrians (and Babylonians) as instruments of his righ-

---

[81] *IDB*, vol. 2, 1000. In general if there are many different words in a language to express a concept, that concept is important to the people who use the language.

[82] The author certainly showed careful historical knowledge on other details.

teous anger in spite of their wicked intentions (Isa 10:7), he can use the usually self-serving benevolence of other pagan authorities as instruments of his favor.[83] God will perform his word.

---

[83] J. G. McConville ("Ezra-Nehemiah and the Fulfillment of Prophecy, 208) writes, "The reference to Darius as 'the king of Assyria' (vi 22) marks him, even in an act of benevolence, as the true descendant of Sennacherib and Shalmaneser." He understands this verse as "perhaps the most significant statement about Persia in the books" and suggests that the author may have had Isa 10 in mind (p. 209).

III. GOD SENDS EZRA TO JERUSALEM (7:1–8:36)
   1. Ezra's Genealogy (7:1-7)
   2. Ezra the Scribe (7:8-10)
   3. Ezra's Commission (7:11-26)
      (1) Introduction (7:11-12)
      (2) The Decree to Return (7:13-17)
      (3) Instructions concerning Silver and Gold (7:18-20)
      (4) Command for Imperial Support (7:21-24)
      (5) Ezra's Royal Authority (7:25-26)
   4. Ezra's Praise and Preparation (7:27-28)
   5. The List of Returnees (8:1-14)
   6. The Recruitment of Levites (8:15-20)
   7. Preparation for the Journey (8:21-30)
      (1) Spiritual Preparation (8:21-23)
      (2) Administrative Preparation (8:24-30)
   8. The Journey (8:31-32)
   9. The Temple Donations Delivered (8:33-34)
   10. Worship and Sacrifices (8:35-36)

———————— **III. GOD SENDS EZRA TO JERUSALEM** ————————
(7:1–8:36)

Finally, in chap. 7 we come to the story of Ezra, for whom this book is named. Fifty-seven years had elapsed between the completion of the temple in chap. 6 and Ezra's journey to Jerusalem at the beginning of chap. 7. The author did not pretend to give a complete history of the period; he was concerned with the happenings that had theological significance for the continued existence of the Jewish community. According to Eskenazi, 7:1–10:44 comprises the second movement of Ezra-Nehemiah, describing the rebuilding of the community. Like the other two movements (1:7–6:22; Neh 1:1–7:5), it begins with preparation in Babylon and the introduction of characters.[1]

---

[1] T. Eskenazi, *In an Age of Prose: A Literary Approach to Ezra-Nehemiah* (Atlanta: Scholars Press, 1988), 38-40.

1. Ezra's Genealogy (7:1-7)

[1]After these things, during the reign of Artaxerxes king of Persia, Ezra son of Seraiah, the son of Azariah, the son of Hilkiah, [2]the son of Shallum, the son of Zadok, the son of Ahitub, [3]the son of Amariah, the son of Azariah, the son of Meraioth, [4]the son of Zerahiah, the son of Uzzi, the son of Bukki, [5]the son of Abishua, the son of Phinehas, the son of Eleazar, the son of Aaron the chief priest— [6]this Ezra came up from Babylon. He was a teacher well versed in the Law of Moses, which the LORD, the God of Israel, had given. The king had granted him everything he asked, for the hand of the LORD his God was on him. [7]Some of the Israelites, including priests, Levites, singers, gatekeepers and temple servants, also came up to Jerusalem in the seventh year of King Artaxerxes.

7:1-5 This genealogy follows that of 1 Chr 6:3-14 from Aaron to Meraioth, but it omits several names between Meraioth and Ezra. The author was primarily interested in showing that Ezra was from the Aaronic-Zadokite high priestly line, although he was not a high priest. T. Eskenazi explains that this sixteen-ancestor genealogy introduces Ezra with fanfare and establishes him as "the most prominent individual in the book." It also "signals that something momentous is to come and Ezra is at the center of it."[2]

Seraiah was high priest in the time of Zedekiah and was killed by Nebuchadnezzar (2 Kgs 25:18-21), nearly one hundred and thirty years before these events. So one or more generations were omitted (see 1 Chr 6:14-15). In Hebrew "son of" often means "descendant of."

The name "Azariah," which is in the center of the genealogy, means "the LORD has helped"; Ezra is a shortened form of the same name. "Hilkiah" was high priest in the time of Joash (2 Kgs 22:4). Zadok was the high priest who replaced the rebellious Abiathar, the last descendant of Eli to occupy the position (1 Kgs 2:35).

The author showed that Ezra had authority both from the Persian king and from his Jewish ancestry as part of the high priestly family. God works in history; the Bible constantly exhorts God's people to re-

---

[2] Eskenazi, *Age of Prose*, 63. Commentators have found difficulties with Ezra 7:1-7 because of the awkward construction: the genealogy is inserted between the name Ezra in v. 1 and the main verb, "came up," in v. 6. The author, likely Ezra himself, probably added the genealogy when he incorporated the Ezra Memoirs into the book. H. G. M. Williamson (*Ezra, Nehemiah*, WBC [Waco: Word, 1985], 95-106) says the editor included the letter from Artaxerxes (7:12-26) before using the rest of the memoirs. However, Ezra's thanksgiving in vv. 27-28 suggests that the Ezra Memoirs already had included the letter from Artaxerxes.

member their history, to learn from it, and to praise God for his work in that history. God chooses leaders such as Ezra to influence his people, and Ezra left a lasting influence on the Jewish community.

7:6-7 Later Nehemiah came from Susa, but Ezra came from Babylon. Most of the Jewish exiles lived in the Babylon area, and many had not returned to Jerusalem in 538 (Ezra 1–2). The Jewish community there continued to worship Yahweh and continued their religious traditions. Verse 7 indicates that distinctions between priests, Levites, singers, gatekeepers, and temple servants were maintained. The fact that Ezra was well versed in the law also shows that the Jews used and studied the *Torah*. We can assume they also used at least some of the Prophets and other writings.

Scholars debate how the Pentateuch was formed and how much of it Ezra had. Here the Pentateuch certainly does not appear to have been something new; Ezra and Nehemiah did not need to convince the people of its authority. The most reasonable conclusion is that Ezra had the entire Pentateuch, which already was understood as authoritative by the Jewish community.

The Hebrew *sōpēr* is translated "teacher" in the NIV. Others translate "scribe." The word was used originally to refer to the "state secretary" (2 Sam 20:25) or a royal private secretary (2 Sam 8:17; 2 Kgs 22:3-13).[3] In the Elephantine Papyri it was used for secretaries of the treasury or of the province. It can also mean "scribe" or "clerk" in the Aramaic Papyri.[4] The word came to mean "one who studies, interprets, and copies Scripture." Even by the time of Jeremiah this work must have been institutionalized and sometimes corrupted (Jer 8:8).

Ezra uniquely combines the two meanings of *sōpēr*. He was given a high office by Artaxerxes; in Judah he must have been something like "secretary on behalf of religious institutions." At the same time he was a priest "well versed in the Law of Moses," a scholar of God's law. "Well versed" (or "skilled," from a verb meaning "hasten"; cf. Prov 22:29) indicates that Ezra was "a professional of the highest order."[5] He knew thoroughly the law of God and how to apply it.

Beginning with Ezra, there arose a class of specialists who were

---

[3] The "scribe" or "secretary" had an important role in the government as noted in the time of David (2 Sam 8:17; 20:25), Solomon (1 Kgs 4:3), Hezekiah (Isa 36:1-22), Josiah (2 Kgs 22:3-20), and Jehoiakim (Jer 36:20-21).

[4] Fensham, *Ezra and Nehemiah*, 99-100.

[5] Ibid., 100.

teachers of the law; they were scholars who studied, interpreted, and copied the Scriptures.[6] In the New Testament we see that these "scribes" were greatly revered by the people.

Teaching is an important task throughout the Bible. But teaching also carries great responsibility; for if one teaches error, he can lead astray those whom he teaches. The prophets condemned those who handled Scripture but did not "know God": "The priests did not ask, 'Where is the LORD?' Those who deal with the law did not know me" (Jer 2:8). Those who faithfully expound Scripture must do so from a perspective, or worldview, that is consistent with the Bible's own point of view.[7]

"The king had granted him everything he asked," but there is no specific record of what Ezra asked. Evidently the letter of Artaxerxes, 7:12ff., represents these things. This letter then must be in response to requests Ezra had made.

The phrase "the hand of the LORD his God was on him" is repeated in Ezra 7:9,28; 8:18,22,31; and Neh 2:8,18. The author continually emphasized God's providential favor upon the restoration. The Jewish community has been preserved because of God's action.

2. Ezra the Scribe (7:8-10)

[8]Ezra arrived in Jerusalem in the fifth month of the seventh year of the king. [9]He had begun his journey from Babylon on the first day of the first month, and he arrived in Jerusalem on the first day of the fifth month, for the gracious hand of his God was on him. [10]For Ezra had devoted himself to the study and observance of the Law of the LORD, and to teaching its decrees and laws in Israel.

7:8 The seventh year of King Artaxerxes I was 458 B.C. As noted in the Introduction, some think Ezra could not have been in Jerusalem be-

---

[6] S. Talmon ("Ezra and Nehemiah," *IDBSup* [Nashville: Abingdon], 317) says that in Ezra and Nehemiah we see the beginnings "of an ongoing reinterpretation of tradition in its application to changing circumstances." He notes the public reading of the law in Neh 8, Ezra's confession in Ezra 9–10, the enforcement of Sabbath laws in Neh 13:15-21, and the application of the laws against intermarriage in Neh 13:23-28. He says we have here "the beginnings of the exegetical and hermeneutical techniques of the midrash *halachah* later fully developed and applied by the sages to the interpretation of biblical, legal literature."

[7] By "worldview" we mean what one believes about God, about humanity, about nature, and about history. The Bible presents an amazingly unified perspective on these matters. See especially A. Holmes: *Faith Seeks Understanding* (Grand Rapids: Eerdmans, 1971) and idem, *Contours of a World View* (Grand Rapids: Eerdmans, 1983).

fore Nehemiah; therefore they think this was Artaxerxes II. Others suggest that it was Artaxerxes I but that it should be the thirty-seventh year (428 B.C.), so the "thirty" dropped out of the text. Since there is no textual evidence or evidence from other versions for this, it is best to accept Jewish tradition that it was Artaxerxes I.[8] Therefore the date was the first day of Ab (or Aug. 4) 458 B.C.

7:9 The Hebrew of v. 9a reads literally, "For on the first of the first month that was the founding of the going up from Babylon." Many emend the vowels of the noun "founding of" (*yĕsud*) to a verb, yielding either "he had determined [*yissad*] the going up" or "it was determined [*yussad*], the going up." All three readings of the verse reflect what happened. The date of his departure seems to have been set for the first day of Nisan or April 8, 458 B.C. Although everything was ready for a departure on that date (8:15), there was a delay while Ezra looked for Levites and persuaded them to go to Jerusalem (8:15-30). Then, according to 8:31, "On the twelfth day of the first month we set out from the Ahava Canal."[9] The dates suggest comparison with the exodus from Egypt (cf. Exod 12:2; Num 33:3), a connection also found in the Prophets (e.g., Isa 11:11-16).[10] This was to be a new beginning for Israel.

The trip, by way of Carchemish, would have been some eight or nine hundred miles. It was a long, hot, dangerous trip (8:21-22), but it only took the group a little more than three and a half months to travel to Jerusalem, averaging about ten miles a day. Again we have the author's emphasis on God's providence in working out all the details and in protecting Ezra and those with him. The next verse explains why God's hand was upon Ezra.

7:10 "Had devoted himself to" is literally "had set his heart on." Ezra had dedicated all of himself and all his life to this wonderful ministry. In "study, observance of the Law . . . and to teaching" we have the secret of Ezra's impact. He loved God's Word and God's people. He had "devoted himself" to the three things mentioned, but not as a hobby or pastime activity. He had devoted himself to the "study" of God's law, to its "observance," and to "teaching" it.

---

[8] See the description in J. Blenkinsopp, *Ezra-Nehemiah* (Philadelphia: Westminster, 1988), 140-44.

[9] See Williamson, *Ezra, Nehemiah,* 89; Fensham, *Ezra and Nehemiah,* 101; Blenkinsopp, *Ezra-Nehemiah,* 138-39.

[10] McConville, "Ezra-Nehemiah and the Fulfillment of Prophecy," *VT* 36 (1986): 219, relates the verse particularly to Isa 2:3 and Jer 31:6, which prophesy a going up to Zion (cf. also Isa 60:7). The point of the connection is that "the promised return of the exiles is indeed under way—Ezra's return is its 'foundation'—but it is by no means a *fait accompli.*"

Ezra was not just an editor; he devoted himself to "study" (from *dāraš*, "seek," describing a careful search) God's revelation, which had been handed down from his ancestors. All the Bible emphasizes the "Word of God." By his word he created everything, by his word he directs history, and through the inspired word of his prophets he has chosen to reveal himself. God has seen fit to give special place to his written Word.

Ezra also dedicated himself to the "observance of the Law of the LORD." Ezra put emphasis on God's commands, on the legal content; but the "law of the LORD" must include at least all of the Pentateuch (see Introduction). Study is of little value if one does not also obey God's will, which is made known in his Commandments. The Old Testament does not look upon the law as a heavy weight or something negative but as a guide to a healthy society. It is truthfully the royal law of liberty, a divinely inspired ethical guide. Most of the legal material in the Pentateuch shows the application of these ethical principles to specific life situations. It is in the area of ethics where theology most affects everyday life. To study or "seek" the law means to determine its implications for daily life. As McConville has written, "The model teacher in Ezra is a doer. And the doer can be no mere demonstrator. He must *be* what he would have his disciples be."[11]

God's people always need "teaching." A great percentage of the work of the church is discipling, nurturing, teaching. More than just the imparting of facts, this involves training in righteousness and motivating believers to love and obey God. It includes learning what a biblical view signifies for practical life today.

Study, observe (obey), then teach is the correct order. God's revelation has for its purpose the ordering of his people's lives. There are no easy solutions or quick recipes to solve life's problems. God needs men and women who will devote their lives to this ministry. These three aspects of ministry are interdependent. One called by God to teach must also study and obey.

"Decrees" (*ḥōq*) refers to statutes or appointed regulation of conduct; "laws" (*mišpaṭ*) means "ordinances or duties and rights determined by custom and authority."[12] But while they no doubt designate the legal emphasis of Ezra, they are used together to refer to all the requirements of God's law.

---

[11] McConville, "Ezra-Nehemiah and the Fulfillment of Prophecy," *VT* 36 (1986): 47.

[12] J. J. Slotki, *Daniel, Ezra and Nehemiah,* Soncino Books of the Bible (London: Soncino, 1951), 152.

In preexilic times the priests were the guardians of the law; the Levites also taught the law (cf. Hos 4:4-6). After the exile the scribes became more important (Sir 38:34b–39:11). According to Jewish tradition, Ezra marks this transition and sets the pattern for future scribal activity.

We can be thankful that Ezra's influence helped the Jewish community maintain its biblical "worldview." The scribal tradition became too legalistic, however, and ended up in a pharisaism that missed the spirit of the law. In fact, the Jewish leaders took pride in their theological correctness and meticulous observance of outward ritual so that they did not even recognize their Messiah when he came. How does the church in any generation maintain the correct balance? The other extreme—assimilation or syncretism with a "pagan" worldview—also loses the biblical message. This latter appears to be the greatest danger in our time. Few people think "Christianly" in our modern Western world. All religion, even Christianity, is evaluated from the viewpoint of "scientific naturalism" when a biblical perspective demands that the reverse be true.[13]

3. Ezra's Commission (7:11-26)

(1) Introduction (7:11-12)

[11]This is a copy of the letter King Artaxerxes had given to Ezra the priest and teacher, a man learned in matters concerning the commands and decrees of the LORD for Israel:

[12] Artaxerxes, king of kings,

To Ezra the priest, a teacher of the Law of the God of heaven:

Greetings.

7:11-12 The NIV again translates "teacher" for *hassōpēr*. The next word in Hebrew is again *sōpēr*, literally "teacher of," here translated "a man learned." The man is learned in regard to "the commands and decrees of the LORD for Israel." God makes behavioral demands of his people. God made humankind, and he knows what is best for human society. Therefore we must take seriously his moral demands.

Some scholars have considered it impossible that this letter (vv. 12-26) could come from a Persian king of the fifth century B.C., for it con-

---

[13] In *Foolishness to the Greeks* (Grand Rapids: Eerdmans, 1990), Bishop Newbigin asks: "As people who are part of modern Western culture, with its confidence in the validity of its scientific methods, how can we move from the place where we explain the gospel in terms of our modern scientific worldview to the point of view of the gospel?" (p. 22).

tains too many details with which only Jews would be familiar. However, we know that these kings had advisors for their different subject peoples.[14] So a Jewish advisor, possibly Ezra himself, prepared the first draft of this letter. In addition the letter contains some typically Persian expressions that indicate it came from the Persian court—for example, "king of kings" and "seven counselors."[15]

"King of kings" was a title used especially by the Persian kings. Since it was not used later by Greek Hellenistic rulers, its use here helps confirm the authenticity of the decree.[16] The word translated "Law" is a loan word from Persian.[17] The whole phrase must have been an official Persian title for Ezra, perhaps like "secretary of state for Jewish affairs."[18] The word *gĕmîr,* translated "greetings," is difficult to understand, and several suggestions have been made. The word itself means "complete" or "perfect" and is often taken as a greeting similar to "cordial greetings" in 5:7 (cf. 1 Esdr 8:9).[19]

(2) The Decree to Return (7:13-17)

[13]Now I decree that any of the Israelites in my kingdom, including priests and Levites, who wish to go to Jerusalem with you, may go. [14]You are sent by the king and his seven advisers to inquire about Judah and Jerusalem with regard to the Law of your God, which is in your hand. [15]Moreover, you are to take with you the silver and gold that the king and his advisers have freely given to the God of Israel, whose dwelling is in Jerusalem, [16]together with all the silver and gold you may obtain from the province of Babylon, as well as the freewill offerings of the people and priests for the temple of their

---

[14] Notice Neh 11:23, which calls Pethahiah "the king's agent in all affairs relating to the people."

[15] Fensham, *Ezra and Nehemiah,* 103. Verses 12-26 are again in Aramaic. The Aramaic sections of Ezra are 4:8–6:18 and 7:12-26.

[16] Williamson (*Ezra, Nehemiah,* 100) notes that the title was occasionally used by Babylonian kings.

[17] Aramaic דָּתָא is from Persian and was used of law in a wide sense (Fensham, *Ezra and Nehemiah,* 104).

[18] Williamson, *Ezra, Nehemiah,* 100.

[19] שְׁלָמָא כְלָּא in 5:7 is literally "well-being completely." Since גְּמִיר is in the same semantic range as כְלָּא the expressions may be equivalent, with שְׁלָם either intentionally or accidentally deleted (Blenkinsopp, *Ezra-Nehemiah,* 148; E. Vogt, *LLAVT* [1971]: 35). Hence NASB and NKJV translate "perfect peace" and NRSV "peace." Another possibility is that גְּמִיר is used adverbially like the rabbinic term וגמר, which means "et cetera." The idea would be "and so on, with all the proper formulas of greeting to be supplied." See F. Rosenthal, *A Grammar of Biblical Aramaic* (Wiesbaden: Otto Harrassowitz, 1974), 88; Slotki, *Daniel, Ezra and Nehemiah,* 151.

God in Jerusalem. **¹⁷With this money be sure to buy bulls, rams and male lambs, together with their grain offerings and drink offerings, and sacrifice them on the altar of the temple of your God in Jerusalem.**

The letter contains five stipulations: (1) it authorizes Ezra (and others with him) to go to Jerusalem to see that God's law was observed (vv. 14,25); (2) it provides a grant to buy sacrifices and temple vessels (vv. 15-19); (3) it commands the treasurers in the provinces to give supplies to Ezra (vv. 21-23); (4) it frees all temple officials from taxation (v. 24); and (5) it authorizes Ezra to set up a judicial system to see that the Jews obeyed these laws (it included teaching the content of the laws, vv. 25-26).

7:13 This verse indicates that many Jews still lived in Mesopotamia. It was to the Persian king's advantage to have a strong friendly community in Jerusalem since he was concerned about rebellions in Egypt.

Ezra was given two basic tasks (vv. 14-15): (1) to check into the religious condition of the Jewish community and (2) to take the gifts of gold and silver from the king to the temple in Jerusalem.

7:14 Esther 1:14 also mentions "the seven nobles of Persia and Media who had special access to the king and were highest in the kingdom." Herodotus wrote that the king had an advisory council made up of the heads of the seven leading families in Persia.[20] "The Law of your God, which is in your hand" indicates that it was in written form, not just oral.

7:15 Ezra was to take the silver and gold the king had "freely given." Political governments sometimes oppose God's people, but many times God uses rulers to benefit his people.

7:16-17 How did Artaxerxes know what sacrifices were needed? He must have had a Jewish advisor, possibly Ezra himself, to help draft the decree. The phrase in v. 6, "The king had granted him everything he asked," also suggests that it was Ezra.

The king wanted to be sure the Jews could buy the sacrifices needed. The Persian kings took seriously the religious rites of their subjects. We have examples of this from Darius II; "The Passover Papyrus," one of the Elephantine letters, says that King Darius authorized a festival of unleavened bread for the Jewish garrison there.[21]

(3) Instructions concerning Silver and Gold (7:18-20)

¹⁸You and your brother Jews may then do whatever seems best with the

---

[20] Herodotus 3.31, 71, 83-84; also cf. Xenophon, *Anabasis* 1.6.4-5.
[21] *ANET,* 491.

rest of the silver and gold, in accordance with the will of your God. [19]Deliver
to the God of Jerusalem all the articles entrusted to you for worship in the
temple of your God. [20]And anything else needed for the temple of your God
that you may have occasion to supply, you may provide from the royal treasury.

7:18 The king trusted Ezra to use wisely the money he sent. The
phrase "in accordance with the will [or desire] of your God" probably refers to the ordinances that the Torah requires.

7:19 "All the articles" may refer to the vessels mentioned in 8:27;
those that Nebuchadnezzar carried away had already been sent back in
the first return (1:7-8).

7:20 The phrase "anything else needed" seems too generous, but the
Persians were careful to support the religious celebrations of the people
they ruled. In Egypt also they made arrangements for supplies for the religious practices. When Cambyses lessened the revenue from what the
former Persian king had provided, the people considered him harsh. Later the Jews of Elephantine were boastful about the fact that when Cambyses invaded Egypt, the Egyptian temples were destroyed but their
Jewish temple was spared.[22]

(4) Command for Imperial Support (7:21-24)

[21]Now I, King Artaxerxes, order all the treasurers of Trans-Euphrates to
provide with diligence whatever Ezra the priest, a teacher of the Law of the
God of heaven, may ask of you— [22]up to a hundred talents of silver, a hundred cors of wheat, a hundred baths of wine, a hundred baths of olive oil,
and salt without limit. [23]Whatever the God of heaven has prescribed, let it
be done with diligence for the temple of the God of heaven. Why should
there be wrath against the realm of the king and of his sons? [24]You are also
to know that you have no authority to impose taxes, tribute or duty on any
of the priests, Levites, singers, gatekeepers, temple servants or other workers at this house of God.

7:21 Part of the purpose for such an amazingly generous order to the
treasurers of the province may have been to provide supplies on the journey. Thus Ezra could show this decree to the Persian officials during the
journey of nearly four months.

7:22 "Up to a hundred talents of silver" seems very high. According
to Herodotus the annual tribute for the whole province of Beyond the

---

[22] A. T. Olmstead, *History of the Persian Empire* (Chicago: University Press, 1948),
91-92.

River was only 350 talents.[23] However, the fact that specific limits are mentioned (to the amount Ezra could request) is another indication of the authenticity of the text. A hundred cors of wheat would be about 380 bushels. A hundred baths was about 480 gallons.

7:23 In 6:10 Darius had asked for prayer for his well-being and that of his sons. Here Artaxerxes wanted God's protection even though he also feared other gods. It was important to him that God's wrath in the form of catastrophes on Jerusalem be avoided. There had been a revolt in Egypt in 460 B.C.; and in this same year, 458, a Persian army was sent to Egypt. Nevertheless, it is interesting that the king of one of the greatest empires the world has ever known should care about the God of such a seemingly insignificant people.

7:24 All the people involved in temple service were to be free from taxes. That this was Persian policy is seen in other cases. Olmstead notes that Darius I scolded a servant in western Turkey, Gadatas, for exacting tribute from the "sacred cultivators of Apollo."[24]

(5) Ezra's Royal Authority (7:25-26)

25And you, Ezra, in accordance with the wisdom of your God, which you possess, appoint magistrates and judges to administer justice to all the people of Trans-Euphrates—all who know the laws of your God. And you are to teach any who do not know them. **26**Whoever does not obey the law of your God and the law of the king must surely be punished by death, banishment, confiscation of property, or imprisonment.

7:25 The king recognized that Ezra had good judgment and that the source of his wisdom was God's word ("which you possess" is literally "which is in your hand"). Because of this wisdom, the king gave him ample authority, although he was not called a governor.[25] His jurisdiction no doubt included authority over Jews who had remained in Palestine during the exile but who had neglected the law and, in some cases, had intermarried with non-Jews. Some of them may have been living in areas outside of Judah since the verse says "Trans-Euphrates" instead of Judah.

---

[23] Williamson, *Ezra, Nehemiah,* 102.

[24] Olmstead, *History,* 156.

[25] S. Talmon, in *IDBSup,* 317-28, analyzes the history of Ezra's time. It has long been thought that after Zerubbabel, Judah must have been incorporated into the province of Samaria. Then, in 445, Nehemiah tried to make it a separate province again. But Talmon, using jar handles and bullae from the fifth century B.C., points out that we now know that Judah continued to be a province. It appears that a certain Ahzai was governor when Ezra arrived. Later Nehemiah was governor.

The king was concerned that all the Jews be under the same law. From extrabiblical sources we also have evidence that the Persian kings were concerned that each subject people take seriously their own laws.[26]

7:26 This may not mean that Ezra could punish in the ways listed but that the governor and Persian authorities were to back him up with these punishments. This authority was invoked in 10:8, where the question of mixed marriages is involved.

Ezra, like Joseph many years before, had authority in a foreign government. In God's providence both were used to fulfill God's purposes for his people. But depending on a secular government to enforce Christian or "biblical" principles can be dangerous. God's laws give us the blueprint for a healthy society. But they, at the same time, are a part of the covenant "I-thou" relationship between God and his people.

When a political government forces on "unregenerate" people these biblical principles, however, the inward motivation may be lacking. The results are (1) the development of a people or "church" with the inclusion of "pagan" elements (church history shows this happened after Constantine made Christianity the official religion of the Roman Empire) and (2) a reaction against biblical norms and biblical ethics. Christians should be concerned about ethical norms in society as a whole; but we must also remember that only a personal relationship with God can provide genuine motivation for godly living.[27]

4. Ezra's Praise and Preparation (7:27-28)

[27]Praise be to the LORD, the God of our fathers, who has put it into the king's heart to bring honor to the house of the LORD in Jerusalem in this way [28]and who has extended his good favor to me before the king and his advisers and all the king's powerful officials. Because the hand of the LORD my God was on me, I took courage and gathered leading men from Israel to go up with me.

Here we return to Hebrew, and while the first part of chap. 7 probably is based on Ezra's own account, the Ezra Memoirs may actually begin

---

[26] A text from Egypt notes that in 519 Darius ordered a satrap of Egypt to assemble the wise men "from among the warriors, the priests and the scribes of Egypt so that they may set down in writing the ancient laws of Egypt." It specifically mentions "the law of the Pharaoh, of the temples and of the people" (R. De Vaux, *The Bible and the Ancient Near East* [Garden City: Doubleday, 1971], 74).

[27] F. C. Holmgren, *Israel Alive Again: A Commentary on Ezra & Nehemiah* (Grand Rapids: Eerdmans, 1987), 61.

here in 7:27 and continue to the end of chap. 9.

7:27 "To bring honor to the house of the LORD" is literally "to beautify the house of the LORD" (cf. Isa 60:7,13[28]). This may explain the inclusion of Artaxerxes in 6:14. No doubt repairs were made and perhaps some embellishing of the temple. Ezra emphasized God's providence and God's goodness. God works in secular rulers to make provision for his people and for his work. Indicative of Ezra's devotion and sincerity is the fact that he began with praise to God.

7:28 Ezra recognized God's goodness to him and God's work on his behalf. He also realized that his work was in accordance with God's promise. Furthermore, he chose leaders and shared the responsibility in God's work.

5. The List of Returnees (8:1-14)

[1]These are the family heads and those registered with them who came up with me from Babylon during the reign of King Artaxerxes:

[2]of the descendants of Phinehas, Gershom;
of the descendants of Ithamar, Daniel;
of the descendants of David, Hattush; [3]of the descendants of Shecaniah;

of the descendants of Parosh, Zechariah, and with him were registered 150 men;
[4]of the descendants of Pahath-Moab, Eliehoenai son of Zerahiah, and with him 200 men;
[5]of the descendants of Zattu, Shecaniah son of Jahaziel, and with him 300 men;
[6]of the descendants of Adin, Ebed son of Jonathan, and with him 50 men;
[7]of the descendants of Elam, Jeshaiah son of Athaliah, and with him 70 men;
[8]of the descendants of Shephatiah, Zebadiah son of Michael, and with him 80 men;
[9]of the descendants of Joab, Obadiah son of Jehiel, and with him 218 men;
[10]of the descendants of Bani, Shelomith son of Josiphiah, and with him 160 men;
[11]of the descendants of Bebai, Zechariah son of Bebai, and with him 28 men;
[12]of the descendants of Azgad, Johanan son of Hakkatan, and with him 110 men;
[13]of the descendants of Adonikam, the last ones, whose names were Eliph-

---

[28] See Eskenazi, *Age of Prose,* 72, for other connections between Ezra 7 and Isa 60.

elet, Jeuel and Shemaiah, and with them 60 men; [14]**of the descendants of Bigvai, Uthai and Zaccur, and with them 70 men.**

8:1 The emphasis on the "family heads" reminds us of the great responsibility of being head of a family. The family is the basis of society, and the father is the head of the family. As such he has a tremendous responsibility under God to direct and teach his family. Ezra's carefulness about registering each family should be a challenge for Christians today to take seriously each family in the church community.

8:2-14 Some question the genuineness of this list since it differs from that of Ezra 2 and Neh 7. But this list is not based on Ezra 2 and Neh 7. It is an independent list included to show the genealogical legitimacy of those who went with Ezra to Jerusalem.

The differences between this list and that of Ezra 2 and Neh 7 are significant. In this one the priests' families are mentioned first (v. 2), then the royal line, a descendant of David (vv. 2b-3a), and then twelve lay families (vv. 3b-14). In Ezra 2 the laity is first, then priests and Levites, temple servants, and sons of Solomon's servants. Also the priests here are counted in the Aaronite line, while in Ezra 2 they follow the Zadokite line. Here also Joab (v. 9) is considered an independent family instead of part of the Pahath-Moab family as in Ezra 2. In Ezra 2 the females are included in the numbers, but here only the men are listed.[29] Two priestly families are mentioned (v. 2). Phinehas, in whose line Ezra was counted, was the son of Eleazar, Aaron's third son (Exod 6:23-25), and Ithamar was Aaron's fourth son (Exod 6:23).

Hattush was a great-great-grandson (fourth generation) of Zerubbabel,[30] in the line of David. The construction here gives the impression that some other name should follow Shecaniah. However, the punctuation in NIV indicates that Hattush himself was a descendant of Shecaniah, and this in confirmed in 1 Chr 3:21-22. Notice that although Hattush was a direct descendant of David, he was not in a position of leadership as was Zerubbabel many years earlier.[31]

In vv. 3b-14 twelve families are listed. Many believe this emphasizes

---

[29] The Hebrew word for "men," which appears in each verse from 3-14, is זָכָר, which means "male."

[30] Fensham notes that if Zerubbabel was born ca. 560 B.C. and if we count about twenty-five years for a generation, the date for Hattush coincides with the 458 B.C. date for Ezra (Fensham, *Ezra and Nehemiah,* 111).

[31] Holmgren comments that by this time the expectancy of putting a descendant of David on the throne as king was replaced by other priorities. Now the priests were the most important leaders (Holmgren, *Ezra & Nehemiah,* 65).

that they represent all of Israel, which was made up of twelve tribes. W. J. Dumbrell has observed, "It is a notable feature of postexilic eschatology that projections are shaped in terms of an ideal 12-tribe Israel."[32] He also noted that "the 'all Israel' tradition is very vigorously preserved and indeed promoted by Ezra as he returns."[33] While Ezra material uses the term "Israel" twenty-four times, "Judah" is referred to four times. For these twelve families, the number of men registered in each is given (vv. 3-14), but for the two priestly families and for Hattush (vv. 1-2), numbers are not given. The total number of men in the twelve families was fifteen hundred. If we add women and children, there must have been more than five thousand people in the caravan that made its way from Babylon to Jerusalem.[34]

The name "Zebadiah" (v. 8) has been found on an ostracon from Ashdod, dated in the fifth century B.C.[35] Some scholars suggest emending "Shelomith" (v. 10) to Shelomot since Shelomith is a feminine name; however, it can also be a man's name.

In place of "110 men" (v. 12) some manuscripts (the Lucianic recension of the Septuagint and Syriac) have "120."

The text does not explain what is meant by "last ones" (v. 13). It most likely indicates that these descendants of Adonikam were the last ones who remained in Babylon.

All the names in this list (vv. 3-14) are also found in Ezra 2. So those who returned to Jerusalem with Ezra must have had relatives in Jerusalem from the first return (eighty years earlier). We can imagine what a time of getting acquainted and reviewing family history they must have had when in Jerusalem they discovered relatives of whom they may have had little knowledge before.

6. The Recruitment of Levites (8:15-20)

[15]**I assembled them at the canal that flows toward Ahava, and we camped there three days. When I checked among the people and the priests, I found no Levites there.** [16]**So I summoned Eliezer, Ariel, Shemaiah, Elnathan, Jarib, Elnathan, Nathan, Zechariah and Meshullam, who were leaders, and Joiarib and Elnathan, who were men of learning,** [17]**and I sent them to Iddo, the leader in Casiphia. I told them what to say to Iddo and his kinsmen, the**

---

[32] W. J. Dumbrell, "Malachi and the Ezra-Nehemiah Reforms," *RTR* 35 (1976): 44-45. Cf. also F. Koch, "Ezra and the Origin of Judaism," *JSS* 19 (1974): 193-94.

[33] Dumbrell, "Malachi and the Ezra-Nehemiah Reforms," 45.

[34] Williamson, *Ezra, Nehemiah,* 110.

[35] Myers, *Ezra. Nehemiah,* 67.

temple servants in Casiphia, so that they might bring attendants to us for the house of our God. [18]Because the gracious hand of our God was on us, they brought us Sherebiah, a capable man, from the descendants of Mahli son of Levi, the son of Israel, and Sherebiah's sons and brothers, 18 men; [19]and Hashabiah, together with Jeshaiah from the descendants of Merari, and his brothers and nephews, 20 men. [20]They also brought 220 of the temple servants—a body that David and the officials had established to assist the Levites. All were registered by name.

8:15 Preparation time ("I assembled them at the canal") is not lost time. Ezra was eager to go to Jerusalem, but he knew the importance of careful planning. With a group of over five thousand people, careful plans were needed. The "three days" they camped near the canal must have been days of intense preparation. There Ezra organized the entire group. That was when he discovered that there were no Levites.

A rabbinic legend says that there were Levites in the group but that none were qualified to carry out temple duties, for they had all bitten off the fingers of their right hands so the Babylonians could not force them to play temple music on their harps.[36] Nevertheless, we should not be surprised that no Levites were in the group of returnees. No doubt a certain amount of prosperity in Babylon and the kind of servile work assigned to Levites did not make it easy to recruit them to return to Jerusalem.

The Hebrew word "river" is similar to the Babylonian word for "canal" (v. 15).[37] There were canals in the city of Babylon, around it, and several that extended out from the city. Although the place cannot be pinpointed by historians, we can assume it was an open area along one of these canals.

8:16 Some names of "leaders" are in v. 16 that are not mentioned in vv. 1-14. The ones mentioned here are "heads,"[38] but they are not necessarily heads of families. Some commentators think this list was corrupted since Elnathan appears three times. However, it was a common name and could easily refer to three different men.

Slotki translates "men of learning" (v. 16) as "teachers";[39] Fensham

---

[36] The story is found in a Midrash to Ps 137: "By the rivers of Babylon . . . our tormentors demanded songs of joy. . . . How can we sing the songs of the Lord while in a foreign land?" (Slotki, *Daniel, Ezra and Nehemiah,* 158).

[37] Hebrew נָהָר ("river") is similar to Akkadian *nāru,* "canal."

[38] The same Hebrew word רָאשִׁים ("heads") is used.

[39] Slotki, Daniel, *Ezra and Nehemiah,* 158.

calls them "interpreters of the Law."[40] Since the same word[41] in Neh 8:7-9 refers to the interpretation and teaching of the law, it likely carries that idea here. Joiarib and Elnathan, then, had some special teaching function, although they were not Levites.

8:17 "The leader" indicates a certain amount of organization among the Jews living there. They had their own leaders. In fact, apparently there was a concentration of Levites in Babylon.

"Casiphia" must have been a village not far from Babylon where there was a large community of Jews. Literally v. 17 says, "Casiphia, the place." The expression "the place"[42] often designates in the Old Testament a sanctuary (e.g., Deut 12:5; Jer 7:3,6-7). There may have been a temple there like the one at Elephantine or simply a place of worship that later developed into one of the first synagogues. Blenkinsopp suggests Casiphia may have had a school for training temple personnel.[43]

8:18-19 Sherebiah is called "a capable man" (lit. "a man of understanding," *śekel*). The term *śekel* can refer to practical wisdom as the ability to act wisely with common sense, avoiding foolish and harmful behavior (1 Sam 25:3; Prov 19:11). It can also refer to the spiritual insight of one who knows and obeys the Lord (1 Chr 22:12; 2 Chr 30:22; Neh 8:8; Ps 111:10).[44] Sherebiah appears several times in the Ezra narrative as a leader or instructor of the people (Ezra 8:24; Neh 8:7; 9:4-5; 10:12; 12:8,24).

Again, Ezra gave God the credit ("the good hand of our God") for success in acquiring Levites to go to Jerusalem. In all there were thirty-eight Levites to accompany Ezra. He must have been disappointed in the number but only recorded his thanks that there were some. If God was responsible for assembling the group, it must have been enough. Besides, those who responded were willing to leave with only three day's preparation.

8:20 The "temple servants" ("Nethinim") were assistants to the Levites in the many tasks involved with temple sacrifices and temple upkeep. The only indication of their origin is given here. As in Ezra 2, a large number of them (220) joined Ezra's group.

---

[40] Fensham, *Ezra and Nehemiah*, 113-14.
[41] Hebrew מְבִינִים.
[42] In Hebrew הַמָּקוֹם.
[43] Blenkinsopp, *Ezra-Nehemiah*, 144.
[44] See *TWOT*, 7.

7. Preparation for the Journey (8:21-30)

(1) Spiritual Preparation (8:21-23)

²¹**There, by the Ahava Canal, I proclaimed a fast, so that we might humble ourselves before our God and ask him for a safe journey for us and our children, with all our possessions. ²²I was ashamed to ask the king for soldiers and horsemen to protect us from enemies on the road, because we had told the king, "The gracious hand of our God is on everyone who looks to him, but his great anger is against all who forsake him." ²³So we fasted and petitioned our God about this, and he answered our prayer.**

8:21 Fasting seems to have been more prominent after the exile than before. Before the exile we find fasts on special occasions (Judg 20:26; Jer 14:12; 36:6,9; Pss 35:13; 69:11), but the only fast for the whole community was the Day of Atonement. After the exile fasting was given more emphasis (Jer 41:4-5; Zech 7:2-7; Ezra 10:6; Neh 9:1; Esth 4:3,16). Zechariah 8:19 mentions "the fasts of the fourth, fifth, seventh and tenth months." Here the fast indicates Ezra's humble spirit of dependence on God[45] (cf. Ps 35:13).

These people were making a momentous decision to leave the security of their relatively comfortable life, make a dangerous four-month trip, and live in Judah, which still had a precarious existence. Yet as with the first return in Ezra 1, this decision was important in God's plan of redemption, for it was through the continuance of this Jewish community that Jesus came to this world and brought redemption for all humankind.

Ezra challenges us with his emphasis on humility and worship. Before he launched any project related to God's work, he sought God's guidance and worshiped.

8:22 In saying "I was ashamed to ask the king for soldiers," Ezra was not bragging about his faith, nor was he regretting his earlier statement to the king. He simply was explaining that the king might have misunderstood if he had asked for a military escort. We must admire Ezra for being consistent. Often we do not give God a chance to show his power. As he said to Paul, "My power is made perfect in weakness" (2 Cor 12:9).

It is enlightening to compare Ezra with Nehemiah. Later Nehemiah

---

[45] Yamauchi ("Ezra," 660) explains that "fasting implies an earnestness that makes one oblivious to food." See comments on Ezra 10:6 for more on fasting. "Safe journey" is lit. a "straight or level way." Cf. Isa 40:3. This was John Robinson's text as he preached to the departing pilgrims in Leiden in 1620 (J. Bowman, "Ezra," *IB*, 638).

carefully planned his trip to Jerusalem, but he asked the king for a military escort. In fact, Nehemiah saw the escort as part of God's provision. Of course, Nehemiah went as a political official and was governor of Judah. Thus two of God's servants acted differently; both were following God's leading, and God used both of them.

8:23 Ezra again leaves us a challenge to seek earnestly God's will, his guidance, and his power. "He answered our prayer" has been the testimony of God's people throughout the centuries.

(2) Administrative Preparation (8:24-30)

[24]Then I set apart twelve of the leading priests, together with Sherebiah, Hashabiah and ten of their brothers, [25]and I weighed out to them the offering of silver and gold and the articles that the king, his advisers, his officials and all Israel present there had donated for the house of our God. [26]I weighed out to them 650 talents of silver, silver articles weighing 100 talents, 100 talents of gold, [27]20 bowls of gold valued at 1,000 darics, and two fine articles of polished bronze, as precious as gold.

[28]I said to them, "You as well as these articles are consecrated to the LORD. The silver and gold are a freewill offering to the LORD, the God of your fathers. [29]Guard them carefully until you weigh them out in the chambers of the house of the LORD in Jerusalem before the leading priests and the Levites and the family heads of Israel." [30]Then the priests and Levites received the silver and gold and sacred articles that had been weighed out to be taken to the house of our God in Jerusalem.

Following Ezra's example, Christian leaders should delegate responsibility. Ezra carefully chose the people to whom he gave responsibility. It may seem exaggerated to have taken such precautions with the money, to weigh it out carefully, to record every detail. However, to do things carefully, with decisions and transactions documented in writing, is a sign of wisdom rather than a lack of confidence. It protects everyone involved. Many present-day scandals could be avoided if Christian leaders would learn from Ezra.

8:24 Sherebiah, Hashbiah, and the ten were Levites. According to Num 4, the priests were in charge of the tabernacle furnishings; but the Levites were to carry them. Ezra was careful to include both priests and Levites in the group responsible for delivering these treasures to Jerusalem.

8:25-27 The amount of silver (650 talents or 25 tons) and gold (100 talents or 3 3/4 tons) indicated in v. 26 seems excessive. Clines gives the estimate that "Ezra's treasure . . . would represent the annual income of,

say, between 100,000 and 500,000 men."[46] Many scholars think there is
a textual error in the numbers or that "talents" has replaced the original
"minas."[47] The phrase "silver articles weighing 100 talents" is literally
"silver vessels, one hundred, worth talents." Williamson believes the
amount has dropped out and translates this as "100 silver vessels weighing . . . talents."[48] Fensham, however, notes that the Persian rulers gave
generously for their subjects' religious practices and that in addition
there were many donations given by Jews who were financially prosper-
ous. For example, from texts discovered in Nippur we know that some
Jewish families participated in a banking business in 455–403 B.C.[49]

8:28-30 Both the articles and the men in charge were consecrated to
the Lord. Consecrated men and women are needed to handle correctly offerings and donations for the Lord's service. Ezra also made sure that
there were sufficient witnesses when the donations were deposited in the
temple. In addition to the religious leaders, the family heads[50] were also
to be present. Evidently Ezra sensed the need for exact records, careful
auditing, and doing everything possible to avoid suspicions of wrong use
of money and goods given to the Lord's service.[51] This is an example of
faithful, responsible stewardship.

8. The Journey (8:31-32)

**[31]On the twelfth day of the first month we set out from the Ahava Canal
to go to Jerusalem. The hand of our God was on us, and he protected us
from enemies and bandits along the way. [32]So we arrived in Jerusalem,
where we rested three days.**

---

[46] Clines, *Ezra, Nehemiah, Esther,* 113.

[47] Ibid.

[48] Williamson, *Ezra, Nehemiah,* 114.

[49] Fensham, *Ezra and Nehemiah,* 118. The Murashu documents include some seven
hundred and thirty tablets found in Nippur in 1893. They date from the reigns of Artaxerxes I (464–424) and Darius II (424–404). They are records of a certain Murashu banking
family and are of interest to Bible scholars because they include some Jewish names. They
indicate that some Jews reached relatively important positions. For example, a Jew, El-ya-
din, is named as cocreditor in a transaction with a member of the Murashu family (M. D.
Coogan, "Life in the Diaspora: Jews at Nippur in the Fifth Century B.C.," *BA* 37/1 [1974],
6-12; reprinted in *The Biblical Archaeologist Reader* IV [Sheffield: The Almond Press,
1983], 249-56).

[50] Because "family heads" does not appear in v. 33, some scholars suggest that it is an
addition here. But in v. 33 Ezra did not pretend to list all the witnesses present.

[51] Notice Solomon's attention to details in 2 Chr 8–9; also notice the quantities of gold
and silver mentioned.

8:31 On the twelfth of Nisan (Apr. 19) Ezra and his large caravan finally set out on their nearly four-month trip to Jerusalem. In 7:9 it says Ezra had begun his journey on the first of Nisan (Apr. 8), but the gathering together by the Canal of Ahava, the preparations there, and the search for Levites (8:15-30) account for the delay.

Again Ezra gave thanks for God's protection. The dangerous route from Babylon to Palestine was plagued with bands of robbers. When Ezra said God protected them from enemies and bandits, he did not specify whether they were attacked and were protected or were free from attacks, but the latter is more likely the meaning. Certainly Ezra was correct in attributing this miracle to God, for such a group (over five thousand) without armed escort and carrying large quantities of gold and silver over nine hundred miles would have been an inviting target for robbers. Again, Ezra demonstrated that even in dangerous situations God is able to protect his children.

8:32 No more details of the journey are given. The trip must have been long and tedious. The group left Babylon on April 19 and arrived in Jerusalem on August 4 (7:8; the fifth of Ab, the fifth month). They deserved the three days of rest when they arrived, even before delivering the money and goods to the temple (cf. Neh 2:11).[52]

9. The Temple Donations Delivered (8:33-34)

[33]**On the fourth day, in the house of our God, we weighed out the silver and gold and the sacred articles into the hands of Meremoth son of Uriah, the priest. Eleazar son of Phinehas was with him, and so were the Levites Jozabad son of Jeshua and Noadiah son of Binnui. [34]Everything was accounted for by number and weight, and the entire weight was recorded at that time.**

8:33 Meremoth may have been the high priest, or he may have been the temple treasurer. In Neh 3:4 a Meremoth, son of Uriah, son of Cos, was building the wall. He was not called a priest but was building on the part where the priests worked. In Ezra 2:61 the sons of Cos were not qualified for priestly work because they did not have the register of their genealogy. There has been much discussion about Meremoth;[53] these could have been different men since the name was common. If they refer

---

[52] Some scholars suggest that if the Jubilee calendar was followed by the returnees (it is known from Qumran), the arrival would have been on a Friday. Thus there would not have been time to weigh out and register the money and goods before the Sabbath (Fensham, *Ezra and Nehemiah,* 120).

to the same Meremoth, from Ezra 2:61 Meremoth must have been accepted as an officiating priest and had an important position.

8:34 In Babylonian practice most transactions, such as sales and marriages, had to be recorded; and the Persians continued Babylonian legal tradition. So Ezra probably had to send to King Artaxerxes signed certification that these treasures had been received in the temple. Christians must learn from Ezra to be circumspect in all their accounting: today's civil law requires it, non-Christians expect it, God's people want it, and God requires it.

10. Worship and Sacrifices (8:35-36)

[35]Then the exiles who had returned from captivity sacrificed burnt offerings to the God of Israel: twelve bulls for all Israel, ninety-six rams, seventy-seven male lambs and, as a sin offering, twelve male goats. All this was a burnt offering to the LORD. [36]They also delivered the king's orders to the royal satraps and to the governors of Trans-Euphrates, who then gave assistance to the people and to the house of God.

The style, especially the use of the third person, suggests these verses are comments added by the author to the original Ezra Memoirs.

8:35 The first thing the returnees did was worship God. For those who love God, the first response before, during, or after any project such as this must be worship.

Again there is emphasis on the number twelve, which stands for the twelve tribes. The author emphasized that this exilic community represented all Israel. All the numbers here are multiples of twelve except "seventy-seven," but in 1 Esdr 8:66 it is seventy-two (thus a multiple of twelve). However, there is no textual evidence for the change. Since seventy-seven is often used to denote a large number, most scholars think the original text must have had "seventy-seven."[54]

8:36 These "orders" probably were the documents that gave Ezra authority to administer Jewish law to his fellow Jews primarily in the area of Palestine. The fact that it says "to the royal satraps and to the governors of Trans-Euphrates" may indicate that this also included Jews in other satrapies such as Egypt where a number of Jews lived. Since it was an order from the king, the governors had to comply; they "gave assistance to the people and to the house of God."

---

[53] Some have used the data to argue a later date for Ezra, and some have used the same data to argue the opposite (Williamson, *Ezra, Nehemiah*, 121-22).

[54] Fensham, *Ezra and Nehemiah*, 122.

—————— **IV. KEEPING THE COVENANT: THE PROBLEM** ——————
OF INTERMARRIAGE (9:1–10:44)

What should a leader and a community of believers do when an issue arises that threatens the life and effectiveness of the community? That was the problem facing Ezra and the people of Israel on the occasion recounted in these chapters. Their solution was to take immediate decisive action.

The issue was brought to light by Ezra's teaching of Scripture. Four months had passed between the events of chaps. 8 and 9. According to 7:9, Ezra arrived in Jerusalem in the fifth month, and the present episode is dated in the ninth month (10:9). Many commentators believe that Neh 8, which recounts Ezra's public reading of the Law, was originally part of the Ezra Memoirs and was found between Ezra chaps. 8 and 9, since in Neh 8 the seventh month is mentioned. Also, the emphasis in Neh 8 on obeying God's Law would help explain why the leaders became concerned about intermarriage and approached Ezra in Ezra 9. However, it is also possible that the Law was read on more than one occasion.[1] Certainly Ezra was busy teaching the Law from the beginning of his work in Jerusalem. According to these chapters, at last Ezra's teaching of Scripture was bearing fruit.

---

[1] See the discussion in the Introduction.

1. Ezra's Humility and Consternation (9:1-5)

[1]After these things had been done, the leaders came to me and said, "The people of Israel, including the priests and the Levites, have not kept themselves separate from the neighboring peoples with their detestable practices, like those of the Canaanites, Hittites, Perizzites, Jebusites, Ammonites, Moabites, Egyptians and Amorites. [2]They have taken some of their daughters as wives for themselves and their sons, and have mingled the holy race with the peoples around them. And the leaders and officials have led the way in this unfaithfulness."

[3]When I heard this, I tore my tunic and cloak, pulled hair from my head and beard and sat down appalled. [4]Then everyone who trembled at the words of the God of Israel gathered around me because of this unfaithfulness of the exiles. And I sat there appalled until the evening sacrifice.

[5]Then, at the evening sacrifice, I rose from my self-abasement, with my tunic and cloak torn, and fell on my knees with my hands spread out to the LORD my God.

9:1   T. Eskenazi has noted that one strong characteristic of Ezra was that he taught Scripture and worked with leaders instead of trying to do everything himself.[2] Although Ezra was a strong leader, he delegated work and authority to other leaders. Here the effect of Ezra's teaching and influence is seen in these leaders with whom he worked closely. They became concerned about wrong practices in the community.

The list of foreign peoples given in v. 1 is similar to the list of peoples in Canaan that appears several times in the Pentateuch; but here the Ammonites, Moabites, and Egyptians are added.[3] Throughout the Bible, God calls his people to separate themselves from the world (1 John 2:15-17). Of course some, like the Essenes of Jesus' time, were extremists who isolated themselves from the rest of society, which in New Testament terms negates the mandate to disciple all peoples. At the same time, Christians must take seriously ethical and cultural factors that result in disobedience to God's will. The correct interpretation and the application of Scripture's ethical teaching is a constant challenge. Being a disciple of Jesus implies a distinctive life-style because one's values are different from those of the world. The neighbors of Israel had a different life-style.

---

[2] T. Eskenazi, *In an Age of Prose* (Atlanta: Scholars Press, 1988), 64, 66.

[3] The Ammonites, Moabites, and Egyptians still existed as distinct peoples in Ezra's time; but the others no longer existed as such. Since in the Pentateuch these names commonly refer to the surrounding pagans, the same names are used in this sense here. Notice this further indication of the long-standing influence of the Pentateuch on the people's way of expressing themselves.

"A covenant community that allows its leaders to adopt a life-style that threatens the central covenant torah traditions is sacrificing its future."[4]

The Old Testament did not completely forbid intermarriage with foreigners. Indeed several important "men of faith" had non-Israelite wives (Gen 16:3; 41:45; Exod 2:21; Num 12:1; 2 Sam 3:3). The most striking example is in the Book of Ruth, which shows that David was a descendant from such a relationship. But when it would involve a compromise of faith or practice, intermarriage with the pagan peoples of Canaan was forbidden. The phrase "with their detestable practices" suggests that more was involved than simply sexual intercourse. Deuteronomy 7:3-4 makes it clear: "Do not intermarry with them. Do not give your daughters to their sons or take their daughters for your sons, for they will turn your sons away from following me to serve other gods, and the LORD's anger will burn against you and will quickly destroy you." This passage and others (e.g., Exod 34:11-16; Deut 20:10-18) must have been included in Ezra's teaching of the Law.

9:2 "The holy race" is literally "the holy seed." "The term 'holy' shows that the term 'seed' has nothing to do with racial prejudice. . . . It was a question of the living relation between the LORD and his people, and not of who one's ancestors might be."[5] The same expression is used in Isa 6:13. God chose Israel to be a holy nation (Exod 19:6; Lev 19:2; Deut 7:6). They were to be different because their relation to God was different. The same word, "mingled," is used in Ps 106:35: "They mingled with the nations and adopted their customs." This is why Ezra was so upset. The intermarriage would result in adopting customs (the lifestyle) of those who did not know God. Righteousness and purity of religion were in question.[6] The term translated "unfaithfulness" (*ma⁽al*) refers to a breach of trust and is used elsewhere only of persons violating their covenant relationship with God (cf. Lev 5:15; 26:40; Num

---

[4] F. C. Holmberg, *Israel Alive Again: A Commentary on the Books of Ezra and Nehemiah* (Grand Rapids: Eerdmans, 1987), 73. The relevance of this for today is evident. Christians who adopt a life-style that negates Jesus' commands are sacrificing both the future of the church and that of the peoples it should be reaching with the gospel.

[5] F. C. Fensham, *The Books of Ezra and Nehemiah,* NICOT (Grand Rapids: Eerdmans, 1982), 125.

[6] Of course, Ezra's emphasis on genealogies indicates his concern for covenant continuity, although proselytes were admitted into the Jewish nation. Still, what concerned Ezra and the other leaders was the influence that a "pagan" mother had on her children; notice this concern in Neh 13:23-24. Later in Jewish tradition it was decreed that in mixed marriages "one who is born of a Jewish mother" is a Jew (F. C. Holmgren, *Ezra and Nehemiah* [Grand Rapids: Eerdmans, 1987], 73).

5:6,12,27; Josh 7:1; 22:16,20,22; 1 Chr 10:13).

The New Testament also commands believers not to intermarry with those who do not have faith in Jesus Christ.[7] The same problems that faced the Israelites face the community of faith today, in a culture that is increasingly given to an anti-Christian worldview. Paul's warning is of utmost importance: "Do not be yoked together with unbelievers" (2 Cor 7:14). Any commitment we make that competes with our commitment to Christ amounts to unfaithfulness.

Leadership is a serious responsibility. Leaders are accountable for what they do and what they teach because they affect many people. Here the "leaders and officials" had led the people wrongly. Williamson suggests that these officials were leaders who were in the land before and not those who came with Ezra.[8] The prophet Malachi likely preached to the people around the time of Ezra or perhaps a little earlier. Malachi 2:10-16 indicates that some of the people had divorced their Jewish wives in order to marry the foreigners.[9]

9:3 Ezra must have known something of this before, but here he responded to the extent and seriousness of the problem. He tore his tunic and cloak and pulled out hair from his head. These are signs of great consternation and mourning. The tunic was the undergarment, and the cloak was a long, flowing robe used over other garments. Clines points out that it was customary in times of distress to rend one's garment, but Ezra's response showed extreme grief. Such "stylized stripping oneself naked" was a "token of humiliation and death."[10] It is revealing to compare Ezra's action with that of Nehemiah (Neh 13:25). Nehemiah pulled the hair of the offenders but out of indignation; Ezra pulled his own hair in sorrow.

9:4 The phrase "everyone who trembled at the words of God" was used, especially in the postexilic community, of those who strictly observed the law. It denotes an attitude of openness to what God says and a readiness to obey. A number of people were concerned about the problem and began gathering around Ezra. They needed a leader to express the problem and take the necessary initiative. We might think that Ezra was overly dramatic, but the response shows the attractiveness of holy zeal. D. Kidner has observed that in a sense Ezra did nothing. Yet his inaction

---

[7] The New Testament does not say anything against intermarrying between different ethnic groups.

[8] H. G. M. Williamson, *Ezra, Nehemiah,* WBC (Waco: Word, 1985), 130.

[9] On divorce see comments on Ezra 10:44.

[10] D. J. A. Clines, *Ezra, Nehemiah, Esther,* NCB (Grand Rapids: Zondervan, 1984), 121.

was "more potent than a flurry of activity, since it drew out of other people the initiatives that could best come from them."[11] Those who tremble at the Word of God will tremble at human sin. Today's spirit of acceptance and broad-mindedness has much to learn from Ezra's "immoderate godliness."[12]

Ezra sat there a long time, until the evening sacrifice. Sitting in silence for an extended time also shows grief and mourning (Job 2:13; Ezek 26:16). The "evening sacrifice," according to Num 28:4, was offered at twilight.

9:5 The Bible does not command a special physical posture for prayer. Falling to his knees showed Ezra's attitude of humility before God, and spreading out his hands indicated his need of God's help.

Ezra and Nehemiah constantly turned to God in prayers of worship, confession, praise, petition, and thanksgiving. They show us the importance of an implicit trust in a personal God and that God's work depends on the prayer of his people. Prayer founded on biblical theology assumes that God is omniscient and hears each prayer. It also assumes that God acts in historical events in response to the prayers of his people.

2. Ezra's Prayer of Confession (9:6-15)

(1) Confession of Sin (9:6-7)

⁶and prayed:

"**O my God, I am too ashamed and disgraced to lift up my face to you, my God, because our sins are higher than our heads and our guilt has reached to the heavens. ⁷From the days of our forefathers until now, our guilt has been great. Because of our sins, we and our kings and our priests have been subjected to the sword and captivity, to pillage and humiliation at the hand of foreign kings, as it is today.**

Ezra's prayer gives us insight into his character and his theology. It dealt with (1) a confession of sin (vv. 6-7a); (2) punishment for sin (v. 7b); (3) God's graciousness in using the Persian kings to restore the remnant (vv. 8-9); (4) another confession of sin, the sin of disobeying God's command against intermarriage (vv. 10-14); and (5) a doxology recognizing God's righteousness (v. 15).[13]

---

[11] D. Kidner, *Ezra and Nehemiah,* TOTC (Downers Grove: InterVarsity, 1979), 68.

[12] J. G. McConville, *Ezra, Nehemiah, Esther* (Philadelphia: Westminster, 1985), 62.

[13] Fensham, *Ezra and Nehemiah,* 128. Ezra's prayer must have been a part of the Ezra Memoirs and was written originally for its inclusion here. That is, it was not a later addition. One might wonder if this was a prayer or a sermon. Perhaps the term *sermon-prayer* is appropriate.

9:6 Although Ezra was not personally guilty, he identified with the community; he considered himself guilty before God along with the whole community. Ezra teaches us the importance of identification with the community of which we are a part or of which we are leaders. In one sense each one is responsible for his own faults, but in another sense the whole community is guilty when one member fails. Both emphases are taught throughout the Bible. Clines explains: "It is not simply that certain individuals have broken the law, but that the community has sinned in being the kind of community where such actions could occur and be tolerated"[14] (cf. 1 Cor 5:1-8).

9:7 Ezra had just returned to Jerusalem after years of captivity in Babylon. He recognized that all this came upon his people because they turned away from God. Furthermore, their present subservience to Persia was the direct result of sin.

"Humiliation" is literally "shame of face," which is also found in Jer 7:19; Ps 44:16; Dan 9:7-8. In 2 Chr 32:21 it is translated "disgrace." "At the hands of foreign kings" is literally "at the hands of the kings of the nations." Ezra had in mind the nations of Assyria, Babylon, and Persia.

(2) Recognition of God's Goodness (9:8-9)

8"But now, for a brief moment, the LORD our God has been gracious in leaving us a remnant and giving us a firm place in his sanctuary, and so our God gives light to our eyes and a little relief in our bondage. **9**Though we are slaves, our God has not deserted us in our bondage. He has shown us kindness in the sight of the kings of Persia: He has granted us new life to rebuild the house of our God and repair its ruins, and he has given us a wall of protection in Judah and Jerusalem.

9:8 Ezra recognized God's mercy in restoring the people to their own land. He had just talked of God's great work in keeping him and his company safe as they traveled to Jerusalem.

Ezra's prayer at this point was based on several theological premises: (1) God makes ethical demands on his people; (2) God's righteousness requires punishment for transgression, and he even uses other nations to punish his own people; (3) God is merciful, forgiving sin and making provision for salvation and restoration.

"Leaving us a remnant" (also translated "an escaped remnant"[15]) refers here to those who returned from Babylon, escaping from the exile.

---

[14] Clines, *Ezra, Nehemiah, Esther,* 120.
[15] Fensham, *Ezra and Nehemiah,* 129.

The term "remnant" is significant in the theology of the prophets, such as Isaiah, Jeremiah, and Zechariah. The prophets lost hope in political Israel for the future of God's kingdom. They prophesied that God would continue his plan through a "remnant." Sometimes this refers to a remnant that will return to God (Isa 10:21, e.g., in Hezekiah's reform); sometimes it refers to those who will return from exile (Jer 42:2; Zech 8:6,11-12); sometimes it speaks of another "return" in which Gentiles will participate (Isa 11:10-16); and at times, to Israel in the messianic age (Jer 23:3; 31:7; Zech 14:2).[16] Ezra knew how important this "remnant" was for God's plan. Only a pure and separate "remnant" would be useful to God in his plan of redemption, which was to provide the Scriptures and the Savior for all the world. This helps explain Ezra's seemingly "radical" policies.

McConville has noted the prophetic character of Ezra-Nehemiah. A subtle but clear message recurs that the restoration period was but one step in God's new program to produce righteousness on earth by faith. A clue of the incompleteness of prophetic fulfillment during those days occurs in v. 7 in the phrase "as it is today." Another is in the recognition in v. 8 that God's favor was being experienced "for a brief moment," that they had received "a little [$m\check{e}^c a t$] relief." Ezra's prayer here and Nehemiah's in Neh 9 "leave no doubt that the exiles' situation, which could be worse (cf. Ezra 9:13), could equally be rather better."[17] The book's alternation between glory and grief, rejoicing and repentance can be understood only by reading it against the background of the prophetic promises of a complete salvation. The recurring sins of the people explained the obstacles they were facing and that the salvation promised in the Prophets had not yet fully arrived.

"Firm place" is literally a "tent peg"; Fensham translates "a foothold."[18] Having their own sanctuary gave the Jews a renewed sense of security.

"Give light to our eyes" is literally "make our eyes shine." It means "to revive the spirit of a person" (1 Sam 14:29; Isa 13:3).

9:9 Even though the Jews were still subject to the Persian Empire, Ezra recognized that God had blessed them and given them new life as a religious community. The word for "wall of protection," *gādēr*, is generally used of a fence or a wall around a vineyard. Ezra here was not talk-

---

[16] Notice Paul's use of the remnant "chosen by grace" in Rom 11.

[17] J. G. McConville, "Ezra-Nehemiah and the Fulfillment of Prophecy," *VT* 36 (1986): 209-10.

[18] Fensham, *Ezra and Nehemiah*, 126, 129.

ing about the Jerusalem wall but about God's protection for the Jewish community.

(3) Recognition of Disobedience (9:10-12)

[10]"But now, O our God, what can we say after this? For we have disregarded the commands [11]you gave through your servants the prophets when you said: 'The land you are entering to possess is a land polluted by the corruption of its peoples. By their detestable practices they have filled it with their impurity from one end to the other. [12]Therefore, do not give your daughters in marriage to their sons or take their daughters for your sons. Do not seek a treaty of friendship with them at any time, that you may be strong and eat the good things of the land and leave it to your children as an everlasting inheritance.'

9:10-11 Ezra acknowledged that his people had neglected to take seriously God's commands. He mentioned some of these commands in vv. 11-12 and referred to various passages (Lev 18:25ff.; 2 Kgs 16:3; Deut 7:1-3; 11:8; 23:6; 2 Kgs 21:16; Isa 1:19), thus testifying to the unity of Scripture. We must know God's Word so we can heed the warnings that are applicable to the present dangers. We need to remember that God has given specific ethical commands that should be followed in order to do his will.

9:12 "Do not seek a treaty of friendship with them" was implied by the command against making treaties with the Ammonites and Moabites in Deut 23:6.

(4) Plea for God's Mercy (9:13-15)

[13]"What has happened to us is a result of our evil deeds and our great guilt, and yet, our God, you have punished us less than our sins have deserved and have given us a remnant like this. [14]Shall we again break your commands and intermarry with the peoples who commit such detestable practices? Would you not be angry enough with us to destroy us, leaving us no remnant or survivor? [15]O LORD, God of Israel, you are righteous! We are left this day as a remnant. Here we are before you in our guilt, though because of it not one of us can stand in your presence."

9:13 "You have punished us less than our sins have deserved" is literally, "You have withheld [our punishment] below our iniquities." Ezra recognized that it was God's mercy, not the people's merit, that had made possible their reestablishment in Jerusalem. There is unity in biblical teaching. The New Testament also emphasizes that every human being has sinned and deserves eternal punishment. Only by God's mercy are we saved from that condemnation if we are in Christ (Rom 3:21-26).

9:14 The Old Testament passages mentioned earlier warn that God's anger will be kindled if his people disobey him. God is not capricious like human beings; his anger is his just reaction to disobedience and evil. Ezra recognized the seriousness of their condition. They had been punished for disobedience and had experienced God's mercy in reestablishing them. Therefore, to commit the same sins like intermarriage with pagans would demand renewed punishment. Grace ought to result in obedience (Ps 130:4; Rom 12:1; 1 Cor 6:11). Believers must learn how serious it is to go back to the evils from which God has delivered and cleansed them.

The words for "remnant" and "survivor" are almost synonymous. The first means "something left over after destruction," and the second refers to something that escapes from destruction.[19]

9:15 Ezra could only throw himself on God's mercy and plead that he not destroy the people. He mentioned God's righteousness "not to supplicate pardon, as Neh. 9:33, for the righteousness of God would impel Him to extirpate the sinful nation, but to rouse the conscience of the community, to point out to them what, after this relapse into their old abominations, they had to expect from the justice of God."[20] A vision of God's holiness such as Ezra had would indicate that our society and our culture are also subject to God's judgment.

God is "righteous" in several senses. He is righteous and thus must punish sin and evil. The root *ṣādaq* means "to conform to an ethical norm."[21] It is often applied to God himself. "Righteousness and justice are the foundation of his throne" (Ps 97:2). "They always characterize his actions."[22] But God's righteousness is also manifest in salvation. The psalmist said, "Save me from blood guilt, O God, the God who saves me, and my tongue will sing of your righteousness" (Ps 51:14). And 1 John 1:9 says that if we confess our sins, God is "righteous" and "just" to forgive our sins. Under the covenant, God is righteous when he delivers his people. So while Ezra primarily was thinking of God's righteousness in judging Israel for sin, he also must have included this covenant-salvation meaning. The contrast between God's righteousness and Israel's sin is

---

[19] J. J. Slotki, *Daniel, Ezra and Nehemiah,* Soncino Books of the Bible (London: Soncino, 1951), 168.

[20] Keil and Delitzsch, *The Book of Ezra,* in *Commentary on the Old Testament,* vol. 3 (Grand Rapids: Eerdmans, 1980), 125.

[21] Harris, Archer, and Waltke, *TWOT,* 752.

[22] Ibid., 754.

apparent. Because of God's character, there is punishment, but there is preservation for the remnant for their faithfulness.

3. The Covenant to Change (10:1-6)

[1]While Ezra was praying and confessing, weeping and throwing himself down before the house of God, a large crowd of Israelites—men, women and children—gathered around him. They too wept bitterly. [2]Then Shecaniah son of Jehiel, one of the descendants of Elam, said to Ezra, "We have been unfaithful to our God by marrying foreign women from the peoples around us. But in spite of this, there is still hope for Israel. [3]Now let us make a covenant before our God to send away all these women and their children, in accordance with the counsel of my lord and of those who fear the commands of our God. Let it be done according to the Law. [4]Rise up; this matter is in your hands. We will support you, so take courage and do it."

[5]So Ezra rose up and put the leading priests and Levites and all Israel under oath to do what had been suggested. And they took the oath. [6]Then Ezra withdrew from before the house of God and went to the room of Jehohanan son of Eliashib. While he was there, he ate no food and drank no water, because he continued to mourn over the unfaithfulness of the exiles.

In most of chap. 9 Ezra himself is speaking in the first person; now chap. 10 is written in the third person. Similar changes are found in Ezra 7:1-10; 8:35-36; and Neh 8. Several theories have been presented to explain the change. Some think chap. 10 is not part of the Ezra Memoirs. Others think the whole narrative is so well integrated that it is better to consider it part of the Ezra Memoirs. If it is, the final author changed this part to third person because he abbreviated it in some places and inserted comments in others.[23] Eskenazi follows Mowinckel in arguing that the recurring shift between first and third person is a literary device enabling the reader to view events from different perspectives.[24]

10:1 The narrative here takes up from 9:5, explaining the events that followed Ezra's prayer. In one of the courts of the temple Ezra had prayed, identifying with the people and accepting the principle of collective responsibility. The whole atmosphere reminds us of Ps 51:17, "A broken and contrite heart, O God, you will not despise."

Ezra was a respected leader, and his extreme distress caught the people's attention. In fact, such an uninhibited demonstration of emotion "proved infectious."[25] "Instead of whipping a reluctant people into ac-

[23] See Williamson, *Ezra, Nehemiah*, 148.
[24] Eskenazi, *Age of Prose*, 127-35.
[25] Fensham, *Ezra, Nehemiah*, 133.

tion, Ezra has pricked their conscience to the point at which they now urge *him* to act."[26] McConville has pointed out further that "it was the godliness and commitment of Ezra, testifying more powerfully than any harangue to the reality of God, of right and wrong and of judgment, that brought others to repentance."[27] Such, in fact, is the power of all who practice godliness.

One wonders if some of the foreign wives the Jews had married were among the women who gathered around Ezra in tears. Ezra's nearness to the temple, however, may have excluded the presence of foreigners.

10:2 A large number of the family of Elam are registered in 2:7 as returning from Babylon, and a smaller number went up with Ezra (8:7). Since this Shecaniah was a member of this family, he probably was not the person by this name mentioned in 8:3 or 8:5. Some of the Elamites were found guilty of marrying foreign wives, one of whom had the same name as Shecaniah's father, Jehiel (10:26). We are not sure it is the same Jehiel; but if it is, then Shecaniah denounced the sin of his own father.[28] Shecaniah seems to have been a spokesman for those concerned; his drastic solution was accepted.

The Hebrew *nōšeb* ("marrying") means literally "cause to dwell (in one's house)" or "give a home."[29] Shecaniah and the other leaders recognized that in taking foreign women into their homes they had been unfaithful (*māʿal*) and had broken the covenant with God.

10:3 According to Blenkinsopp, making a covenant here involved collectively swearing to observe certain stipulations of law and having names of those taking the oath recorded (cf. 2 Chr 15:8-15; 29:10; Neh 9:38).[30] A number of revivals in the Old Testament consisted mainly of a renewal of the covenant with God.[31] Since the covenant theme is central in the Bible, the prophets saw Israel's apostasy as a breaking of their covenant with God. Ezra understood intermarriage with "pagan" women

---

[26] Kidner, *Ezra and Nehemiah*, 69-70.

[27] McConville, *Ezra, Nehemiah, and Esther*, 69.

[28] Several individuals by this name in are found in Scripture. See 2 Chr 15:18,20; 16:5; 23:8; 27:32; 29:8; 2 Chr 21:2; 29:14; 31:13; 35:8; Ezra 8:9; 10:21,26.

[29] Only in this chapter and Neh 13 is it used this way and translated "marry." Also the word for "send away" in v. 3 is not the usual word for divorce. Therefore some have suggested that these were not true marriages (see Williamson, *Ezra, Nehemiah*, 150). However, the whole context, the seriousness of the situation, and the similar situation reflected in Malachi indicate that they were considered real marriages. Clearly it was cause for concern, repentance, and reform.

[30] Blenkinsopp, *Ezra-Nehemiah*, 188.

[31] For example, Josh 24.

as a breach of the covenant.

"Send away" is literally "cause to go out." Definite action was needed in a crisis situation. The action may seem harsh, but the continuity of the Jewish community was at stake.

The law referred to may be the law against intermarriage. Deuteronomy 7:3, speaking about the people of Canaan when the Israelites entered, says, "Do not intermarry with them." Also Deut 24:1-4 gives laws for divorce (cf. also 22:19,29; Isa 50:1; Jer 3:8). Furthermore, Deut 29:10-13 gives instructions for men, women, and children making a covenant with the Lord. The returned exiles under Ezra's instruction took seriously God's commandments.

10:4 Shecaniah urged Ezra to act, but the responsibility was Ezra's. A leader whom God has called cannot escape making decisions and taking action that affects people. But others are also important in encouraging that action. "So take courage" reminds us of God's words to Joshua (Josh 1:7). This verse has a series of action verbs in the imperative mood, emphasizing that Ezra must act now.

10:5-6 Ezra took definite action, but first he secured the support of the leaders and all the people.

In the temple complex were various rooms. Some served as storerooms, but some were occupied by priests.[32] Ezra went alone to fast and pray, which shows that his weeping and mourning outside was not just superficial or a "show" to produce an effect on the people. He was sincerely mourning for the returned exiles who had so soon forgotten why they were punished; now they again were unfaithful to God.

In the Old Testament the only day of fasting required by all the Israelites was on the Day of Atonement (see comments on 8:21). However, many special occasions of personal or national fasting are described, and numerous motives are noted. Fasting was often a manifestation of total or partial repentance (1 Sam 7:6; Dan 9:3; 2 Chr 20:3; Neh 9:1), of grief (1 Sam 31:13; 1 Kgs 21:27,29; 1 Chr 10:12; Ezra 8:21). It was practiced in preparation for revival or special encounters with God (Exod 34:28; Deut 9:9-18) and was called forth by a remembrance of national disasters (Zech 7:3; Esth 9:31). It also could accompany prayer before a critical decision or ominous course of action (Neh 1:4). The prophets condemned the people's fasting when it was a mere ritual without sincere dedication

---

[32] Those who argue for the late date of Ezra rely heavily on v. 6, arguing that this Eliashib was the same one who was high priest in Neh 12:22 and that Jehohanan was a grandson of this Eliashib. For discussion see "The Chronology of Ezra and Nehemiah" in the Introduction.

to the Lord (Isa 58:1-14; Jer 14:12; 36:1-10; cf. Matt 6:16-18). Ezra's intense consternation concerning the sin of the people brought him to a profound attitude of remorse. Because he was a man of prayer and deep devotion to God, his natural response was to fast and pray.

4. The Assembly of the People (10:7-11)

[7]A proclamation was then issued throughout Judah and Jerusalem for all the exiles to assemble in Jerusalem. [8]Anyone who failed to appear within three days would forfeit all his property, in accordance with the decision of the officials and elders, and would himself be expelled from the assembly of the exiles.

[9]Within the three days, all the men of Judah and Benjamin had gathered in Jerusalem. And on the twentieth day of the ninth month, all the people were sitting in the square before the house of God, greatly distressed by the occasion and because of the rain. [10]Then Ezra the priest stood up and said to them, "You have been unfaithful; you have married foreign women, adding to Israel's guilt. [11]Now make confession to the LORD, the God of your fathers, and do his will. Separate yourselves from the peoples around you and from your foreign wives."

10:7-8 After the crowd that had gathered had dispersed, Ezra and the leaders decided what action to take, and the proclamation was sent to "all the exiles." The postexilic community had not expanded very far, so all could arrive within three days.

The word for "forfeit" is *ḥerem,* which refers to putting something "under the ban." Anything under the ban was devoted to the Lord either by destruction or by giving it to the temple treasury (cf. Lev 7:21). This seems drastic, but it was in keeping with the authority given to Ezra in 7:26. As in the law against marrying non-Jews, this warning was given to keep the covenant community unique and free from outside pressures.

10:9 "The ninth month" was a little more than four months after Ezra's arrival in Jerusalem (Ezra 7:8-9) "In the square before the house of God" is the same place they gathered when Ezra read the Law to them (Neh 8:1).

Their "distress" was twofold: inwardly emotional and outwardly physical from the rain. The ninth month is November-December, which is part of the rainy season and often is cold. For "rain" the Hebrew uses the plural of intensity, suggesting that the rain was heavy. Although this rain made the people uncomfortable, rain could suggest God's blessing; for Deut 11:10-17 says God will send rain for fertility when the people obey.

10:10 Ezra spoke directly to the heart of the matter. He could not forget all God's punishment in the exile. Now the people were heaping up more guilt by taking to themselves foreign women.

10:11 The Hebrew *todâ* (here "confession") usually is translated "give thanks" or "praise." Although Fensham translates "thank the LORD,"[33] "confession" makes the best sense here. Nevertheless, it is true that only the sinner who confesses can truly praise God "and do his will." Genuine repentance is always related to obeying God's ethical commands, which indicate his will.

5. Positive, Orderly Response (10:12-17)

[12]The whole assembly responded with a loud voice: "You are right! We must do as you say. [13]But there are many people here and it is the rainy season; so we cannot stand outside. Besides, this matter cannot be taken care of in a day or two, because we have sinned greatly in this thing. [14]Let our officials act for the whole assembly. Then let everyone in our towns who has married a foreign woman come at a set time, along with the elders and judges of each town, until the fierce anger of our God in this matter is turned away from us." [15]Only Jonathan son of Asahel and Jahzeiah son of Tikvah, supported by Meshullam and Shabbethai the Levite, opposed this.

[16]So the exiles did as was proposed. Ezra the priest selected men who were family heads, one from each family division, and all of them designated by name. On the first day of the tenth month they sat down to investigate the cases, [17]and by the first day of the first month they finished dealing with all the men who had married foreign women.

10:12 God used individual leaders to bring community unity. In God's work it is important to seek community decisions that indicate a unity of thought and heart.

10:13 The decision on what to do was made quickly, but the details of carrying it out needed time. The people wisely decided to proceed carefully and with sufficient time.

10:14 The guilty men had to come with the elders and judges of their town who would know the individual circumstances. This shows a genuine interest in justice for each case since these elders and judges would consider each individual situation.

10:15-16 Since the Hebrew literally says "stood against" (or alongside of), it has been suggested that it does not mean they were opposed.

---

[33] Fensham, *Ezra and Nehemiah*, 137.

However, the normal reading of the verse is that these men did oppose the decision. The text does not say why they opposed it; they may have objected to taking the time the assembly requested. However, the sense of the verse is that they opposed the whole decision to put away the foreign women. The emphasis here is on the unity of the community with little opposition.[34]

If "Meshullam" was the same Meshullam as in v. 29, we could see why he would oppose the resolution, for there he had to give up his foreign wife. However, there are at least ten Meshullams in Ezra-Nehemiah. This one in v. 15 had come with Ezra to Jerusalem, so he probably was not the same one as in v. 29.

10:17 The commission worked for three months. Fensham notes that it took about seventy-five days and that would only be about two cases a day (of those who had to send away their foreign wives).[35] He suggests that there may have been more cases but that not all were found guilty.[36] Others think the list in vv. 18-44 is not complete, that there must have been many more than some 111 persons guilty in a group of some thirty thousand.[37] There is no evidence to suggest that there were more. Ezra was concerned about stopping the erroneous practice before it became more widespread. As the rest of Scripture shows (the cases of Achan in Josh 7 and Ananias and Saphira in Acts 5), one person's sin affects the whole community of faith.

6. Those Guilty of Intermarriage (10:18-44)

[18]**Among the descendants of the priests, the following had married foreign women:**

> **From the descendants of Jeshua son of Jozadak, and his brothers: Maaseiah, Eliezer, Jarib and Gedaliah.** [19]**(They all gave their hands in pledge to put away their wives, and for their guilt they each presented a ram from the flock as a guilt offering.)**
> [20]**From the descendants of Immer:**
>   **Hanani and Zebadiah.**
> [21]**From the descendants of Harim:**
>   **Maaseiah, Elijah, Shemaiah, Jehiel and Uzziah.**

---

[34] See Num 13–14 with regard to Caleb and Joshua.

[35] No doubt the commission's work included many economic and social details involved in this decision, such as the inheritance rights of the children and the return of dowries to the wives who were sent away.

[36] Fensham, *Ezra and Nehemiah,* 142.

[37] Myers, *Ezra, Nehemiah,* 87.

[22]From the descendants of Pashhur:
   Elioenai, Maaseiah, Ishmael, Nethanel, Jozabad and Elasah.

[23]Among the Levites:
Jozabad, Shimei, Kelaiah (that is, Kelita), Pethahiah, Judah and Eliezer.

[24]From the singers:
   Eliashib.
From the gatekeepers:
   Shallum, Telem and Uri.
[25]And among the other Israelites:
   From the descendants of Parosh:
   Ramiah, Izziah, Malkijah, Mijamin, Eleazar, Malkijah and Benaiah.
[26]From the descendants of Elam:
   Mattaniah, Zechariah, Jehiel, Abdi, Jeremoth and Elijah.
[27]From the descendants of Zattu:
   Elioenai, Eliashib, Mattaniah, Jeremoth, Zabad and Aziza.
[28]From the descendants of Bebai:
   Jehohanan, Hananiah, Zabbai and Athlai.
[29]From the descendants of Bani:
   Meshullam, Malluch, Adaiah, Jashub, Sheal and Jeremoth.
[30]From the descendants of Pahath-Moab:
   Adna, Kelal, Benaiah, Maaseiah, Mattaniah, Bezalel, Binnui and Manasseh.
[31]From the descendants of Harim:
   Eliezer, Ishijah, Malkijah, Shemaiah, Shimeon, [32]Benjamin, Malluch and Shemariah.
[33]From the descendants of Hashum:
   Mattenai, Mattattah, Zabad, Eliphelet, Jeremai, Manasseh and Shimei.
[34]From the descendants of Bani:
   Maadai, Amram, Uel, [35]Benaiah, Bedeiah, Keluhi, [36]Vaniah, Meremoth, Eliashib, [37]Mattaniah, Mattenai and Jaasu.
[38]From the descendants of Binnui:
   Shimei, [39]Shelemiah, Nathan, Adaiah, [40]Macnadebai, Shashai, Sharai, [41]Azarel, Shelemiah, Shemariah, [42]Shallum, Amariah and Joseph.
[43]From the descendants of Nebo:
   Jeiel, Mattithiah, Zabad, Zebina, Jaddai, Joel and Benaiah.
[44]All these had married foreign women, and some of them had children by these wives.

10:18-44 In all there were 110 or 111 (depending on the understanding of the text in v. 40) men who had taken foreign women: there were seventeen priests, ten Levites, and eighty-three or eighty-four lay Israelites.

Correction of a community problem must start with the leaders. Even some of the priestly families were guilty. The family of "Jeshua" (v. 18) was an important family; Jeshua was coleader with Zerubbabel in the time of Zechariah, shortly after the first return under Cyrus.

Fensham mentions that there are no families of temple servants in the list (there are also only one of the singers in v. 24 and three gatekeepers found guilty). Although we do not have much information concerning the social stratification of the community, the impression is that the people of the land were better off economically than the exiles; thus Fensham suggests that the upper classes of exiles would have been the ones most tempted to take foreign women.[38]

The symbolic use of the handshake ("hands in pledge" in v. 19) is seen in 2 Kgs 10:15 and Ezek 17:18. These priests also offered "a guilt offering." Some think that only the priestly families had to present an offering for their sin since the same is not mentioned again in this chapter. However, Lev 5:14-16 shows that this sacrifice was required of anyone who was unfaithful.

There seems to be a textual difficulty at v. 40. "Macnadebai" may not be a proper name but may mark the division of another family.[39]

The Hebrew text at v. 44 reads "Some of them had children by these wives." Here, the Greek text of 1 Esdr 9:36 says, "They sent them and the children away." This seems to be implied by the Hebrew text, even though it appears harsh; however, we are not familiar with the arrangements that might have been made for these women and children. In the ancient world a woman had a guardian (usually her father or brother) who was responsible to see that the woman's husband fulfilled the marriage contract. Perhaps in this case arrangements were made with the women's families.

Ezra knew that marriage was instituted by God and considered a permanent and exclusive relationship (Gen 2:24, quoted in Matt 19:5; Eph 5:31). If Malachi preached about Ezra's time or just before, Ezra was surely familiar with his teaching on divorce in 2:16 ("'I hate divorce,' says the LORD God of Israel"). Much of biblical ethics has to do with the sanctity of the marriage relationship. In fact, God even uses marriage to illustrate his own relationship to his people (Hos 1–3; Eph 5). Since the family is the basis of society, any offense against the family is an offense against God.

---

[38] Fensham, *Ezra and Nehemiah*, 144.

[39] W. Rudolph, in *BHS*, makes two suggestions. First, וּמִבְּנֵי זַכָּי ("from the descendants of Zakkai"); the second option, וּמִבְּנֵי עַזּוּר is taken by Williamson on the basis of 1 Esdr 9:34, and he translates, "Of the family of Azzur" (Williamson, *Ezra, Nehemiah*, 144). One of the two suggestions seems appropriate because otherwise the list of the family of Binnui is exceptionally large.

The moral dilemma Ezra faced, however, was caused by the pagan influence these foreign women would have on the children of these mixed marriages and on the newly reestablished community of faith. Ezra knew the story of Solomon and his foreign wives and the devastating effect this had had on Israel (1 Kgs 11:1-11; cf. Neh 13:26-27).[40] The family and the convictions of the whole religious community were at stake. Ezra's action was drastic, but he chose the path most likely to protect the covenant community from pagan syncretism (cf. Gal 3:23; 1 Cor 5). There is wisdom in Holmgren's statement: "Sometimes preservation of a way of life dictates a policy which disappoints the democratic, ecumenical spirit."[41]

Nevertheless, if Ezra emphasized God's law, how could he support the decision to divorce these foreign wives? Deuteronomy 24:1-4 indicates that sometimes divorce was permitted in the Old Testament (also 22:19,29; Isa 50:1; Jer 3:8). Also, the situation in Ezra was different from that envisioned elsewhere, for in Ezra pagan wives were involved.[42] These marriages were wrong from the outset. Malachi's statement that God hates divorce, although true in an absolute sense, is given in response to Jews who had divorced their Jewish wives in order to take foreign women. In this historically unique case, Ezra and the Jewish leaders considered that the importance of maintaining the purity of the religious community superceded that of these marital relationships.[43]

In the New Testament, Jesus plainly teaches that divorce is not God's will: "What God has joined together, let not man separate" (Matt 19:6). Especially in our times when irresponsibility and selfishness are often renamed "individual freedom," the sanctity and permanence of marriage must be emphasized. Yet Matt 19:9 and 1 Cor 7:11,15 recognize that in certain cases divorce will occur. Churches have differed concerning the toleration of divorce and remarriage. The Catholic Church has consistently prohibited it, as have some Protestant groups. It has become an ever-increasing moral issue. The teaching of the Old and New Testaments has led many Christians to accept that in some circumstances di-

---

[40] Compare Gen 36:1-9 with 24:3 in light of the adversarial role played by Edom throughout Scripture. See also Num 25; Josh 23:11-13; 1 Kgs 16:31-33.

[41] Holmgren, *Ezra and Nehemiah,* 85.

[42] W. C. Kaiser, Jr., however (*Hard Sayings of the Old Testament* [Downers Grove: InterVarsity, 1988], 142), suggests that Ezra's action was based on his exegesis of Deut 24:1-4, understanding "something indecent about her" in that passage to be "the breaking of the covenant relationship."

[43] If the situations in Malachi and Ezra were related, there is irony in the necessity of saving the community through divorce, the very thing that had led to the threatening crisis.

vorce may be accepted as a tragic last resort when the marriage has completely broken down and no possibility of restoration exists. These chapters in Ezra, however, are descriptive, not prescriptive. They cannot be taken as authorization for divorcing an unbelieving spouse. In 1 Cor 7:12-16 Paul exhorts one who has an unbelieving partner not to divorce; but if the unbelieving partner leaves, the believer is "not bound in such circumstances."[44] Most Christian leaders agree that each case must be studied carefully in light of Scripture and in light of its own particular situation.

This episode shows the danger of moral and spiritual apathy and the importance of maintaining the identity of the believing community in a pagan world. The commission of Artaxerxes to Ezra was to develop Judaism as a religious community. According to Malachi, some men already had divorced their Jewish wives to take foreign women, and the process of assimilation had already begun (Mal 2:10-17; 3:13-15). So the threat to the community was real. It also shows the seriousness with which the Bible treats marriage between believers and unbelievers (2 Cor 6:14-18). Furthermore, this episode also shows the wisdom of Ezra's leadership. As vital as his leadership was, he did not force his decision on the people. Rather, he influenced the leaders and people, relying on the power of God's Word and Spirit; and the decision was made by the community of believers. We can learn from his teaching, his patience, and his example. This shows how strong convictions, held deeply by one leader or a minority, can influence the future of the whole community's life and thought. Just as in Ezra's time, the believing community today often faces crises that demand strong leadership and decisive, united community action.

---

[44] Kaiser (*Hard Sayings*, 143) interprets 1 Cor 7:15 to mean the believer may "sadly accept the divorce with the right to be married to another."

V. RESTORING JERUSALEM: NEHEMIAH BUILDS THE WALLS
   (1:1–7:73a)
   1. News from Jerusalem (1:1-3)
   2. Nehemiah's Concern and Prayer (1:4-11)
      (1) Confession of Sin (1:4-7)
      (2) Plea for God's Help (1:8-11)
   3. Nehemiah's Mission and Commission (2:1-10)
      (1) Nehemiah's Sadness (2:1-2)
      (2) Nehemiah's Request (2:3-5)
      (3) The Requests Granted (2:6-8)
      (4) Action and Opposition (2:9-10)
   4. Nehemiah Surveys the Walls (2:11-20)
      (1) The Secret Inspection by Night (2:11-16)
      (2) Nehemiah Presents the Challenge (2:17-18)
      (3) Opposition by Ridicule (2:19-20)
   5. Building for Unity: The Community Rebuilds the Wall (3:1-32)
      (1) Repairing the Northern and Western Walls (3:1-15)
      (2) The Construction of the Eastern Wall (3:16-32)
   6. Opposition to Building the Wall (4:1-23)
      (1) Opposition by Ridicule (4:1-6)
      (2) Opposition by Plot (4:7-9)
      (3) Internal Opposition: Discouragement and Fear (4:10-15)
      (4) Diligence and Readiness in the Work (4:16-23)
   7. Problems within the Community (5:1-19)
      (1) Extortion by the Rich (5:1-5)
      (2) Nehemiah Rebukes the Creditors (5:6-11)
      (3) The Offenders Accept the Exhortation (5:12-13)
      (4) Nehemiah's Unselfish Leadership (5:14-19)
   8. More Opposition from Without (6:1-19)
      (1) Opposition by Trickery (6:1-9)
      (2) Opposition by Intimidation (6:10-14)
      (3) The Wall Completed (6:15-16)
      (4) Opposition by Intrigue (6:17-19)
   9. Nehemiah Organizes the Community (7:1-73)
      (1) Organization for Conservation (7:1-3)
      (2) The Registration of the People (7:4-73a)

────────── **V. RESTORING JERUSALEM: NEHEMIAH** ──────────
BUILDS THE WALLS (1:1–7:73a)

Like the Book of Ezra, the Book of Nehemiah may be understood in
terms of the faithfulness and holiness of God. The first part of Nehemiah
is concerned primarily with the rebuilding of the walls. Once the people
had returned and worship had been reestablished, the city of David, Jerusalem, had to be rebuilt. Passages such as Isa 65:17-25; Jer 33:1-13;
Amos 9:11-15; Mic 7:11-20 speak clearly of a new Jerusalem inhabited
by the community of God. The servant of God used to instigate this restoration was Nehemiah, the cupbearer to the king in Susa (Neh 1:11).
Nehemiah proved to be a capable leader, diligent in God's work both for
the community of God and the city of David. Glory should not be given
to Nehemiah, however, but rather to God, who directed and brought
about this event. Just as in Ezra, the providence of God, his loving care,
and discipline were the real forces behind the events recorded in these
chapters of the Book of Nehemiah.

1. News from Jerusalem (1:1-3)

[1]The words of Nehemiah son of Hacaliah:

**In the month of Kislev in the twentieth year, while I was in the citadel of
Susa, [2]Hanani, one of my brothers, came from Judah with some other men,
and I questioned them about the Jewish remnant that survived the exile, and
also about Jerusalem.**
**[3]They said to me, "Those who survived the exile and are back in the prov-
ince are in great trouble and disgrace. The wall of Jerusalem is broken down,
and its gates have been burned with fire."**

1:1 "Nehemiah" means "The LORD comforts." The Lord used Nehemiah to revive the spirit of the discouraged exiles and bring them
hope (cf. Isa 57:14-21). The first seven chapters of Nehemiah as well as
12:31–13:31 are written in the first person. This, as well as all or part of
Neh 11 and the rest of Neh 12, constitutes what is called the Nehemiah
Memoirs. As such it offers an extensive look into the life and heart of an
outstanding servant of God that is unique to the Old Testament. Nehemiah was an energetic leader who combined a deep trust in the Lord with
precise planning, careful organization, and discreet but energetic action.
Christian leaders find inspiration in Nehemiah's life and character.

The month of Kislev, spanning parts of November-December, would be the third month if the year started with Tishri; but it would be the ninth month if it started from Nisan, the more common reckoning. However, 2:1 indicates the former was in use since Nisan is still counted as the twentieth year.[1] The fact that the text does not say "the twentieth year of Artaxerxes" suggests that there could be either a textual problem here or an editorial abbreviation of the Nehemiah Memoirs at this point. A more recent suggestion considers that Nehemiah, working in the Persian court, was thinking of regnal years.[2]

The twentieth year of Artaxerxes I was 445 B.C. The years immediately before this had been difficult. In 460 B.C. there was a revolt in Egypt that was not quelled until 455. In 448 Megabyzus, satrap of Trans-Euphrates, rebelled but was later reconciled to the king. Therefore at this point the king of Persia would have been interested in having loyal supporters in Jerusalem in case of more trouble in Egypt or anywhere in the west (see Introduction).

The citadel of Susa (v. 1) was the winter residence of the Persian kings; Ecbatana was their summer residence. The events of Esther took place in Susa, as did the vision of Dan 8.[3]

1:2 Hanani was either a real brother, a kinsman, or a fellow Jew. All are possible ways of understanding the text; however, the fact that he called him "my brother" in 7:2 when he appointed him to a high office supports the first meaning.

"Questioned them" indicates Nehemiah's deep concern for his own people, even those who lived far away. From the beginning it is evident that Nehemiah's interest was not only himself or his immediate family; his vision included God's people even though far away. Christian leaders today must also have a global concern for God's work.

1:3 Verse 3 would seem to indicate that by "Jewish remnant" Ne-

---

[1] Some have suggested that the text should read "the nineteenth year" in 1:1 since we know that the twentieth year is correct for 2:1.

[2] As noted in Neh 5:14. E. Bickerman ("En marge de l'Ecriture. I.—Le comput des annees de regne des Achemenides [Neh., i, 2; ii, 1 et Thuc., viii, 58]," *RB* 88 [1981]: 19-23) presents this argument and says that Artaxerxes became king in the month of Ab (July-Aug.), so both months mentioned by Nehemiah were in the same regnal year (H. G. M. Williamson, *Ezra, Nehemiah*, WBC [Waco: Word, 1985], 170).

[3] Susa is 150 miles (241 km.) north of the Persian Gulf. In 521 B.C., Darius I made Susa his administrative capital. From 518 to 512 he built a palace there. The events of Esther occurred in Susa, where Xerxes apparently had his winter capital. Artaxerxes I (464–423) also lived in Susa. During his reign the palace of Darius was destroyed by fire. Later Artaxerxes II (404–360) rebuilt the palace (E. Yamauchi, "Susa" in *The New International Dictionary of Biblical Archaeology*, ed. E. M. Blaiklock and R. K. Harrison [Grand Rapids: Zondervan, 1983], 426-30).

hemiah was referring to the returned exiles in Jerusalem and Judea rather than those who were not carried into captivity.

The province to which Nehemiah refers probably was the whole province of Trans-Euphrates.

Was "the broken wall" the result of the destruction by Nebuchadnezzar in 587? Or were some walls built at a later time, such as in the episode mentioned in Ezra 4:12? Nehemiah seems to have been surprised and appalled; therefore it is reasonable to suppose that Ezra 4:12 refers to a partial building of walls at some time after the first return in 538 that had been destroyed, perhaps by Rehum and Shimshai when they interceded according to Ezra 4:23.

2. Nehemiah's Concern and Prayer (1:4-11)

(1) Confession of Sin (1:4-7)

⁴When I heard these things, I sat down and wept. For some days I mourned and fasted and prayed before the God of heaven. ⁵Then I said:

"O LORD, God of heaven, the great and awesome God, who keeps his covenant of love with those who love him and obey his commands, ⁶let your ear be attentive and your eyes open to hear the prayer your servant is praying before you day and night for your servants, the people of Israel. I confess the sins we Israelites, including myself and my father's house, have committed against you. ⁷We have acted very wickedly toward you. We have not obeyed the commands, decrees and laws you gave your servant Moses.

1:4 Nehemiah displays here his profound concern, his sensitivity and his intense feeling. Certainly it is easier to pray about something when one feels deep concern for it; however, one should pray even when the feeling is not profound. More concern about God's honor and more time in communion with God in prayer will result in more intense concern about prayer needs.

Nehemiah was a man of faith, and we can find two sources of his steadfast trust in God. The first is at the beginning of his prayer—his deep understanding of who God is. The second is seen throughout the prayer—his thorough knowledge of God's word.

Nine prayers of Nehemiah are recorded in this book.[4] Most of them are quite short. Because this one is long and similar to the prayers of Ezra, some think it was composed or amplified by the author. However, its similarities to other prayers (including those of Daniel) simply repre-

---

[4] The others are found in Neh 2:4; 4:4-5; 5:19; 6:14; 13:14,22,29,31.

sent the custom of the time and the influence of the Deuteronomic theology.[5]

1:5 Nehemiah's prayer (vv. 5-11) reminds us of psalms classified as Community Laments (e.g., Pss 74; 79; 80; 85); however, this prayer lacks the complaint element common to those psalms. Westermann notes that in the time of Ezra and Nehemiah the Prayer of Repentance was taking the place of the Community Laments.[6] This prayer is actually a prayer of repentance. It can be outlined as follows: (a) invocation to God; (b) confession of sins; (c) request to the LORD to remember his people; (d) request for success.

"LORD" is the Tetragrammaton (Yahweh), which carries the ideas of love and personal relationship. The phrase "God of heaven" was commonly used in the Persian Empire even by the Persians in speaking of their god. This prayer shows it had been accepted in the religious language of the Jews. However, it was not altogether new since it is used in Gen 24:7.

"The great and awesome God" indicates Nehemiah's appreciation of who God is: the one whom Nehemiah feared and the source and object of his deep faith. God's awesomenes is the impression his total character and person leaves on all who encounter him. Those who know and trust God are those who fear him (cf. Mal 1:14; 4:5; Exod 15:11; Deut 28:58; Ezra 9:4).[7] The order of the prayer is significant: praise then petition.

One central theme of the Old Testament is God's special covenant relation with his people. The word *ḥesed* (translated here "love" in "covenant of love") is used frequently in the Old Testament. It is closely related to the covenant and contains the idea of loyalty.[8] It emphasizes God's mercy and love to his people. "With those who love him and obey his commands" shows that covenant love or loyalty was to be reciprocal. God's people are to obey God's commands, which express his will. The

---

[5] Note the similarities between the prayers of Ezra, Nehemiah, and Daniel: (1) identification with the guilty people (Ezra 9:6-15; Neh 9:32-37; Dan 9:4-19); (2) the captivity is attributed to the sins of the people (vv. 7-8; Ezra 9:7; Neh 9:29-30; Dan 9:7-8); (3) a remnant dependent on God's grace is mentioned (v. 10; Ezra 9:8,15; Neh 9:31; Dan 9:15); (4) the covenant is reaffirmed (v. 5; Neh 9:32; Dan 9:4); (5) healing for the people is sought in confession and repentance (vv. 6-9; Ezra 9:15; Neh 9:32-37; Dan 9:15-19). See E. W. Hamrick, "Ezra-Nehemiah," BBC, vol. 3 (Nashville: Broadman, 1970), 472.

[6] C. Westermann, *The Psalms: Structure, Content and Message* (Minneapolis: Augsburg, 1980), 31.

[7] "Awesome" (וְהַנּוֹרָא) translates the niphal participle of יָרֵא, "fear."

[8] On חֶסֶד see K. D. Sakenfeld, *The Meaning of Ḥesed in the Hebrew Bible* (Missoula: Scholars Press, 1978), and N. Glueck, *Hesed in the Bible*, tr. A. Gottschalk (Cincinnati: Hebrew Union College, 1967).

mention of the covenant should always cause us to recognize God's faithfulness and our responsibility. As Fensham says, "Love and the Law are the two pillars on which the covenant rests."[9]

1:6 Nehemiah knew that God would hear; he was asking God to take action. One of the utterly astounding characteristics of biblical psalms is that the psalmist never doubted that God heard his prayer. How great is God that he can pay attention to each of our prayers, millions of them around the world, individually and simultaneously! Our minds cannot comprehend it, but God is beyond our comprehension.

Even though he was a leader, Nehemiah emphasized his identification with the people and with their sins. Leaders must not consider themselves superior to others; admission of fault will not ruin effectiveness. Corporate solidarity is an important part of the Old Testament view of things, although not to the extent of minimizing individual responsibility. Each of God's children is a part of the believing community and is identified with that community. Nehemiah identified with his people in humility as Jesus did at his baptism. Even though he did not sin, he so identified with the people who were coming to repent of their sins that he insisted on being baptized by John the Baptist.

1:7 In Job 34:31[10] the word translated "acted wickedly" (*ḥābal*) means to "offend." Nehemiah was speaking to God here as to a master he has offended by disregarding his commands. The concept of disobedience goes right to the heart of the matter. God's commands are not capricious; he knows what is best for his people and for all society. Nehemiah recognized the seriousness of disobeying God's ethical demands. Many ethical dilemmas of our day are not easily solved; however, we often make them more difficult by not accepting as relevant ethical commands that are clear in Scripture. In this case "the commands, decrees and laws" refer to the Pentateuch.[11]

(2) Plea for God's Help (1:8-11)

8"Remember the instruction you gave your servant Moses, saying, 'If you are unfaithful, I will scatter you among the nations, 9but if you return to me and obey my commands, then even if your exiled people are at the farthest horizon, I will gather them from there and bring them to the place I have

---

[9] F. C. Fensham, *The Books of Ezra and Nehemiah*, NICOT (Grand Rapids: Eerdmans, 1982).

[10] The only other use of the verb in the qal. In the piel it means "destroy, ruin."

[11] On the concept of law see D. J. Wiseman, "Law and Order in Old Testament Times" *VE* 8 (1973): 5-21.

chosen as a dwelling for my Name.'

^{10}"They are your servants and your people, whom you redeemed by your great strength and your mighty hand. ^{11}O L$_{ORD}$, let your ear be attentive to the prayer of this your servant and to the prayer of your servants who delight in revering your name. Give your servant success today by granting him favor in the presence of this man."

I was cupbearer to the king.

1:8-9 Nehemiah's prayer was based on God's Word. As Kidner notes, even though Nehemiah, like all of us, had to come before God empty-handed, with nothing deserving the Lord's favor or even attention (indeed, just the opposite), he nevertheless did not come uninvited. Most of this prayer is based on Deuteronomy, many phrases of which are practically the same.[12] Nehemiah realized that God justly punished Israel, but he reminded God that this very situation had been anticipated in Deut 4:25-31 and of his promise of mercy, faithfulness, and forgiveness.

Nehemiah realized that God had fulfilled much of Deut 30:1-10; but he was convinced that God's promise included more than the situation in which the Jerusalem community found itself at that moment. Thus, Nehemiah's prayer shows a profound understanding and faith in what God had promised in his Word. Nehemiah challenges us to prayer based on an understanding of God's purpose and will as found in his Word. He also reminds us that we can always begin again in our relationship with God if we return to him in humility.

1:10 This verse is almost a copy of Deut 9:29. Redemption involves the payment of a price to reclaim a person from slavery. Here reference is made to God's act in delivering Israel from slavery in Egypt. The exodus theme is used many times in the New Testament to emphasize redemption from the power and judgment of sin and the resultant relationship between the Redeemer and the redeemed (1 Pet 1:18; Rev 5:9; 14:3-4).

1:11 Nehemiah had prayed for days, but now he was arriving at a decisive moment. After prayer was to come action, and Nehemiah had determined that the time was "today." He asked that King Artaxerxes might be divinely moved to act on behalf of God's people. Humanly speaking, Nehemiah had no reason to expect such favor.

According to Ezra 4:21, this same Artaxerxes had earlier issued a decree to stop work on the city of Jerusalem, perhaps on the wall itself.[13]

---

[12] Note Deut 4:27; 6:1; 7:9,21; 9:29; 10:17; 12:5; 21:15; 28:64; 30:1-4.

To make such a request clearly contrary to royal policy might even prove dangerous. But Nehemiah called him "this man," perhaps to stress that he was only a human under God's sovereignty. Nehemiah knew the seriousness of his undertaking and put his case in God's hands. Like many since his time, Nehemiah's greatness came from asking great things of a great God and attempting great things in reliance on him.

Nehemiah's final comment, however ("I was a cupbearer to the king"), may be an acknowledgment that God had already begun to move on Israel's behalf by placing Nehemiah in such a strategic position with access to the king. This would have encouraged Nehemiah at the same time it terrified him (cf. Esth 4:12-14).

3. Nehemiah's Mission and Commission (2:1-10)

(1) Nehemiah's Sadness (2:1-2)

[1]In the month of Nisan in the twentieth year of King Artaxerxes, when wine was brought for him, I took the wine and gave it to the king. I had not been sad in his presence before; [2]so the king asked me, "Why does your face look so sad when you are not ill? This can be nothing but sadness of heart."

I was very much afraid,

2:1 Since "Nisan" spans parts of our March-April, four months had passed since Nehemiah received news from Jerusalem. He had been praying and planning during these four months so that he would be ready when the opportunity arose.

When a servant brought the wine, Nehemiah, as official cupbearer, tasted it and gave it to the king.[14] This most likely took place during a feast. Some question whether Nehemiah had not had occasion to serve the king during the four months that passed. No doubt Nehemiah served the king constantly but was waiting for the right time to present his peti-

---

[13] The events of Ezra 4:7-23 may have taken place during the time that Egypt rebelled against Artaxerxes, so it is understandable that he would not want walls built around Jerusalem. But then some ask why the same king would have commissioned Nehemiah to rebuild the walls in 445 B.C. Yamauchi notes that by then "both the Egyptian revolt and the rebellion of Megabyzus had been resolved" (E. M. Yamauchi, *Persia and the Bible*, [Grand Rapids: Baker, 1990], 251). Artaxerxes no doubt was more willing to commission the building of the walls at this time.

[14] The official cupbearer had a position of honor and influence in the king's court. In fact, in Persian art he is shown to be next to the crown prince in attending the king (Hamrick, "Ezra-Nehemiah," 472). The fact that the king immediately noticed Nehemiah's sadness indicates that the king knew Nehemiah very well.

tion. Williamson notes that Persian kings regularly had special feasts; according to Herodotus (9.110), at a certain feast in the year, the Persian king showed special generosity. The feast may have been related to the New Year. (Nisan was the first month in the Persian calendar.)[15]

Some commentators translate "I had not been sad" as "Verily I was depressed in his presence."[16] But the plain sense of the Hebrew, as in NIV, is not a problem. Up until now Nehemiah had controlled his feelings; 1:11, along with this verse, gives the impression that he wanted the king to notice his grief this day, which was part of Nehemiah's plan of action.

2:2 When one acts according to God's will, others will take notice. In this case Nehemiah was risking his life. The king might have become suspicious of some kind of a plot. "Sadness of heart"[17] can also mean "a bad (or evil) heart."

(2) Nehemiah's Request (2:3-5)

[3]but I said to the king, "May the king live forever! Why should my face not look sad when the city where my fathers are buried lies in ruins, and its gates have been destroyed by fire?"
[4]The king said to me, "What is it you want?"
Then I prayed to the God of heaven, [5]and I answered the king, "If it pleases the king and if your servant has found favor in his sight, let him send me to the city in Judah where my fathers are buried so that I can rebuild it."

2:3 "May the king live forever" was the common formula for addressing the king as we see in Dan 2:4. Nehemiah went on to say he was sad because of the condition of the city "where my fathers are buried." Such a description showed both Nehemiah's respect for his ancestors and also his sense of shame at the condition of his native city. Nehemiah's request no doubt touched the sentiments of the king. He carefully avoided raising the king's suspicions by mentioning Jerusalem by name and so reminding him of his earlier decree, though of course the king knew Nehemiah's background. Nehemiah showed his great ability in communication and delicate diplomacy. He first had to get the king's sympathy before going on to details.

2:4 The king knew that Nehemiah wanted to make a request. This question could be the first hint that the king would listen favorably.

---

[15] Williamson, *Ezra, Nehemiah,* 178.
[16] See J. Myers, *Ezra, Nehemiah,* AB (Garden City: Doubleday, 1965), 97-98.
[17] רֹעַ לֵב.

Quick prayers are possible and valid if one has prayed sufficiently beforehand. In this case Nehemiah's prayer is evidence of a life lived in constant communion with God. Nehemiah had prayed for months, but he knew he was completely dependent on God's work in the king's heart at this moment.

2:5   No doubt when Nehemiah began to pray about the condition of Jerusalem, he had no idea that he would be the one to do the work. But such is God's way of working. Perhaps while Nehemiah was praying he realized that he should go. Now he presented the petition to the king. Nehemiah's concern and submission resulted in his action. "If it pleases the king" indicates that he was also submissive to the king.

(3) The Requests Granted (2:6-8)

6Then the king, with the queen sitting beside him, asked me, "How long will your journey take, and when will you get back?" It pleased the king to send me; so I set a time.

7I also said to him, "If it pleases the king, may I have letters to the governors of Trans-Euphrates, so that they will provide me safe-conduct until I arrive in Judah? 8And may I have a letter to Asaph, keeper of the king's forest, so he will give me timber to make beams for the gates of the citadel by the temple and for the city wall and for the residence I will occupy?" And because the gracious hand of my God was upon me, the king granted my requests.

2:6   The word *šēgal* is not the usual word for "queen." In Ps 45:10 it appears to refer to the chief member of the royal harem.[18] We do not know whether it was his official queen, Damaspia, or some favorite from his harem. But why was she mentioned here? Some suggest she may have favored Nehemiah and thus helped his cause.[19] Others suggest her significance was as a witness of the king's words to Nehemiah. The detailed questions and answers and the fact that the queen was not usually present at the great feasts suggest that this may have been a more private scene. It is possible that Nehemiah's account has combined two different conversations with the king.[20]

The text does not give Nehemiah's answer to the question of how long

---

[18] J. Slotki, *Daniel, Ezra and Nehemiah*, Soncino Books of the Bible (London: Soncino, 1951), 188.

[19] According to Yamauchi ("Ezra-Nehemiah," EBC, vol. 4, ed. F. E. Gaebelein [Grand Rapids: Zondervan, 1988], 4:685), "Extrabiblical sources reveal that the Achaemenid court was notorious for the great influence exercised by the royal women."

[20] See Williamson, *Ezra, Nehemiah*, 180.

the work would take. In Neh 5:14 we learn that he was governor in Jerusalem for twelve years. No doubt the time he asked was much shorter. Kidner suggests that he reported back to the king after the dedication of the walls, within the year, and then his appointment as governor was renewed.[21]

2:7 Nehemiah had planned carefully and knew his precise needs. First he needed letters of safe conduct, especially since Artaxerxes had previously had the building stopped (Ezra 4:17-22).

2:8 "Asaph" is a Hebrew name, so a Jew must have held this position. The Persian word *pardes* ("forest") is used also in Song 4:13 and Eccl 2:5. Some take for granted that the king's forest would have been located in Lebanon; however, there must have been other official reserves, and the name of the keeper suggests it could have been in Judah, although in the time of Cyrus timber for the temple was sent from Lebanon (Ezra 3:7). The timber was needed for three types of construction: for the gates of the citadel, for the wall and for Nehemiah's residence. We can readily understand the first and last, but it may surprise us that wood was needed for the city wall. Several studies have shown that in the ancient Near East it was customary to use timber in the walls.[22]

"The citadel by the temple" was a fortress on the north side of the temple. This side of the city and temple mount was always the hardest to defend. This citadel probably was a precursor and on the same site as the later Roman tower, Antonia.[23]

Nehemiah was realistic, giving God the credit for causing the king to grant his requests (cf. Prov 21:1). Because Nehemiah was sure this was of God, he had no problem accepting what the king offered. In the Bible, God often uses the king of a country in the divine plan (e.g., Exod 6:1; 10:1; 14:4; Isa 45:1-7).

God's work and our planning are not contradictory. J. White notes, "Prayer is where planning starts."[24] Nehemiah modeled good leadership; he prayed, planned, and acted in dependence on God and submission to his guidance. Neither is research contrary to dependence on God. Nehemiah knew who the officials were with whom he would have to deal, so he requested the credentials he would need as the project progressed.

---

[21] D. Kidner, *Ezra and Nehemiah*, TOTC (Downers Grove: InterVarsity, 1979), 81.

[22] Fensham, *Ezra and Nehemiah*, 163.

[23] We know that around 250 B.C. a fortress existed there, according to the letter of Aristeas (a writer from Alexandria, Egypt, 285–246 B.C.). It was located at the place where the present "Via Dolorosa" begins (G. Báez-Camargo, *Comentario arqueológico de la Biblia* [Miami: Editorial Caribe, 1979], 155).

[24] J. White, *Excellence in Leadership* (Downers Grove: InterVarsity, 1986), 35ff.

(4) Action and Opposition (2:9-10)

⁹**So I went to the governors of Trans-Euphrates and gave them the king's letters. The king had also sent army officers and cavalry with me.**

¹⁰**When Sanballat the Horonite and Tobiah the Ammonite official heard about this, they were very much disturbed that someone had come to promote the welfare of the Israelites.**

2:9 Ezra had not asked for a military escort, and we are not told that Nehemiah did either, but he had one. It may have been the king's idea.[25] The context suggests that its significance was to convince Sanballat and others that Nehemiah had the king's authority and support. There is no reason to interpret the use of the escort as a sign of Nehemiah's lack of faith.

2:10 "Sanballat the Horonite" probably was from one of the Beth-horons about eighteen miles northwest of Jerusalem, although some suggest the Moabite town of Horonaim. According to an Elephantine Papyrus, Sanballat was governor of Samaria in 408 B.C. Since his sons were acting for him at that time, he probably was elderly.[26] These verses imply that he already was governor of Samaria in Nehemiah's time.

"Tobiah the Ammonite official"[27] was likely governor of Ammon, although he may have been an Ammonite official under Sanballat's authority. Tobiah is a Jewish name and not Ammonite, but the Tobiad family was to have influence in Ammon for a long time.[28] These Tobiads may have been descendants of the Tobiah who in Ezra 2:60 was rejected from the Jewish community because "they could not show that their families

---

[25] J. Blenkinsopp (*Ezra-Nehemiah*, OTL [Philadelphia: Westminster, 1988], 216) refers to evidence that "an armed escort, together with guides and travel rations, was standard procedure."

[26] Williamson, *Ezra, Nehemiah*, 182. Blenkinsopp (*Ezra-Nehemiah,* 217) notes that whether Sanballat was still alive in 408 is "neither stated nor implied" in that letter. In another letter written in response to the first the governor or acting governor of Samaria is named as Delaiah.

[27] Literally "Tobiah, the servant, the Ammonite." Likely the term "servant" refers to his being a servant of the king of Persia (B. Mazar, "The Tobiads," *IEJ* 7 [1957]:144). In Nehemiah's response to their opposition in v. 20 he called himself and his colleagues the servants of the God of heaven.

[28] Blenkinsopp concludes (*Ezra-Nehemiah,* 219) that "Tobiah belonged to a distinguished Jerusalemite family with close ties to the high priesthood and the aristocracy." Documents from 'Araq el-Emir and the Zenon Papyri from 259 B.C. indicate the Tobiads were in office under Ptolemy II. They again exercized negative influence on the religion of Jerusalem just before the Maccabean period (Kidner, *Ezra and Nehemiah,* 82).

were descended from Israel." If so, their long-standing enmity against the Jewish community may have begun at that time.[29]

Earlier in the reign of Artaxerxes their complaints against Jerusalem had been accepted by the king, who decreed that the Jews stop building. So a Jew coming now as governor, with authorization to build, greatly disturbed them. Likewise, today some are disturbed when God blesses his work, but Ezra-Nehemiah reminds us we should not fear that the work of God is finally dependent upon human attitudes. We are involved in a spiritual conflict of cosmic proportions, but God's armor is available, and his victory is assured (Eph 6:10-18).[30]

4. Nehemiah Surveys the Walls (2:11-20)

(1) The Secret Inspection by Night (2:11-16)

[11]I went to Jerusalem, and after staying there three days [12]I set out during the night with a few men. I had not told anyone what my God had put in my heart to do for Jerusalem. There were no mounts with me except the one I was riding on.

[13]By night I went out through the Valley Gate toward the Jackal Well and the Dung Gate, examining the walls of Jerusalem, which had been broken down, and its gates, which had been destroyed by fire. [14]Then I moved on toward the Fountain Gate and the King's Pool, but there was not enough room for my mount to get through; [15]so I went up the valley by night, examining the wall. Finally, I turned back and reentered through the Valley Gate. [16]The officials did not know where I had gone or what I was doing, because as yet I had said nothing to the Jews or the priests or nobles or officials or any others who would be doing the work.

2:11 We are not told what Nehemiah did in these three days. He may have rested like Ezra (Ezra 8:32) and met the leaders of the Jewish community.[31] Rest also is an important part of the schedule of a servant of God. Jesus said to his disciples, "Come with me by yourselves to a quiet place and get some rest" (Mark 6:31).

2:12 Nehemiah was to prove himself to be a hard worker. But hard

---

[29] For a thorough discussion of the Tobiads, see Mazar, "The Tobiads," 137-45, 229-38.

[30] J. G. McConville (*Ezra, Nehemiah, Esther,* DSB [Philadelphia: Westminster, 1985], 82) discusses the chapter's focus on the conflict between טוֹב, "good," and רַע, "evil" (somewhat obscured in translation), especially clear in this verse. Note the alternation between the two also in vv. 1-3,5-8,17-18.

[31] Fensham suggests he rested and obtained information about the situation in Jerusalem (Fensham, *Ezra and Nehemiah*, 165).

work alone will not ensure success. It must be the right work at the right time done in the right way. That takes planning. Praying and trusting God does not mean that research is not necessary. Nehemiah wanted to assess the situation before presenting his project to the officials and the people. Specifically, Nehemiah needed to know where to rebuild the old walls and where to construct the new one. He used only one mount so as not to call attention to what he was doing. He did not want opposition before he started as in Ezra 4:12. Nehemiah's wise leadership is evident here. Some things are better not publicized before their time.

Nehemiah was to face many problems and much opposition, but his sense of divine direction would give him confidence. He was humbly aware that it was God who had entrusted the project to him and would give him the wisdom by which it would be accomplished. His mission was to restore Jerusalem to an environment pleasing to God. Ezra had begun to work, but Nehemiah was to finish rebuilding the city. The temple was the place of worship, but the city of Jerusalem was the home of the temple. The walls would serve not only as protection but would also symbolize the boundaries of religious belief. Later in chap. 8 the boundaries were reinstated by the reading of the Torah, the five books of Moses.

2:13 The "Valley Gate" is considered to have been the chief gate in the western wall overlooking the Tyropoeon Valley. A gate in this area was found in excavations.[32]

"The Jackal Well" has often been considered to be near En-rogel, but it can hardly be a site so far down the valley. Rather, it may have been a well, now unknown, on the east side of the Tyropoeon Valley and west or southwest of the wall. It also could be translated "the Dragon's Eye" and thus may refer to some other landmark.

"The Dung Gate" must have been at the southern end of the city where the Tyropoeon and Hinnom valleys meet.[33] It is usually equated with the Potsherd Gate of Jer 19:2. There has been some discussion about the extent of the city enclosed by Nehemiah's wall. The old city of Jerusalem had at first occupied only the eastern hill between the Tyropoeon Valley on the west and the Kidron Valley on the east. It had been expanded later to encompass the western hill beyond the Tyropoeon Valley, but recent studies confirm that Nehemiah's city did not include the western hill but only the eastern hill (the ancient City of David) and the temple

---

[32] B. Mazar, *The Mountain of the Lord* (Garden City: Doubleday, 1975), 167, 182, 193; Williamson, *Ezra, Nehemiah*, 188.

[33] Mazar, *Mountain of the Lord*, 194-95.

mount to the north of it.[34]

2:14 "The Fountain Gate" was on the east near the south end of the city, not too far from En-rogel, the fountain that is located some 220 meters to the south of where the Kidron and Hinnom valleys meet.

"The King's Pool" is often considered to be at or near what was later the Pool of Siloam. But if that were the case, Nehemiah would have had to go back inside the wall. More likely the pool was a type of receiving pool for the overflow of the Pool of Siloam and located outside the wall (cf. 3:15).

The debris from the destruction obstructed the valley. The houses built on the terraces on the hillside were destroyed when the walls fell. Archaeologists found much rubbish and many large stones here.[35] Nehemiah decided to build not where the former wall was located but farther up near the crest of the hill. Thus the city of Nehemiah was smaller than the preexilic city.[36]

2:15 Nehemiah was now following the Kidron Valley farther down rather than along the wall because of all the debris. Apparently Nehemiah did not make the complete circuit of the city but retraced his steps and entered the city where he had gone out.

2:16 "Officials" here must be used in a general sense to speak of all the leaders. Nehemiah was adept in communication and public relations. He knew when to keep quiet and when to present his project. "Nobles or officials" may have been the same group (cf. 13:11,17; 5:7).

(2) Nehemiah Presents the Challenge (2:17-18)

17Then I said to them, "You see the trouble we are in: Jerusalem lies in ruins, and its gates have been burned with fire. Come, let us rebuild the wall of Jerusalem, and we will no longer be in disgrace." **18**I also told them about the gracious hand of my God upon me and what the king had said to me.

They replied, "Let us start rebuilding." So they began this good work.

2:17-18 Nehemiah was able to discern the proper time to present the building project, and he knew how to motivate the leaders and the peo-

---

[34] See Y. Aharoni, et al. eds., *The Macmillan Bible Atlas*, 3d ed. (New York: Macmillan, 1993), 127-30, and Williamson, *Ezra, Nehemiah*, 188. For additional information on the geography of ancient Jerusalem, see W. H. Mare, *The Archaeology of the Jerusalem Area* (Grand Rapids: Baker, 1987); N. Avigad, *Discovering Jerusalem* (Nashville: Nelson, n.d.).

[35] K. Kenyon, *Jerusalem, Excavating 3000 Years of History* (New York: McGraw-Hill, 1967), 108.

[36] Ibid., 108-9. See also McConville, *Ezra, Nehemiah, and Esther,* 84.

ple. He used four incentives:[37] (1) He identified with the people; he
spoke of "the trouble *we* are in." (2) He stressed the seriousness of the
situation. A leader must be realistic and honestly assess the facts. People
will have confidence in such a leader. (3) Nehemiah was committed to
taking definite action. (4) He used his personal testimony of God's grace
to assure them of God's favor on the project (v. 18). A Christian leader
must encourage trust in God by leading in faith as well as in action.

If we analyze the social processes in Nehemiah, we can see that chaps.
1–2 describe the "innovation process." When Nehemiah was in Susa and
heard of the situation in Jerusalem, his anguish over the deplorable condition of God's people and his desire for God's glory resulted in a spiritual experience that gave him a new vision of what God desired for his
people in Judah. He set about to transform his vision into social reality.
Part of that task was sharing his vision with the community and motivating the people to work together to change the situation.[38]

As another sign of God's "gracious hand" at work, the leaders and
people responded to Nehemiah. He came to them with compassion, realism, conviction, and faith; thus God used him to communicate his own
vision and motivate the people to begin the "good work."

(3) Opposition by Ridicule (2:19-20)

[19]**But when Sanballat the Horonite, Tobiah the Ammonite official and
Geshem the Arab heard about it, they mocked and ridiculed us. "What is this
you are doing?" they asked. "Are you rebelling against the king?"**

[20]**I answered them by saying, "The God of heaven will give us success. We
his servants will start rebuilding, but as for you, you have no share in Jerusalem or any claim or historic right to it."**

These enemies, especially Sanballat and Tobiah, knew that Nehemiah
had credentials from the king. Thus they tried to stop the work by dis-
heartening the people who were building. They used ridicule as their
tool. The enemies even accused the Jews of rebellion, which would have

---

[37] Suggested in White, *Excellence in Leadership,* 47-48.

[38] According to K. Tollefson: "This segment of the Nehemiah account (1:1–2:20) un-
derscores the need for creative planners to communicate effectively in solving community
problems. Societies begin to change when individuals become concerned enough to probe
the problems, seek solutions, and become catalysts for change. To involve the members of
the community, such solutions must then be explained in terms of their immediate interests. Nehemiah effectively followed this innovation process" (Tollefson, "Nehemiah,
Model for Change Agents," *CSR,* XV [1986]: 110).

brought back memories of the official action against Jerusalem noted in Ezra 4:12.

When the enemies of God's work can find no legitimate basis for opposition, they may use ridicule, questioning the significance of our labors. This sometimes does more harm than even questioning one's credentials or good intentions (which Nehemiah's enemies also did) because it attacks the very impetus for action. Ridicule is especially hard to endure when the recipients are in the minority. Christians experiencing it should remember what Heb 11:38-39 says about the biblical heroes of faith: "Some faced jeers and flogging. . . . The world was not worthy of them. . . . These were all commended for their faith." Jesus also suffered ridicule and mocking on many occasions (Luke 22:63-64; 23:11), and his followers can expect to face the same kind of opposition.

Nehemiah's enemies were well informed of his activities, no doubt by friends within Jerusalem. Apparently both Sanballat and Tobiah considered themselves Yahwists, if we can judge by the names of their children; but they were syncretistic. Such a mixture of worship of Yahweh along with adherence to other gods and pagan customs really was paganism. Nehemiah would not accept their brand of syncretistic Yahwism but testified that God would prosper the Jews who served him alone. Some of the Jewish families, however, did form relationships with those of mixed allegiance, and they faced the anger of Nehemiah. Later one of Sanballat's daughters was married to a member of the Jewish high priest's family (Neh 13:28).

2:19 "Geshem" was a powerful chieftain of Qedar in northwest Arabia. He was somewhat under the control of the Persians but had great freedom to govern over a confederation of Arab tribes that included Edom and the southern part of Judah.[39]

2:20 For the sake of the workers, Nehemiah's response to this first oppositional strategy was important. His answer had three parts: (1) He did not speak of his authority or the king's but of his trust in "the God of heaven." (2) Nehemiah advised his people to ignore the ridicule and threats and simply *work*. (3) He refused to compromise. He denied his opponents a share in the work, the land, or the worship of the Jewish community (cf. Ezra 4:3).

---

[39] J. Bright, *A History of Israel*, 3d ed. (Philadelphia: Westminster), 382. Geshem's name was found on a silver vessel at Tell el-Maskhuta in Lower Egypt. Another probable reference to him was found in an inscription from Dedan in Arabia (Williamson, *Ezra, Nehemiah*, 192). See also Blenkinsopp, *Ezra-Nehemiah*, 225-27; W. J. Dumbrell, "The Tell el-Maskhuta Bowls and the 'Kingdom' of Qedar in the Persian Period," *BASOR* 203 (1971): 33-44.

In former years Sanballat and Tobiah may have had some jurisdiction over the affairs of Judah, but now Nehemiah was in charge, commissioned by the king. The "historic right" Nehemiah mentioned is the term *zikaron*, which can mean "a reminder." The word can refer to historic rights (property, participation in the community, etc.) but probably was used in the sense of a right to participate in the temple worship.[40] The Passover Feast was such a reminder (Exod 12:14), as was the Feast of Unleavened Bread (Exod 13:9).[41]

This chapter is packed with action. It depicts Nehemiah as a model leader—humble, trusting God, willing to act, carefully planning his project, and wisely sharing both his vision and faith with the leaders and the community of God's people.

5. Building for Unity: The Community Rebuilds the Wall (3:1-32)

This chapter shows Nehemiah was an outstanding organizer. Some forty-five sections of construction are mentioned, including ten gates.[42] Planning all this building activity, organizing the groups, plus arranging the infrastructure to supply materials was no small accomplishment.

Nehemiah 3:1–7:4 describes the second important social process in community change (see comments on 2:17-18), the "community development process." Tollefson notes that "Nehemiah skillfully divided the work force into some forty manageable work crews (3:1-32) organized by common interests and geography. The way Nehemiah confronted opposition both from without and from within and the way he organized the community were significant ingredients in the realization of his vision."[43]

Chapter 3 contains one of the most detailed biblical descriptions of Jerusalem. Yet many of the exact locations cannot be identified with certainty today, for archaeologists have not discovered many remains in Jerusalem from the Persian period. Of course, it is hard to find sites to excavate in a city as populated as modern Jerusalem. K. Kenyon's excavations on the eastern slope have shown that Nehemiah's wall was farther up the side of the hill than the former wall had been. The wall she uncovered was about eight feet thick.[44]

---

[40] Fensham, *Ezra and Nehemiah*, 169.

[41] *TWOT*, 242.

[42] Gates are mentioned in vv. 1,3,6,13-15, 26, 28-29,31.

[43] Tollefson, "Nehemiah, Model for Change Agents," 115.

[44] Kenyon, *Jerusalem*, 111.

The entire province of Judah was not very large. Aharoni and Avi-Yonah use the evidence from this chapter and from the places in which seal impressions from this time have been found to trace the boundaries of Judah. It reached from Jericho and Mizpah in the north to Beth-zur (just north of Hebron) and En-gedi in the south. In the northwest the province included Gezer, Lod, and extended as far as Ono, not far from Joppa.[45]

Some think this chapter was not originally written by Nehemiah because it is in third, rather than first, person. Also its point of view is post-construction; it mentions the finishing touches of gates, bolts, and doors, which according to 6:1 and 7:1 were completed later. It may have been taken from temple archives. However, it is reasonable to assume that Nehemiah included it when he wrote his memoirs. Although it appears to be a complete description of the wall, it is possible that some descriptive details have dropped out or were omitted. This is suggested by the fact that in a number of cases where a man or group is said to have built "another section" ("a second section"), no first section has been mentioned.[46]

(1) Repairing the Northern and Western Walls (3:1-15)

[1]Eliashib the high priest and his fellow priests went to work and rebuilt the Sheep Gate. They dedicated it and set its doors in place, building as far as the Tower of the Hundred, which they dedicated, and as far as the Tower of Hananel. [2]The men of Jericho built the adjoining section, and Zaccur son of Imri built next to them.

[3]The Fish Gate was rebuilt by the sons of Hassenaah. They laid its beams and put its doors and bolts and bars in place. [4]Meremoth son of Uriah, the son of Hakkoz, repaired the next section. Next to him Meshullam son of Berekiah, the son of Meshezabel, made repairs, and next to him Zadok son of Baana also made repairs. [5]The next section was repaired by the men of Tekoa, but their nobles would not put their shoulders to the work under their supervisors.

[6]The Jeshanah Gate was repaired by Joiada son of Paseah and Meshullam son of Besodeiah. They laid its beams and put its doors and bolts and bars in place. [7]Next to them, repairs were made by men from Gibeon and Mizpah—Melatiah of Gibeon and Jadon of Meronoth—places under the authority of the governor of Trans-Euphrates. [8]Uzziel son of Harhaiah, one of the goldsmiths, repaired the next section; and Hananiah, one of the perfume-makers,

---

[45] Aharoni, *Macmillan Bible Atlas,* 109.

[46] For example, where this phrase appears in vv. 11,19- 20,30 there are no antecedents, but those of vv. 21, 24,27 have their antecedents in vv. 4,18, and 5, respectively. See comments on v. 11.

made repairs next to that. They restored Jerusalem as far as the Broad Wall. [9]Rephaiah son of Hur, ruler of a half-district of Jerusalem, repaired the next section. [10]Adjoining this, Jedaiah son of Harumaph made repairs opposite his house, and Hattush son of Hashabneiah made repairs next to him. [11]Malkijah son of Harim and Hasshub son of Pahath-Moab repaired another section and the Tower of the Ovens. [12]Shallum son of Hallohesh, ruler of a half-district of Jerusalem, repaired the next section with the help of his daughters.

[13]The Valley Gate was repaired by Hanun and the residents of Zanoah. They rebuilt it and put its doors and bolts and bars in place. They also repaired five hundred yards of the wall as far as the Dung Gate.

[14]The Dung Gate was repaired by Malkijah son of Recab, ruler of the district of Beth Hakkerem. He rebuilt it and put its doors and bolts and bars in place.

[15]The Fountain Gate was repaired by Shallun son of Col-Hozeh, ruler of the district of Mizpah. He rebuilt it, roofing it over and putting its doors and bolts and bars in place. He also repaired the wall of the Pool of Siloam, by the King's Garden, as far as the steps going down from the City of David.

3:1 "Eliashib" was the grandson of Jeshua (Neh 12:10), the leader in the time of the construction of the temple. The priests, even the high priest, did not just direct others, but they themselves "went to work and rebuilt the Sheep Gate." The Sheep Gate (cf. John 5:2) was near the northeast corner of the wall and near the temple area. It probably was so named because sheep destined for sacrifice usually were brought in there to the market.

There were two towers on the north wall since this was the only side not naturally defended by a steep hill. The "Tower of Hananel" probably was the same as "the citadel by the temple" in 2:8 (cf. 7:2).[47] T. Eskenazi observes that this tower is mentioned in only two places outside Nehemiah (cf. 12:39): Jer 31:38 and Zech 14:10. The context of both these texts is the eschatological restoration of Jerusalem. Its mention in the ceremony of dedication in 12:39, "combined with the consecretation in Neh 3:1, gathers around it associations and expectations that extend beyond mere architectural information. Such clustering of associations casts the sanctification and the repair or restoration of the Tower of Hananel as the enactment of a larger theological-salvific vision."[48] Building the wall was part of the fulfillment of the word of Jeremiah (Ezra 1:1) and its completion would mean the restoration of the holy city (11:1,18), despite the in-

---

[47] D. J. A. Clines, *Ezra, Nehemiah, Esther,* NCB (Grand Rapids: Eedrmans, 1984), 151.

[48] T. Eskenazi, *In an Age of Prose* (Atlanta: Scholars Press, 1988), 86.

completeness of that restoration due to the continuing sins of the people.

When the people finished the whole wall, they had a dedication ceremony. This is the only section where a separate dedication is mentioned.[49] T. Eskenazi believes that this amounted to the high priest's dedication of the whole project and that it shows its religious significance. The walls, she argues, were regarded as an extension of the house of God.[50]

3:2 This was a cooperative effort. People from all professions and trades helped, coming from many villages and outlying areas of Judah. In some cases the names of the leaders are not mentioned.

3:3 The "Fish Gate" was near the northwest corner, probably also called the Ephraim Gate (8:16; 12:39; 2 Kgs 14:13) and the Middle Gate (Jer 39:3).[51] There probably was a fish market there at one time. It is thoght to have been near the location of the present-day Damascus Gate.

3:4 "Meremoth" was known to both Ezra and Nehemiah. "Repaired," literally "to make firm or strong," is used many times in the following verses. At times, especially in vv. 16-31, it is used even if the old wall was located at a different place and a completely new section of wall had to be built.

3:5 "Tekoa," located southeast of Bethlehem, was the home of the prophet Amos. Since it was close to the area controlled by Geshem the Arab, perhaps the nobles who "would not put their shoulders to the work" were influenced by or afraid of him. Whatever their reason, it indicates that some of the Jews did not support Nehemiah's plan.

3:6 The name "Jeshanah gate," is often understood as an abbreviated form of "the gate of the old city" or slightly emended to read "the Mishneh Gate," opening into the second (*mišneh*) district of Jerusalem on the western hill (2 Kgs 22:14; Zeph 1:10).[52] It was near the northwest corner of the walled city.

3:7 Gibeon, modern El-Jib, was about six miles northwest of Jerusalem. Originally a Canaanite city that tricked Joshua into an alliance (Josh 9–11), it was made a levitical city in Benjamin (Josh 18:25; 21:17).

---

[49] The term קִדְּשׁוּהוּ ("they dedicated it") occurs twice in the verse. Williamson (*Ezra, Nehemiah*, 195) emends the first occurrence to קֵרְשׁוּהוּ ("they boarded it").

[50] Eskenazi, *Age of Prose*, 84-85. She suggests that the wall's being viewed as an extension of the house of God explains the unusual appointing of Levites to guard the gates of the city (7:1; 13:22).

[51] Clines, *Ezra, Nehemiah, Esther*, 151. See, however, the very helpful diagram in R. W. Wood, *New Bible Atlas* (Leicester: InterVarsity, 1985), 102.

[52] Blenkinsopp, *Ezra-Nehemiah*, 234; Williamson, *Ezra, Nehemiah*, 196. The emendation involves the change of הַיְשָׁנָה to הַמִּשְׁנֶה.

"Mizpah," probably the modern Tell en-Nasbeh, was located in the territory of Benjamin (Josh 18:26) about seven and a half miles northwest of Jerusalem. It was fortified by King Asa (1 Kgs 15:22), and Gedaliah governed there after the fall of Jerusalem (2 Kgs 25:23). Meronoth was probably nearby. "Places under the authority of the governor of Trans-Euphrates," a difficult phrase to translate, is literally "to the seat of the governor of Trans-Euphrates." Fensham translates "up to the quarters of the governor of TransEuphrates," which gives the impression that the governor had a place to stay in Jerusalem.[53] Mizpah probably was the governor's residence when he visited the province.[54]

3:8 Guilds such as "goldsmiths" and "perfume-makers" have been known since ancient Sumer. The social organization also must have included many other guilds such as potters and bakers, who may have contributed to the building project by working at their trade.

"They restored Jerusalem"[55] may also be rendered, "They left out" or "abandoned [part of] Jerusalem" (the more common meaning; see NIV text note). If this is the intended meaning, it suggests that the builders left the course of the old wall at this point or that they left part of the former city outside the wall.

3:9 The word "district," *pelek*, refers to the countryside near a town or city.[56] The province of Judah was subdivided into smaller administrative areas.[57] The Persians often left the administration of these units in the hands of the local people, so some of these may have been Jews who had not gone into captivity. Whatever their background, the involvement of rulers (cf. vv. 12-19)—along with priests, merchants, and people from outlying towns—shows an amazing cooperative spirit as well as Nehemiah's administrative skill.

3:10 Naturally those with homes near the wall would have been most enthusiastic about making repairs in that area (cf. vv. 23,28-30).

3:11 "Repaired another section" also can be translated "repaired a second section," meaning that these men finished one section and then

---

[53] Fensham, *Ezra and Nehemiah*, 169. Blenkinsopp (*Ezra-Nehemiah*, 235) rejects this translation, explaining that it would require עַד־כִּסֵּא rather than לְכִסֵּא.

[54] Williamson, *Ezra, Nehemiah*, 197.

[55] The Hebrew is וַיַּעַזְבוּ.

[56] Fensham (*Ezra and Nehemiah*, 175) translates "half of the territory of Jerusalem."

[57] Blenkinsopp (*Ezra-Nehemiah*, 235-36) claims that "the province was divided into six districts and twelve subdistricts each with its principal and secondary administrative center: Jerusalem (Netophah), Beth-zur (Tekoa), Keilah (Adullam), Beth-haccherem (Zanoah), Mizpah (Gibeon), and Jericho (Senaah). Of these all but two (Netophah and Adullam) provided manpower."

worked on another. A number of men and groups are named as doing the same.[58] The ovens referred to in this verse (also 12:38) would have been either for baking bread or for firing pottery.

3:12 "Shallum," as was Rephaiah in v. 9, was ruler of part of the countryside around Jerusalem. Some understand *běnôt*, "daughters," as "small towns" and translate "he and men from small towns."[59] It is true that *běnôt* is used of "daughter" towns, but here the masculine suffix argues for the NIV translation.[60] If Shallum had no sons, his daughters would have inherited his property (Num 27:1-11). This mention of women involved in the work again demonstrates the extent of Nehemiah's support and his mobilization of the people.[61]

3:13 Zanoah" was about thirteen miles southwest of Jerusalem. The "five hundred yards" was a long sector, which may indicate much of the old wall at that point was still in good condition.[62]

3:14 "Beth Hakkerem," the capital of a district of Judah, has not been identified with certainty. It may have been at Ramat Rahel three miles south of Jerusalem near Bethlehem, about five miles west of Jerusalem at Ein Karim, or at a site yet to be identified.[63]

3:15 The "district" of Mizpah was distinct from the town and had its own ruler (see v. 19 and comments at 3:9). "The City of David" refers to the eastern hill, the original City of David, which was a small area south of the temple.

(2) The Construction of the Eastern Wall (3:16-32)

[16]**Beyond him, Nehemiah son of Azbuk, ruler of a half-district of Beth Zur, made repairs up to a point opposite the tombs of David, as far as the artificial pool and the House of the Heroes.**

[17]**Next to him, the repairs were made by the Levites under Rehum son of Bani. Beside him, Hashabiah, ruler of half the district of Keilah, carried out repairs for his district.** [18]**Next to him, the repairs were made by their countrymen under Binnui son of Henadad, ruler of the other half-district of Keilah.** [19]**Next to him, Ezer son of Jeshua, ruler of Mizpah, repaired another section, from a point facing the ascent to the armory as far as the angle.**

---

[58] See the introduction to this section and n. 36.

[59] Fensham, *Ezra and Nehemiah*, 176.

[60] See Williamson, *Ezra, Nehemiah*, 207.

[61] Clines (*Ezra, Nehemiah, Esther*, 154) believes the daughters were mentioned only because Shallum had no sons. There is no reason to think they were the only women involved in the construction.

[62] On the Valley Gate and the Dung Gate, see the comments at 2:13.

[63] See Blenkinsopp, *Ezra-Nehemiah*, 236.

²⁰Next to him, Baruch son of Zabbai zealously repaired another section, from the angle to the entrance of the house of Eliashib the high priest. ²¹Next to him, Meremoth son of Uriah, the son of Hakkoz, repaired another section, from the entrance of Eliashib's house to the end of it.

²²The repairs next to him were made by the priests from the surrounding region. ²³Beyond them, Benjamin and Hasshub made repairs in front of their house; and next to them, Azariah son of Maaseiah, the son of Ananiah, made repairs beside his house. ²⁴Next to him, Binnui son of Henadad repaired another section, from Azariah's house to the angle and the corner, ²⁵and Palal son of Uzai worked opposite the angle and the tower projecting from the upper palace near the court of the guard. Next to him, Pedaiah son of Parosh ²⁶and the temple servants living on the hill of Ophel made repairs up to a point opposite the Water Gate toward the east and the projecting tower. ²⁷Next to them, the men of Tekoa repaired another section, from the great projecting tower to the wall of Ophel.

²⁸Above the Horse Gate, the priests made repairs, each in front of his own house. ²⁹Next to them, Zadok son of Immer made repairs opposite his house. Next to him, Shemaiah son of Shecaniah, the guard at the East Gate, made repairs. ³⁰Next to him, Hananiah son of Shelemiah, and Hanun, the sixth son of Zalaph, repaired another section. Next to them, Meshullam son of Berekiah made repairs opposite his living quarters. ³¹Next to him, Malkijah, one of the goldsmiths, made repairs as far as the house of the temple servants and the merchants, opposite the Inspection Gate, and as far as the room above the corner; ³²and between the room above the corner and the Sheep Gate the goldsmiths and merchants made repairs.

The style of this section of the text is somewhat different from vv. 1-15. The most evident difference is that the landmarks are now primarily houses and other buildings instead of gates. Some scholars think they were originally two different lists; however, a better explanation is that the wall on the east side of the city did not follow the old wall but was built farther up on the crest of the hill.

3:16 Beth Zur was a town some thirteen miles south of Jerusalem and marked the southern limits of the province of Judah. The Nehemiah mentioned here is a different "Nehemiah" from the one we have been following. "The artificial[64] pool" may have been the same as the King's Pool of 2:14.

3:17-21 Hashabiah was a Levite who was ruler of his territory. The high priest's house is mentioned in v. 20. On one side of the house the Levites built the wall (vv. 17-19), and the priests built on the other side

---

[64] This is a qal passive participle from עָשָׂה ("do, make"). NKJV translates "man-made." The name distinguishes it from the Pool of Siloam.

(vv. 20-22). In 10:1-8 Baruch (3:20) and Meremoth (3:21) are listed among the priests.

As the NIV text note indicates, the Hebrew has "Bavvai" in v. 18, which is considered a scribal error for "Binnui." Verse 24 says he also restored another section. Ezer probably was ruler of the city of Mizpah as opposed to the countryside (v. 15).

It must have been a great honor for Baruch (whose name meant "blessed") to have been commended for zeal by Nehemiah (v. 20). His zeal for such "menial tasks" as building a wall for the Lord must have inspired those who worked with him.[65]

3:22-27 "The surrounding region" (v. 22) must refer to the rural area around Jerusalem.[66] The "court of the guard" (v. 25) is mentioned in Jer 32:2. "The hill of Ophel" was part of the east ridge between the City of David and the temple area (2 Chr 27:3; 33:14). It had been included in the city by Solomon.[67]

Fensham suggests that "opposite the Water Gate" refers to a turn in the wall so that it was "opposite" the Water Gate.[68] However, if the new wall was farther up the slope than the old wall, then "opposite" the gate may simply mean "up the hill" from that gate ("above" in v. 28 may be equivalent to "opposite" in v. 31). The "Water Gate" led from the palace-temple complex to the Gihon Spring (cf. 8:1,3,16; 12:37).

3:28-29 The text of 2 Chr 23:15 gives the impression that the "Horse Gate" was an entrance to the palace, but Jer 31:40 indicates it was a gate in the city wall.

"The East Gate" in v. 29 is related to "the east gate of the LORD's house" in Ezek 10:19[69] (cf. also 11:1; 40:6,10). It is thought to have been where the Golden Gate later stood.

3:30-31 There were chambers or rooms in the temple construction as indicated by Ezra 10:6 and Neh 12:44. Tobiah's family was related by marriage to Meshullam (Neh 6:18), who even gave Tobiah the use of one of these rooms (13:4-9). "The Inspection Gate" in v. 31 is sometimes translated "Muster Gate" or "Watch Gate." Blenkinsopp suggests it may

---

[65] Williamson (*Ezra, Nehemiah*, 198) thinks that הֶחֱרָה ("zealously") is a dittography from the preceding word אַחֲרָיו or a scribal gloss on the end of v. 19.

[66] The word הַכִּכָּר is used in Gen 13:10 of the lower plain of the Jordan (hence RSV "men of the Plain," but "men of the surrounding area" in NRSV). NIV translation is correct here. The term probably included priestly villages like Anathoth (Jer 1:1).

[67] Blenkinsopp, *Ezra-Nehemiah*, 240.

[68] Fensham, *Ezra and Nehemiah*, 178.

[69] The word there for "east," however, is הַקַּדְמֹנִי rather than הַמִּזְרָח, which occurs here.

have been "a designated point for assembly and review, perhaps for the temple or palace guard."[70]

Despite its mundane appearance, this chapter is more than a construction record. Although the walls and gates would serve a military purpose (cf. Neh 4), the book's concern for separation from pagan influence suggests it also had symbolic significance (cf. 13:19-22). Rather than simply providing security, the walls encouraged in the people of God a sense of identity and distinctiveness. Their restoration also represented a reversal of the humiliation of defeat and destruction suffered because of Israel's sin (cf. 2:3,17). Like the restored temple, the rebuilt walls would assure the Jews of God's redemptive presence among them.[71] For the Christian, however, the continuing demonstration of God's powerful and loving presence is the cross (Rom 5:5-11).

This chapter also contains important teachings for Christians today. One reason the work progressed was that everyone took part, from rulers and temple personnel to merchants and citizens with their families (cf. 1 Cor 12:4-13,27-30). Even the people from the villages who lived a distance from Jerusalem also helped. They felt part of the community, even though they personally received fewer direct benefits. McConville suggests that "their co-operation on the walls is one of the Old Testament's finest pictures of its ideal of Israelite brotherhood"[72] (cf. John 17:21-23; 1 Thess 1:7-8; 2 Cor 8:3-5; 9:1-2). Even their enemies were amazed at the results (notice the same in Acts 2:43-47; 4:32). In order not only to survive but also to be effective in the midst of opposition from a hostile secular culture, the church must exhibit a cooperative spirit. Another reason for the Jews' success was Nehemiah's wise delegation of labor. He knew how to choose leaders and to delegate authority (cf. 2 Tim 2:2). Also, many built the part nearest their own house. A leader must take into account family and incentive factors in planning and delegating responsibilities (cf. Eph 4:11-13).

6. Opposition to Building the Wall (4:1-23)

(1) Opposition by Ridicule (4:1-6)

¹When Sanballat heard that we were rebuilding the wall, he became angry and was greatly incensed. He ridiculed the Jews, ²and in the presence of his

---

[70] Blenkinsopp, *Ezra-Nehemiah*, 239.

[71] McConville (*Ezra, Nehemiah, and Esther,* 88) explains that "the Lord was giving his people a badge, a further token—alongside the Temple—that they *were* his people."

[72] Ibid., 89.

associates and the army of Samaria, he said, "What are those feeble Jews doing? Will they restore their wall? Will they offer sacrifices? Will they finish in a day? Can they bring the stones back to life from those heaps of rubble—burned as they are?"

³Tobiah the Ammonite, who was at his side, said, "What they are building—if even a fox climbed up on it, he would break down their wall of stones!"

⁴Hear us, O our God, for we are despised. Turn their insults back on their own heads. Give them over as plunder in a land of captivity. ⁵Do not cover up their guilt or blot out their sins from your sight, for they have thrown insults in the face of the builders.

⁶So we rebuilt the wall till all of it reached half its height, for the people worked with all their heart.

The real test of a leader is how he or she faces crises and reacts to opposition. This chapter recounts several forms of opposition and how Nehemiah confronted them. In Nehemiah we have a prime example of a dedicated, faithful, wise, and energetic leader.

Progress in building is given in stages in response to opposition. Despite ridicule, half the construction was completed (4:1-6; in the Hebrew Bible this section is 3:33-38, and chap. 4 begins with our 4:7). Then, despite plots from enemies causing discouragement and fear, the work continued (4:7-23). Overcoming internal economic obstacles (5:1-19), the wall was finished except for the gates (6:1). Finally, the entire task was completed (6:15) despite trickery (6:1-9) and intimidation (6:10-14).

4:1 Sanballat knew that a restored Jerusalem would lessen his influence in the area. Thus he was greatly angered[73] and intent on discouraging Nehemiah's project, even though he knew that it had the approval of the Persian court. Anger will often be the world's response to God's work because it challenges worldviews and values. Much of the opposition to the project consisted of psychological warfare. The first opposition came in the form of ridicule, often sufficient to stifle the spirit and work of anyone.[74]

4:2 Sanballat began the campaign of ridicule, encouraging his colleagues to follow his example. He used rhetorical questions designed to drive home the opposition. The first one took advantage of a "truth"

---

[73] The two verbs used to describe Sanballat's response, חרה ("become hot") and כעס ("be angry"), are synonyms. Especially used together with the adverbial infinitive absolute הַרְבֵּה ("greatly") they emphasize the intensity of his anger.

[74] On the nature of intimidation, see White, *Excellence in Leadership,* 69.

about which the Jews were sensitive, "those feeble Jews." They knew they were not strong or numerous. The job was more than they should have undertaken. Then Sanballat asked, "Will they restore their wall?"[75] He wanted to instill doubts about the wisdom of the project. They were fools, he chided, wasting effort on a hopeless project. The third rhetorical question, "Will they offer sacrifices?" ridiculed their "pretended" trust in God. Did they think prayer and sacrifice could make the wall grow?

His final question, "Can they bring the stones back to life . . . burned as they are?" used some wrong information to discourage the builders. Most of the stones were still in good condition. They had not all disintegrated from the fire as he suggested. Psychological warfare can use truths to which people are sensitive or half-truths or falsehoods to intimidate the enemy.

4:3 Tobiah echoed Sanballat's first argument and exaggerated it. The wall, he claimed, was so weak that even a small animal would knock it down. This of course was not at all true, for archaeological excavations found Nehemiah's wall to be about nine feet thick.[76]

4:4-5 The first thing Nehemiah did was to turn to God in prayer. God's people should always regard prayer not as a last resort but as our primary weapon against opposition.

Nehemiah's prayer has much in common with imprecations in the Psalms[77] and in Jeremiah (11:18-20; 15:15; 17:18; 18:19-23).[78] Such requests seem at odds with the teaching of Christ on loving our enemies. A number of points in response to this issue should be made: (1) Nehemiah's request, like imprecations elsewhere, was for divine judgment against sin, a clear teaching in Scripture. The prayer in v. 5 for God not to cover their enemies' guilt was not a prayer against their salvation but

---

[75] The question is difficult to translate. The NIV and many others take for granted the meaning of הַיְעַזְבוּ as "restore" or "repair" (see *TWOT* 2:659).

[76] Kenyon, *Jerusalem*, 111.

[77] See Pss 5:10; 28:4-5; 31:17-18; 35:4-8; 58:6-11; 59:5,11-13; 69:22-28; 79:6-7,12; 83:9-18; 109:6-15; 137:7-9; 139:19-22; 140:9-11. On the imprecations in Psalms, see W. A. VanGemeren, "Psalms," EBC, ed. F. E. Gaebelein (Grand Rapids: Zondervan, 1991), 5:830-32; J. C. Laney, "A Fresh Look at the Imprecatory Psalms," *BSac* 138 (1981): 35-45; C. Martin, "The Imprecations in the Psalms," in *Classical Essays in Old Testament Interpretation*, ed. W. C. Kaiser Jr., 113-32 (Grand Rapids: Baker, 1972); J. G. Vos, "The Ethical Problems of the Imprecatory Psalms," *WTJ* 4 (1942): 123-38.

[78] There is a striking similarity between Neh 4:5 [Heb 3:37] and Jer 18:23:

Neh 4:5 [3:37]: וְאַל־תְּכַס עַל־עֲוֺנָם וְחַטָּאתָם מִלְּפָנֶיךָ אַל־תִּמָּחֶה

"Do not cover up their guilt or blot out their sins from your sight,"

Jer 18:23: אַל־תְּכַפֵּר עַל־עֲוֺנָם וְחַטָּאתָם מִלְּפָנֶיךָ אַל־תֶּמְחִי

"Do not forgive their crimes or blot out their sins from your sight."

for divine justice. (2) It was a prayer for God to act, not for permission to take personal vengeance (cf. Rom 12:19-21). (3) It expressed zeal for God's work and God's honor. Nehemiah had no doubts that the building of the wall was God's doing, so opposition to it was opposition to God. (4) It may have had a rhetorical function to encourage confidence before opposition. D. Kidner explains that in the Old Testament imprecations, "horror may be piled on horror more to express the speaker's sense of outrage than to spell out the penalties he literally intends"[79] (cf. Jer 20:15-17).

Christians are under the new covenant and are admonished to love our enemies and to make it our primary concern to lead a wicked world to faith and forgiveness through the message of the cross. Nevertheless, God's people can ask him to judge injustice and to thwart the plans of those who would hinder God's work.

In his use of the first person ("we are despised" in v. 4; "we rebuilt the wall" in v. 6; "we prayed . . . and posted a guard" in v. 9; "we all returned to the wall" in v. 15; "we continued the work" in v. 21), Nehemiah showed his identification with the people; he faced the same dangers and sacrifices and confronted the same tests of faith as everyone else. Nehemiah could have shut himself up in the governor's quarters and let others solve the problems. But "by remaining close to those he would lead, Nehemiah preserved their confidence and spirit in the face of opposition."[80]

4:6 "So we rebuilt the wall" is a commendation of God's faithfulness in response to prayer and of the people's courage and determination. The people continued steadfastly toward the goal even in the face of ridicule. The faith, unity, and energy of the small group prevailed. In the face of ridicule today, the same faith and energetic work toward a clear objective will have the same results.

(2) Opposition by Plot (4:7-9)

⁷But when Sanballat, Tobiah, the Arabs, the Ammonites and the men of Ashdod heard that the repairs to Jerusalem's walls had gone ahead and that the gaps were being closed, they were very angry. ⁸They all plotted together to come and fight against Jerusalem and stir up trouble against it. ⁹But we prayed to our God and posted a guard day and night to meet this threat.

4:7 When Sanballat and his friends realized that their ridicule was

---

[79] D. Kidner, *Psalms 1–72* (London: InterVarsity Press, 1973), 27.

[80] Tollefson, "Nehemiah, Model for Change Agents," 112.

not successful in stopping the work on the wall, their anger increased, and their plans escalated.

Sanballat had succeeded in enlisting others in his malevalent alliance. Jerusalem was now surrounded by enemies: the Samaritans on the north, the Ammonites on the east, the Arabians on the south, and the men of Ashdod on the west. Since the time of the Assyrian conquest of Palestine, the Philistine territory had been a separate province and was called Ashdod.

4:8 How serious Sanballat's supporters were about actually fighting is not clear; they could have destroyed all the people and sent an excuse to the king that Jerusalem was rebelling. (They would have had the precedent of Ezra 4:19-22, where Artaxerxes had issued a command to stop building.) This must be what is meant by "stir up trouble against it."[81] Their only hope was to do something quickly and completely, thus avoiding Persian reprisal. Or they could have influenced the Persian king to make another decree similar to Ezra 4:22. The Jews also remembered that occasion; so the whole plot would have made them think that continuing the building was useless.

4:9 Nehemiah's response was clear: prayer and precaution, trust and good management. He trusted God, but he also was aware of the dangers and took the necessary precautions. To be sure, the dangers were real. As the following verses indicate, the enemies could attack at any moment.

(3) Internal Opposition: Discouragement and Fear (4:10-15)

[10]**Meanwhile, the people in Judah said, "The strength of the laborers is giving out, and there is so much rubble that we cannot rebuild the wall."**

[11]**Also our enemies said, "Before they know it or see us, we will be right there among them and will kill them and put an end to the work."**

[12]**Then the Jews who lived near them came and told us ten times over, "Wherever you turn, they will attack us."**

[13]**Therefore I stationed some of the people behind the lowest points of the wall at the exposed places, posting them by families, with their swords, spears and bows.** [14]**After I looked things over, I stood up and said to the nobles, the officials and the rest of the people, "Don't be afraid of them. Remember the LORD, who is great and awesome, and fight for your brothers, your sons and your daughters, your wives and your homes."**

[15]**When our enemies heard that we were aware of their plot and that God had frustrated it, we all returned to the wall, each to his own work.**

---

[81] "Against it" is problematic in the Hebrew text because of the masculine suffix, which should be feminine to refer to Jerusalem (לוֹ). Some emend the text to "against me" or "against us." In any case the meaning of the phrase is clear.

4:10 Internal problems can be more serious than those from the outside. The people were becoming discouraged. The people's saying is in poetic form in the Hebrew text, which Myers attempts to reproduce:[82]

> The strength of the burden bearer is drooping,
> The rubbish heap so vast;
> And we are unable by ourselves
> To rebuild the wall.

We can imagine the people singing this lament as they worked on the wall.[83] In addition to building, they had to remove mounds of rubbish from the old destruction.

4:11 The rumors of impending surprise attack added to the discouragement caused by the natural hardships. Of course, that is what the enemies intended. External pressure amplifies internal weakness.

4:12 "The Jews who lived near them" must refer to those who lived in villages that bordered on the territories of the enemies. What they told the workers may be rendered literally, "From all the places where you turn against us." The difficulties of this text have led to several different translations, some involving emendation.[84] Apparently the enemies were spreading rumors of attack to dishearten the people (cf. Josephus, *Ant.* 11.175). "Ten times over" would suggest that these enemies constantly reiterated the rumors so the people in the villages would pass them on to their friends in Jerusalem.

4:13 Nehemiah took definite action. He had to sacrifice some labor from building the wall, but the precaution was necessary. Grouping them according to families would strengthen the motivation to fight (see v. 14).

---

[82] J. Myers, *Ezra-Nehemiah*, AB (Garden City: Doubleday, 1965), 122.

[83] McConville (*Ezra, Nehemiah, and Esther*, 91) believes it is "a kind of chorus chanted during the work. Despite its rather negative tone it may actually have had the function of keeping the men going—not unlike the 'spirituals' which encouraged enslaved labourers of more recent times." He thinks this view of the verse makes more sense in view of v. 6, where Nehemiah testified that the people "worked with all their heart."

[84] The LXX has Ἀναβαίνουσιν ἐκ πάντων τῶν τόπων ἐφ᾽ ἡμᾶς, "They are coming against us from all sides." W. Rudolph (*BHS*) emends to read "all the plots [changing מִכָּל־הַמְּקֹמוֹת to כָּל־הַמְּזִמּוֹת] they have devised [תָּשׁוּבוּ to חָשְׁבוּ] against us." NRSV has, "From all the places where they live [reading יֵשְׁבוּ rather than תָּשׁוּבוּ] they will come up against us." Fensham (*Ezra and Nehemiah*, 183) translates, "From everywhere they are coming against us." Williamson (*Ezra, Nehemiah*, 220) translates the verse, "When the Jews who lived near them came and said to us time and again from all sides, 'You must return to us.'" Thus he insists the verse is a subordinate clause with the independent clause following in the next verse. Concerned relatives and people in the outlying villages were imploring those in Jerusalem to abandon the city and return to the villages (p. 226).

4:14 Nehemiah called the people together (see also v. 15), which had the effect of showing their strength and giving Nehemiah an opportunity to encourage them by emphasizing God's great delivering power and by appealing to the defense of their families.[85] The language of Nehemiah ("Don't be afraid") is reminiscent of words of reassurance and victory from other leaders in Scripture (cf. Exod 14:13; Num 14:9; Deut 20:3; 31:6; Josh 10:25).

4:15 Verse 15 shows the results of Nehemiah's prayer and action. When the enemies realized they could not surprise the Jews, their plot withered away because "God had frustrated it." Again, Nehemiah gave God the credit. God used Nehemiah's faith and leadership, but it was God who brought success (Phil 2:13). So they "all returned to the wall." It was necessary to sacrifice some time and effort to confront the crisis, but Nehemiah never took his eyes off the goal.

(4) Diligence and Readiness in the Work (4:16-23)

[16]**From that day on, half of my men did the work, while the other half were equipped with spears, shields, bows and armor. The officers posted themselves behind all the people of Judah** [17]**who were building the wall. Those who carried materials did their work with one hand and held a weapon in the other,** [18]**and each of the builders wore his sword at his side as he worked. But the man who sounded the trumpet stayed with me.**

[19]**Then I said to the nobles, the officials and the rest of the people, "The work is extensive and spread out, and we are widely separated from each other along the wall.** [20]**Wherever you hear the sound of the trumpet, join us there. Our God will fight for us!"**

[21]**So we continued the work with half the men holding spears, from the first light of dawn till the stars came out.** [22]**At that time I also said to the people, "Have every man and his helper stay inside Jerusalem at night, so they can serve us as guards by night and workmen by day."** [23]**Neither I nor my brothers nor my men nor the guards with me took off our clothes; each had his weapon, even when he went for water.**

4:16 The arrangements described in the following verses apply to all of the remaining work on the wall. Nehemiah had a deep trust in God; but at the same time, he was careful to take all of the precautions the situation required.

"My men" is literally "my youths" or "my servants" (cf. NRSV). The term must refer to a special group of helpers or a bodyguard (cf. 5:10,16;

---

[85] Blenkinsopp, *Ezra-Nehemiah*, 249-50.

13:19). These helpers apparently had more armor than the average worker. "The officers" posted behind the builders may have represented Nehemiah's armed men or another defense force. Blenkinsopp thinks it was "the other half" who were "posted" there, and that the term translated "the officers" was accidentally added to the text.[86]

4:17-20 Those who carried materials could carry a weapon in one hand, but those who were building needed both hands free, so they carried a sword at their side. Verse 20 suggests that besides Nehemiah's trumpet bearer there were others with trumpets at different places along the wall. In Nehemiah's assurance that "our God will fight for us," he was surely thinking of earlier occasions when God fought for Israel (cf. Deut 1:30; 3:22; 20:4; 2 Chr 32:8).

4:21-23 These verses show the exemplary dedication and diligence with which the people worked. "Till the stars came out" came to be used in rabbinic literature to designate a specific time in the evening.

Nehemiah and his group of personal helpers set an example for the whole community. As the NIV note indicates, the last phrase, "even when he went for water," is difficult in the Hebrew. Literally it says, "A man his weapon the water." But the intent of the verse is clear: each one kept himself in constant readiness.

7. Oppression within the Community (5:1-19)

(1) Extortion by the Rich (5:1-5)

¹Now the men and their wives raised a great outcry against their Jewish brothers. ²Some were saying, "We and our sons and daughters are numerous; in order for us to eat and stay alive, we must get grain."

³Others were saying, "We are mortgaging our fields, our vineyards and our homes to get grain during the famine."

⁴Still others were saying, "We have had to borrow money to pay the king's tax on our fields and vineyards. ⁵Although we are of the same flesh and blood as our countrymen and though our sons are as good as theirs, yet we have to subject our sons and daughters to slavery. Some of our daughters have already been enslaved, but we are powerless, because our fields and our vineyards belong to others."

In chap. 4 and again in chap. 6 Nehemiah faced external opposition. In chap. 5 he had to deal with internal difficulties. The inequality and injus-

---

[86] He suggests dittography because of the similarity of וְהַשֹּׁרִים ("the officers") and the previous word וְהַשִּׁרְיֹנִים ("and armor").

tice that transpired during the building of the wall developed over a period of time. But the wall building and external opposition put more strain
on the economic substructure of the community. The culmination of
these problems may have occurred shortly before the wall was finished in
August-September.[87] This would have been near the end of the harvest,
and the creditors would have required payment of capital and interest on
loans. According to 4:22, Nehemiah had asked the workers to stay in
Jerusalem and not return to their villages. This must have caused a short-
age of workers for the harvest. The extra labor on the wall no doubt affected the efficiency of the harvest and the income many families
normally would have received from working in the harvest. In short, the
economic situation was more critical because the people dedicated so
much labor to the wall. The completion of the wall was necessary to fulfill both the word and the will of God. In the midst of the building, however, power became a threat as the "nobles and officials" (v. 7) began to
oppress the people in a variety of ways.

5:1   Husbands and wives worked together, and both had a right to be
heard. The extra manpower needed on the wall may have meant that
more women had to help in the harvest.

The same word "outcry" also describes the complaint of the Israelites
under Egyptian oppression in Exod 3:9. One of the most damaging evils
inherent in the human race since the fall is exploitation (oppression) by
one's fellow human beings. The great cry throughout the world in our
time is for justice. The complaint here was not against Nehemiah but
against "their Jewish brothers." The text says literally "their brothers, the
Jews." Although the term "Jews" is usually used in a general sense, it can
also refer to a more select group, as here (cf. 2:16; 5:17). Blenkinsopp
defines its meaning here as "a privileged stratum of the population, most
probably the more affluent of those who had returned from the Babylonian diaspora."[88]

5:2   There are several different groups or situations represented in
vv. 2-4. First, in v. 2 are the wage earners whose families were becoming

---

[87] See the discussion in Yamauchi, *Persia and the Bible;* Williamson, *Ezra, Nehemiah,*
236; Clines, *Ezra, Nehemiah, Esther,* 165-66. Some observe, however, that there is no explicit statement in the text that this crisis arose while the wall was being built. There was
certainly conflict during the building of the wall. Nevertheless, it may have been later that
it reached the climax recounted here. Nehemiah may have described it at this point in the
account in order to qualify the impression of chaps. 3-4 that the people were experiencing
total unity. See McConville, *Ezra, Nehemiah, and Esther,* 96-97; Blenkinsopp, *Ezra-Nehemiah,* 255-56.

[88] Blenkinsopp, *Ezra-Nehemiah,* 256.

destitute. The economic crisis was especially difficult for large families. During the months they were working on the wall, they could not produce enough grain; therefore they had to buy it even though they were poor. Little money buys little grain. This whole episode in Nehemiah teaches us that we cannot ignore the needs of people, even when involved in a special project. The conditions here are similar to those described in Mal 3:5-15.

5:3-4 The second group in trouble consisted of landowners. In order to get loans to buy grain, they had to mortgage their property. Others had to borrow money to pay the taxes on their property. The Babylonians had taxed real estate, and the Persians continued the same practice. Darius had instituted a tax on the past harvest plus the present yield. In the time of Artaxerxes taxation was heavy throughout the Persian Empire; many landowners fell into the hands of "loan sharks" who made enormous profits. Heavy taxation is a form of socioeconomic oppression (cf. Prov 22:7). Sometimes the charge was as much as 40 percent interest instead of the normal 20 percent.[89] The result was a form of slavery (cf. Neh 9:37).

5:5 At times a family was forced to resort to debt slavery. This practice was common in the ancient Near East, and in the laws of the Pentateuch it was controlled but not prohibited (Exod 21:1-11). The son or daughter had to work for the creditor until the debt was paid (cf. 2 Kgs 4:1). In many cases the daughter was taken as wife by the creditor or for one of his sons. The law of the Sabbatical Year required that debt slaves be released in the seventh year (Lev 25:39-43).

One of the curses for disobedience to God was that the people's sons and daughters would be given "to another nation," and they would be "powerless to lift a hand" (Deut 28:32); but here it was happening between those of the same Jewish community (cf. 2 Chr 28:10-11). Although a cooperative spirit was one of the characteristics of the restoration community as observed in chap. 3, it did not characterize ev-

---

[89] A. T. Olmstead, *History of the Persian Empire* (Chicago: University Press, 1948), 297-99. Although the Persian kings were quite benevolent to their subject peoples in regard to religion, they were more severe in regard to taxes. These taxes gave the Persian rulers enormous wealth. When Alexander conquered Susa, he found there some 270 tons of gold and twelve hundred tons of silver. The political elite and large economic establishments, such as the Murashu firm, profited from the situation; but small landowners did not. The interest rates were high; they rose from 20 percent in the time of Cyrus and Cambyses to 40 or 50 percent at the end of the fifth century B.C. Documents from Babylon confirm that even there some landowners had to mortgage their property in order to pay their taxes. Many times it meant they became hired laborers rather than landowners.

eryone in the community, especially as the work continued. There will always be some ready to capitalize on the misfortune of others. That is why Nehemiah was so disturbed and why we should be concerned about injustice within the Christian community. Sometimes members of the Christian community are insensitive to the needs (material or educational, for example) of other members of the same community.

(2) Nehemiah Rebukes the Creditors (5:6-11)

⁶When I heard their outcry and these charges, I was very angry. ⁷I pondered them in my mind and then accused the nobles and officials. I told them, "You are exacting usury from your own countrymen!" So I called together a large meeting to deal with them ⁸and said: "As far as possible, we have bought back our Jewish brothers who were sold to the Gentiles. Now you are selling your brothers, only for them to be sold back to us!" They kept quiet, because they could find nothing to say.

⁹So I continued, "What you are doing is not right. Shouldn't you walk in the fear of our God to avoid the reproach of our Gentile enemies? ¹⁰I and my brothers and my men are also lending the people money and grain. But let the exacting of usury stop! ¹¹Give back to them immediately their fields, vineyards, olive groves and houses, and also the usury you are charging them— the hundredth part of the money, grain, new wine and oil."

5:6 Nehemiah was angry (cf. Mark 3:5) because the behavior was wrong and because he realized the danger of the community's slipping into serious inequality and upsetting the economic infrastructure. Also, the harmony among fellow members of the community was breaking down. Action had to be taken before this ruined the community.[90]

5:7 Nehemiah again served as an example of one who considers things carefully before acting.[91] He was facing a conflict between social classes, which he solved on the basis of principles taught in the Pentateuch, especially the sense of community equality and the importance of the covenant. E. A. Martens points out that the covenant formula (e.g., Lev 26:12, "I will walk among you and be your God, and you will be my people") "envisages a people; not an individual, but a community."[92] Individuals, while important, were expected to act for the benefit of the group. McConville observes that the Book of Deuteronomy characteristi-

---

[90] See Fensham, *Ezra and Nehemiah,* 193.

[91] "I pondered them in my mind" is literally "my heart took counsel upon me." It may also be translated "I considered carefully." See BDB, 576.

[92] E. A. Martens, *God's Design: A Focus on Old Testament Theology* (Grand Rapids: Baker, 1981), 66.

cally refers to fellow Israelites as "brothers" (*ʾāḥîm*) "regardless of social status or tribal divisions." This included kings and priests (e.g., Deut 1:16; 3:12-20; 10:9; 15:3-11; 17:15; 18:2). This, together with the "tendency to speak of Israel as a single whole," had a "levelling function in Israel."[93] This relationship of a unified people bound to God by covenant meant, according to Tollefson, that "relations between Jews should never be treated purely as business transactions, but rather as spiritual service that is pleasing to God and blessed by Him."[94] That such is also the case in the church is suggested by 1 Cor 6:1-11.

Tollefson's sociological reading of Nehemiah reveals a model for conflict resolution: (1) "Separate the people from the problem." Instead of seeing the problem as a class conflict, Nehemiah treated it as a community problem (v. 8). (2) "Focus on interests, not positions." Nehemiah showed the rich that their actions were hurting the whole community (v. 9). (3) "Generate a variety of possibilities before deciding what to do." Nehemiah proposed a solution that benefited the whole community (vv. 10-12). (4) "Insist that the results be based on some objective standard, tradition, or authority." Nehemiah based his solution on biblical principles (v. 13).[95]

"Then [they] accused the nobles and officials." It always takes courage to oppose the influential members of a community, but leaders whose allegiance is to God cannot fail to do so when necessary (cf. Prov 14:20-21; Luke 14:12-14; 1 Thess 2:4; Jas 2:1-9). Nehemiah needed the support of these important people. It is a tribute to his leadership that he confronted them despite the serious consequences that could have resulted.

The charge was "exacting usury." This phrase employs a verb (*nāšāʾ* or *nāšâ*) and a noun (*maššāʾ*) of the same root. The meaning varies with context, and even then it is disputed. The term can refer to making loans as in v. 10 (cf. Deut 24:10). It can also refer to loaning at interest (Exod 22:25), a practice that was forbidden to a fellow Israelite since it would mean profiting from the misfortune of one's brother (Deut 23:19). The verb phrase "exacting usury" in Neh 5:7, however, and the noun *maššāʾ* in v. 10, translated "exacting of usury," may refer in this context not just to lending or lending at interest but to lending against a pledge (Deut 24:10).[96] Taking pledges to assure repayment was allowed in the law but

---

[93] J. G. McConville, *Law and Theology in Deuteronomy* (Sheffield: JSOT Press, 1984), 19.

[94] Tollefson, "Nehemiah, Model for Change Agents," 113.

[95] Ibid.

was regulated. One could not accept a millstone as collateral since that was a necessary tool for a family's daily bread (Deut 24:6). Nor could a creditor enter a borrower's house to seize anything in pledge (Deut 24:10-11) nor keep a cloak as pledge overnight, thus depriving one of protection from the cold (Exod 22:26-27; Deut 24:12-13). The principle involved in these rules, which Nehemiah was applying, is the importance of generosity and kindness toward those in need.[97] This certainly would have been contrary to the practice of seizing persons or property for failure to repay.

5:8 It is not clear whether "our Jewish brothers who were sold to the Gentiles" refers to the experience in Babylon and Persia or to debt slavery in the hands of neighboring peoples. The latter probably is the case. Apparently the returned exiles had made a special effort to redeem their fellow Jews who had been in debt slavery to the surrounding people. Nehemiah was incensed that now the rich Jewish landowners were not only causing them to go back into debt slavery but also selling them as slaves to others (cf. Ezek 27:13; Joel 3:3-8; Amos 1:9).[98] One's "legal rights" can cause oppression and be morally wrong in God's sight. Often Christians do not realize how serious and sinful "indirect" oppression can be.

5:9 Nehemiah's statement, "What you are doing is not right," is an example of how a leader can assume the role of a moral teacher. The "officials and nobles" (v. 7) had done wrong, and Nehemiah confronted them with the truth, not with what was pleasing to them. The primary problem was that what was happening would obstruct their ultimate mission to the Gentiles. To "walk in the fear of our God" is a concept taken from the wisdom literature of the Old Testament (e.g., Proverbs, Job) and means "to live in awe of and devotion to God and with kindness and integrity toward men" (cf. Deut 10:12; 2 Chr 6:31; Lev 25:36; Neh 7:2). Such a life-style would be a witness to the Gentiles and would fulfill the election of Israel (Gen 12:1-3; Isa 42:6-9).

5:10 "My brothers" must have been a separate group from "my men." Nehemiah seems to have belonged to a wealthy family. He had also been lending money and grain. Whatever is meant by the terminolo-

---

[96] Clines, *Ezra, Nehemiah, Esther*, 168-69; Williamson, *Ezra, Nehemiah*, 233; McConville, *Ezra, Nehemiah, and Esther*, 98. Blenkinsopp (*Ezra-Nehemiah*, 259) says they were "acting the part of the *nōśeh*, the seizer of persons and property pledged against nonpayment of debt."

[97] P. C. Craigie, *The Book of Deuteronomy*, NICOT (Grand Rapids: Eerdmans, 1976), 306-309. Williamson (*Ezra, Nehemiah*, 233) suggests that the practice facing Nehemiah may have been more inappropriate than illegal.

[98] Blenkinsopp, *Ezra-Nehemiah*, 259.

gy (see on v. 7), we might assume that Nehemiah had been acting in accordance with the Law. This would mean he was not charging interest, although he may have been loaning against a pledge. However, he realized that the situation now required giving, not lending. Sometimes one can help others by lending, but at other times even that is not enough; we must be willing to give unselfishly (cf. Deut 15:7-18).

5:11 The main question in interpreting vv. 10-11 is whether Nehemiah was asking that all loans be forgiven[99] or that pledges and interest be returned. Clines thinks Nehemiah was only asking pledges to be returned. He favors emending *mĕʾat,* "the hundredth part" (usually interpreted as a reference to interest), to *maššaʾt,* "pledge of."[100] Presumably "the hundredth part" would mean 1 percent per month or 12 percent annually. However, the normal interest in the Persian Empire was much higher. At Elephantine it could be as high as 60 to 75 percent.[101] Therefore the phrase may simply mean "interest"; they were to waive interest and to give back all they had charged in money or in kind.[102] Kidner perfers to understand it as "the income derived by the creditors from the property they have taken in pledge (cf. NEB)."[103] It is clear at least that Nehemiah was enjoining property and proceeds (and certainly persons, although they are not mentioned) to be returned. In times of crisis or at any time the well-being of the community of faith is more important than the comfort and security of the affluent; they must be willing to sacrifice (cf. Prov 22:16).

(3) The Offenders Accept the Exhortation (5:12-13)

[12]"We will give it back," they said. "And we will not demand anything more from them. We will do as you say."

Then I summoned the priests and made the nobles and officials take an oath to do what they had promised. [13]I also shook out the folds of my robe and said, "In this way may God shake out of his house and possessions every man who does not keep this promise. So may such a man be shaken out and emptied!"

At this the whole assembly said, "Amen," and praised the LORD. And the people did as they had promised.

---

[99] Fensham, *Ezra and Nehemiah,* 195.

[100] Clines, *Ezra, Nehemiah, Esther,* 169.

[101] Blenkinsopp, *Ezra-Nehemiah,* 257.

[102] Williamson, *Ezra, Nehemiah,* 240-41.

[103] Kidner, *Ezra and Nehemiah,* 97.

5:12 The nobles and officials accepted Nehemiah's challenge and promised to pay back the interest and collateral they had taken. Here Nehemiah's humility and sense of social responsibility were crucial in solving long-term social-economic problems that surfaced under the added stress of building the wall. These leaders were willing to work together, even at great personal cost.

Nehemiah knew that promises made under emotional pressure are not always kept. As Clines says, "Nehemiah was not prepared to trust the moneylenders further than he could see them."[104] Nehemiah called the priests and had the men take an oath "to do what they promised." The priests normally administered oaths (Num 5:19). Nehemiah had proceeded wisely. First he called a large assembly (v. 7) to deal with the problems, for a problem that affects the public should involve the public in its solution. Then after these leaders promised to rectify the situation, Nehemiah took measures to assure that they would do it.

5:13 "Shook out the folds of my robe" was a symbolic act to announce effectively the curse on those who disobeyed, that God would take away their houses and possessions. The unselfish leadership and courageous action of Nehemiah bore fruit: not only did the offenders do as they had promised, but they also restored unity and praised the Lord.

(4) Nehemiah's Unselfish Leadership (5:14-19)

[14]**Moreover, from the twentieth year of King Artaxerxes, when I was appointed to be their governor in the land of Judah, until his thirty-second year—twelve years—neither I nor my brothers ate the food allotted to the governor. [15]But the earlier governors—those preceding me—placed a heavy burden on the people and took forty shekels of silver from them in addition to food and wine. Their assistants also lorded it over the people. But out of reverence for God I did not act like that. [16]Instead, I devoted myself to the work on this wall. All my men were assembled there for the work; we did not acquire any land.**

[17]**Furthermore, a hundred and fifty Jews and officials ate at my table, as well as those who came to us from the surrounding nations. [18]Each day one ox, six choice sheep and some poultry were prepared for me, and every ten days an abundant supply of wine of all kinds. In spite of all this, I never demanded the food allotted to the governor, because the demands were heavy on these people.**

[19]**Remember me with favor, O my God, for all I have done for these people.**

---

[104] Clines, *Ezra, Nehemiah, Esther*, 170.

This paragraph describes Nehemiah's style of leadership during the time he was governor in Jerusalem, not just the short period during the building of the wall. Verses 1-13 describe a crisis during the building project; later Nehemiah added this section, which covers a longer period. Blenkinsopp observes that the reference to "this wall" in v. 16 suggests this was written in Jerusalem. If so, it was written after his return from Babylon recounted in 13:6-7.[105]

5:14 The specific detail that Nehemiah had been appointed governor by Artaxerxes has not been mentioned before. The dialogue with King Artaxerxes in Neh 2 does not lead us to expect that Nehemiah would be in Jerusalem twelve years (445-433 B.C.). It is possible that he returned to Susa after a year or so and then was reappointed for a longer time. Or his appointment as governor may have been made after he was in Jerusalem.

The governor, under Persian policy, had the right to receive taxes from the people to support his own household, servants, and diplomatic expenses. But Nehemiah did not use this prerogative; he forfeited his "rights" in order to help the people (cf. 1 Cor 9).

5:15-16 Who were the "governors" who preceded Nehemiah? Some commentators since Alt (1934) and Rudolph (1949) have argued that they were officials from Samaria who had charge of Judah before Nehemiah arrived. However, it is not likely he would refer to these as "early governors–those preceding me." Besides, a number of discoveries have confirmed that there had been governors of Judah since the beginning of the Persian Empire. Therefore these were the former governors of the province of Judah since the time of the first return from exile.[106]

The term "assistants" translates the same word (*na'ar*) that is translated "men" in vv. 10 and 16. They were officials who owed personal allegiance to the governor. The other governors' assistants used their position to enhance their own power and "lorded it over the people." But Nehemiah and "all [his] men" dedicated themselves to work on the wall with all the people instead of looking for personal gain. The land Nehemiah refers to is that which governors could accumulate from people's failure to pay taxes or to repay debts.

5:17 Nehemiah was supporting the officials and employees of the government as well as Jews who migrated to Judah. As governor Ne-

---

[105] Blenkinsopp, *Ezra-Nehemiah*, 264.

[106] Ibid. Blenkinsopp thinks Judah may have been under Samarian control temporarily from the time of Rehum and Shimshai's complaint (Ezra 4:8-16) to the appointment of Nehemiah as governor. See also the Introduction, 22-23.

hemiah had to take care of them until they could be settled in Judah. Also as governor he had to entertain visitors and officials from other parts of the Persian Empire.

5:18 The amount of food required "each day" was significant but considerably less than that of Solomon (1 Kgs 4:22-23).[107] Usually a well-to-do person uses political power to increase his wealth, but Nehemiah "never demanded the food allotted to the governor." He explained his motives as the fear of the Lord (v. 15) and compassion on the people. Nehemiah knew God's concern for justice, compassion, and equality. The depth of one's reverence for God will determine one's decisions.

Nehemiah also realized that the taxes and the demands of work on the wall were already heavy. Therefore he not only sacrificed the taxes he was entitled to, but he also underwrote government expenses from his personal savings. Nehemiah reminds us of 1 John 3:17: "If anyone has material possessions and sees his brother in need but has no pity on him, how can the love of God be in him?" Nehemiah is a worthy example for Christian leaders today. "Leadership means going further than those one is leading."[108]

5:19 "Remember me with favor," like Nehemiah's prayers in the concluding chapter (13:14,22,31; cf. 1:18), has been criticized as self-glorification.[109] We might counter with Blenkinsopp, however, that "if Nehemiah's desire to be acknowledged by God is venal and self-serving, the same must be said of many of the psalms and indeed of much of Chrisitan prayer from the beginnings down to the present." McConville explains that "the invocation of God's favour is not so much a plea for a reward as an emphatic way of claiming that he has acted in good faith and from right motives. It is a statement of confidence that God is judge, and judges favourably those who sincerely seek to do his will."[110]

Even though Nehemiah knew how to take definite action and exert courageous leadership, his dependence was on God. The Christian leader faces many delicate matters. The internal problems of greed, inequality, and injustice that Nehemiah faced were delicate and serious. But he reacted carefully yet swiftly and decisively, trusting in God's help and the guidance of his Word. He confronted the offender privately and made the

---

[107] Reference to "poultry" is questioned by some, but from around 600 B.C. there is evidence that domesticated fowl was eaten in Palestine (Fensham, *Ezra and Nehemiah*, 198).

[108] Williamson, *Ezra, Nehemiah*, 246.

[109] Eskenazi, *Age of Prose*, 151.

[110] McConville, *Ezra, Nehemiah, and Esther*, 102.

matter clear (the implication of v. 7). Then he called an assembly, since public issues must be dealt with in public. Yet he exhibited a humble attitude throughout. He was an example of generosity, setting an example of unselfish service.

8. More Opposition from Without (6:1-19)

(1) Opposition by Trickery (6:1-9)

[1]When word came to Sanballat, Tobiah, Geshem the Arab and the rest of our enemies that I had rebuilt the wall and not a gap was left in it—though up to that time I had not set the doors in the gates— [2]Sanballat and Geshem sent me this message: "Come, let us meet together in one of the villages on the plain of Ono."

But they were scheming to harm me; [3]so I sent messengers to them with this reply: "I am carrying on a great project and cannot go down. Why should the work stop while I leave it and go down to you?" [4]Four times they sent me the same message, and each time I gave them the same answer.

[5]Then, the fifth time, Sanballat sent his aide to me with the same message, and in his hand was an unsealed letter [6]in which was written:

"It is reported among the nations—and Geshem says it is true—that you and the Jews are plotting to revolt, and therefore you are building the wall. Moreover, according to these reports you are about to become their king [7]and have even appointed prophets to make this proclamation about you in Jerusalem: 'There is a king in Judah!' Now this report will get back to the king; so come, let us confer together."

[8]I sent him this reply: "Nothing like what you are saying is happening; you are just making it up out of your head."

[9]They were all trying to frighten us, thinking, "Their hands will get too weak for the work, and it will not be completed."

[But I prayed,] "Now strengthen my hands."

The work on the wall had reached a crucial stage and was almost complete. Failing in every previous attempt to halt the work, Sanballat and his malevolent allies determined that the final solution would be to murder Nehemiah, either outside the city (6:1-9) or inside the temple (6:10-14). However, despite all their efforts, even with inside help (6:17-19), the wall was completed with the Lord's strength and the people's courage (6:15-16).

6:1 Nehemiah was not taking credit here for rebuilding the wall singlehandedly. He was only speaking from the viewpoint of the enemies who understood that stopping the work would mean stopping Nehemiah.

In any great work of God the leaders are strategic; the enemy, whether human or satanic, will try to cause the leader to fall, lose credibility, or disappear altogether. Leadership always involves stress. Here Nehemiah's personal danger added to his stress, but he was able to confront it, trusting the Lord and continuing to work toward the God-given goal.[111]

6:2 Nehemiah's enemies first attempted to lure him outside the city with a pretense of peacemaking. "Ono" was about seven miles southeast of Joppa. It may have been in neutral territory between Judah and Samaria, although the references to Jews living in Ono (Ezra 2:33; Neh 11:35) make it more likely that it was in the extreme northwestern part of Judah. As the NIV note indicates, the phrase "in one of the villages" is a translation of one Hebrew word, kĕphîrîm, which can be a place name. It was evidently not difficult for Nehemiah to determine from past experience that "they were scheming to harm" him.

6:3-4 A more foolish leader bloated with his own importance might have convinced himself that this was an important opportunity to take time out from construction for diplomacy.[112] Nehemiah's answer was polite but firm and somewhat ironic, since leaving the work was the very object of their overtures.

These men repeated their invitation "four times," which shows their desperation to halt the work. Repeated temptation can also weaken one's resistance. Nehemiah stood firm and was careful not to let the opposition divert him from his main purpose.

6:5 On their next attempt, they tried a different motivation to get Nehemiah to respond. An open letter can be a vicious way to attack a leader. If Sanballat had been interested in reconciliation, he could have gone to Jerusalem. But now he and Geshem dropped their pretense of friendliness and tried to spread rumors that would damage the work. This strategy was very subtle; on the one hand, it could have diverted Nehemiah from his purpose. On the other hand, the rumors, if left unchecked, could affect public support and bring down the wrath of the Persian king on the Jewish community. After the events of Ezra 4, when similar reports resulted in a Persian decree to stop the work, this seemed to be an excellent plan.

6:6-7 The reported rumors were serious accusations. Jerusalem had a history of rebelling against controlling empires. A strong wall around Jerusalem would have made rebellion more viable. No doubt some of the Jews were remembering the prophecies of restoration of the Davidic

---

[111] See White, *Excellence in Leadership,* 93.
[112] Ibid., 97.

kingship; some commentators think Nehemiah was a descendant of David, although there is no biblical evidence that he was.

6:8 Slander and gossip usually play on some kernel of truth or some weak point of the leader. How should the leader react? It is legitimate to defend oneself against inaccurate slander, but it is often better to ignore it if possible. Knowing the accusations to be lies, Nehemiah was able simply to deny them and continue the work.

6:9 Nehemiah recognized the psychological warfare of the enemies. The same verb translated "frighten" in v. 9 is repeated again in vv. 13,14,19, where it is translated "intimidate" (lit., "to make afraid"). The different forms of opposition in this chapter were all intended to instill fear in Nehemiah and his helpers so they would not continue the work.

The words "but I prayed" are not in the Hebrew text but are added to identify the clause "now strengthen my hands" as a prayer to God.[113]

(2) Opposition by Intimidation (6:10-14)

10One day I went to the house of Shemaiah son of Delaiah, the son of Mehetabel, who was shut in at his home. He said, "Let us meet in the house of God, inside the temple, and let us close the temple doors, because men are coming to kill you—by night they are coming to kill you."

11But I said, "Should a man like me run away? Or should one like me go into the temple to save his life? I will not go!" **12**I realized that God had not sent him, but that he had prophesied against me because Tobiah and Sanballat had hired him. **13**He had been hired to intimidate me so that I would commit a sin by doing this, and then they would give me a bad name to discredit me.

14Remember Tobiah and Sanballat, O my God, because of what they have done; remember also the prophetess Noadiah and the rest of the prophets who have been trying to intimidate me.

6:10 Nehemiah's enemies would not give up but kept trying different strategies. Some people within the Jewish community were not in favor of the building project; so Sanballat and Tobiah tried to use them against Nehemiah's leadership (see v. 14). Nehemiah accepted Shemaiah's invitation to see him, thinking he was a true prophet. But Shemaiah had sold out to the opposition. He used his influence to undermine Ne-

---

[113] This is so only if the verb חֲזַק is understood as an imperative. Williamson (*Ezra, Nehemiah*, 247) translates the verb as in infinitive absolute, "I continued with even greater determination" (following the LXX καὶ νῦν ἐκραταίωσα τὰς χεῖράς μου). See also Blenkinsopp, *Ezra-Nehemiah*, 267. The similarity with other short prayers of Nehemiah in situations of crisis would favor the NIV translation of the verb as an imperative.

hemiah. He may have thought he was doing the right thing, but he simply joined the ranks of the betrayers in the Scriptures and in the world. "The lure to betray the sacred is a continuing one."[114]

The whole phrase "shut in at his home" represents one word in Hebrew ($^c\bar{a}\d{s}\hat{u}r$). There has been much discussion of why Shemaiah was shut in (how could he flee with Nehemiah to the temple if he was ritually unclean or incapacitated in some way?) and even about the meaning of the word. Perhaps Shemaiah's confinement was symbolic to impress upon Nehemiah the danger.[115]

If Shemaiah's father, Delaiah, is the same one mentioned in 1 Chr 24:18, then Shemaiah was a priest and had special access into the temple. Nehemiah could not enter legitimately. Many years before, Uzziah went into the temple and was stricken with leprosy.[116]

6:11-12 Nehemiah "realized that God had not sent" Shemaiah. He was able to discern that Shemaiah was a fraud. Shemaiah's proposal constituted a subtle temptation. Nehemiah was sensitive to do God's will. He did not want to be closed to what could have been God's message through a prophet. How then could he discern whether or not the message was from God (and how can we)? His two questions in v. 11 indicate the answer: (1) "Should a man like me run away?" This show of fear, and even cowardice, would be a lack of trust in God and would undermine the confidence of the people in his leadership. (2) "Should one like me go into the temple to save his life?" It was not lawful for him to enter the temple.[117] According to Deut 18:20 and Isa 8:19-20, if a word that claims to be a prophecy from God is in contradiction with what God has already revealed, we should be suspicious of it.

6:13-14 The strategy to "discredit" the leader is a subtle one and is common today. Against such attacks we can again learn from Nehemiah's decision to do what was right and leave the outcome to God. Thus he again prayed that God "remember Tobiah and Sanballat . . . the prophetess Noadiah and the rest of the prophets" who were opposed to his

---

[114] F. C. Holmgren, *Israel Alive Again: Ezra and Nehemiah* (Grand Rapids: Eerdmans, 1987), 119.

[115] E. Kutsch, "Die Wurzel עצר im Hebräischen," *VT* (1952): 57-69.

[116] Some think that Nehemiah was a eunuch because of the position he had in Artaxerxes' court and thus would have had double reason to be barred from entering the temple (Fensham, *Ezra and Nehemiah*, 204). See the argument against this, however, in E. Yamauchi, "Was Nehemiah the Cupbearer a Eunuch?" *ZAW* 92 (1980): 132-42.

[117] It is true that in certain circumstances provision was made to seek asylum at the altar. But that was not inside the temple, and Nehemiah did not fit the conditions for that kind of asylum. See Exod 21:13-14; 1 Kgs 1:50-53; 2:28-34; 2 Chr 26:16-20; 27:2.

leadership and opposed God's work. Vengeance was left to God (cf. Deut 32:35; Ps 94:1; Rom 12:19).

(3) The Wall Completed (6:15-16)

¹⁵So the wall was completed on the twenty-fifth of Elul, in fifty-two days. ¹⁶When all our enemies heard about this, all the surrounding nations were afraid and lost their self-confidence, because they realized that this work had been done with the help of our God.

6:15 What a note of victory! The best answer to opposition is to keep working and fulfill God's will; thus others will see God's power.

"The twenty-fifth of Elul" has been determined to correspond with October 2, 445 B.C., although the date is disputed.[118] Elul was the sixth month starting with Nisan as the first (2:1); so all the events of chaps. 2–6 fit into these six months. "In fifty-two days" seems very short, but there is no good reason to doubt it.[119] It shows what can be accomplished when the community works together under good leadership.

6:16 Why do people oppose God's work? If they admit that it is God working, that admission implies that they recognize his power (cf. Acts 5:34-39). If they can continue to convince themselves that the gospel really is not true or that this work is not God's work, then they can remain comfortable in their unbelief or indifference. But this self-confidence receives a blow when they understand that God has really been working in and through his people.

Judah's enemies tried to make Nehemiah and the Jews afraid; but in the end they were the ones who feared (cf. Deut 2:25; 1 Chr 14:17; Ps 126:2; Mal 1:11,14)[120] because they realized God had done something astonishing in this community. The phrase "and lost their self-confidence" is literally "and they fell very much in their eyes," an unfamiliar idiom but one suggesting their pride had suddenly vanished (cf. Prov 16:18-19; 29:23).[121] Though the enemies increased because of San-

---

[118] R. A. Parker and W. H. Dubberstein, *Babylonian Chronology 626 B.C.–A.D. 75*, *Brown University Studies* 19 (Providence: Brown University Press, 1956). Blenkinsopp (*Ezra-Nehemiah*, 273) defends the older mid-September date, arguing that October 2 would be too late since Elul, the sixth month, ran from mid-August to mid-September.

[119] Josephus said it took two years and four months; but he had no other evidence, and it is better to take Nehemiah's word. Thucydides (1.89-93) says the wall around Athens was built in one month.

[120] The verb וַיִּֽרְא֣וּ is read by the Massoretes as being from יָרֵא, "fear" (several Hebrew manuscripts have the plene spelling). The LXX has ἐφοβήθησαν. Without *meteg*, however, the word could be taken from רָאָה "see," thought by many (e.g., Rudolph in *BHS*) to be more likely.

ballat, the result was that more people were impressed with God's power
(4:1,7).

(4) Opposition by Intrigue (6:17-19)

[17]Also, in those days the nobles of Judah were sending many letters to Tobiah, and replies from Tobiah kept coming to them. [18]For many in Judah
were under oath to him, since he was son-in-law to Shecaniah son of Arah,
and his son Jehohanan had married the daughter of Meshullam son of Berekiah. [19]Moreover, they kept reporting to me his good deeds and then telling
him what I said. And Tobiah sent letters to intimidate me.

6:17 The phrase "in those days" means "throughout that period." It
suggests that events mentioned in this paragraph did not necessarily happen after those recorded in the first part of the chapter. However, the fact
that opposition is again discussed after recounting the completion of the
walls suggests that it continued to be a problem. Throughout Nehemiah's
troublesome work in Judah, all his enemies were not outsiders. This added to the pressure Nehemiah had to bear.

6:18 The phrase "under oath" is literally "masters of oath." It does
not refer to the marriage vow but to an agreement with Tobiah, perhaps
in both economic and political matters.

The strategy of the enemies here seems to have been that of causing
division between Nehemiah and the priestly families. Nehemiah 13:4
shows that Tobiah (see comments at 2:10) had family ties not only with
Arah (Ezra 2:5; Neh 7:10) and Meshullam (3:4) but also with the high
priestly family of Eliashib, apparently by marriage. Judging from Tobiah's name and that of his son, Jehohanan ("the LORD has shown mercy"),
he must have considered himself a worshiper of God. The nobles of
Judah (v. 17) may have compromised because of the threats of Sanballat
(v. 5). After all, if Nehemiah was friendly with the Persians, could not
they have been friendly with Tobiah? Moreover, some, like Meshullam
(3:4,30), who gave his daughter in marriage to Tobiah's son, helped on
the wall but may not have supported Nehemiah's separatist policies. So it
is evident that some people among the Jews did not support Nehemiah.

Was Nehemiah too separatist? How does one know where to draw the
line? Certainly decisions of this kind require a discernment of the situation in which people find themselves. "There is a time for flexibility and
a time for firmness; wisdom is knowing when to prefer the one to the

---

[121] The idiom is similar to "his countenance fell" (e.g., Gen 4:5, rendered in NIV "his
face was downcast").

other."[122]

6:19 Tobiah must have had many good traits, and some of the people were led astray by him; nevertheless, he was trying to hinder Nehemiah's leadership. His involvement may be "the most sinister aspect of the story." Only Nehemiah's faith and "clear-headed resoluteness" equipped him for the challenge.[123]

9. Nehemiah Organizes the Community (7:1-73)

Most commentators accept that vv. 1-5 of this chapter are part of the Nehemiah Memoirs. However, there is much discussion over vv. 6-73, which include virtually the same genealogical list as Ezra 2. The narrative of the organization of the community for choosing which families should live in Jerusalem continues in chap. 11. Some think the link to chap. 11 is found in v. 5; however, v. 73 serves better as the connection.[124] If that assumption is correct, then Nehemiah probably included this genealogical list in his original memoirs.

(1) Organization for Conservation (7:1-3)

[1]After the wall had been rebuilt and I had set the doors in place, the gatekeepers and the singers and the Levites were appointed. [2]I put in charge of Jerusalem my brother Hanani, along with Hananiah the commander of the citadel, because he was a man of integrity and feared God more than most men do. [3]I said to them, "The gates of Jerusalem are not to be opened until the sun is hot. While the gatekeepers are still on duty, have them shut the doors and bar them. Also appoint residents of Jerusalem as guards, some at their posts and some near their own houses."

7:1 Nehemiah did not let problems go and grow; he confronted the inequality and injustice even while building. He also continued strong leadership after the building project was finished. He realized that a great success can still be followed by a great failure. He had apparently also not allowed his focus to be on the project instead of on the Lord.

"The gatekeepers" usually were responsible for guarding the entrance to the temple. But because of the dangers of the situation, Nehemiah put them in charge of the city gates (also see comments on 3:1). Many consider "the singers and the Levites" an addition to the text taken from vv.

---

[122] F. C. Holmgren, *Ezra and Nehemiah,* 117.

[123] McConville, *Ezra, Nehemiah, and Esther,* 104-5.

[124] See the discussion in Williamson, *Ezra, Nehemiah,* 268-69, 271-74.

43-45.[125] However, if Nehemiah used the trained temple guard for special protection because of the continuing danger of attack, it is logical that he would reinforce that guard with the singers and Levites who always worked closely with the gatekeepers. D. Kidner also suggests that the singers and Levites shared the priority with the gatekeepers because the purpose of the Jerusalem community was to worship God.[126]

7:2 As the NIV note indicates, some think that "Hanani" and Hananiah" refer to the same person. However, the phrase in v. 3, "I said to them," would indicate that they were two different men. "Hananiah the commander of the citadel" was the officer in charge of the men who guarded the city. Because there was still danger from within and from without, Nehemiah carefully selected these men.

Nehemiah again showed qualities of good leadership in delegating authority. At the same time, he was careful to select men of integrity who feared God.

7:3 There is uncertainty about who is speaking in this verse. Whereas the Masoretic tradition reflected the verb "and I said," the consonantal text of the Masoretes read "and he said." It is possible that Hananiah gave the following commands. "While the gatekeepers are still on duty" is literally "until [or while] they are standing." The verse can mean that the gates were to be shut during the hottest part of the day or during the time after lunch when the guard tended to be lax.[127] However, the sense given in the NIV (before it grew dark in the evening) is entirely satisfactory.

"Appoint residents . . . some near their own houses" was a wise move since it involved the residents themselves in rotating guard duty. If their own houses were involved, they would be even more loyal. It is important to give responsibility to people where they are.

(2) The Registration of the People (7:4-73)

⁴Now the city was large and spacious, but there were few people in it, and the houses had not yet been rebuilt. ⁵So my God put it into my heart to assemble the nobles, the officials and the common people for registration by families. I found the genealogical record of those who had been the first to return. This is what I found written there:

⁶These are the people of the province who came up from the captivity of

---

[125] Blenkinsopp, *Ezra-Nehemiah*, 275.

[126] Kidner, *Ezra and Nehemiah*, 102.

[127] Williamson, *Ezra, Nehemiah*, 263, 266; Blenkinsopp, *Ezra-Nehemiah*, 275.

the exiles whom Nebuchadnezzar king of Babylon had taken captive (they returned to Jerusalem and Judah, each to his own town, [7]in company with Zerubbabel, Jeshua, Nehemiah, Azariah, Raamiah, Nahamani, Mordecai, Bilshan, Mispereth, Bigvai, Nehum and Baanah):

The list of the men of Israel:

[8]the descendants of Parosh	2,172
[9]of Shephatiah	372
[10]of Arah	652
[11]of Pahath-Moab (through the line of Jeshua and Joab)	2,818
[12]of Elam	1,254
[13]of Zattu	845
[14]of Zaccai	760
[15]of Binnui	648
[16]of Bebai	628
[17]of Azgad	2,322
[18]of Adonikam	667
[19]of Bigvai	2,067
[20]of Adin	655
[21]of Ater (through Hezekiah)	98
[22]of Hashum	328
[23]of Bezai	324
[24]of Hariph	112
[25]of Gibeon	95

[26]the men of Bethlehem and Netophah	188
[27]of Anathoth	128
[28]of Beth Azmaveth	42
[29]of Kiriath Jearim, Kephirah and Beeroth	743
[30]of Ramah and Geba	621
[31]of Micmash	122
[32]of Bethel and Ai	123
[33]of the other Nebo	52
[34]of the other Elam	1,254
[35]of Harim	320
[36]of Jericho	345
[37]of Lod, Hadid and Ono	721
[38]of Senaah	3,930

[39]The priests:

the descendants of Jedaiah (through the family of Jeshua)	973
[40]of Immer	1,052
[41]of Pashhur	1,247
[42]of Harim	1,017

43The Levites:

the descendants of Jeshua (through Kadmiel through the line
of Hodaviah)   74

44The singers:

the descendants of Asaph   148

45The gatekeepers:

the descendants of Shallum, Ater, Talmon, Akkub,

Hatita and Shobai   138

46The temple servants:

the descendants of Ziha, Hasupha, Tabbaoth,
47Keros, Sia, Padon,

48Lebana, Hagaba, Shalmai,
49Hanan, Giddel, Gahar,

50Reaiah, Rezin, Nekoda,
51Gazzam, Uzza, Paseah,
52Besai, Meunim, Nephussim,
53Bakbuk, Hakupha, Harhur,
54Bazluth, Mehida, Harsha,

55Barkos, Sisera, Temah,
56Neziah and Hatipha
57The descendants of the servants of Solomon:
the descendants of Sotai, Sophereth, Perida,
58Jaala, Darkon, Giddel,
59Shephatiah, Hattil, Pokereth-Hazzebaim and Amon
60The temple servants and the descendants of the servants of Solomon 392

61The following came up from the towns of Tel Melah, Tel Harsha, Kerub,
Addon and Immer, but they could not show that their families were descended from Israel:

62the descendants of Delaiah, Tobiah and Nekoda 642

63And from among the priests:

the descendants of Hobaiah, Hakkoz and Barzillai (a man who had married a
daughter of Barzillai the Gileadite and was called by that name).

64These searched for their family records, but they could not find them
and so were excluded from the priesthood as unclean. **65**The governor, there-

fore, ordered them not to eat any of the most sacred food until there should be a priest ministering with the Urim and Thummim.

[66]The whole company numbered 42,360, [67]besides their 7,337 menservants and maidservants; and they also had 245 men and women singers. [68]There were 736 horses, 245 mules, [69]435 camels and 6,720 donkeys.

[70]Some of the heads of the families contributed to the work. The governor gave to the treasury 1,000 drachmas of gold, 50 bowls and 530 garments for priests. [71]Some of the heads of the families gave to the treasury for the work 20,000 drachmas of gold and 2,200 minas of silver. [72]The total given by the rest of the people was 20,000 drachmas of gold, 2,000 minas of silver and 67 garments for priests.

[73]The priests, the Levites, the gatekeepers, the singers and the temple servants, along with certain of the people and the rest of the Israelites, settled in their own towns.

7:4 Nehemiah was sensitive to the long-term needs of the community. The wall was necessary, but Jerusalem was not safe if it was underpopulated. The Hebrew construction translated "had not yet been built" can mean that there were simply not enough houses,[128] The previous verse as well as the building account in chap. 3 (see 3:20,29; cf. Hag 1:4) shows that some houses did exist. The population and housing problems referred to here are dealt with in chap. 11.

7:5 Apparently the people preferred to live in the surrounding villages and not in Jerusalem. Yet the defense of Jerusalem was important for all their security. So Nehemiah wanted the sacrifice of living in Jerusalem to be distributed justly among the families. The genealogical list here has a different purpose from the one in Ezra 2; here it is used to choose those who would live in Jerusalem. Nehemiah makes clear that the census was approved by the Lord and not Satan, as in 1 Chr 21:1.

7:6-32 This list is practically the same as that of Ezra 2:1-70 but with some slight differences of names and numbers.[129] For a discussion of the origin of the list and comments on some of the names, see comments on Ezra 2.

7:33-67 "Of the other Nebo" is literally "the men of the other Nebo"; in each case the NIV does not repeat "men of" or "children of." Ezra 2:29 simply has "the children of Nebo."

7:68 As the NIV note indicates, most Hebrew Bibles do not include

---

[128] Fensham, *Ezra and Nehemiah*, 211. Williamson also takes this meaning (*Ezra, Nehemiah*, 267).

[129] See Blenkinsopp, *Ezra-Nehemiah*, 280-81 for a list of differences.

this verse. It is found in the Septuagint and Vulgate versions. At some stage of transmission, it must have dropped out of the Hebrew text.[130] Thus vv. 69-73 in NIV are numbered 68-72 in the Hebrew text.

7:70-72   The end of these verses reads in Hebrew "garments of priests thirty and five hundred." Since the "five hundred" would normally come before the "thirty," many think that "five hundred" originally went with "minas of silver," which dropped out of the text. So the phrase probably should read "30 priestly garments and 500 minas of silver."[131]

Verses 70-72 are summarized in Ezra 2:68-69, which again indicates that Ezra 2 depends on Neh 7. In Ezra 2:69 the total is sixty-one thousand drachmas instead of the forty-one thousand mentioned here. Apparently in Ezra 2:69 the fifty bowls were valued at twenty thousand drachmas and were included in the total.[132]

7:73a   This verse has caused much discussion because neither the Hebrew text here nor in Ezra 2:70 seems to be original. Some wish to add the words "in Jerusalem" after "along with certain of the people"; thus all those mentioned in the first part of the verse settled in Jerusalem while the rest of the Israelites settled in their own towns (following 1 Esdr 5:46). Williamson gives strong arguments against this proposal[133] and endeavors to reconstruct the process by which the text arrived at its present form. It seems best to keep the sense as translated in NIV.

The last part of v. 73 is really part of the following narrative; the continuation of Nehemiah's narrative is taken up in chap. 11.

---

[130] The translators of the LXX and Vulgate either had a Hebrew text that still contained the verse or they took it from the parallel passage in Ezra 2:66.

[131] Myers, *Ezra and Nehemiah,* 145; Williamson, *Ezra, Nehemiah,* 267. The LXX, however, omits "five hundred" and simply reads καὶ χοθωνωθ τῶν ἱερέων τριάκοντα, "and thirty priestly garments."

[132] Myers, *Ezra and Nehemiah,* 148.

[133] Williamson, *Ezra, Nehemiah,* 272.

VI. THE COVENANT RENEWED (7:73b–10:39)
1. The Law Read and Explained (7:73b–8:12)
2. The Feast of Tabernacles Celebrated (8:13-18)
3. The Israelites' Prayer of Confession (9:1-37)
    (1) The Assembly for Confession and Worship (9:1-5a)
    (2) Prayer of Confession (9:5b-37)
4. The Agreement of the People (9:38–10:39)
    (1) Introduction (9:38)
    (2) The Chief Leaders and Priests Who Signed (10:1-8)
    (3) The Levites Who Signed (10:9-13)
    (4) The Other Leaders Who Signed (10:14-27)
    (5) The Solemn Promise (10:28-29)
    (6) Specific Examples of Separation (10:30-31)
    (7) The Temple Taxes (10:32-33)
    (8) Offerings in Kind (10:34-39)

VI. THE COVENANT RENEWED (7:73b–10:39)

As noted earlier, one of the most difficult problems in analyzing Ezra and Nehemiah is to ascertain how chaps. 8–10 of Nehemiah fit in the present context (see the Introduction). However, they were related to the memoirs of Ezra and Nehemiah, these chapters were placed here for theological reasons to emphasize the renewal of the covenant and the events associated with it. B. Childs has explained how all the rest of Ezra-Nehemiah leads up to chaps. 7–13, which describe the reordering of the community's life.[1] T. Eskenazi views Neh 7:73–13:37 as the third part of Ezra-Nehemiah's tripartite structure: Part I is "potentiality: decree to the community to build the house of God" (Ezra 1:1-4). Part II is "the process of actualization: the community builds the house of God according to the decree" (Ezra 1:5 to Neh 7:72). And part III is "success: the community celebrates the completion of the house of God according to Torah" (7:73–13:31).[2] This final section, therefore, should be read as a

---

[1] B. Childs, *Introduction to the Old Testament as Scripture* (Philadelphia: Fortress, 1979), 632-33.

[2] T. Eskenazi, *In an Age of Prose* (Atlanta: Scholars Press, 1988), 37-39.

time of celebration and dedication of what God had done. The reading of
Scripture (Neh 8) and the act of prayer (Neh 9) followed by community
commitment (Neh 10) is a model for worshiping communities.

In studying the social process of community development and transformation, K. Tollefson emphasizes that the present sequence of chapters
in Nehemiah exemplifies in a program for "total physical and cultural
transformation that rebuilt the city and revitalized the people's attitudes,
values, and beliefs."[3]

Clearly we have here a revival of the community. Several times
throughout the Old Testament a covenant renewal implies or is accompanied by a spiritual awakening (Exod 34; Josh 24; 2 Kgs 18; 22–23).
Though revival is God's work, we should also take into account the role
of the leader, the role of Scripture, and the changes revival brings. Christian revivals are always related to a return to the Scriptures. The Reformation in the sixteenth century was brought about by and caused a great
turning to God's Word. The turning to God's Word as evidenced here in
Neh 8 serves as a paradigm for us to study and follow.

1. The Law Read and Explained (7:73b–8:12)

**When the seventh month came and the Israelites had settled in their
towns,**
**¹all the people assembled as one man in the square before the Water Gate.
They told Ezra the scribe to bring out the Book of the Law of Moses, which
the LORD had commanded for Israel.**

**²So on the first day of the seventh month Ezra the priest brought the Law
before the assembly, which was made up of men and women and all who were
able to understand. ³He read it aloud from daybreak till noon as he faced the
square before the Water Gate in the presence of the men, women and others
who could understand. And all the people listened attentively to the Book of
the Law.**

---

[3] K. Tollefson, "Nehemiah, Model for Change Agents: A Social Science Approach to
Scripture," *CSR* XV (1986): 124. Tollefson says: "The internal organization of the book
[Nehemiah] is marked by an integration of social processes, decisions, and responses. Each
subsequent chapter seems to be a logical outgrowth of the previous ones. If a single chapter were missing, there would need to be something similar reported in the data for the
book to make sense, for the succeeding situation to occur, or for the project to progress toward completion. The book reads much like a contemporary field project of planned social
change and reveals a grasp of sophisticated methods and concepts." Tollefson sees the third
social process in community development described in Neh 7:5–10:39; he calls it "The
Cultural Revitalization Process." The fourth process, "The Consolidation Process," is described in 11:1–13:31.

[4]Ezra the scribe stood on a high wooden platform built for the occasion. Beside him on his right stood Mattithiah, Shema, Anaiah, Uriah, Hilkiah and Maaseiah; and on his left were Pedaiah, Mishael, Malkijah, Hashum, Hash-baddanah, Zechariah and Meshullam.

[5]Ezra opened the book. All the people could see him because he was standing above them; and as he opened it, the people all stood up. [6]Ezra praised the LORD, the great God; and all the people lifted their hands and responded, "Amen! Amen!" Then they bowed down and worshiped the LORD with their faces to the ground.

[7]The Levites—Jeshua, Bani, Sherebiah, Jamin, Akkub, Shabbethai, Hodiah, Maaseiah, Kelita, Azariah, Jozabad, Hanan and Pelaiah—instructed the people in the Law while the people were standing there. [8]They read from the Book of the Law of God, making it clear and giving the meaning so that the people could understand what was being read.

[9]Then Nehemiah the governor, Ezra the priest and scribe, and the Levites who were instructing the people said to them all, "This day is sacred to the LORD your God. Do not mourn or weep." For all the people had been weeping as they listened to the words of the Law.

[10]Nehemiah said, "Go and enjoy choice food and sweet drinks, and send some to those who have nothing prepared. This day is sacred to our LORD. Do not grieve, for the joy of the LORD is your strength."

[11]The Levites calmed all the people, saying, "Be still, for this is a sacred day. Do not grieve."

[12]Then all the people went away to eat and drink, to send portions of food and to celebrate with great joy, because they now understood the words that had been made known to them.

7:73b Regardless of its original connection with the Ezra Memoirs, this account does not describe an event immediately following Ezra's return to Jerusalem but a revival that occurred years later (see Introduction). The seventh month was important in the Jewish calendar. The first day was the Feast of Trumpets, later celebrated as the New Year. On the tenth day the Day of Atonement was celebrated, and on the fifteenth the Feast of Tabernacles began. According to Deut 31:11-13, the proclamation of the cancellation of debts for each sabbatical year was made during the Feast of Tabernacles.[4] During the same feast every seventh year, the law was to be read to "men, women and children."

8:1 The "people" dominate these verses. The word "people" occurs thirteen times in 8:1-12. The phrase "all the people" occurs in nine of

---

[4] See J. Blenkinsopp, *Ezra-Nehemiah*, OTL (Philadelphia: Westminster, 1988), 282-87. For the view that this was not a special day but rather was one of the new moon days, see D. J. A. Clines, *Ezra, Nehemiah, Esther*, NCB (Grand Rapids: Eerdmans, 1984), 182-83.

those instances. This fact leads Eskenzai to determine that the most important character in this section is the people. The character Ezra functions here only for the purpose of reading the book to them.[5]

Williamson has suggested that we have here almost the same elements as in a typical synagogue service: (1) the assembly of the people; (2) the request for reading of the Torah; (c) the opening of the scroll; (d) the people standing; (e) the praise (by Ezra); (f) the response of the people; (g) sermon instruction; (h) reading the law; (i) oral explanation and exhortation; (j) departure for a fellowship meal (v. 10).[6]

Just as these people took the initiative, we should encourage all Christian believers to take the initiative in seeking spiritual revival. The people already respected the law of Moses and recognized its authority for their community. It is significant that this reading of the law and the worship service were not centered in the temple and not controlled by the priesthood. From this time on in Judaism, the Torah was more important than the temple. Likewise, for Christians, the living power of the Bible should be more important than any church building. Through Scripture the Holy Spirit brings people to abundant life.

8:2 "Men and women and all who were able to understand" involved the entire community, including young people and children. The Jews became known as "the people of the book." The Old Testament emphasizes that God's Word is to be known and used by all the people, not only the priests and leaders. Early Christians adopted this same principle. This changed as time went on as fewer and fewer people had access to the Bible. The Protestant Reformation, with its emphasis on *sola scriptura* (on the Bible as the *sole* authority for faith and practice) returned to the biblical principle that every believer should read Scripture as God's Word for their lives.

8:3 "He read it" is literally he read "in it." It must have been a large scroll, for it was read for some six hours. Some argue that it could not have been the whole Pentateuch because that would have taken much longer than six hours. But if he read "in" it, we should conclude that he read selected parts. The people "listened attentively" because they firmly believed the message to be God's revelation. God's Word preached in the power of the Holy Spirit and with authority will command attention. The reading of God's Word brings revival.

8:4 "Ezra . . . on a high wooden platform" shows that preparation

---

[5] Eskenazi, *Age of Prose*, 96-99. On "book" see comment on 8:5.

[6] Williamson, *Ezra-Nehemiah*, 281-82. But Williamson observes that this does not include all we know from later synagogue services.

had been made for this event. This was the prototype pulpit but may have originated during the Babylonian exile along with the beginnings of the synagogue.[7] "Beside him" were thirteen other men. Some think the men named here were priests; however, other references specify when they are priests or Levites. Most likely these were influential lay leaders in the community. It is important for God's people to prepare special times for seeking his will and searching his Word.

8:5 "Ezra opened the book," which, of course, was a scroll; the codex or book form was not yet used.[8] Standing in reverence and acceptance of God's authority in the Scripture must have been customary. In Neh 9:3 we note the same tradition of standing for reading the Torah, for confession of sin, and for worship.

8:6 This verse makes clear that the respect the people had for "the book" came not because they considered it an object of veneration but because it was their word from God who deserved their praise and worship.

"All the people . . . responded" is a splendid example of unified worship as the leader raised his voice in praise and the people responded. They responded (1) by lifting their hands in worship and showing a sense of need; (2) by saying, "Amen! Amen!" and thus affirming their submission to the authority of Scripture; and (3) by bowing down to the ground with a sense of humility and submission before God.

8:7 Even then Scripture needed to be explained. The Old Testament was written in the Hebrew language. Since the people had lived in a foreign country all of their lives, they had lost some of their ability to understand Hebrew. Regardless, the Levites had the job of making sure the people knew what was being said. They were helping them bridge the cultural gap between the last seventy years in Babylonia with their cultural heritage as found in Scripture. It could not have been easy. Although God's Word is authoritative for life and faith and all matters of knowing God, it frequently takes hard work to understand the message of God written in a foreign language in a distant time and place.

8:8 This verse summarizes what already was said in vv. 5-7, but it

---

[7] J. G. McConville, *Ezra, Nehemiah, and Esther*, DSB (Philadelphia: Westminster 1985), 116-17. The lists in 1 Esdr 9:43-44, in the LXX text of Neh 8:4, and in the Massoretic text differ slightly. It is best to stay with our Massoretic text as translated in the NIV.

[8] Early Christians had a large part in developing the codex form in the first three centuries A.D. A fragment of papyrus codex (P. Yale 1) has been dated A.D. 80–100. The Hebrew codices that are known are all from several centuries after the time of Christ. An early example of a codex is the Roman parchment notebook from the first century B.C.

adds detail. Scholars discuss the phrase "making it clear." The root *pārāš* means "to break up." Williamson translates "paragraph by paragraph."[9] However, it is better to take it to mean "translating" as in the NIV note. Since the Jews in captivity would have used Aramaic along with Hebrew, parts of Ezra are in Aramaic—the international diplomatic language of the time. Part of the work of the Levites was to give them an Aramaic translation.[10] We know that this was the custom a little later, which resulted in the formation of the Targums—Aramaic paraphrases of the Old Testament. According to a rabbinic tradition, the Targum was first mentioned here in Neh 8:8. At any rate, the leaders helped the people understand by "making it clear" (or translating) and by "giving the meaning." All translations, however, are to some degree "interpretation." But beyond that the exposition helps students of the Word understand the overall message and the implications of the text for doctrine and practice. Furthermore, although the message and content of Scripture does not change, it does need fresh application in every situation.

8:9 Some commentators suggest that if this chapter originally stood with Ezra 8, Nehemiah was not yet present; so this is a scribal addition. They point out that the verb "said" is singular and argue that the phrase "Nehemiah and the Levites" was added later.[11] However, as Kidner points out, this construction is quite common with a verb preceding a string of subjects. In fact, Ezra 8:20 is another case where a singular verb is used with "David and his officials."[12]

Although there are slight variants in 3 Esdras and the Septuagint, both Kidner and Fensham agree that "not enough textual-critical evidence can be presented to delete either name [Ezra or Nehemiah]."[13] If we read with the Hebrew text we must conclude that Ezra and Nehemiah worked together on this occasion. Several points support this conclusion: (1) the position of this narrative in Nehemiah; (2) after Nehemiah finished re-

---

[9] Williamson, *Ezra, Nehemiah,* 277.

[10] The use of the additional word (וְיָבִ֫ינוּ) translated "giving the meaning" in the NIV would confirm the rendering "translating" for מְפֹרָשׁ as Fensham suggests (F. C. Fensham, *The Books of Ezra and Nehemiah,* NICOT [Grand Rapids: Eerdmans, 1982], 218).

[11] Williamson considers "Nehemiah, the governor, an addition by the editor" (Williamson, *Ezra, Nehemiah,* 279); Myers also considers it a secondary addition (J. Myers, *Ezra, Nehemiah,* AB [Garden City: Doubleday, 1965], 151).

[12] D. Kidner, *Ezra and Nehemiah,* TOTC (Downers Grove: InterVarsity, 1979), 149. According to Gesenius (G-K 145 o), "Variations from the fundamental rule [that the verb agrees in number with its subject] very frequently occur when the predicate precedes the subject (denoting animals or things)." But then he gives cases where a singular verb is used in this way before collectives and mixed subjects.

building the wall, the people called on Ezra to read the Law (Neh 8:1-12); (3) Nehemiah was active in helping instruct the people (Neh 8:9); (4) Nehemiah is first on the list of those who signed the covenant (10:1); (5) both Ezra and Nehemiah participated in the processions at the dedication of the wall (Neh 12:31, 36,38,40).[14]

There are two reasons for the exhortation to rejoice: (1) the people had repented, and (2) this was the first day of the seventh month, the Feast of Trumpets, which was to be a day of rejoicing (Lev 23:23-25; Deut 16:15). The people must have been repentant for disobeying the law (v. 10). A similar reaction occurred in the time of Josiah (2 Kgs 22:11-13,19). The Word of God, when read, has the power to transform lives today just as it had in the time of both Josiah and Ezra. The Bible convicts, changes, and guides lives. In the time of Ezra the people realized that the Babylonian captivity was a result of disobedience. Only genuine repentance before God could bring about a real change in the community. The living power of the Word of God still liberates people from their own various forms of captivity. Leaders pointed out God's mercy to the people. Those who teach must show God's justice and the need for repentance but must not forget to emphasize God's love and mercy.

8:10-11 The Hebrew text of v. 10 begins, like v. 9, with the singular verb "said." It has no subject specified, however. The NIV has supplied "Nehemiah" on the assumption that he is the one speaking. Some think the subject here could be Ezra. In either case, the leaders wanted the people to rejoice and enjoy a fellowship meal.

The peace offering, or fellowship offering, explained in Lev 3 was often accompanied by a meal. Most of the meat of the offering was eaten by the one who offered the sacrifice. The peace offering, or fellowship offering, is mentioned together with feasting in 2 Sam 6:18-19; 1 Chr 29:22; 2 Chr 30:21-26. Here, too, there may have been a combination of

---

[13] Fensham notes that 3 Esdras 5:40 does not have "Nehemiah"; the LXX does not have "who was governor," but the 3 Esdras passage instead of "governor" has "Attharates." This shows that the text used by the author of 3 Esdras did have the word "governor" and no doubt "Nehemiah" also (Fensham, *Ezra and Nehemiah*, 218). Also Kidner, *Ezra and Nehemiah*, 148.

[14] See Kidner, *Ezra and Nehemiah*, 148-52. Those who deny that Ezra and Nehemiah were together on this occasion consider Neh 8 as misplaced and delete the name of Ezra from all the texts mentioned. As noted there simply is not sufficient textual-critical evidence to justify this. In fact, Kidner points out more textual evidence in the opposite direction. The LXX text of Neh 12:31 has "they" instead of Nehemiah's "I," so Nehemiah is omitted from the record of the dedication of the wall; but in 12:36 (in the uncorrected text of the LXX) Ezra is present (ibid., 148).

fellowship offering and fellowship meal. Some must have prepared it, but they were to share with those who did not have it prepared, perhaps in some cases because they were too poor. The day was "sacred" and deserved to be celebrated. God calls his people to the celebration of new life (Luke 19:1-10). One's faith is optimistic because of God's power. Real joy is an expression of faith in what God can do and is doing.

8:12 What a difference it makes when God's people "understand" God's Word and apply it to their particular situations. Allowing the use of the Bible to become routine and ritualistic is a violation of its nature and message. The prophet Hosea said to those who were supposed to teach Scripture to God's people, "My people are destroyed from lack of knowledge" (Hos 6:6; Mal 2:1-9). The biblical text needs to be applied by each generation and in each situation without falling into legalism or accepting a syncretism in which one loses the Scripture's authority and distinctive message. Jesus used the same Old Testament Scriptures as the Pharisees, but the people listened with attention and marveled because he taught with authority (Matt 7:29).

2. The Feast of Tabernacles Celebrated (8:13-18)

[13]On the second day of the month, the heads of all the families, along with the priests and the Levites, gathered around Ezra the scribe to give attention to the words of the Law. [14]They found written in the Law, which the LORD had commanded through Moses, that the Israelites were to live in booths during the feast of the seventh month [15]and that they should proclaim this word and spread it throughout their towns and in Jerusalem: "Go out into the hill country and bring back branches from olive and wild olive trees, and from myrtles, palms and shade trees, to make booths"—as it is written.

[16]So the people went out and brought back branches and built themselves booths on their own roofs, in their courtyards, in the courts of the house of God and in the square by the Water Gate and the one by the Gate of Ephraim. [17]The whole company that had returned from exile built booths and lived in them. From the days of Joshua son of Nun until that day, the Israelites had not celebrated it like this. And their joy was very great.

[18]Day after day, from the first day to the last, Ezra read from the Book of the Law of God. They celebrated the feast for seven days, and on the eighth day, in accordance with the regulation, there was an assembly.

8:13 The majority of the people must have gone home, as v. 15 suggests. But the "heads of all the families, along with the priests and the Levites," stayed with Ezra for further instruction. They were not satisfied with a superficial revival but wanted to be obedient in every detail.

The family heads were responsible for the life-style of their families. Here they wanted to practice what Deut 6:4-9 commands, that all the people, not just the priests, were to know and talk about "these commands." Today, even more, not just the pastors and "experts" but all believers should "do theology," reflecting together on the application of biblical, ethical principles to every area of life. To do theology or theologize is to apply biblical principles to every aspect of life. The Bible must never be allowed to become the sole property of scholars and ministers. Such occurred during the Middle Ages and the people were at the mercy of those "elite." The Bible was given to all believers, and all believers have the responsibility to study God's Word and need the grace to live by it.

8:14 This was the second day of the seventh month. The seventh month included the Day of Atonement and the Feast of Tabernacles (cf. Ezra 3). The Day of Atonement is not mentioned, perhaps because it had more to do with priestly activity; here the emphasis is on what the community did. It also did not fit the theme of celebration. The people still had time to prepare and proclaim the Feast of Tabernacles, which started on the fifteenth day of the month. They were zealous to do exactly what God commanded.

8:15 The emphasis on bringing branches and living in booths is found in Lev 23:33-43, but Deut 16 emphasizes celebrating with joy. No attempt is made here to quote these passages verbatim; the people wanted to do God's will, so they applied these passages of Scripture to their present situation. Deuteronomy 16:15 says they were to celebrate the feast at "the place the LORD will choose, which they know to be" Jerusalem.[15]

8:16 The "roofs" of houses in the ancient Near East usually were flat. The booth would be a temporary "hut" structure that would remind them of the temporary nature of Israel's dwelling in the wilderness following the exile from Egypt. Such an act was a deep expression of their faith in God, who dwelt with them in their booths. It perhaps also was to remind them "that their continuing existence was more fragile than the security of a regular pattern of life could suggest. . . . It is far more difficult to hear the message of fragility of life and the fact of dependence upon God in each succeeding breath amid the settled affluence and long life-expectancy that so many in the modern western world

---

[15] See the discussion in Williamson, *Ezra, Nehemiah,* 293-95. Scholars have discussed whether this verse reflects the influence of Lev 23 or Deut 16 and why Jerusalem is mentioned here, but not in those passages.

would enjoy."[16]

8:17   Other Scripture passages indicate that the Feast of Tabernacles
had been celebrated regularly (by Solomon in 2 Chr 8:13, Hezekiah in 2
Chr 31:3, Josiah in 2 Chr 35:18, and the future celebration in Zech
14:16-18).[17] What was different? The feast had two principal meanings:
(1) it was an agricultural festival to commemorate the "ingathering" of
the harvest (Exod 34:22); (2) it was a memorial celebration of the wilderness wanderings. Apparently through the years the harvest application
had been emphasized, but the living in booths to remember the wilderness wanderings had been neglected. As the people examined Scripture
here, they returned to that emphasis, which was appropriate after their
new exodus in returning from the Babylonian captivity.[18] One effect of
the continued study of Scripture is that it helps us adjust our traditions
according to the divine standard.

When the people began to celebrate the feast with new understanding
and a new sense of obedience, it gave them great joy. Obedience to God
as a community brings God's blessing and great joy. Deuteronomy
16:13-15 commands, "Be joyful at your Feast" and concludes, "Your joy
will be complete."

8:18   Deuteronomy 31:12-13 commands the reading of the Law every seventh year at the Feast of Tabernacles: "So they can listen and
learn to fear the LORD your God and follow carefully all the words of
this law. Their children, who do not know this law, must hear it and learn
to fear the LORD."

Nehemiah 8 emphasizes that all the people of God must know his
Word. Surveys have shown the appalling lack of biblical knowledge
among Christians today. At the same time there is a deep hunger for the
Word among Christians. Religious leaders today must take seriously their
responsibility as shepherds to feed the flock (John 21:15-17; Acts 20:28-
31; Heb 5:12-14; 1 Pet 2:2).

Paul's command to Timothy is still valid for ministers, "Preach the
Word!" (2 Tim 4:2); and James's word is valid for all believers, "Be do-
ers of the word, and not merely hearers who deceive themselves" (Jas
1:22, NRSV).

This chapter also stresses the need for exhortation based on the Word
(Neh 8:9-12). Ezra's helpers explained the meaning of the Law and its

---

[16] McConville, *Ezra, Nehemiah, Esther,* 20.

[17] Instructions concerning the Feast of Tabernacles are given in Exod 23:14-17; 34:22;
Lev 23:23-25; Deut 16:13-15; 31:10-13.

[18] Williamson, *Ezra-Nehemiah,* 296. Booths are mentioned in Ezra 3.

relevance for the people in their situation. They first understood their need for forgiveness; then they needed an explanation of God's forgiveness and his grace.

3. The Israelites' Prayer of Confession (9:1-37)

Chapter 9 fits precisely into the author's purpose to show the place of Scripture reading and confession in the covenant renewal explained in chap. 10. However, it seems odd that a day of fasting would come two days after the close of the Feast of Tabernacles, which was a time of rejoicing.

We must remember that the people's first reaction to the reading of the Law was sorrow and weeping (8:9); however, Nehemiah and the Levites exhorted the people to rejoice in the Lord. So they had a joyous Feast of Tabernacles. It was natural that after that joyous occasion they should again turn to a repentant attitude.[19]

Some accept 9:1-5 as the setting for chap. 9 but think the long prayer (vv. 5b-37) was composed at a different time. There would be no difficulty in using on this occasion a psalm that already existed, but neither is it difficult to think that Ezra could have composed it for this occasion. There is no compelling reason to remove this chapter from its present context.[20] Instead, its place here makes perfect sense. This section has the third reading of the Law (9:3). The first reading was in 8:4-8. The second reading was in 8:14-15. After the first reading, celebration was called for (8:12). After the second reading, Tabernacles was celebrated. The third reading (9:3) would be followed by a prayer of confession (9:5b-37).[21] This is not a text that had any separate origin but is the result of the intention of the author of the text. As it stands, it continues the worshipful devotion of the community in its third stage. It is followed by the community writing a pledge to both Torah and the house of God.[22]

(1) The Assembly for Confession and Worship (9:1-5a)

---

[19] See Fensham, *Ezra and Nehemiah*, 222.

[20] Williamson agrees that the final editor of Ezra-Nehemiah carefully chose this material, but he thinks that the original setting of chap. 9 was different from Neh 7; 11 and even different from Neh 8 (Williamson, *Ezra, Nehemiah*, 308). Fensham says chaps. 8–9 have a similar liturgical approach, which would indicate that they came from the same historical origin (Fensham, *Ezra and Nehemiah*, 223). We can consider chap. 8 part of the Ezra Memoirs and chap. 9 at least based on the same. Fensham's argument is accepted here.

[21] Eskenazi, *Age of Prose*, 96.

[22] Ibid.

¹On the twenty-fourth day of the same month, the Israelites gathered together, fasting and wearing sackcloth and having dust on their heads. ²Those
of Israelite descent had separated themselves from all foreigners. They stood
in their places and confessed their sins and the wickedness of their fathers.
³They stood where they were and read from the Book of the Law of the LORD
their God for a quarter of the day, and spent another quarter in confession
and in worshiping the LORD their God. ⁴Standing on the stairs were the Levites—Jeshua, Bani, Kadmiel, Shebaniah, Bunni, Sherebiah, Bani and Ke-
nani—who called with loud voices to the LORD their God. ⁵And the Levites—
Jeshua, Kadmiel, Bani, Hashabneiah, Sherebiah, Hodiah, Shebaniah and
Pethahiah—said: "Stand up and praise the LORD your God, who is from everlasting to everlasting."

9:1   In these chapters we have a revival that occurred when the people gathered as a community of believers for a special time of prayer, including self-examination, repentance, and confession (cf. Job 1:21; Joel
1:8;13; Jonah 3:5,8).

"Wearing sackcloth" symbolized mourning and humility. Reading the
Book of the Law (v. 3) made the people realize that they and their ancestors had constantly failed to keep the covenant with God.

9:2   Since this had to do with the covenant between God and Israel,
only the covenant people could participate in this time of repentance and
confession.²³ There was a sense of solidarity in the community. Such
continuity and solidarity with past generations is constantly emphasized
in Ezra-Nehemiah. The Christian community today has lost this sense of
shared history and continuity with Jews. This view of history is shaped
by a view of God based on written revelation and expresses the role of
God in world events.

9:3   "They stood . . . and read." The people must have had a genuine
hunger to know God's will and his promises because they read for several hours. Their example presents two challenges: (1) Allow God to speak
through his Word. That is the only sure basis for revival and for correction of the life and mission of the church. (2) Read widely in God's
Word, not just brief portions. At times we need to read long sections at
one sitting to get a broad perspective. We can learn from the balance here
between hearing God's Word, worship, and confession. Each one is important, and all are imperative.

---

²³ Blenkinsopp (*Ezra-Nehemiah,* 296) explains that "those of foreign descent who, according to Deut 16:14, participated in Sukkoth (though according to Lev 23:42 they did not
dwell in booths), could not be expected to identify with the collective and cumulative sin
of Israel confessed in the prayer which follows."

9:4 The Levites were the leaders of the worship services. Leaders in the church today also must take the lead in humble confession and in praising God. In Israel the Psalms, used in their worship, played a significant role in shaping the way the community viewed the world.[24] Any society shapes its own values and priorities. In Israel their worship formed their "world" of values and priorities. In the life of the church, the worship service fulfills the same role; it shapes the "world" of the Christian community. Thus the ministry of those who lead worship is of utmost importance.

A more literal rendering of the Hebrew beginning v. 4 would be "on the stairs of the Levites stood Jeshua." It is not known for sure what the "stairs of the Levites" were. They may have been steps from one court of the temple to the other. According to the Mishna, in the Herodian temple the Levites stood to sing on the fifteen steps between the court of the women and the court of Israel.[25]

9:5a Two lists of Levites are given in vv. 4-5, but five of the names are repeated. The two groups probably had different functions, but it is not surprising that the leaders of the Levites would have been involved in both.

(2) Prayer of Confession (9:5b-37)

"Blessed be your glorious name, and may it be exalted above all blessing and praise. [6]You alone are the LORD. You made the heavens, even the highest heavens, and all their starry host, the earth and all that is on it, the seas and all that is in them. You give life to everything, and the multitudes of heaven worship you.

[7]"You are the LORD God, who chose Abram and brought him out of Ur of the Chaldeans and named him Abraham. [8]You found his heart faithful to you, and you made a covenant with him to give to his descendants the land of the Canaanites, Hittites, Amorites, Perizzites, Jebusites and Girgashites. You have kept your promise because you are righteous.

[9]"You saw the suffering of our forefathers in Egypt; you heard their cry at the Red Sea. [10]You sent miraculous signs and wonders against Pharaoh, against all his officials and all the people of his land, for you knew how arrogantly the Egyptians treated them. You made a name for yourself, which remains to this day. [11]You divided the sea before them, so that they passed

---

[24] See, for example, works by W. Brueggemann, *Israel's Praise* (Philadelphia: Fortress, 1988) and W. Holladay, *The Psalms through Three Thousand Years: A Prayerbook of a Cloud of Witnesses* (Minneapolis: Fortress, 1993) for a history of the use of the Book of Psalms in both Jewish and Christian history. Also see comments at 11:16-18.

[25] *Middoth* 2.5.

through it on dry ground, but you hurled their pursuers into the depths, like a stone into mighty waters. [12]By day you led them with a pillar of cloud, and by night with a pillar of fire to give them light on the way they were to take.

[13]"You came down on Mount Sinai; you spoke to them from heaven. You gave them regulations and laws that are just and right, and decrees and commands that are good. [14]You made known to them your holy Sabbath and gave them commands, decrees and laws through your servant Moses. [15]In their hunger you gave them bread from heaven and in their thirst you brought them water from the rock; you told them to go in and take possession of the land you had sworn with uplifted hand to give them

[16]"But they, our forefathers, became arrogant and stiff-necked, and did not obey your commands. [17]They refused to listen and failed to remember the miracles you performed among them. They became stiff-necked and in their rebellion appointed a leader in order to return to their slavery. But you are a forgiving God, gracious and compassionate, slow to anger and abounding in love. Therefore you did not desert them, [18]even when they cast for themselves an image of a calf and said, 'This is your god, who brought you up out of Egypt,' or when they committed awful blasphemies.

[19]"Because of your great compassion you did not abandon them in the desert. By day the pillar of cloud did not cease to guide them on their path, nor the pillar of fire by night to shine on the way they were to take. [20]You gave your good Spirit to instruct them. You did not withhold your manna from their mouths, and you gave them water for their thirst. [21]For forty years you sustained them in the desert; they lacked nothing, their clothes did not wear out nor did their feet become swollen.

[22]"You gave them kingdoms and nations, allotting to them even the remotest frontiers. They took over the country of Sihon king of Heshbon and the country of Og king of Bashan. [23]You made their sons as numerous as the stars in the sky, and you brought them into the land that you told their fathers to enter and possess. [24]Their sons went in and took possession of the land. You subdued before them the Canaanites, who lived in the land; you handed the Canaanites over to them, along with their kings and the peoples of the land, to deal with them as they pleased. [25]They captured fortified cities and fertile land; they took possession of houses filled with all kinds of good things, wells already dug, vineyards, olive groves and fruit trees in abundance. They ate to the full and were well-nourished; they reveled in your great goodness.

[26]"But they were disobedient and rebelled against you; they put your law behind their backs. They killed your prophets, who had admonished them in order to turn them back to you; they committed awful blasphemies. [27]So you handed them over to their enemies, who oppressed them. But when they were oppressed they cried out to you. From heaven you heard them, and in your great compassion you gave them deliverers, who rescued them from the hand of their enemies.

[28]"But as soon as they were at rest, they again did what was evil in your

sight. Then you abandoned them to the hand of their enemies so that they ruled over them. And when they cried out to you again, you heard from heaven, and in your compassion you delivered them time after time.

[29]"You warned them to return to your law, but they became arrogant and disobeyed your commands. They sinned against your ordinances, by which a man will live if he obeys them. Stubbornly they turned their backs on you, became stiff-necked and refused to listen. [30]For many years you were patient with them. By your Spirit you admonished them through your prophets. Yet they paid no attention, so you handed them over to the neighboring peoples. [31]But in your great mercy you did not put an end to them or abandon them, for you are a gracious and merciful God.

[32]"Now therefore, O our God, the great, mighty and awesome God, who keeps his covenant of love, do not let all this hardship seem trifling in your eyes—the hardship that has come upon us, upon our kings and leaders, upon our priests and prophets, upon our fathers and all your people, from the days of the kings of Assyria until today. [33]In all that has happened to us, you have been just; you have acted faithfully, while we did wrong. [34]Our kings, our leaders, our priests and our fathers did not follow your law; they did not pay attention to your commands or the warnings you gave them. [35]Even while they were in their kingdom, enjoying your great goodness to them in the spacious and fertile land you gave them, they did not serve you or turn from their evil ways.

[36]"But see, we are slaves today, slaves in the land you gave our forefathers so they could eat its fruit and the other good things it produces. [37]Because of our sins, its abundant harvest goes to the kings you have placed over us. They rule over our bodies and our cattle as they please. We are in great distress.

This prayer contains some characteristics of poetry but is not as poetic as the Psalms. It is similar in form to the prayers of confession that we find in the historical books. The content is quite similar to historical psalms such as 78; 105; 106; 135; 136.[26] These historical psalms are of two types: some emphasize a thanksgiving theme and others a penitential one. This passage stresses the penitential theme. The prayer is also an example of how the people had learned to "implement the Torah." As Eskenazi has said, "Having learned Torah, having read the book of the Torah (Neh 9:3), the people demonstrate a new competence, a new understanding of what they have read, and prove able to translate these into commitment and action."[27]

The Jewish theologian P. Sigal calls the passage a "prayer-psalm

---

[26] F. C. Fensham, "Neh 9 and Pss 105, 106, and 136: Post-Exilic Historical Traditions in Poetic Form," *JNSL* 9 (1981): 35-51.

[27] Eskenazi, *Age of Prose,* 101.

which affirms the divine role in history and ascribes Israel's historic sufferings to Israel's repeated apostasies." He also considers it a prime source for Jewish theology and finds the following themes: (1) God as Creator (v. 6); (2) God's choice of Abraham and his covenant with him (vv. 7-8); (3) God's miraculous redemption of Israel from Egypt (vv. 9-12); (4) God's revelation at Sinai, mediated by Moses (vv. 13-14); (5) God's ordaining of the Sabbath (v. 14); and (6) God's attributes of grace, compassion, love, and patience (vv. 27-33).[28]

PRAISE TO GOD THE CREATOR (9:5b-6).   **9:5b**   The prayer begins with exaltation of God and the recognition of who he is. In the Lord's Prayer (Matt 6:9-13) Jesus teaches the same truth.

9:6   The doctrine of creation is important because it emphasizes God's sovereignty over all. Blenkinsopp translates the first clause, "You, O, YHVH, are the only God." It points, he says, to the Lord's incomparability and uniqueness (cf. Isa 44:6,8; 45:6,21-22; 46:9).[29] This theme is found also in Pss 95; 104; 136. "Starry host" translates Hebrew ṣĕbāʾām, which can also refer to angelic "hosts"; NIV probably is correct in understanding it as reference to the sun, moon, and stars. The people recognized that no one has life on his own merits; life comes from God.

GOD CHOSE ABRAHAM (9:7-8).   **9:7**   "Abram" is one of only two historical persons mentioned here by name (Moses is in v. 14). This prayer is not about specific persons in the past, but is about what God was doing with the Jews at that time. The emphasis throughout the prayer is on what God has done. It recounts God's actions in and for his people. He is, in fact, the subject of every sentence in vv. 6-15. We also need to remember God's acts in our history and throughout all the history of salvation. As Christians we are grafted into God's family, and thus Israel's history becomes part of our history.

9:8   God's special covenant relation with his people is central in the Bible. This covenant relationship motivates obedience to his commandments. The prophetic warnings of judgment are based on the fact that Israel broke the covenant, and God therefore had to judge the people.

The "land" as part of the covenant promise is the focus in this prayer. The covenant with Abraham is found in Gen 12; 15; 17.[30] The list of na-

---

[28] P. Sigal, *Judaism: The Evolution of a Faith* (Grand Rapids: Eerdmans, 1988), 36-37. Sigal thinks this prayer-psalm was written soon after the destruction of Jerusalem in 587 B.C. and is similar in genre to Lamentations. Others would place its origin later but still before the time of Nehemiah; thus it was used at times in the liturgy of the returned exiles. However, the spiritual circumstances of the particular community confession would recommend that the psalm was penned for this occasion, though clearly echoing exilic sounds.

[29] Blenkinsopp, *Ezra, Nehemiah*, 297.

tions here is abbreviated from Gen 15:19. Throughout this prayer the language is directly reminiscent of and dependent on many specific passages of the Pentateuch; also Joshua, Judges, Samuel, and Kings are used frequently.[31] "You are righteous" is the central topic of this section. There is a parallel emphasis on God's faithfulness and the faithfulness of Abraham.

LIBERATION AND GUIDANCE: EXODUS AND WANDERINGS (9:9-12). **9:9** As God cares for those who suffer (Exod 3:7), so should his people do likewise. One of the lasting impressions the exodus made on Israel was a sense of justice. God later reminded them to remember the oppressed because he had released them from oppression (Deut 15:12-15).

9:10 The exodus experience had a decisive influence on the life and thought of Israel. First, there was great emphasis on the wonders and miracles God did there (Deut 6:20-23). Some forty Hebrew words are used to speak of miracles; they are used approximately five hundred times in the Old Testament. Half of these five hundred occurrences refer to the miracles of the exodus.[32]

The exodus profoundly influenced Israel's theology, especially in three areas: (1) in the way Israel viewed history as God's acts and as a dialogue between God and persons, (2) in Israel's emphasis on justice and freedom, and (3) in the basis for the biblical language of redemption.[33]

9:11-12 These verses refer to Exod 13:1-14:30. God had delivered the Hebrews from the oppression of a foreign land similar to the deliverance of the Jews from Babylon and Persia. The New Testament uses language of deliverance to remember how God liberates us from the oppression of sin and from the fears that are so much a part of life around us (2 Cor 1:9-11; Gal 1:4; Col 1:13; Heb 2:14-15). We also should remember God's daily guidance as a miraculous gift.

GOD'S GIFTS AT SINAI AND LATER (9:13-15).   **9:13** In Exod 20:1-23 God gave the gift of the Commandments. They are not simply negative commands but rather are instructions on how to live the godly life. No more important gift is known in the Old Testament. God is not an im-

---

[30] Nehemiah 9:8 can be considered a commentary on Gen 15:6.

[31] Myers (*Ezra, Nehemiah,* 167-70) fills three pages with the list of parallel passages and concludes: "The author of our prayer psalm drew upon a wide knowledge of the theology and traditions of his people, skillfully weaving into it elements of instruction, exhortation, and confession."

[32] D. Said, "A funçao dos milagres na liberaçao do exodo." Unpublished Ph.D. diss. (Seminario Bóblico Latinoamericano, San José, Costa Rica, 1973), chap. 1.

[33] J. M. Breneman, ed., *Liberación, Exodo y Biblia* (Editorial Caribe, 1975), 14.

personal force but a personal God who communicates with human beings. The God of the Bible acts in history and has spoken, revealing to his people who he is, what he does, and what his will is. This entire chapter emphasizes all that God has given to his people. The Hebrew word *nātan* ("give") is used fifteen times.[34]

The Jews did not see the laws as a burden or something negative but as a gift of God to guide his people in forming a just and good society. As Jesus said, the basis of the law is to love God and love our neighbor (Mark 12:28-34; cf. Matt 5:17-20). The other laws are corollaries of these. We still need specific norms to know God's will in particular areas of life.

The law proves that we need God's grace. But after being reconciled with God through his grace in Christ, we desire to do God's will. The law, encapsulated in the Ten Commandments, indicates what his will is in the important areas of life. In the Sermon on the Mount, Jesus showed the relevance of the Ten Commandments for life under the new covenant (Matt 5-7).

9:14 The Sabbath is mentioned here in a context of grace (cf. 10:31; 13:15-22). Various words for God's commands ("commands, decrees, and laws") are used in this passage as in Ps 119. Each has a slightly different focus but, as in Ps 119, is used here as a synonym to express God's revelation to his people. "Moses holds a special place in the Jewish faith and is no less important for the New Testament, where he is referred to eighty-five times (e.g., John 1:15-18; Heb 3; Rev 15:1-4; in fact, Moses is referred to eighty-five times in the New Testament).

9:15 "Bread from heaven" is a reference to the manna given to the children of Israel during the journey from Egypt to Canaan (Exod 16:4-8). This expression is used in poetic descriptions such as Pss 78:24; 105:40. The concept appears in John 6:22-40 and Rev 2:17. The teaching is that God provides for his people's daily needs. The conquest of the land was to be God's work, but the people had to believe and take initiative. Initiative based on faith was required but was lacking on that occasion. Real faith motivates one to do God's will.

ISRAEL'S DISOBEDIENCE AND GOD'S MERCY (9:16-18).   **9:16** A

---

[34] God gave (1) the land (v. 8; "to give" used twice); (2) miraculous signs and wonders (v. 10; "sent"); (3) regulations, laws, decrees, and commands (v. 13); (4) bread and water (v. 15); (5) land (v. 15); (6) his good Spirit (v. 20); (7) water (v. 20); (8) victory over kingdoms and nations (v. 22); (9) victory over the Canaanites (v. 24; "handed over"); (10) deliverance (v. 27; "handed over"; *nātan* used twice); (11) his great goodness (v. 35); (12) the land (v. 35); (13) the land (v. 36). Cf. F. C. Holmgren, *Israel Alive Again: Ezra and Nehemiah*, ITC [Grand Rapids: Eerdmans, 1987], 133.

major change in thought is signaled in this verse by the initial "but they." What God did for and gave to Israel should have produced thankfulness and humility in them. That it did not was the great tragedy of the Old Testament. "Stiff-necked" is a common biblical expression for stubbornness (cf. Exod 32:9; Jer 7:26; 17:23). The imagery is that of an animal that struggles against having a yoke placed on its neck. This attitude of pride and wickedness was widespread during the monarchical period and is claimed to have been the reason for the fall of both Samaria and Judah (cf. Jer 17:9).

9:17-18 God's people are to "remember" what he has done for them in the past.[35] Forgetfulness of what God has done can cause disobedience (cf. Deut 4:23,31). In spite of all God had given to them, the people of Israel constantly turned away from him. "To return to their slavery" certainly was foolish, but this is a part of human nature. That is why we need to "clothe" ourselves "with the Lord Jesus Christ" and not "think about how to gratify the desires of sinful nature" (Rom 13:14).

"You are a forgiving God" is the key phrase in this section and perhaps in the whole prayer. In spite of all the people's failures, God kept on forgiving; he still guided them and took care of them. The sentence begins with "but you" (we'attâ). This term, also in the Hebrew text of vv. 17,19,27,28,33 (sometimes obscured in translation) and the alternating "but they" (wĕhēm) in vv. 16,35 mark the great tension in this and every confession. Despite our sin, God is gracious; despite God's grace, we continue to sin; despite our continuing sin, God continues to be gracious (Rom 5:20). God's forgiveness is something no human could devise but can experience.

GOD'S PROVISION IN THE DESERT (9:19-21). **9:19** Nehemiah reemphasized that though God in his justice punishes sin, he also is a God of love and compassion. This prayer indicates that to view the Old Testament God as a God of anger and the God of the New Testament as a God of love is a false dichotomy. Even when the people acted rebelliously, God graciously guided them with pillars of cloud and fire (Exod 13:21-22).

9:20 The idea of the Trinity was not revealed in the Old Testament. However, the Old Testament contains many references to the activity of God's Spirit. God is Spirit. There is no separation of God and Spirit, as Gnosticism might suggest.[36]

9:21 The providential care of God is referred to again as is evident

---

[35] The term "remember" is especially prominent in Deuteronomy (e.g., 4:10; 5:15; 7:18) and Psalms (e.g., 77:11). See also Neh 4:14.

[36] Some have suggested that this passage reflects Persian dualism. But there are many references to God's Spirit long before there was a possibility of Persian influence (e.g., Gen 1:2; Num 11:17,25; 1 Sam 16:14; 2 Kgs 22:23; Pss 51:11; 143:10; Isa 43:10. See the comments on v. 30.

in the journey from Egypt to the promised land. The prayer reflects the faith of the people that just as God cared for the children of Israel who came up out of Egypt, they too would be cared for in a similar way. The land is vital to the Jewish faith because it represents their covenant with God.

THE CONQUEST OF CANAAN (9:22-25).   **9:22**   As God later used Assyria and Babylon to judge Israel, he used Israel to judge the moral corruption of the Canaanite society. As a sovereign God he has a right to judge people and entire populations.

9:23   "As numerous as the stars in the sky" is a reference to the promise God made to Abraham (Gen 12:2; 15:5). This entire scene (Neh 7:73–10:39) has the design and look of a covenant renewal ceremony (Exod 34). This phrase is basic to the original covenant made with Abraham. The fulfillment of the covenant is realized in the fact that there were people who had regathered in Israel to renew the covenant.

9:24   The Hebrews, directed and guided by God, took the land. They had been displaced but had now returned to their home, the place of promise.

9:25   The point of this passage is God's abundant provision for Israel so that they "reveled in [his] great goodness." However, Israel took all their prosperity for granted and disobeyed God's commands, which according to the following verses is rebellion.

THE PEOPLE'S PERSISTENCE IN BACKSLIDING (9:26-31).   This section presents a threefold repetition of the same four-step historical cycle evident in the Book of Judges (see Judg 2:10-20): (1) the people were disobedient; (2) God handed them over to their enemies, who oppressed them; (3) they then cried to God for help; (4) God heard and delivered them. The cycle is seen in vv. 26-27 (which begins "but they"), in v. 28, and again in vv. 29-31; but the last cycle is not completed. The cry for help (the third step in the cycle) is the theme of this prayer, and it looks forward to that expected complete deliverance.

9:26   Law was of utmost importance in Israel's context. The whole Mesopotamian culture was characterized by centuries of legal development. The well-known laws of Hammurapi date back to ca. 1700 B.C., but they represent the culmination of work on jurisprudence for centuries before. There were also later collections such as the Middle Assyrian Laws. This background is reflected in the Pentateuch. God used many elements of this background to reveal his will to his people.

When Israel followed God, they were eager to keep his laws because they wanted to please him. But when they neglected their loyalty to God and were guilty of backsliding, they also neglected his laws. The result was a breakdown in society and God's punishment in the form of the Babylonian captivity. When God tried to warn his people, their response was to silence the warning voice (cf. Jer 26:8). The people thought they could live without God's word, but the result was exile.

God's moral imperatives show his will. We must allow God's Spirit to instruct us through his Word. We must take seriously John's admonition: "The man who says, 'I know him,' but does not do what he commands is a liar, and the truth is not in him" (1 John 2:4).

9:27 Israel seems to have needed a crisis to recognize its need of dependence on God. Often we do not realize that we need God until we are under oppression (cf. 2:23-25).

"From heaven you heard them" indicates that again God's mercy and compassion is prominent.

9:28 Thus the cycle repeats itself. When all goes well, it is easy to neglect dependence on God (Deut 6:10-12; 8:11-20; 11:15-16; 31:20).

9:29 "By which a man will live" is a well-known theme in the law (Lev 18:5; Deut 4:1; 30:16). God's word (his laws, his guidance) is the life of his people. One who rejects God's moral instructions is really rejecting life with God.

9:30 The prophetic messages were inspired by God's Spirit. Nevertheless, even revelation through the prophets was not accepted. The Christian community must be receptive to what the Holy Spirit wants to say through the Scriptures.

9:31 This entire prayer emphasizes God's abundant "mercy." The prayer recognizes that God would have been "just" in putting an end to these rebellious people. Yet he kept on loving, guiding, and delivering them (Exod 32:10; 33:5).

A PLEA FOR MERCY (9:32-37).   **9:32** The people could still address God as "our God" because they knew he was merciful. They knew the truth of 2 Chr 7:14: "If my people, who are called by my name, will humble themselves and pray and seek my face and turn from their wicked ways, then will I hear from heaven and will forgive their sin and will heal their land."[37] Now that they were repenting, they could count on the promise; and the third cycle could be completed.

The covenant relation between God and his people is central in the Bible. The people knew God was faithful and merciful because of his action in the past. They recognized that God is "the great, mighty and awesome God," all powerful and sovereign; yet they remembered his

---

[37] Although 2 Chronicles may not have been written at this time, the promise comes from the time of the dedication of Solomon's temple.

covenant of love with his people.

"From the days of the kings of Assyria" includes the whole time of captivity, even the captivity of the Northern Kingdom in 722. "Until now" would be the time of the composition of this prayer of confession.[38]

9:33 The people recognized that God's judgment had been just and that they deserved punishment because their fathers and their leaders did not obey God.

9:34 The wrongdoing was not God's but was that of the kings, leaders, priests, and fathers who did not keep the Torah, the written revelation contained in Genesis through Deuteronomy.

9:35-37 "We are slaves today" is thought by some to contradict what we know about the way the Persians treated their subjects. Some think this indicates that the prayer was composed earlier, while the people were still under Babylonian rule. However, even though the Persians were not as cruel to their subjects as Assyria and Babylon had been, they exacted heavy taxes. The Jews were still their subjects.

It was one thing to be a slave in a foreign land, but to be a slave in their own land was quite another. The Jews still lived under the auspices of the Persian king, but their desire was to live only under the God of their ancestors. The prayer ends on a confessional note, "We are in great distress." Such an end to a prayer is a tremendous sign of faith in God. The people knew that God was their only chance for deliverance, just as he had been for the children of Israel when they were in Egypt.

Nehemiah and the people knew that the inexhaustibility of God's grace did not give them license to sin. It was, in fact, because of sin that they continued to suffer (vv. 33-37). As McConville observes, "The balance of the prayer is intended, therefore, both to point to the open-ended possibilities of future blessing from God and to call the people to set their house in order, so that it might be realized.[39]

This chapter is full of practical theology. It puts the emphasis on three great themes: (1) what God has done, (2) how the people disobeyed God, and (3) what God continues to do in history. These were very important themes for the community of returned exiles as they are for us today. God's providential role in history is displayed with great care in this chapter. What humans may attribute to secular causes, the biblical authors understood to have derived from none other than the living God.

---

[38] As noted above, this could have been anytime from shortly after the fall of Jerusalem to the Babylonians in 587 B.C. but more likely was the time of Ezra and Nehemiah.

[39] McConville, *Ezra, Nehemiah, and Esther*, 128.

4. The Agreement of the People (9:38–10:39)

(1) Introduction (9:38)

38"In view of all this, we are making a binding agreement, putting it in writing, and our leaders, our Levites and our priests are affixing their seals to it."

As noted in the introduction, scholars differ on the origin of chap. 10 (9:38–10:39 in English).[40] Certainly the final author of Ezra-Nehemiah saw this agreement of the people as the culmination of the work of Ezra and Nehemiah.

9:38 "In view of all this" links this chapter with chap. 9. Even though some think Neh 8–10 may not have been composed together, the events certainly could have occurred in this order. The author shows how the emphasis on the Torah resulted in the people's commitment to obey God.

The Hebrew verb *kārat,* used many times in the Old Testament to "make" or "cut" a covenant (*běrît*), is used here with *ʾămānâ* ("agreement").[41] The author may have used it here because in 9:7-8 he remembered Abraham's faithfulness (the same Hebrew root *ʾāmān*) and God's covenant with him. Just as Abraham was faithful, the postexilic covenant community must be faithful to God.

(2) The Chief Leaders and Priests Who Signed (10:1-8)

1Those who sealed it were:

Nehemiah the governor, the son of Hacaliah.

---

[40] According to Williamson, the chapter does not seem to be part of either the Ezra Memoirs or the Nehemiah Memoirs. Neither does it appear to have been part originally of this section. He suggests that originally the chapter was an independent composition; the final author may have taken it from temple archives. It also seems strange, he says, after this solemn agreement, to find again in Neh 13 the problems the agreement was designed to solve. He thinks that chronologically it is best to consider that this agreement was made after the events of Neh 13. There are many parallels with Neh 13 but also some differences (Williamson, *Ezra, Nehemiah,* 330). Myers also notes that Neh 10 coincides better with Neh 13 than with the Ezra material (Myers, *Ezra, Nehemiah,* 165). This is a possible reading of the material; however, we must take seriously the fact that the chapter was placed here by the final author (probably Ezra). The correspondence with Neh 13 can be understood if we consider that in chap. 13 Nehemiah was giving a summary of events that occurred over a considerable period of time; thus some of those events could have occurred before the agreements of Neh 10.

[41] This is the only place in the Old Testament where אֲמָנָה is used as a synonym for בְּרִית (Holmgren, *Ezra and Nehemiah,* 136-37).

Zedekiah, [2]Seraiah, Azariah, Jeremiah,
[3]Pashhur, Amariah, Malkijah,
[4]Hattush, Shebaniah, Malluch,
[5]Harim, Meremoth, Obadiah,
[6]Daniel, Ginnethon, Baruch,
[7]Meshullam, Abijah, Mijamin,
[8]Maaziah, Bilgai and Shemaiah.

These were the priests.

In addition to a discussion about the composition of chap. 10, several theories exist about the relation of the list of signees to the rest of the chapter. Some suggest the list was added later because the grammatical construction of 9:38 continues in 10:28.[42] It must include the leading families of the postexilic community. However, the list in its present location certifies that the events of Neh 8–9 were community oriented and thus it is the establishment of the community of God that stands as the important element in the story. The families returned from Persia and Babylonia to reconvene their life with God in their homeland. Thus the following list signifies that the community as a whole adopted the Word of God as authoritative for their lives.

10:1-8 A seal signified a "legal assent to a written document." Here the "seals" refer to the signatures of these leaders.[43] In Hebrew there is a conjunction ("and") between Nehemiah and Zedekiah, but this does not occur between the other names. Thus it sets off these two who represent the civil government. There are twenty-one priestly names, fifteen of which are names of families. Ezra probably was not named because he belonged to the family of Seraiah, as did the high priest Eliashib.

(3) The Levites Who Signed (10:9-13)

[9] **The Levites:**

**Jeshua son of Azaniah, Binnui of the
sons of Henadad, Kadmiel,
[10]and their associates: Shebaniah,
Hodiah, Kelita, Pelaiah, Hanan,
[11]Mica, Rehob, Hashabiah,
[12]Zaccur, Sherebiah, Shebaniah,**

---

[42] Rudolph and Mowinckel think an independent official list lies behind this list. Williamson concludes that it was taken from the other lists in Ezra and Nehemiah (Williamson, *Ezra, Nehemiah*, 330).

[43] Clines, *Ezra, Nehemiah, Esther*, 200.

¹³**Hodiah, Bani and Beninu.**

10:9 Of the seventeen Levitical names, some are family groups, and some are individual names.[44] Some are families who returned with Zerubbabel (Neh 12:8); six or seven are mentioned in the group that taught the law in Neh 8:7. The lists of Levites vary considerably in Ezra-Nehemiah. In Ezra 2 (and Neh 7) only three families are mentioned; in Neh 9:4-5 there are sixteen names, of which some are repeated here; in Neh 12:8-9 there are eight names, of which four are found here; in Neh 12:24-25 only three names are listed.

10:10-12 "And their associates" is literally "and their brothers," meaning their fellow Levites.

(4) The Other Leaders Who Signed (10:14-27)

¹⁴ **The leaders of the people:**

Parosh, Pahath-Moab, Elam, Zattu, Bani,
¹⁵**Bunni, Azgad, Bebai,**
¹⁶**Adonijah, Bigvai, Adin,**
¹⁷**Ater, Hezekiah, Azzur,**
¹⁸**Hodiah, Hashum, Bezai,**
¹⁹**Hariph, Anathoth, Nebai,**
²⁰**Magpiash, Meshullam, Hezir,**
²¹**Meshezabel, Zadok, Jaddua,**
²²**Pelatiah, Hanan, Anaiah,**
²³**Hoshea, Hananiah, Hasshub,**
²⁴**Hallohesh, Pilha, Shobek,**
²⁵**Rehum, Hashabnah, Maaseiah,**
²⁶**Ahiah, Hanan, Anan,**
²⁷**Malluch, Harim and Baanah.**

10:14-27 "The leaders of the people" (v. 14) were mostly family representatives. The first twenty-one are nearly parallel to the list of Ezra 2:3-30 (and Neh 7). The remaining twenty-three include some families who helped build the wall (Neh 3) and some new ones; perhaps some returned from Babylonia more recently, and others were branches of older families.[45] It is also possible that some could have been families who had remained in Judah during the captivity and now joined the returned exiles.[46]

---

[44] Fensham says all are names of individuals (*Ezra and Nehemiah,* 236).
[45] Kidner, *Ezra and Nehemiah,* 115.

(5) The Solemn Promise (10:28-29)

[28]"The rest of the people—priests, Levites, gatekeepers, singers, temple
servants and all who separated themselves from the neighboring peoples for
the sake of the Law of God, together with their wives and all their sons and
daughters who are able to understand— [29]all these now join their brothers
the nobles, and bind themselves with a curse and an oath to follow the Law of
God given through Moses the servant of God and to obey carefully all the
commands, regulations and decrees of the LORD our Lord.

10:28   The Hebrew begins, "And the rest," which may be a continuation of 9:38. As noted earlier, the list of names may have been added after the rest of the chapter was written. More likely, however, the list in
vv. 1-27 should be understood not so much as having been added but
rather as integral to the intent of the text as a whole. It took agreement
among the leaders in order for the whole community to make this commitment together.

The phrase "all who separated themselves" indicates that this was a
definite community with definite limits. Separation from the neighboring
peoples was important to maintain the distinctive beliefs and ethical principles of the community. God still wants his people to be separate by re-
pudiating values and beliefs that are contrary to his will. We must take
seriously the scriptural emphasis on separation without falling into an
isolationist situation. The other danger is to accommodate the world so
much that we fall into a syncretism that loses our Christian way of thinking and acting. In the situation of Ezra and Nehemiah, separation was imperative to secure the continuity of the redeemed community.

10:29   "Sons and daughters . . . able to understand" reminds us that
the young people and children must be included in community commitment. Why did they include a curse? This was a covenant between the
people and God. Covenant agreements (between kings and nations) in the
ancient world included blessings for keeping the covenant and curses for
breaking it. God's covenant with Israel was presented in the same terms
(note the curses in Deut 27:15-26; 30:19). The people followed this same
pattern and took for granted that the breaking of the oath would incur a
curse, which would be some punishment or judgment from God. The
community pledge that follows presupposes a detailed knowledge of the
law.

Submission to the authority of God's Word is the unmistakable com-

---

[46] The phrase "and all who separated themselves from the neighboring peoples" in v.
28 could support this.

mand here. The postexilic community was experiencing many problems, both ethical and religious. The first step toward solving these problems was a commitment by the whole community to submit to the authority of God's revelation as found in the Scriptures. The same is true for God's people today. This commitment to the authority of Scripture must be applied to present situations, for "true religion cannot be merely general principles."[47] The principles must be applied to specific actions and decisions.

(6) Specific Examples of Separation (10:30-31)

[30]"We promise not to give our daughters in marriage to the peoples around us or take their daughters for our sons.
[31]"When the neighboring peoples bring merchandise or grain to sell on the Sabbath, we will not buy from them on the Sabbath or on any holy day. Every seventh year we will forgo working the land and will cancel all debts.

The specific promises or regulations listed from vv. 30-39 are based on the laws of the Pentateuch but applied to this specific situation.[48] Clines says it appears that the levitical lawyers drew up this document as a group of standards or norms similar to the "halakot" (traditions applying the law to life) of the later rabbis. He suggests that this represents the beginnings of the process of scriptural exegesis and legal definition that developed later into the Mishna and Talmud

10:30 The first rule forbids intermarriage with foreigners. Here it is somewhat modified from the original laws in the Pentateuch (Exod 34:11-16; Deut 7:1-4; 20:10-18), which prohibited intermarriage with the nations of Canaan because that would lead to apostasy. These prohibitions against intermarriage were for religious reasons. Converts like Rahab and Ruth were accepted in the community.

10:31 The laws regarding the Sabbath and Sabbatical Year are based on the laws of the Pentateuch, but they define new cases. The Jews would not have bought and sold among themselves. However, living so close to non-Jews who brought merchandise to sell on the Sabbath presented a new situation. Likewise the decision about the seventh year combines older laws. Exodus 23:10-11 says the land was to rest each seventh year; Exod 21:2-6 includes the release of slaves (who were slaves because of debts); and the cancelation of debts is found in Deut 15:1-2.

---

[47] F. C. Holmgren, *Ezra and Nehemiah*, 138.

[48] D. J. A. Clines, "Nehemiah 10 as an Example of Early Jewish Biblical Exegesis," *JSOT* 21 [1981]: 111-17. See also idem, *Ezra, Nehemiah, Esther*, 204.

Are these laws relevant for us today? As Christians in the new covenant we are not under "law," but the Old Testament is still God's word for our lives. The Old Testament laws contain ethical principles that are valid at all times. The principle of dedicating one day of the week especially to the Lord is still valid. We have nothing directly corresponding to the Sabbatical Year, but certainly it teaches us that commitment to the Lord must influence our social thinking. The prophets pointed out that when the Israelites neglected God's laws (which maintained social equality), they fell into unjust economic practices that resulted in an unjust society. This in turn brought God's judgment on the nation. Although we are saved by grace (John 1:15-18), Jesus did not teach us to live outside of the law but within it (Matt 5:17-20). It is not the letter of the law we live by but the spirit of the law (2 Cor 3:1-6).

(7) The Temple Taxes (10:32-33)

[32]"We assume the responsibility for carrying out the commands to give a third of a shekel each year for the service of the house of our God: [33]for the bread set out on the table; for the regular grain offerings and burnt offerings; for the offerings on the Sabbaths, New Moon festivals and appointed feasts; for the holy offerings; for sin offerings to make atonement for Israel; and for all the duties of the house of our God.

10:32   The temple tax had not been a specific law before Neh 13:10. In the Persian period the economy became more money based; thus temple support was needed both in cash and in kind (animals and grains). However, there is a precedent to this tax in Exod 30:11-16 and 38:25-26; in fact, the language here reflects a knowledge of the Exod 30 passage.

10:33   This verse lists the uses of this temple tax: (a) the bread, or shewbread (Lev 24:6; cf. 1 Sam 21:6), consisted of twelve cakes of fine flour placed on the golden table at the beginning of each Sabbath; (b) the regular grain offerings and burnt offerings (Exod 29:38-42; Num 28:3-8); (c) offerings on the Sabbaths, New Moon festivals, and appointed feasts (Num 28:9-29:39); (d) the holy offerings; (e) the sin offerings (Lev 4:1-5; Num 15:22-29); and (f) all the duties "of the house of our God," which included the upkeep of the temple and temple property. The burnt offering was to be one lamb each morning and evening. In Ezra 6:9 and 7:17 the Persian government provided these animals, though apparently that help did not continue (under Cambyses the Persian, help given to temples in Egypt was greatly reduced).

A community of believers that loves God will not neglect these responsibilities. God is Spirit, but our worship and service, though not ostentatious, do require some structure. In practical terms this means providing the financial support that enables the ministry of the church.

(8) Offerings in Kind (10:34-39)

³⁴"We—the priests, the Levites and the people—have cast lots to determine when each of our families is to bring to the house of our God at set times each year a contribution of wood to burn on the altar of the LORD our God, as it is written in the Law.

³⁵"We also assume responsibility for bringing to the house of the LORD each year the firstfruits of our crops and of every fruit tree.

³⁶"As it is also written in the Law, we will bring the firstborn of our sons and of our cattle, of our herds and of our flocks to the house of our God, to the priests ministering there.

³⁷"Moreover, we will bring to the storerooms of the house of our God, to the priests, the first of our ground meal, of our [grain] offerings, of the fruit of all our trees and of our new wine and oil. And we will bring a tithe of our crops to the Levites, for it is the Levites who collect the tithes in all the towns where we work. ³⁸A priest descended from Aaron is to accompany the Levites when they receive the tithes, and the Levites are to bring a tenth of the tithes up to the house of our God, to the storerooms of the treasury. ³⁹The people of Israel, including the Levites, are to bring their contributions of grain, new wine and oil to the storerooms where the articles for the sanctuary are kept and where the ministering priests, the gatekeepers and the singers stay.

"We will not neglect the house of our God."

10:34 "Each of our families" points to the importance of commitment and contribution by families. The wood offering is not mentioned in the Pentateuch; however, Lev 6:12-13 stipulates that the fire on the altar was to be kept burning at all times, hence the phrase "as it is written in the law." Nehemiah had made some provision for the supply of wood (Neh 13:31). The comment in Neh 13:31 may indicate that Neh 13 includes some events that happened prior to the agreements in this chapter.

Verses 35-39 mention several different firstfruit and tithe offerings. The tithes and offerings of God's people are used to support the worship and work commanded by God. There are various stipulations in the Pentateuch concerning these offerings for support of the Levites, priests, and the sacrifices. Apparently the offerings had not been sufficient. (Nehemiah 13:10 also shows that the offerings were insufficient.) Malachi 3:8-12, generally dated just before Ezra and Nehemiah (around 460), refers to a similar situation. The "firstfruits" (v. 35) offerings are commanded in Exod 23:19; 34:26; Deut 26:1-15. In Num 18:11-15 we are told that these offerings belonged to the priests and Levites.

10:35-36 The people promised, "We will bring." What is the equivalent today? We dedicate our earnings and our possessions to the Lord; we dedicate our children to him. Most of the Israelites' offerings were used to maintain the priests and Levites who were especially called to minister. In the church all believers are priests, but God still calls leaders and workers who are supported by the tithes and offerings of the believing community.

10:37a "The first"[49] can also be "the best of." The same word is used in Num 15:20-21. Numbers 18:21-24 stipulates that these tithes were to be given to the Levites; however, in Deut 14:22-29, where the tithe of produce is also commanded, it did not all go to the Levites. Some was used by the offerer to have a celebration "in the presence of the LORD."

10:37b-39 These verses commanded the Levites to tithe. This tithe went to support the priests as Num 18:25-32 commands. Kauffmann points out that in Num 18 the Levites greatly outnumbered the priests, but here there were fewer Levites. He notes this as evidence against the theory that the Pentateuchal laws were written shortly before the time of Ezra and Nehemiah.[50]

Nehemiah 7:73b–10:39 is a fitting description of events following Ezra 1:1 to Neh 7:73a. Eskenazi summarizes this well: "The confluence of persons and movements . . . is matched by the intensified linking of the people and book and people and the house of God. The commitment to the one is tantamount to a commitment to the other. The community, having coalesced—as a community, around the Torah, and in relation to the house of God—embodies the goals of Cyrus's decree"[51] (Ezra 1:1-4). The decree of Cyrus, Eskenazi suggests, is actually a decree by God through Cyrus (Ezra 6:14; see comment there). The purpose of Ezra-Nehemiah is to show how the community of faith was reestablished around the written Word, the Torah or Law, within the surroundings of God's house, a rebuilt Jerusalem.

Chapter 10 contains many challenges for Christians today: (1) It

---

[49] רֵאשִׁית.

[50] So the tithe by the Levites would not be sufficient here in Nehemiah. Kauffmann says: "In spite of the long conflict over the tithe, the priests did not introduce a new law into Scripture that would decide this vital case. Instead, they kept on record obsolete laws, whose harmonization produced the unnecessary and unbearable annual Levitical tithe. Nothing proves more clearly how mistaken is the view that in postexilic times the Torah book was still being added to and revised" (Y. Kaufmann, *The Religion of Israel* [London: Allen & Unwin, 1960], 193.

[51] Eskenazi, *Age of Prose*, 111.

shows the importance of submission to the authority of God's Word. Christians may differ over minor issues, interpreting some biblical passages differently. However, if they hold firmly to the authority of God's Word, they have the basis for finding agreement and a firm anchor against drifting into a sterile syncretism. (2) It emphasizes the holiness of the believing community—the importance of being separated from the world's values. (3) It challenges us to be faithful in the support of community worship, both in attendance and in monies, for maintaining the priority of worship is critical to the life of the church.

VII. THE RESETTLING OF JERUSALEM AND FURTHER
ACTIVITIES OF NEHEMIAH (11:1–13:31)
   1. The Repopulation of Jerusalem (11:1-24)
      (1) The General Arrangements (11:1-2)
      (2) Lay Families in Jerusalem (11:3-9)
      (3) Priests in Jerusalem (11:10-14)
      (4) Levites and Gatekeepers in Jerusalem (11:15-24)
   2. The Cities of Judah and Benjamin (11:25-36)
   3. Lists of Priests and Levites (12:1-26)
      (1) Priests in the Time of Zerubbabel (12:1-7)
      (2) Levites in the Time of Zerubbabel (12:8-9)
      (3) A List of High Priests (12:10-11)
      (4) Priests in the Days of Joiakim (12:12-21)
      (5) More Information about the Levites (12:22-26)
   4. The Dedication of the Wall (12:27-47)
      (1) Preparation for the Dedication (12:27-30)
      (2) The Processions and Dedication Service (12:31-43)
      (3) The Organization of Worship (12:44-47)
   5. Nehemiah's Further Reforms (13:1-31)
      (1) Separation from Foreigners (13:1-3)
      (2) Eliashib and Tobiah (13:4-9)
      (3) The Portion of the Levites (13:10-14)
      (4) The Question of the Sabbath (13:15-22)
      (5) Separation Restored (13:23-31)

VII. THE RESETTLING OF JERUSALEM AND FURTHER ACTIVITIES OF NEHEMIAH (11:1–13:31)

1. The Repopulation of Jerusalem (11:1-24)

(1) The General Arrangements (11:1-2)

¹Now the leaders of the people settled in Jerusalem, and the rest of the people cast lots to bring one out of every ten to live in Jerusalem, the holy city, while the remaining nine were to stay in their own towns. ²The people commended all the men who volunteered to live in Jerusalem.

Chapter 11 takes up the thought of 7:1-5 and 7:73. In the Nehemiah Memoirs this material probably followed immediately after that of chap. 7 (cf. 7:73). The new arrangement follows a logical order: the construction of the walls in chaps. 1–6; the spiritual revival in chaps. 8–10; and the organization of the community in chaps. 11–13. This latter section emphasizes the representation of the different families and the nature of authority in the organization. Especially here the focus is on the "people" rather than on any single character. As T. Eskenazi has shown, "the lists themselves also emphasize the importance of the community as a whole."[1]

Now that the wall was completed, it was important to secure the permanence and maintenance of the city. There were not enough people living in Jerusalem to do this. Nehemiah (7:4-5) records that he recognized this and took a kind of census, which led up to the decisions described here.

11:1 There is some redundancy at the beginning of the chapter since the ideas of vv. 1-2 are repeated in v. 3.[2] Some scholars such as Rudolph and Brockington suggest that the leaders here were taking the lead in moving to Jerusalem. Others take the verse to mean that the leaders already lived in Jerusalem, and the present effort had to do with the rest of the people.[3] This seems to be the normal sense of the verse. In Nehemiah we constantly read about the "leaders" of the people. God raises up leaders, and those in charge, such as Nehemiah, must pay attention to developing leadership and delegating responsibility to the leaders. Nehemiah teaches us the balance between efficient organization and good leadership and dependence on God at the same time. The two should not and need not be contradictory.

God can use different means to make known his will. The use of the lot is seen a number of times in the Old Testament (e.g., Num 26:55-56; 1 Chr 24:5; 25:8; John 1:7). Today Christians do not depend on this means of ascertaining God's will. Since the Holy Spirit dwells in every believer, we can expect God to make his will known through his Word, through inner conviction, and through his guidance of the circumstances. Nevertheless, we should not limit what God can do; he is sovereign and may use unusual means in specific circumstances. The important matter

[1] T. Eskenazi, *In an Age of Prose* (Atlanta: Scholars Press, 1988), 112.

[2] Some think that vv.1-2 were added by the editor and thus were not part of the Nehemiah Memoirs (H. G. M. Williamson, *Ezra, Nehemiah,* WBC [Waco: Word, 1985], 345). Verse 3 probably is a redactional note inserted by the editor.

[3] J. Myers, *Ezra. Nehemiah,* AB (Garden City: Doubleday, 1965), 186; F. C. Fensham, *The Books of Ezra and Nehemiah,* NICOT (Grand Rapids: Eerdmans, 1982), 242.

is to trust God for guidance.

The leaders and the people decided that 10 percent of the people who lived in the outlying villages should move to Jerusalem. The next verse does not make clear whether "the men who volunteered to live in Jerusalem" were those chosen by lot or others who volunteered in addition to that 10 percent. It most likely refers to the 10 percent who were chosen and who willingly accepted the decision to move to Jerusalem.

Jerusalem is called "the holy city" here and in v. 18. The same expression is not found often in the Old Testament but is found in Isa 48:2; 53:1; Dan 9:24. The job of both Ezra and Nehemiah had been centered around reestablishing Jerusalem as a city set apart (i.e., made holy) from the world and yet in the world. This title "indicates that the city as a whole is now holy, by virtue of its history, action, and relation to God."[4]

11:2 The fact that "the people commended them" confirmed this positive attitude and suggests that this decision entailed some sacrifice. Most people preferred to live in the villages rather than inside Jerusalem. Moving to Jerusalem meant a change of environment, a change of neighbors, a change of friends for the children, and a change of life-style. But their loyalty to the purpose of maintaining the community made them willing to do it.

(2) Lay Families in Jerusalem (11:3-9)

³These are the provincial leaders who settled in Jerusalem (now some Israelites, priests, Levites, temple servants and descendants of Solomon's servants lived in the towns of Judah, each on his own property in the various towns, ⁴while other people from both Judah and Benjamin lived in Jerusalem):

From the descendants of Judah:

Athaiah son of Uzziah, the son of Zechariah, the son of Amariah, the son of Shephatiah, the son of Mahalalel, a descendant of Perez; ⁵and Maaseiah son of Baruch, the son of Col-Hozeh, the son of Hazaiah, the son of Adaiah, the son of Joiarib, the son of Zechariah, a descendant of Shelah. ⁶The descendants of Perez who lived in Jerusalem totaled 468 able men.

⁷From the descendants of Benjamin:

Sallu son of Meshullam, the son of Joed, the son of Pedaiah, the son of Kolaiah, the son of Maaseiah, the son of Ithiel, the son of Jeshaiah, ⁸and his followers, Gabbai and Sallai—928 men. ⁹Joel son of Zicri was their chief officer, and Judah son of Hassenuah was over the Second District of the city.

---

[4] Eskenazi, *Age of Prose*, 114.

11:3 Verse 3 points out that many of the people lived in other towns and villages. The people mentioned include priests, Levites, and temple servants, while those who were now coming to live in Jerusalem were "other people from both Judah and Benjamin." The families dedicated to temple service were not all living together; they were not isolated from the rest of the population. Some of them lived out in the villages, and some of the other people (who were not priests or Levites) lived in Jerusalem. The professional religious workers lived and worked among all of the people and not in a vacuum where they were removed from the rest of society.

11:4 From v. 4 to v. 24 we have another of the lists of Ezra-Nehemiah. This list presents the names of families who moved to Jerusalem. Lists function as reminders that these were real people. The people of Israel, in fact, are some of the main characters in the book. The people function as a whole, a singular character who acts and reacts, initiates and responds. The list is apparently incomplete, for the parallel list in 1 Chr 9 includes more names and even some from other tribes in addition to Judah, Benjamin, and Levi. Some, like Rudolph, think that 1 Chr 9 depends on Neh 11. Others think that both lists had their origin in government archives,[5] the interpretation that seems to be the most acceptable.[6] Williamson sees no reason to conclude that the list is not authentic from the time of Nehemiah.[7]

11:4-5 "Athaiah . . . and Maaseiah" are the only representative families from Judah, but 1 Chr 9:6 includes the clan of Zerah.

11:6 The NEB translates "able men" as "men of substance," which is a possible translation. However, "brave" or "valiant" is the more common meaning and fits the context here. It takes courage to leave a comfortable situation (life in the village) and move the family to a different place.

11:7-9 Verses 7-9 give "the descendants of Benjamin" who moved to Jerusalem, but only one family line is mentioned; 1 Chr 9:7-9 mentions three other family lines. The "chief officer" had to do with the urban government, and "Second District" is better translated "second in command" (Judah was second in command; cf. v. 17).

---

[5] Myers, *Ezra, Nehemiah,* 185.

[6] But notice that the list in 1 Chr 9 apparently represents the first residents in Jerusalem after the return from exile (E. W. Hamrick, "Ezra-Nehemiah," BBC, vol. 3 [Nashville: Broadman, 1970], 498).

[7] Williamson, *Ezra, Nehemiah,* 346.

(3) Priests in Jerusalem (11:10-14)

¹⁰From the priests:

Jedaiah; the son of Joiarib; Jakin; ¹¹Seraiah son of Hilkiah, the son of Meshullam, the son of Zadok, the son of Meraioth, the son of Ahitub, supervisor in the house of God, ¹²and their associates, who carried on work for the temple—822 men; Adaiah son of Jeroham, the son of Pelaliah, the son of Amzi, the son of Zechariah, the son of Pashhur, the son of Malkijah, ¹³and his associates, who were heads of families—242 men; Amashsai son of Azarel, the son of Ahzai, the son of Meshillemoth, the son of Immer, ¹⁴and his associates, who were able men—128. Their chief officer was Zabdiel son of Haggedolim.

11:10-11 This list of priestly families is parallel to the list in 1 Chr 9:10-13, but there are some details that cause difficulties. If we delete "the son of" after "Jedaiah" (v. 10) as suggested in the NIV note, then we have six priestly family heads just as in 1 Chr 9.

11:12 There were different tasks for the priests as there were for the Levites (cf. v. 16). The number indicates that it requires a great deal of harmony for so many to work together as a unit.

11:14 "Able men" in this verse translates *gibbôrê ḥayil,* a stronger phrase than *ʾanšê ḥayil* (also translated "able men") in v. 6. The phrase in v. 14 is usually used of military personnel. These may have been men trained for defending the temple area. It has been suggested that since the purpose for bringing these people to Jerusalem was the defense of the city, the list uses some military terminology and is organized in the traditional form of military lists.[8] "Haggedolim" at the end of the verse is not otherwise known as a personal name. It is literally "the great ones." The GNB understands it as "a leading family." The total number of priests in 1 Chr 9:13 is 1,760; here it is 1,192.[9]

(4) Levites and Gatekeepers in Jerusalem (11:15-24)

¹⁵From the Levites:

Shemaiah son of Hasshub, the son of Azrikam, the son of Hashabiah, the son of Bunni; ¹⁶Shabbethai and Jozabad, two of the heads of the Levites, who had charge of the outside work of the house of God; ¹⁷Mattaniah son of Mica, the son of Zabdi, the son of Asaph, the director who led in thanksgiving and

---

[8] Williamson (*Ezra, Nehemiah,* 348) says, "The associated list was drawn up in terms reminiscent of the musters of the old conscript army." The material is comparable to that of 1 Chr 2-9 and Num 26 and the format used by Nehemiah in defense of the wall (4:7).

[9] D. J. A. Clines, *Ezra, Nehemiah, Esther,* NCB (Grand Rapids: Eerdmans, 1984), 215.

prayer; Bakbukiah, second among his associates; and Abda son of Shammua, the son of Galal, the son of Jeduthun. [18]The Levites in the holy city totaled 284.

[19]The gatekeepers:

Akkub, Talmon and their associates, who kept watch at the gates—172 men.

[20]The rest of the Israelites, with the priests and Levites, were in all the towns of Judah, each on his ancestral property.

[21]The temple servants lived on the hill of Ophel, and Ziha and Gishpa were in charge of them.

[22]The chief officer of the Levites in Jerusalem was Uzzi son of Bani, the son of Hashabiah, the son of Mattaniah, the son of Mica. Uzzi was one of Asaph's descendants, who were the singers responsible for the service of the house of God. [23]The singers were under the king's orders, which regulated their daily activity.

[24]Pethahiah son of Meshezabel, one of the descendants of Zerah son of Judah, was the king's agent in all affairs relating to the people.

11:16-18 "The outside work of the house of God" (v. 16) reminds us of the many different kinds of work committed to the Levites. Here it may include gathering and storing provisions for the temple and caring for the temple building and property.[10] Verse 17 reminds us that the purpose of all these different jobs was to worship God.

"Shabbethai and Jozabad" are mentioned in other passages as contemporaries of Ezra (Ezra 8:33; 10:15; Neh 8:7).[11]

"The director who led in thanksgiving and prayer" had a great influence on the thinking and life of the community. Israel's worship was the maker of its "world."[12] Today those who direct the worship of the church have extensive influence and a great responsibility in forming the values and priorities of the Christian community (see comments at 9:4).

Bakbukiah, as "second among his associates," may have been Mattaniah's substitute or second to him in this service. The small number of Levites in v. 18 in comparison to the priests reflects the situation in Ezra 8:15-20. In earlier times there were more Levites.

11:19 "The gatekeepers" here are not listed as Levites, though they are in 1 Chr 9:23-26; 26:1-19.[13] The passage in 1 Chr 9:17-27 gives

---

[10] Myers, *Ezra, Nehemiah,* 187.

[11] This is an indication that the list is not from a century later, as some think, but had its origin near the time of Nehemiah (Clines, *Ezra, Nehemiah, Esther,* 212).

[12] See W. Brueggemann, *Israel's Praise* (Philadelphia: Fortress, 1988).

more details about the duties of the gatekeepers.

11:20 This verse interrupts the list and seems to be out of place. It would fit better with v. 25. Williamson thinks vv. 21-24 were a later addition. The original list possibly ended with v. 20 and vv. 21-24 perhaps were added later to bring up to date the list of Asaph's descendants.[14] The verse reminds us that not all priests and Levites lived in Jerusalem.

11:21-22 "The temple servants" were the *nĕtînîm* (see Ezra 2:70). They were not included in the original list of vv. 3-20 because they already lived in Jerusalem. "The hill of Ophel" is the hill at the north end of the City of David just south of the temple area.

The importance of the worship service is again emphasized. Since David's time some of the Levites were especially designated as singers. This was continued even in the postexilic community.

11:23 The singers "were under the king's orders." King David had given special orders regarding the singers (1 Chr 25; Neh 12:24), but here the king must refer to the Persian king who was interested in the continuation of cultic practices in all his subject peoples.[15] This understanding is confirmed by v. 24, which mentions Pelaliah as "the king's agent in all affairs relating to the people." He must have been the Persian king's official advisor on Jewish affairs. All this reminds the reader that the Jews were not politically free but were subject to the Persian king. According to Ezra 6:14, however, the Persian king was subject to God.

2. The Cities of Judah and Benjamin (11:25-36)

25As for the villages with their fields, some of the people of Judah lived in Kiriath Arba and its surrounding settlements, in Dibon and its settlements, in Jekabzeel and its villages, **26**in Jeshua, in Moladah, in Beth Pelet, **27**in Hazar Shual, in Beersheba and its settlements, **28**in Ziklag, in Meconah and its settlements, **29**in En Rimmon, in Zorah, in Jarmuth, **30**Zanoah, Adullam and their villages, in Lachish and its fields, and in Azekah and its settlements. So they were living all the way from Beersheba to the Valley of Hinnom.

31The descendants of the Benjamites from Geba lived in Micmash, Aija, Bethel and its settlements, **32**in Anathoth, Nob and Ananiah, **33**in Hazor, Ramah and Gittaim, **34**in Hadid, Zeboim and Neballat, **35**in Lod and Ono, and in the Valley of the Craftsmen.

---

[13] Some think this is another indication that Chronicles was written later than Ezra-Nehemiah (Williamson, *Ezra, Nehemiah,* 345). But note that in Neh 12:26 the gatekeepers are included with the Levites as in 1 Chr 9.

[14] Ibid., 348.

[15] Fensham, *Ezra and Nehemiah,* 248.

³⁶**Some of the divisions of the Levites of Judah settled in Benjamin.**

11:25-36 This list has given rise to much discussion. Most of the Judean cities appear also in the list of Josh 15.¹⁶ This might indicate the extent of the province of Judah at this time, which includes the former area of Benjamin. However, some towns are mentioned that appear to have been outside of Judah, as Ono and cities in the Negev where Geshem and the Arabs must have lived. So the list probably includes some towns that had a partially Jewish population beyond the border of Judah. The Jews were free to move around in the Persian Empire.

3. Lists of Priests and Levites (12:1-26)

The first part of chap. 12 continues with lists of priests and Levites. Verses 1-7 present the family names of the priests at the time of the first return; vv. 8-9 list the Levites of the same time; vv. 10-11 list the line of high priests; vv. 12-21 list the priests in the time of Jehoiakim, the second generation after the return; vv. 22-23 add details about the records; vv. 24-26 continue with the Levites and details on chronology.¹⁷ It may seem tedious to us to find so many lists of genealogies and place names in Ezra and Nehemiah. But it reminds us again that God's work is done by individuals. Even though it is community activity, each person in the community is important and must be given responsibility and must be an integral part of the community's activities.

The material in 11:21-36 and this material (12:1-26) appear to be parenthetical to Nehemiah's account of the resettlement of Jerusalem and the dedication of the wall. So 12:27 continues the account from 11:20.

(1) Priests in the Time of Zerubbabel (12:1-7)

¹**These were the priests and Levites who returned with Zerubbabel son of Shealtiel and with Jeshua: Seraiah, Jeremiah, Ezra, ²Amariah, Malluch, Hattush, ³Shecaniah, Rehum, Meremoth, ⁴Iddo, Ginnethon, Abijah, ⁵Mijamin, Moadiah, Bilgah, ⁶Shemaiah, Joiarib, Jedaiah, ⁷Sallu, Amok, Hilkiah and Jedaiah. These were the leaders of the priests and their associates in the days of Jeshua.**

12:1-7 Some think this list of priests was taken from the list in vv.

---

¹⁶ Ibid., 249 and the discussion in Myers, *Ezra, Nehemiah,* 189-90.
¹⁷ See Williamson, *Ezra, Nehemiah,* 360.

12-21.[18] The author no doubt used archival material as well.

(2) Levites in the Time of Zerubbabel (12:8-9)

⁸The Levites were Jeshua, Binnui, Kadmiel, Sherebiah, Judah, and also Mattaniah, who, together with his associates, was in charge of the songs of thanksgiving. ⁹Bakbukiah and Unni, their associates, stood opposite them in the services.

12:8-9 Ezra 2:40 mentions the Levite families at the first return but includes only those of Jeshua and Kadmiel; the list here includes several other families. Mattaniah and Bakbukiah also appear as directors of worship in Nehemiah's time (Neh 11:17; 12:25).

Mattaniah's family is mentioned as being in charge of worship (cf. 11:17). Bakbukiah and Unni "stood opposite them in the services," providing support and apparently contributing to the worship with antiphonal singing.

(3) A List of High Priests (12:10-11)

¹⁰Jeshua was the father of Joiakim, Joiakim the father of Eliashib, Eliashib the father of Joiada, ¹¹Joiada the father of Jonathan, and Jonathan the father of Jaddua.

12:10-11 We know that Jeshua was high priest at the time of the first return from exile and during the time of Haggai and Zechariah. Eliashib was high priest in the time of Nehemiah. So Joiakim must have been high priest some time before, perhaps at the time of Ezra's arrival in Jerusalem. The other names, compared with v. 22 and names mentioned in the Elephantine letters and in Josephus, have been used to set forth differing theories about chronological details.

According to the Elephantine letters, a Johanan was high priest in 410 B.C.[19] Josephus mentioned a Jaddua as high priest at the time of the fall of the Persian Empire to Alexander Magno (331 B.C.). New evidence shows that these names reappeared in successive generations, so the Jaddua of Josephus must have been from a later generation.[20]

---

[18] Ibid., 361.

[19] Cited in Kidner, *Ezra and Nehemiah*, 144.

[20] Williamson suggests that this list is not complete and that part of it was added at a later date, so this is the Jaddua of whom Josephus spoke (Williamson, *Ezra, Nehemiah*, 363). On the other hand, Kidner doubts this and also mentions that since these same names appear frequently in the genealogy, the Johanan and Jaddua of Josephus might have been different men, high priests of the same name who lived at a later time (Kidner, *Ezra and Nehemiah*, 144-45). Also Josephus sometimes did not have his details correct, especially his history of the Persian period. See the discussion on the repetition of names (pappynomy) in the line of high priests in Williamson, *Ezra, Nehemiah*, 363-65.

(4) Priests in the Days of Joiakim (12:12-21)

[12]In the days of Joiakim, these were the heads of the priestly families: of Seraiah's family, Meraiah; of Jeremiah's, Hananiah; [13]of Ezra's, Meshullam; of Amariah's, Jehohanan; [14]of Malluch's, Jonathan; of Shecaniah's, Joseph; [15]of Harim's, Adna; of Meremoth's, Helkai; [16]of Iddo's, Zechariah; of Ginnethon's, Meshullam; [17]of Abijah's, Zicri; of Miniamin's and of Moadiah's, Piltai; [18]of Bilgah's, Shammua; of Shemaiah's, Jehonathan; [19]of Joiarib's, Mattenai; of Jedaiah's, Uzzi; [20]of Sallu's, Kallai; of Amok's, Eber; [21]of Hilkiah's, Hashabiah; of Jedaiah's, Nethanel.

12:12-21   Joiakim was the son of Jeshua, who was high priest at the time of the first return. This list has similarities with that of 10:2-8, but here it is expanded to include six more names.

(5) More Information about the Levites (12:22-26)

[22]The family heads of the Levites in the days of Eliashib, Joiada, Johanan and Jaddua, as well as those of the priests, were recorded in the reign of Darius the Persian. [23]The family heads among the descendants of Levi up to the time of Johanan son of Eliashib were recorded in the book of the annals. [24]And the leaders of the Levites were Hashabiah, Sherebiah, Jeshua son of Kadmiel, and their associates, who stood opposite them to give praise and thanksgiving, one section responding to the other, as prescribed by David the man of God.

[25]Mattaniah, Bakbukiah, Obadiah, Meshullam, Talmon and Akkub were gatekeepers who guarded the storerooms at the gates. [26]They served in the days of Joiakim son of Jeshua, the son of Jozadak, and in the days of Nehemiah the governor and of Ezra the priest and scribe.

12:22-23   Verse 22 presents the same questions about genealogy and chronology as vv. 10-11. Kidner suggests that this Johanan was a brother of Joiada and followed him as high priest. Verse 23 says Johanan was "son of Eliashib." This could mean "descendant of," but it is better to take it here as "son of."[21] The Elephantine Papyri indicate that a Johanan was high priest in 410 B.C., in the reign of Darius II.[22] "Darius the Persian" is a unique expression. Williamson suggests that the editor used this designation to distinguish Darius I from Darius the Mede mentioned in Daniel.[23]

---

[21] See the discussion in Williamson, *Ezra, Nehemiah,* 152. Williamson takes Johanan as son of Eliashib.

[22] Kidner, *Ezra and Nehemiah,* 124.

[23] Williamson, *Ezra, Nehemiah,* 364.

12:24 "One section responding to the other" refers to antiphonal singing. David had instituted antiphonal singing using different choirs. The author here emphasized that they were following what David had inaugurated (see vv. 8-9).

"David, the man of God" is used only here, in v. 36, and in 2 Chr 8:14, always in relation to his work in organizing worship. The title "man of God" usually refers to prophets, but here the author no doubt was comparing David with Moses, who had founded Israelite worship.[24]

12:25 "Mattaniah, Bakbukiah, Obadiah" should be included with v. 24 because they were singers as Neh 11:17 indicates. The other three were gatekeepers.[25]

12:26 "In the days of Nehemiah . . . and of Ezra" again leads to the discussion about whether Nehemiah and Ezra were in Jerusalem at the same time. Many reject this possibility because they are mentioned together only in this verse. However, Haggai and Zechariah were contemporaries, and neither book mentions the other.[26]

Of course, v. 26 does not in itself necessarily prove that Ezra and Nehemiah were together. The author was giving details covering a rather long span of time. In representing the whole process as a unit, he tended to compress history and include later additions in the lists. The same process is seen in Chronicles. The author did not propose to give us a careful chronology; he was showing the continuity of the community and how God used these leaders during this process.

Not only were the outstanding leaders necessary for God's work in the community; the singers, the gatekeepers, and the Levites were all indispensable. In God's work each believer is important. According to Eph 4 the Lord has given gifts to each one, and the whole body grows together when all these gifts are used and coordinated in God's work. In a time when self-centeredness seems to dominate Western life-styles, the Word of God calls us to work and live together as a community, to be dependent upon one another, and to help one another in achieving the task God has set before us.

4. The Dedication of the Wall (12:27-47)

The completion of the wall of Jerusalem was cause for a time of dedi-

---

[24] Ibid., 365.

[25] The gatekeepers were included with the Levites. In 11:19 they were put in a separate list, but in 1 Chr 9 they were included with the Levites.

[26] See the discussion in the Introduction.

cation and celebration. Music filled the air (vv. 31,38), and there was great joy (v. 43). God calls us to celebration as well as service. The law even commands thankfulness and rejoicing (Deut 12:7,12,18; 14:26; 16:11-15; 26:11; 27:7; cf. 28:47). All had been completed. The decree of Cyrus (Ezra 1:1-4) had been fulfilled (Ezra 1:5 to Neh 7:73a), and the community had been restored (Neh 7:73b–12:26). The prophecy of Jeremiah (Ezra 1:1) had begun to be fulfilled, and the stage was now set for the completion of God's work in Israel (Jer 31:31-34). All of this would be acknowledged in the dedication of the work brought about by God.

(1) Preparation for the Dedication (12:27-30)

[27]At the dedication of the wall of Jerusalem, the Levites were sought out from where they lived and were brought to Jerusalem to celebrate joyfully the dedication with songs of thanksgiving and with the music of cymbals, harps and lyres. [28]The singers also were brought together from the region around Jerusalem—from the villages of the Netophathites, [29]from Beth Gilgal, and from the area of Geba and Azmaveth, for the singers had built villages for themselves around Jerusalem. [30]When the priests and Levites had purified themselves ceremonially, they purified the people, the gates and the wall.

12:27 The text does not tell us how long after the completion of the wall this dedication took place. We can assume it was very soon. Nehemiah did not separate the secular (wall building) from the sacred (worship), which was all part of the community's dedication to God. It was natural and appropriate to call a special worship service at the completion of the wall-building project that God had guided and protected.

The worship leaders are very important in the celebration: "the Levites were sought out." "Songs of thanksgiving" translates the Hebrew word *tôdôt*, which in vv. 31,38,40 is translated "choirs." The term should be translated throughout the passage as "thanksgiving choirs."[27]

12:28-29 "The singers also were brought." It is not clear whether the singers were counted among the Levites or considered a separate group.[28]

These villages were not all in the same area. Netopha was southeast of Bethlehem; Gilgal was near Jericho; Geba and Azmaveth were northeast

---

[27] Fensham, *Ezra and Nehemiah*, 257.

[28] Williamson suggests that here they were beginning to be counted among the Levites, and by the time Chronicles was written they were definitely included with the Levites (Williamson, *Ezra, Nehemiah*, 373).

of Jerusalem in the Benjamite area.[29]

12:30 The text does not give details on exactly what the purification included. It no doubt included fasting, abstaining from marital intercourse, making sacrifices, and perhaps bathing and using clean garments (Gen 35:2-3; Num 8:21-22; 1 Chr 29:15; 35:6; Ezra 6:20; Neh 13:22; Mal 3:3).[30]

Under the new covenant we are not bound by strict regulations regarding sacrifices and cleansings (cf. 1 John 1:7-9). But we should recognize the emphasis here on holiness. The leaders of God's people must be sensitive to things that defile them. They must constantly be cleansed in order to be holy instruments in God's hand. Holiness is one of the central themes of the Bible and something that God calls us to (Lev 11:44; 20:7; 20:26; Rom 7:12; 12:1; 2 Tim 1:9; 1 Pet 1:15-16; 2 Pet 3:11).

(2) The Processions and Dedication Service (12:31-43)

[31]I had the leaders of Judah go up on top of the wall. I also assigned two large choirs to give thanks. One was to proceed on top of the wall to the right, toward the Dung Gate. [32]Hoshaiah and half the leaders of Judah followed them, [33]along with Azariah, Ezra, Meshullam, [34]Judah, Benjamin, Shemaiah, Jeremiah, [35]as well as some priests with trumpets, and also Zechariah son of Jonathan, the son of Shemaiah, the son of Mattaniah, the son of Micaiah, the son of Zaccur, the son of Asaph, [36]and his associates—Shemaiah, Azarel, Milalai, Gilalai, Maai, Nethanel, Judah and Hanani—with musical instruments [prescribed by] David the man of God. Ezra the scribe led the procession. [37]At the Fountain Gate they continued directly up the steps of the City of David on the ascent to the wall and passed above the house of David to the Water Gate on the east.

[38]The second choir proceeded in the opposite direction. I followed them on top of the wall, together with half the people—past the Tower of the Ovens to the Broad Wall, [39]over the Gate of Ephraim, the Jeshanah Gate, the Fish Gate, the Tower of Hananel and the Tower of the Hundred, as far as the Sheep Gate. At the Gate of the Guard they stopped.

[40]The two choirs that gave thanks then took their places in the house of God; so did I, together with half the officials, [41]as well as the priests— Eliakim, Maaseiah, Miniamin, Micaiah, Elioenai, Zechariah and Hananiah with their trumpets— [42]and also Maaseiah, Shemaiah, Eleazar, Uzzi, Jehohanan, Malkijah, Elam and Ezer. The choirs sang under the direction of Jezrahiah. [43]And on that day they offered great sacrifices, rejoicing because God had given them great joy. The women and children also rejoiced. The sound

---

[29] Ibid., 373.

[30] Myers, *Ezra, Nehemiah*, 202.

of rejoicing in Jerusalem could be heard far away.

12:31-43   The first person narrative with "I" appears again, the first time since 7:5. This must be from the Nehemiah Memoirs. No doubt the whole section of vv. 27-47 is based on these memoirs; they have been incorporated into the whole.[31] Nehemiah was careful to give the leaders their proper place and responsibilities.

The walls were wide enough for the processions referred to.[32] According to Kenyon's excavations, Nehemiah's wall was nearly nine feet wide. Although it is not specified, the starting point must have been the Valley Gate (Neh 2:13). The first group, Ezra's procession, went to the south ("to the right") and followed the wall in a counterclockwise direction. The second part of the procession started off to the north and followed the wall in a clockwise direction (v. 38).

"Along with Azariah, Ezra" (v. 33) indicates Ezra apparently continued to live in Jerusalem as part of the priestly community.

This must have been an impressive celebration. We need to find ways to unite the community and glorify God together. Special celebrations are a help to the believing community and a testimony to the unbelievers. The emphasis on continuity with what David had done (v. 36) reminds us that an understanding of our place in history and our solidarity with former generations of Christians are vital. We too must see ourselves as part of God's continuing plan.

Here as elsewhere in the Old Testament, thanksgiving and celebration were expressed through sacrifice. Although the type of sacrifice is different in New Testament worship, sacrifice is still important (Rom 12:1; Phil 4:18; Heb 13:15). If we love God, we must give ourselves and our goods to him. The joy that God gives is genuine and can best be experienced in fellowship with the community of God's people. We should not be ashamed to be heard when we praise God.

"God had given them great joy" is the climax of the work of Ezra and Nehemiah. Psalm 48 relates to this situation well, especially vv. 12-14:

Walk about Zion, go around her, count her towers,
consider well her ramparts, view her citadels,
    that you may tell of them to the next generation.
For this God is our God for ever and ever;
    he will be our guide even to the end.

---

[31] Williamson, *Ezra, Nehemiah*, 370.
[32] K. Kenyon, *Jerusalem, Excavating 3000 Years of History* (New York: McGraw-Hill, 1967), 111. The NIV notes indicate that the translation "alongside" is also possible.

(3) The Organization of Worship (12:44-47)

[44]At that time men were appointed to be in charge of the storerooms for the contributions, firstfruits and tithes. From the fields around the towns they were to bring into the storerooms the portions required by the Law for the priests and the Levites, for Judah was pleased with the ministering priests and Levites. [45]They performed the service of their God and the service of purification, as did also the singers and gatekeepers, according to the commands of David and his son Solomon. [46]For long ago, in the days of David and Asaph, there had been directors for the singers and for the songs of praise and thanksgiving to God. [47]So in the days of Zerubbabel and of Nehemiah, all Israel contributed the daily portions for the singers and gatekeepers. They also set aside the portion for the other Levites, and the Levites set aside the portion for the descendants of Aaron.

12:44-47 The priests and Levites pleased the people because they "performed the service of their God . . . according to the commands of David." Their goal was not to please people but God; their model for worship was not the current fad but biblical instruction. They were careful to follow what was stipulated in God's Word. The ministers may have been torn between scriptural authority and the pull of creativity to adapt to a new situation. God is pleased with creativity; but more importantly he demands faithfulness to his revelation. The combination of the two is a constant challenge to those in charge of leading worship.

The result of a ministry that aimed to please God and to be faithful to his Word was that "all Israel contributed the daily portions" (v. 47). Faithful ministers encourage faithful worshipers.

5. Nehemiah's Further Reforms (13:1-31)

We may assume that most of chapter thirteen originated in the Nehemiah Memoirs. Like Ezra 9–10, it is anticlimactic after the dedication of the wall in chap. 12. Chapter 13 teaches the need for ongoing efforts to conserve revival. McConville is surely correct that such a disappointing conclusion to a book full of many triumphs causes in the reader a longing for the more complete and lasting spiritual restoration Scripture promises.[33]

(1) Separation from Foreigners (13:1-3)

---

[33] J. G. McConville, "Ezra-Nehemiah and the Fulfillment of Prophecy," *VT* 36 (1986): 223.

¹On that day the Book of Moses was read aloud in the hearing of the peo-
ple and there it was found written that no Ammonite or Moabite should ever
be admitted into the assembly of God, ²because they had not met the Israelites with food and water but had hired Balaam to call a curse down on them.
(Our God, however, turned the curse into a blessing.) ³When the people heard
this law, they excluded from Israel all who were of foreign descent.

13:1   There is no indication that this was a special occasion. Rather it
was the regular liturgical reading from Scripture, the source of encouragement and the standard of behavior of every healthy community of
God's people.

One encouraging fact from these verses is the apparent eagerness with
which the people observed God's Word when they heard it. The Bible
constantly emphasizes obedience and warns against disobedience. God's
revelation is always related to making known his will.

"No Ammonite or Moabite . . . into the assembly of God" is taken
from Deut 23:3-6. No Ammonite or Moabite should enter the assembly
or congregation of God (*qāhāl ĕlohîm*). This must refer to exclusion
from ceremonial worship. Foreigners were prohibited from the worship
service. Apparently some foreigners were allowed to remain in the city.³⁴

13:2   The decision of the Ammonites and Moabites (Num 22:3-11)
had a long lasting influence on their descendants. Each person is responsible for his or her own decisions, but history and the Bible show that decisions people make will affect the lives of their children, their
grandchildren, indeed of future generations.

13:3   Removal of foreigners should not be viewed as racial exclusiv-
ism. As always, foreigners could become part of Israel by conversion (cf.
Ezra 6:21; Ruth 1:16-17).

(2) Eliashib and Tobiah (13:4-9)

⁴Before this, Eliashib the priest had been put in charge of the storerooms
of the house of our God. He was closely associated with Tobiah, ⁵and he had
provided him with a large room formerly used to store the grain offerings
and incense and temple articles, and also the tithes of grain, new wine and oil
prescribed for the Levites, singers and gatekeepers, as well as the contributions for the priests.

⁶But while all this was going on, I was not in Jerusalem, for in the thirty-
second year of Artaxerxes king of Babylon I had returned to the king. Some

---

³⁴ F. C. Holmgren (*Israel Alive Again: Ezra and Nehemiah*, ITC [Grand Rapids: Eerd-
mans, 1987], 148) notes that the people applied this to all foreigners although Deut 23:7-8
allows the third generation of Edomites and Egyptians to participate.

time later I asked his permission [7]and came back to Jerusalem. Here I learned about the evil thing Eliashib had done in providing Tobiah a room in the courts of the house of God. [8]I was greatly displeased and threw all Tobiah's household goods out of the room. [9]I gave orders to purify the rooms, and then I put back into them the equipment of the house of God, with the grain offerings and the incense.

Although the first person appears again only in v. 6, we can assume that most of the material from v. 4 to the end of chap. 13 is from the Nehemiah Memoirs. Different community problems are mentioned (beg. in 12:44), but in relating them the author formed a coherent literary unity.

13:4 The identity of "Eliashib the priest" is not clear. An Eliashib was high priest (Neh 3:1,20-21; 12:10; 13:28), but this one most certainly is not the same man. The high priest would not have been in charge of the storerooms. We can assume some period of time had elapsed since the assignment of the storerooms in 12:44, especially clear from vv. 5-6.

13:5 This Eliashib "was closely associated with Tobiah, "who was an Ammonite (providing the connection with the previous verses). He had provided Tobiah "with a large room." From Neh 6:10 we know that Tobiah was married to a Jew and was a key person in the opposition to Nehemiah's reforms. The priest, Eliashib, had given Tobiah a foothold right in the center of the Jewish community. All this distressed Nehemiah. Certainly the high priest must have known about the matter and even permitted it. Nehemiah saw all this as laxity in regard to maintaining cultic and religious purity. Eliashib was given a job—to be in charge of the storerooms of the temple. His lack of responsibility allowed Tobiah to gain more and more influence in the community.

13:6 Nehemiah's absence had made possible the increasing abuses mentioned in this chapter. He had been governor in Jerusalem for twelve years, from 445 to 433 and then returned to King Artaxerxes.[35] Sometime later he asked permission to go back to Jerusalem. We do not know for how long a time he was absent. The fact that he asked permission to return would imply that he was not expected to go back and perhaps did not return as governor.[36] The leaders in Jerusalem no doubt were not expecting Nehemiah's return. Yet he seems to have possessed enough authority to get things done, as the following verses indicate.

---

[35] It seems strange that he called Artaxerxes the "king of Babylon." Cyrus had also taken this title (Ezra 5:13; *ANET*, 316). Perhaps Artaxerxes was living in Babylon at this time.

[36] According to the Elephantine Papyri, Bagohi was governor in Jerusalem in 407 B.C. We do not know if Nehemiah was governor when he was in Jerusalem the second time; if he was, his term must have ended before 407.

One wonders if Nehemiah had not prepared other strong leaders. Why did his reforms lapse when he was absent? Certainly a leader must prepare other leaders who will share his same vision and continue his work after he is gone from the scene.

13:7 "The evil thing Eliashib had done" apparently did not seem evil to the men in charge, but Nehemiah saw the dangers involved in allowing Tobiah's "opposing" influence to take hold.

13:8 Nehemiah's reaction seems strong. We also should be concerned about things that dishonor God and be willing to take definite action, and we also need to distinguish between peacemaking and compromising with evil. This episode reminds us of the time Jesus cleansed the temple. Jesus also was angered "by those who mock God by using sacred space for personal use."[37] Perhaps Nehemiah could have used a more diplomatic approach, but sometimes such action is required to illustrate the seriousness of the present crisis.

13:9 Having spoken of one "room" that Tobiah had, here Nehemiah also ordered the adjoining "rooms" (plural) purified. This suggests the desecration extended beyond the rooms Tobiah had occupied. Compromising with the neighboring people, especially Tobiah's activities, endangered religious purity. Throughout Ezra and Nehemiah the author was concerned about maintaining the purity of the Jewish community.

(3) The Portion of the Levites (13:10-14)

10I also learned that the portions assigned to the Levites had not been given to them, and that all the Levites and singers responsible for the service had gone back to their own fields. **11**So I rebuked the officials and asked them, "Why is the house of God neglected?" Then I called them together and stationed them at their posts.

12All Judah brought the tithes of grain, new wine and oil into the storerooms. **13**I put Shelemiah the priest, Zadok the scribe, and a Levite named Pedaiah in charge of the storerooms and made Hanan son of Zaccur, the son of Mattaniah, their assistant, because these men were considered trustworthy. They were made responsible for distributing the supplies to their brothers.

14Remember me for this, O my God, and do not blot out what I have so faithfully done for the house of my God and its services.

13:10 As Clines suggests, it may have been when Nehemiah restored the storerooms to their proper function that he learned of the additional laxity in providing for the Levites (cf. 12:47).[38] Nehemiah was

---

[37] Holmgren, *Ezra and Nehemiah,* 151.

right in saying that laxity on the part of the officials in maintaining religious purity resulted in spiritual carelessness in the whole community. When the spiritual life of leaders diminishes because of sin or carelessness, God's provision for his work also decreases. The Levites were supported by the tithes of the people (Num 18:21). In Neh 9:38–10:39 the people had agreed to faithfully give their portion to the Levites. In Neh 12:44 the people were giving their tithes joyfully. But now this was neglected. Chapter 10 closes with the people's promise: "We will not neglect the house of our God." Laxity in one area led to decline and stagnation in others.

13:11-13 A strong and courageous leader is often needed to restore order and bring revival. God's people responded when godly leadership put things in order. Verse 13 shows how Nehemiah put persons who "were considered trustworthy" in responsible positions. Part of the work of continuing revival is that of putting men of integrity in leadership positions.

13:14 As a man of prayer, Nehemiah committed to God what he had "so *faithfully* done." The key word is *hesed,* usually used of God's "steadfast love" or "faithfulness." Nehemiah is a good example of someone who personified *hesed*.[39]

(4) The Question of the Sabbath (13:15-22)

[15]In those days I saw men in Judah treading winepresses on the Sabbath and bringing in grain and loading it on donkeys, together with wine, grapes, figs and all other kinds of loads. And they were bringing all this into Jerusalem on the Sabbath. Therefore I warned them against selling food on that day. [16]Men from Tyre who lived in Jerusalem were bringing in fish and all kinds of merchandise and selling them in Jerusalem on the Sabbath to the people of Judah. [17]I rebuked the nobles of Judah and said to them, "What is this wicked thing you are doing—desecrating the Sabbath day? [18]Didn't your forefathers do the same things, so that our God brought all this calamity upon us and upon this city? Now you are stirring up more wrath against Israel by desecrating the Sabbath."

[19]When evening shadows fell on the gates of Jerusalem before the Sabbath, I ordered the doors to be shut and not opened until the Sabbath was over. I stationed some of my own men at the gates so that no load could be brought in on the Sabbath day. [20]Once or twice the merchants and sellers of all kinds of goods spent the night outside Jerusalem. [21]But I warned them and said, "Why do you spend the night by the wall? If you do this again, I

---

[38] Clines, *Ezra, Nehemiah, Esther,* 240.

[39] See further the comments at 5:19 on Nehemiah's prayers for remembrance.

will lay hands on you." From that time on they no longer came on the Sabbath. ²²Then I commanded the Levites to purify themselves and go and guard the gates in order to keep the Sabbath day holy.

13:15-17 This section begins with the phrase "in those days," similar to the beginning of 12:44; 13:1,15,23. This indicates that the author intended this entire section of 12:44–13:31 to be a unit. The reference to time is general; no information is given about the exact time or occasion.

The expression "I saw men" (13:23) suggests another good characteristic of Nehemiah's leadership—the awareness of what was happening among the people. The keeping of the Sabbath is greatly emphasized in the Old Testament (Gen 2:2; Exod 16:23-29; 31:14-16; 35:2-3; Num 15:32-36). Amos (8:5), Isaiah (58:13-14), and Jeremiah (17:19-27) warned the people against their laxity in keeping the day set apart for rest and worship. This Sabbath of rest and worship—one day of seven separated for God—is unknown in the ancient world outside of Israel. As part of the Ten Commandments (Exod 20:8-11) it emphasizes the moral principle that all of our time belongs to God. This is symbolized by setting apart one day of each week. The prophets recognized that when the people became careless about the Sabbath, it was an indication of their indifference to God's will in other areas of life as well.

Nehemiah mentioned everyday chores that could be done other days; doing them on the Sabbath deprived that day of its special value. Apparently these things had become customary. Nehemiah had the courage to go against the tide and rebuke even the leaders for their laxity.

13:18 Nehemiah pointed out that the downfall of Jerusalem and the captivity were a result of this same carelessness about obeying God's standards. Christians differ on their understanding of our responsibility toward the scriptural emphasis on keeping the Sabbath or Lord's Day. The Ten Commandments give a synopsis of God's will. One's application of this principle will depend on one's theology of the Lord's Day. As a theological principle, Scripture teaches the importance of dedicating one day of seven to the Lord. Under Jesus' teaching the first Christians did not feel obliged to keep the Sabbath legalistically; rather they began to meet for worship on the first day of the week to commemorate Jesus' resurrection. Several of Jesus' postresurrection appearances to the disciples occurred on the first day of the week. Sunday became the day dedicated to worshiping God. Gradually Christians began to apply Old Testament teachings about the Sabbath to their Sunday observance. Theologically this does justice to the new covenant and the new situation brought about in the New Testament as well as to the ethical principles taught in the

Old Testament. Christians should follow Jesus' example; he was not concerned about "how not to desecrate the Sabbath" but rather "how to sanctify the Lord's Day." Christians today "sanctify" the Lord's day by making it a day of rest, a day of worshiping together, and serving the Lord.

13:19 Again Nehemiah took definite action. He "ordered the doors to be shut." When the believing community falls into disobedience, definite action must be taken.

13:20 Some conformed to the rules legalistically by not selling on the Sabbath, but they worked just the same and even spent the night by the walls so they could obtain an advantage in the market the following day. God does not want mere legalistic compliance. Real trust in God will lead to doing his will even if it appears to bring financial disadvantage. In today's consumer society the goddess of "economic security" has so captured even Christians' affection that we are often blind to what God really wants in our lives.

13:21-22 Nehemiah enlisted help when he "commanded the Levites." A united effort among the leaders was needed to bring the community back to the principles Ezra and Nehemiah had established.

Why did they have to "purify" themselves just to guard the gates on the Sabbath? Their work was holy since its purpose was to sanctify the Sabbath. Nehemiah wanted them to be ritually clean.

(5) Separation Restored (13:23-31)

23Moreover, in those days I saw men of Judah who had married women from Ashdod, Ammon and Moab. **24**Half of their children spoke the language of Ashdod or the language of one of the other peoples, and did not know how to speak the language of Judah. **25**I rebuked them and called curses down on them. I beat some of the men and pulled out their hair. I made them take an oath in God's name and said: "You are not to give your daughters in marriage to their sons, nor are you to take their daughters in marriage for your sons or for yourselves. **26**Was it not because of marriages like these that Solomon king of Israel sinned? Among the many nations there was no king like him. He was loved by his God, and God made him king over all Israel, but even he was led into sin by foreign women. **27**Must we hear now that you too are doing all this terrible wickedness and are being unfaithful to our God by marrying foreign women?"

28One of the sons of Joiada son of Eliashib the high priest was son-in-law to Sanballat the Horonite. And I drove him away from me.

29Remember them, O my God, because they defiled the priestly office and the covenant of the priesthood and of the Levites.

[30]So I purified the priests and the Levites of everything foreign, and assigned them duties, each to his own task. [31]I also made provision for contributions of wood at designated times, and for the firstfruits.

Remember me with favor, O my God.

13:23   Nehemiah was aware of what was happening, even outside of Jerusalem. Both Nehemiah and Ezra had taken strong measures to stop mixed marriages. Now he again saw men who married women from Ashdod, Ammon, and Moab. There is no indication of how widespread this problem was, but it probably only involved a few cases. Several passages in Ezra and Nehemiah, however, indicate that the problem was persistent (Ezra 9–10; Neh 6:18; 10:30). According to Josephus, some problem of intermarriage persisted throughout the Persian period.[40]

Cultic purity is constantly threatened by family relationships and economic interests. Nehemiah had to confront both. He was concerned about the effects on the next generation. He knew that one generation's decisions would affect the beliefs and the life of the coming generations.

13:24   We have little evidence to indicate what language the people of Ashdod spoke, but the difference from the language spoken by the returned exiles must have been only a variation in dialect.[41] From Ashdod the few seals and stamped jar handles that we have are in Aramaic.[42] Some ostraca from Arad in the fifth or fourth century also are in Aramaic. No doubt most of the people in both areas spoke Aramaic with some dialectic variations, but some may have still spoken Hebrew and other local dialects such as Ammonite, Moabite, or "Ashdodite."

13:25   Nehemiah took direct action against those who had taken foreign wives. Although Nehemiah's particular action should not be considered a pattern for us, we should see that in such cases action is necessary. Complacency in the spiritual life can make one numb to the effects of sin.

13:26-27   Nehemiah recalled lessons from past history. If the nation was punished for such sins before, let us not repeat the same thing. The New Testament does not condemn intermarriage between different races. But it does warn against intermarriage with unbelievers. Some of the same dangers that worried Nehemiah are inherent in such intermarriages.

---

[40] Williamson, *Ezra, Nehemiah,* 398.

[41] Myers, *Ezra, Nehemiah,* 217.

[42] See D. N. Freedman, "Ashdod," *IDBS* (Nashville: Abingdon, 1976), 72. An ostracon in Nebi-Yunus was in Aramaic and probably is similar to the language in the rest of the area.

One of the most serious is that it denies the children the blessing of being brought up in a family where faith is consistently encouraged. That is why the children's different "language" bothered Nehemiah.

13:28 Even the family of the high priest had fallen into this error. Some commentators have thought this Sanballat was the same one mentioned in the story in Josephus,[43] where he tells of a Manasseh, brother of Jaddua the high priest, who was married to Nikaso, daughter of Sanballat. The elders of Jerusalem made him leave the city. Sanballat built him a temple (Samaritan) on Mount Gerizim. But Josephus did not connect this story with Nehemiah. We now know there were several Sanballats from Nehemiah's time until 331 B.C. Probably Josephus's story has little or nothing to do with this episode.[44]

13:29 Again Nehemiah prayed and committed the matter to God. We must take action where necessary, as did Nehemiah; but we must ask God to correct things and trust him for permanent changes.

13:30-31 Verses 30-31 serve as a short conclusion to the Nehemiah Memoirs and the Book of Nehemiah. Nehemiah is known for building the walls of Jerusalem. However, he finished his report with more emphasis on the establishment and purification of the community's worship. Nehemiah was persistent in seeking this goal.

Nehemiah also "made provision." He knew that the lack of sensitivity to the needs of fellow leaders can cause tensions that will hinder God's work and dampen continuous revival.

We can learn many practical lessons in Christian leadership from Nehemiah. Nehemiah reminds us that the tolerance of evil leads to spiritual stagnation, which leads to indifference on doctrinal matters; the final result is moral and spiritual degeneration.[45]

In order to have lasting results, reform and revival require constant renewal and constant courage. It takes work to maintain the correct priorities. Kidner says of Nehemiah, "His reforming zeal, partnered by the educative thoroughness of Ezra, gave to postexilic Israel a virility and clarity of faith which it never wholly lost."[46]

Certainly Ezra and Nehemiah had a lasting influence on the Jewish community of faith. God did answer Nehemiah's prayer: "Remember me with favor, O my God." The Book of Nehemiah begins with prayer and

---

[43] Josephus, *Antiquities* 11.306-12.

[44] Williamson thinks that Josephus's account is a garbled variant of this story in Nehemiah (Williamson, *Ezra, Nehemiah,* 401).

[45] See the comments in C. J. Barber, *Nehemiah and the Dynamics of Effective Leadership* (Neptune, N. J.: Loizeaux Brothers, Inc., 1976), chap. 17.

[46] Kidner, *Ezra and Nehemiah,* 133.

closes with prayer. For lasting results, ministry can never be separated from prayer.

Esther

―――――――――――― **INTRODUCTION** ――――――――――――

The Book of Esther is the story of a woman and her role in the deliverance of the Jews from the murderous plan of Haman in the Persian Empire during the reign of Xerxes (485–464 B.C.). In the Old Testament, Esther resembles the stories of Ruth and Deborah, two women whom God used for his plan. With Esther, however, there is a unique twist in that "God" is not referred to even once in the entire narrative.[1] It is for this reason, presumably, that Esther apparently was not used at Qumran (since no fragments of Esther were found there). One purpose of the book seems to be to explain the origin of the Feast of Purim (celebrated

―――――――――――――――――――――――――

[1] In the Apocrypha there are additions to Esther which do include references to the God of Israel.

in Feb.-Mar.). This feast is a non-Mosaic feast, that is, a feast not mentioned in the Torah or Pentateuch. This could be another reason for its absence at Qumran. Regardless of its status at Qumran, Esther belongs in our Old Testament. It is a story of faithfulness, courage, and irony. Most of all, it is the story of how the Jewish people survived a planned pogrom that would have meant their end. Only one conclusion can be reached when the book is read: God was behind it all.

1. Historical Background

According to the first verse, the events of the Book of Esther took place during the reign of Xerxes (who sometimes is called Ahasuerus), king of Persia (486–465 B.C.). That would place the events between the completion of the temple construction under Zerubbabel (in 516 B.C., during the reign of Darius I) and the arrival of more returnees to Jerusalem under Ezra in 458 B.C. (during the reign of Artaxerxes I). Contingents of Jews returned to Judea in 538. Many, however, continued to live in Babylon and throughout the eastern part of the Persian Empire. The Murashu texts from Nippur show that some Jews were prospering in the Persian Empire.[2]

The introduction to Ezra-Nehemiah contains a brief history of the Persian Empire. After Cyrus, Cambyses reigned (530–522 B.C.), followed by Darius I (522–486). Xerxes was Darius I's son, though not the eldest. Here we only wish to note some specific characteristics of Xerxes' reign.

The empire reached its peak organization and power under Darius I; however, Xerxes also could boast some significant military and artistic accomplishments. Herodotus described extensively Xerxes' Greek expedition (480–479), which ended in dismal failure. But at the beginning of Xerxes' reign, he had reconquered Egypt, which had rebelled under Darius I. And he also suppressed an important rebellion in Babylon. In this process he further strengthened the powerful military force Darius had built up.

Perhaps Xerxes' greatest achievement was the completion of the palace complex Darius began in Persepolis, a marvel of grandeur, beauty, and luxury. A foundation stone contained the following inscription:

---

[2] See M. Stolper, "Murashu, Archive of," in *ABD*, vol. 4, ed. D. N. Freedman (New York: Doubleday, 1992): 927-28. These texts are Babylonian legal documents compiled in the last half of the fifth century.

I am Xerxes, the great king. The only king, the king of (all) countries (which speak) all kinds of languages, the king of this (entire) big and far-reaching earth—the son of King Darius, the Achaemenian, a Persian, son of a Persian, an Aryan of Aryan descent.

Thus speaks King Xerxes: These are the countries—in addition to Persia—over which I am king under the "shadow" of Ahuramazda, over which I hold sway, which are bringing their tribute to me—whatever is commanded them by me, that they do and they abide by my law(s): Media, Elam, Arachosia, Urartu, Drangiana, Parchia, (H)aria, Bactria, Sogdia, Chorasmia, Babylonia, Assyria, Sattagydia, Sardis, Egypt (Misir), the Ionians who live on the salty sea and (those) who live beyond . . . the salty sea, Maka, Arabia, Gandara, India, Cappadocia, Da'an, the Amyrgian Cimmerians . . . (wearing) pointed caps, the Skudra, the Akupish, Libya, Banneshu (Carians) (and) Kush.[3]

Herodotus basically confirmed Xerxes' claims of extensive political power. On the other hand, Xerxes did not measure up to the moral qualities of his predecessors. G. Ricciotti says that he inherited none of the good qualities of his predecessors "but only a love of opulent display which progressively sapped his moral fiber."[4] After reconquering Egypt and Babylon, he treated their people cruelly. Herodotus recounts quite a few bizarre episodes that have to do with his wives and concubines. C. E. Van Sickle says the first signs of decay in the empire appear in Xerxes' reign. Xerxes "had the weakness, tyrannical character, and love of luxury to be expected in a prince reared at court."[5] As noted earlier his Greek campaign ended in a series of disastrous defeats.

In 470 B.C. the Persian army again suffered defeats at the hands of the Greeks, first at Eurymedon on the coast of Pamphylia and later at Salamis in Cyprus. This ended the fifty-year struggle with Greece. Persia maintained control over Egypt and Cyprus but lost influence over the Greek colonies in Asia Minor.[6] Xerxes was killed in a conspiracy in 465 and was succeed by his son Artaxerxes I (465–424). The events of Ezra 7 to the end of Nehemiah occurred during the reign of Artaxerxes I.

2. The Historicity of Esther

The most debated issue concerning the Book of Esther is whether or

---

[3] C. A. Moore, "Archaeology and the Book of Esther," *BA* 38 (1975): 70-71.

[4] G. Ricciotti, *The History of Israel,* vol. II (Milwaukee: Bruce, 1955), 16.

[5] C. E. Van Sickle, *A Political and Cultural History of the Ancient World* (Boston: Houghton Mifflin, 1947), 151.

[6] Ricciotti, *History,* II, 17.

not the book relates actual historical events. Many critics almost completely reject any historical basis for the Esther narrative. For example, after giving a series of reasons for rejecting the historicity of Esther, Paton says, "In view of these facts the conclusions seem inevitable that the Book of Esther is not historical and that it is doubtful whether even a historical kernel underlies its narrative."[7]

A number of reasons are given for believing that Esther is fictional: (1) Some details seem improbable, such as the six months of feasting (1:4), beauty preparation for a year (2:12), the height of Haman's gallows (5:14), and the great number of men killed by the Jews (9:16). (2) Some details of Esther contradict what Herodotus wrote. For example, Herodotus said Amestris was Xerxes' queen (*History* 7.114; 9.112), and it appears difficult to equate Esther with Amestris. Also the division of the Persian Empire into 127 provinces (1:1; 8:9) seems to contradict the twenty satrapies that Herodotus mentioned. (3) Some inconsistencies within the book are pointed out, such as Mordecai's being one of the captives in the time of Jehoiachin, which would make Mordecai about 120 years old (2:5).

Answers can be given to these critical difficulties, although the issue of *proving* the historicity of the Book of Esther is another matter. Some commentators have tried to make Amestris equivalent to Esther, but that is difficult. One would not expect of Esther the horrible deeds attributed to Amestris. Also the third son of Xerxes and Amestris was Artaxerxes I, who was born about 483, before Esther became queen.[8] J. S. Wright argues that Vashti and Amestris were the same.[9] Another explanation is that the king had more than one wife.[10]

Some of the objections to the historicity of Esther have simple answers. One example is the so-called contradiction that Mordecai was among the captives from Jerusalem over a century before this story (2:5). It is just as possible that the relative pronoun and phrase "who had been carried into exile" refers to Kish, the great grandfather of Mordecai.

It is also argued that a banquet that lasted 180 days (1:4) is absurd, but that may be a misunderstanding of the text. The text may either refer to

---

[7] L. B. Paton, *The Book of Esther*, ICC (Edinburgh: T & T Clark, 1908), 75, and, in agreement with Paton, M. V. Fox, *Character and Ideology in the Book of Esther* (Columbia: University of South Carolina Press, 1991), 131-39.

[8] J. S. Wright, "The Historicity of the Book of Esther," in *New Perspectives on the Old Testament*, ed. J. B. Payne (Waco: Word Books, 1970), 40-41

[9] Ibid., 40-43. See also W. H. Shea, "Esther and History," *AUSS* 14 (1976): 235-37.

[10] J. B. Baldwin, *Esther: An Introduction and Commentary* (Downers Grove: InterVarsity, 1984), 20-21.

two banquets, one before the 180 days and the other after, or two descriptions of one banquet at the end of the 180 days. The text says Xerxes displayed his wealth for 180 days. F. B. Huey suggests that guests may have come in rotation, "as it would have been difficult for all administrative officials to be away from their posts for six months at the same time."[11] This also may have been the occasion of gathering his officials and military leaders to plan the campaign against Greece in 483 B.C.

Another detail that has been considered improbable is that Haman cast lots to determine the date for the execution of the Jews eleven months in advance (Esth 3). However, additional knowledge of the ancient world helps us understand this. Gordis uses an example from Antiochus II of Syria in February 193 B.C. The king issued an order that "was forwarded by his viceroy in Persia four months later on June 25th."[12] The close connection of dice with the selection and installation of high officials in Assyria has led to the conclusion that lots were cast at the beginning of the year to determine important positions and events for the following twelve months.[13] This helps explain Haman's action almost a year in advance of the selected date.

Some think it unlikely that a Jew such as Mordecai could have held such a high position in the Persian Empire. But the Murashu documents show that in Nippur at least two Jews had relatively important positions.[14] Two other examples are in the Bible. There is Joseph, who served as a high official in the court of Pharaoh (Gen 37–50). The other is Daniel, close to Esther chronologically, who served in an official capacity in the court of Nebuchadnezzar among others (Dan 1–6).

Details such as these have tended to change the critical climate. Today few would take the extreme position of completely denying a historical basis for the story.[15] The book is often called a "historical novel," with some writers putting more emphasis on "novel" and others on "historical." B. Childs says there is a "growing consensus forming around a compromise position which shares neither the traditional position of the

---

[11] F. B. Huey, "Esther," EBC, vol. 4, ed. F. E. Gaebelein (Grand Rapids: Zondervan, 1988), 789.

[12] R. Gordis, "Religion, Wisdom and History in the Book of Esther—A New Solution to an Ancient Crux," *JBL* 100/3 [1981]: 383.

[13] W. W. Hallo, "The Die of Iahali," *BA* 46/1 (1983): 27.

[14] M. D. Coogan, "Life in the Diaspora: Jews at Nippur in the Fifth Century B.C.," *BA* 37 (1974):10.

[15] See, however, M. V. Fox's arguments against Esther's historicity in his *Character and Ideology in the Book of Esther*, SPOT (Columbia: University of South Carolina Press, 1991), 131-39.

book's complete historicity (Keil) nor the theory of its whole fabrication (Semler)."[16] R. Gordis says, "It represents a traditional reworking of what may well have been a real historical incident."[17] He regards it as a historical and typological account because it has to do with anti-Semitic outbursts that were to be a part of Jewish experience for millennia.[18]

Moore, after giving a brief summary of the story of Esther, asks: "Is this story essentially true? It certainly could be."[19] Moore continues to show that much of the Esther narrative concurs with what we know of Xerxes and his reign: the greatness of Xerxes' empire (1:1,20), his quick and sometimes irrational temper (1:12; 7:7-8), his almost unlimited promises and generous gifts (5:3; 6:6-7), his drinking feasts, his seven princely advisers (1:14), an efficient postal system (3:13; 8:10), and Persian words.[20] However, Moore also recognizes that some happenings in the book seem improbable. He believes there is a historical basis for the story but that many details are not confirmed by external evidence.

Many details accurately portray conditions in Susa and the Persian Empire. In addition to those mentioned earlier, many more have come to light. For example, our knowledge of Persia confirms Esther's description of the luxuriousness of Xerxes' court (1:5-6). Archaeology has given us some knowledge of the palace at Susa. Unfortunately the excavations at Susa were done before 1900 when careful stratigraphic work had not yet been developed. Susa had been the site of many palaces from ancient times. Darius placed his citadel on the mound, which by then rose one hundred feet above the river Choasps. Archaeologists found an inscription of Darius on the artificial mound to the north of the citadel. It was inscribed on part of the foundation of the palace. Darius explained the construction of his palace at Susa:

This is the *hadish* palace which at Susa I built. From afar its ornamentation was brought. Deep down the earth was dug, until rock bottom I reached. When the excavation was made, gravel was packed down, one part sixty feet, the other thirty feet in depth. On that gravel a palace I built. And that the earth was dug down and the gravel packed and the mud brick formed in molds, that the Babylonians did. The cedar timber was

---

[16] B. S. Childs, *Introduction to the Old Testament as Scripture* (Philadelphia: Fortress, 1979), 603.

[17] Gordis, "Esther—A New Solution," 388.

[18] Ibid.

[19] Moore, "Archaeology," 68. Also see Moore, "Eight Questions Most Asked about the Book of Esther," *BR* 3 (1987): 16-31.

[20] Moore, "Archaeology," 69-70.

brought from a mountain named Lebanon; the Assyrians brought it to
Babylon, and from Babylon the Carians and Ionians brought it to Susa.
Teakwood was brought from Gandara and from Carmania. The gold which
was used here was brought from Sardis and from Bactria. The stone—la-
pis lazuli and carnelian—was brought from Sogdiana. The turquoise was
brought from Chorasmia. The silver and copper were brought from Egypt.
The ornamentation with which the wall was adorned was brought from
Ionia. The ivory was brought from Ethiopia, from India, and from Arachosia. The stone pillars were brought from a place named Abiraduch in
Elam. The artisans who dressed the stone were Ionians and Sardians. The
goldsmiths who wrought the gold were Medes and Egyptians. Those who
worked the inlays were Sardians and Egyptians. Those who worked the
baked brick (with figures) were Babylonians. The men who adorned the
wall were Medes and Egyptians. At Susa here a splendid work was ordered; very splendid did it turn out. Me may Ahuramazda protect, and
Hystaspes, who is my father, and my land.[21]

Records show that Xerxes completed the work his father began in
Susa. The description of luxury with gold and expensive curtains appear
accurate. An inscription of Artaxerxes II says that the palace of Xerxes
was destroyed by fire in the reign of Artaxerxes I. Within thirty years after the time of Esther, the palace had been destroyed, and memory of the
details soon would have disappeared.[22] Although the excavations at Susa
were carried out before the precise scientific methods of today, "the main
features of the palace complex have been identified. These include the
throne room, the harem and the position of the paradise or garden, wa-
tered by the nearby river" (cf. Esth 1:5; 7:7).[23]

To those who have doubts about the possibility of such a massacre of
Jews or their enemies as the book describes, Keil reminds us of the Pa-
risian massacre of St. Bartholomew when Carlos IX put thousands of
Protestants to death and banished hundreds of thousands from France.[24]
He also notes that Ferdinand the Catholic banished three hundred thou-
sand Jews from Spain. Keil suggests that the population of the Persian
Empire from Ethiopia to India must have been at least one hundred mil-
lion. The Jews must have numbered between two and three million.[25]

---

[21] Cited in A. T. Olmstead, *History of the Persian Empire* (Chicago: University Press,
1948), 168.

[22] G. L. Archer, *A Survey of Old Testament Introduction* (Chicago: Moody, 1970), 406.

[23] Baldwin, *Esther,* 20.

[24] C. F. Keil and F. Delitzsch, *Esther,* in *Commentary on the Old Testament,* vol. III
(Grand Rapids: Eerdmans, 1980), 306.

[25] Ibid., 308.

So perhaps the number of enemies killed need not be considered so improbable.[26]

Some have tried to find the origin of Esther in Babylonian mythology. They suggest that the name "Esther" is the goddess Ishtar; and "Mordecai," the god Marduk. But the argument that the book is based on Babylonian mythology is not as popular as it once was. Records indicate that many Jews gave their children Babylonian or Persian names. "Esther" could also come from the Persian word for "star."[27]

Regarding Mordecai, archaeology has provided details that indicate the historical credibility of the story. Besides being found among the exiles who returned to Judah (Ezra 2:2; Neh 7:7), a similar name is found in treasury tablets from Persepolis (Mar-du-uk-ka, Mar-duk-ka, and Mar-du-kan-na-sir). Sixty-six of these Persian treasury tablets (written by Elamite scribes and accountants from Susa) are dated in the reign of Xerxes. The name Marduka or Marduku is found in at least thirty of them and can refer to as many as four different men, indicating that the name was fairly common.[28] Another document from either the end of Darius I's reign or the first part of Xerxes' mentions a *Marduka* who served as an accountant on a tour of inspection from Susa.[29] This could have been the Mordecai of our narrative, since the phrase "sat at the king's Gate" is mentioned several times in regard to Mordecai. Persian officials were required to remain at the gate of the royal palace according to Herodotus.[30]

Archaeology sheds light on a number of details explaining Babylonian cosmetics. In Esth 2:12 the word translated "perfumes" should be "cosmetic burner" according to Albright. Moore says we should translate the phrase "for this was the prescribed length for their treatment: six months with oil of myrrh, and six months fumigation with other cosmetics for women."[31] Similar customs have been found among seminomadic Arab

---

[26] Many who accept the historicity of the narrative would admit that the numbers may be hyperbole. Some, however, understand that אֶלֶף can mean "group" or "family" (see Harrison, *Introduction*, 1092, and Archer, *Introduction*, 428), thereby greatly reducing the actual number being discussed.

[27] Baldwin, *Esther,* 21.

[28] E. M. Yamauchi ("Mordecai, the Persepolis Tablets, and the Susa Excavations," *VT* XLII, 2 [1992]: 273). Yamauchi goes on to indicate ten other Persian names found in Esther (Mehuman, Bigtha, Carcis, Hathach, Meres, Marsena, Memukan, Mammedatha, Aridai, Aridatha) of which parallel names are found in the Elamite Persepolis texts.

[29] Moore, "Archaeology," 74.

[30] Herodotus, *History* 3.120.

[31] Moore, "Archaeology," 78.

women of the eastern Sudan in modern times.[32]

Other details would tend to confirm the historicity of the story: the character of Xerxes, the extent of his empire, his capital city, details of customs at court, the excellent postal system (3:13; 8:10), mourning prohibited (4:2), the death penalty of hanging (5:14), the word *puru* discovered on dice, and new discoveries concerning the use of dice and lots in ancient times. Also the gap between the third year of Xerxes (Esth 1:3) and the seventh year (2:16) may be explained by the Greek campaign (including its preparation) from 483 to 479. Ezra 4:6 also provides other evidence of opposition to Jews in the reign of Xerxes.

If it were possible or necessary to prove the historical accuracy of an ancient document in every detail, the document, then, would be only a collection of facts we could obtain elsewhere. The arguments against Esther's historicity are based primarily not on evidence but on the absence of confirming evidence, in some cases, and on improbabilities judged from our limited knowledge of the ancient world. On the contrary, three basic points lead us to the conclusion that the book is a trustworthy witness to history. (1) Research has demonstrated the author's credibility as a witness to Persian affairs and culture. (2) The viewpoint of Jesus and the apostles is that Old Testament history as a whole is an unquestionably reliable guide to the events of the past.[33] (3) There is no indication that the book is intended to be taken other than as a straightforward narrative of events as they occurred. It goes to great lengths to include places, names, and events, so much so that the text seems to be making a point about its own historical value. Therefore, instead of doubting the details of the Book of Esther until they are confirmed by external sources, we will proceed on the assumption that Esther is a trustworthy witness to history.

---

[32] Ibid., 78.

[33] As C. H. Pinnock wrote: "One good indication of Christ's high regard for the biblical text is found in his complete trust in the literal truth of biblical *history*. He always treats the historical narratives as factually truthful accounts. In the course of his teachings he makes reference to: Abel (Lk. 11:51), Noah (Mt. 24:37), Abraham (Jn. 8:56), Sodom and Gomorrah (Lk. 10:12), Lot (Lk. 17:28), Isaac and Jacob (Mt. 8:11), David eating the shewbread (Mk. 2:25), and many other persons and incidents. It is not too much to say that he accepted without reservation the entire historical fabric of the Old Testament, including those aspects of it most troublesome to modern minds" ("The Inspiration of Scripture and the Authority of Jesus Christ," in *God's Inerrant Word*, ed. J. W. Montgomery [Minneapolis: Bethany, 1974], 202).

3. The Literary Genre of Esther

In later Jewish exegesis the rabbis talked of the *halaka,* which had to do with one's "walk," and is comprised of commands and principles one should follow. The rabbis, on the other hand, classified Esther as *haggada. Haggada* is narrative that is instructive, by example, in the way one is to live. In modern times various suggestions are offered in regard to the genre of Esther. In the nineteenth century European community, novels were a growing genre of stories that represented the reality of the age in which they were produced. As a result, Esther was classified as a novella along with other books such as Judith and Tobit of the Apocrypha.

S. Talmon calls Esther a historicized wisdom tale and compares it to the Joseph narrative, which also has wisdom motifs. He also finds parallels between the Mordecai-Esther-Xerxes court relationship and that of Ahikar-Nadin-Esarhaddon in the Ahikar wisdom texts.[34] Gordis, on the other hand, while accepting that there are parallels in the Joseph story with its wisdom motifs, points out fundamental differences.[35] The first part of Ahikar is in first person and is an introduction to his sayings. But in Joseph and Esther there are no wisdom sayings. Also, the Ahikar material is full of proverbs and aphorisms, whereas the stories of Joseph and Esther are clearly lacking in such material. Gordis has raised serious questions for Talmon's thesis. Gordis concludes that Esther is a unique literary genre not formerly recognized.

He claims that a Jewish author undertook to write his book in the form of a chronicle of the Persian court, meant to appear to have been written by a Gentile scribe. Gordis says he was a Jew of the Eastern Diaspora who wanted to increase confidence in the narrative and help establish Purim as a feast among all Jews. He wrote the book "as though it were an excerpt from the official chronicles of 'the kings of Media and Persia'" (10:2). The writer used the model of the Hebrew historians who often used the "Chronicles of the Kings of Judah" and "The Chronicles of the Kings of Israel."[36] The use of Mordecai the Jew (5:13; 6:10; 8:7; 9:29,31; 10:3) confirms that he was writing as from a viewpoint of a non-Jew and uses the third person throughout the narrative.

Gordis also contends that the establishment of a Jewish festival would

---

[34] Ahikar/Ahiqar was a wise man who lived in the seventh century B.C. His nationality is unknown, but his legacy of wisdom is well remembered (see Tob 1:21), and he is mentioned in the Elephantine Papyri in the Jewish settlement in upper Egypt of the fifth century B.C.

[35] "Gordis, "Esther—A New Solution," 375.

[36] Ibid., 375.

not be part of a Persian chronicle; thus the establishment of Purim is placed in two appendixes, the letters of Mordecai (9:22-28) and of Esther (9:29-31). The absence of detail would be normal for a court chronicle. Esther's refusal to reveal her origin avoids the restriction of having to take the wife from one of the leading families as mentioned in Herodotus. Xerxes' name appears twenty-one times, and he is always called the king, as would be normal in a court chronicle. The mention of the king's counselors (1:10,14) captures the flavor of court protocol. The naming of Haman's sons also underlines the official character of the document. Official legal terminology like "to each province in its script and to each people in its language" and synonyms like "to destroy, kill and annihilate" support the same conclusion. Verbatim quoting of edicts like Haman's and that of Mordecai help give authority and court flavor.

We can agree with Gordis that the author must have been a Jew living in the Persian Empire, but we need not postulate that the author was posing as a Gentile. Geographically, the Persian context may account for most of the details Gordis mentions. That God is not mentioned fits well with this context. It also adds to the effect of the narrative on the believing Jewish community; for although done in a subtle manner, the author constantly reminds the reader of God's providence without mentioning God.

The genre of the Book of Esther is historical narrative. As such, biblical narrative is characterized by the cooperation of three components: ideology (socioreligious perspective), historiography (use of historical persons and events in a narrative), and aesthetic appeal (its influence and persuasion of the reader).[37] Each of these three elements can be readily seen in Esther. The ideology is the orthodox faith of ancient Israel. The book is theological in that its primary purpose is to teach about God and his continuing relationship with his people. It is historiographical in that it is an account of historical persons and historical events as they occurred. It is aesthetic because it is full of drama and suspense and draws its readers to anticipate happenings and events that often are the reverse of what the reader expects.

It is interesting to compare Esther with Daniel 1–6 and the Joseph story in Genesis, since all have to do with Israelites who held important positions in foreign governments. Parallels between the stories of Joseph and Esther were recognized in Jewish tradition and have been noticed again in recent times.[38] Certain details also find parallels in the Book of Jonah, which narrates events in a land outside of Israel. In all these

---

[37] M. Sternberg, *The Poetics of Biblical Narrative* (Bloomington: Indiana University Press, 1987), 41-57.

[38] In recent works like S. Talmon, "Wisdom in the Book of Esther," *VT* 13 (1963): 419-55 and S. B. Berg, *The Book of Esther* (Missoula, Mont.: Scholars Press, 1979).

books the hand of God is seen working in human affairs, for it is God who controls history. The idea of providence is the key element in the ideological nature of this narrative, representing the theological perspective on history.

4. Literary Features in Esther

To say that the story of Esther is well told is an understatement. It is "by any standards a brilliantly written story, to be savored—even chuckled over."[39] The author sustained a swift flow of action, concentrating on events and not on motivations, on incidents and not on character description.[40]

Good stories present problems to be resolved; Esther does this. The solution is unexpected, which adds interest to the narrative. The author repeats certain phrases to draw attention to contrasts: compare 3:10 with 8:2a; 3:12-13 with 8:9-11; 3:14 with 8:13.[41]

A "chiastic" structure in the whole book, indicating a fine degree of literary art, has been observed. The pivotal point is the king's sleepless night (6:1-3), around which the chiastic structure is built.

A   Opening and background (chap. 1)
  B   The king's first decree (chaps. 2–3)
    C   The clash between Haman and Mordecai (chaps. 4–5)
     D   "On that night the king could not sleep" (6:1)
    C'   Mordecai's triumph over Haman (chaps. 6–7)
  B'   The king's second decree (chaps. 8–9)
A'   Epilogue (chap. 10)[42]

Literary elements that help in reading Esther include the viewpoints of characters, narrator, and readers. In such a story suspense and foreshadowing are used repeatedly for aesthetic and interpretive appeal. Historical epithets (e.g., 1:1-3) are used to anchor the story in specific historical contexts. Finally, the story has a unique rhetorical quality that correctly and convincingly persuades the reader that the Jews have been dealt with cruelly and unjustly and that the outcome is just as it should be.[43]

---

[39] McConville, *Ezra, Nehemiah, and Esther,* 154.

[40] R. Gordis, "Studies in the Esther Narrative," *JBL* 95/1 (1976): 45.

[41] Baldwin, *Esther,* 30.

[42] Ibid. If we could be sure the author had in mind such a chiastic structure, it would effectively eliminate any theories that relegate chaps. 9–10 to a later author.

[43] These elements are discussed at length in Sternberg, *Poetics.*

Find def. of Canonnicity

5. The Purpose of the Book

The purpose of the Book of Esther is twofold: (1) to demonstrate God's providential care of his people, even those outside the land of Israel, and (2) to commend the observance of the Feast of Purim by relating how it originated (9:24-28). Baldwin has noted that Herodotus's *Histories* were written "for public recitation at private gatherings or public festivals."[44] Esther was written for the same purpose. Purim is the celebratory festival commemorating the deliverance of the Jews from certain annihilation at the hand of Haman. Esther is clearly the heroine of the story because she did what she was led to do (4:14): deliver her people, which in turn, initiated the Feast of Purim. All of the characters acted and spoke at her discretion. The king was willing to give her up to half of his kingdom (5:6; 7:2). Haman begged for life at Esther's mercy (7:7). Even Mordecai understood the significance of Esther's role in the events at hand (4:9-17).

Gordis notes that the festival of Purim advanced more rapidly in the Diaspora than in Palestine. For example, "the day of Mordecai" occurs in 2 Macc 15:36, which is an abridgment of the larger work of a Diaspora author, Jason of Cyreine. But it does not appear in 1 Maccabees, which is from Palestine. "Anti-Semitic encounters with a dominant non-Jewish majority were recurring phenomena in the history of Diaspora Jewry."[45]

6. Author and Date

Many suggestions have been offered about the author and date of Esther. Augustine thought Ezra was the author. The Talmud says the men of the Great Synagogue were its authors. Clement of Alexandria suggested Mordecai, and many of the ancient Jewish and Christian scholars followed this view.

Paton is among those who date Esther in the Greek period, more exactly in or after the time of the Maccabees.[46] He gives the following data to suggest this date: (1) The book does not say who wrote it or when. (2) There is no external evidence of the book before the beginning of the Christian era. Esther is not mentioned in Chronicles, Ezra, Nehemiah, Daniel, Philo, or the Apocryphal books. It is first mentioned in 2 Macc 15:36. Even this does not prove that Purim was observed in the time of

---

[44] Ibid.,19.

[45] Gordis, "Esther—A New Solution," 381.

[46] Paton, *Book of Esther,* 61.

Judas Maccabee. (3) Some passages (1:1,13-14; 4:11; 8:8) give the impression that the reign of Xerxes was long past at the time of writing. Conversion of Gentiles to Judaism did not take place in the Persian period but in the Greco-Roman period. (4) From an intellectual standpoint, there is no messianic text, the hatred toward the Gentiles is a product of Antiochus Epiphanes (167 B.C.), and the financial considerations of 3:9 are indicative of the Greek period. All three of these suggest a date either late in or just following the Maccabean period. (5) The language of the book resembles that of Ecclesiastes, Daniel, and Chronicles; and many words are only attested to in the Mishna and other early rabbinical texts.

However, a different opinion can be seen in recent works on Esther. Moore points out that earlier scholars said it could not have been written before 300 B.C., but there is increasing evidence for an earlier date.[47] The Hebrew is not similar to that of second century B.C. as known from the Qumran texts, so the suggested second-century date has to be ruled out. There is no Greek vocabulary. The Hebrew of Esther has some affinities with that of the Chronicler, which is often dated around 400 B.C.

Archer agrees with this; he points out that Esther must have been written before 330 B.C. because there are no traces of Greek influence in language or in thought. In 332 B.C. Alexander began his march eastward with Hellenistic reforms. Therefore Greek influence would not have been in Israel before 330. The omission of Mordecai and Esther in Herodotus is not conclusive for a late date. On the basis of Herodotus's omission, many scholars denied the existence of Belshazzar; later archaeological discoveries confirmed the historicity of Daniel 5.[48]

Baldwin gives a similar opinion. She says it should not be dated in the Maccabean times, and "in any case the favorable relationship between the Jews and the Persian king makes the story unsuitable as the product of Palestine in the Maccabean period."[49] Though no words are of Greek origin, many Persian words are included. The linguistic evidence as well as the accurate knowledge of life in Susa in the time of Xerxes suggests a date in the latter half of the fifth century B.C. or the early fourth century.

LaSor, Bush, and Hubbard mention some additional reasons for ascribing to Esther a date earlier than the Greek period. (1) The Greek additions already were in the Septuagint in the second century B.C. and definitely were not part of the original Hebrew text. (2) The Judaism of that time was becoming legalistic, but the Book of Esther gives no evi-

---

[47] C. A. Moore, *Esther*, AB (Garden City: Doubleday, 1971), LVII.

[48] Archer, *Old Testament Introduction*, 403.

[49] Baldwin, *Esther*, 48.

dence of that emphasis. (3) The book has no apocalyptic elements. No angel comes to solve the Jews' problem. No mention is made of Satan. "Elements commonly found in second century Palestine—dualism, angelology, and satanology[50]—are not even hinted at in this work which shows so many indications that it originated in, or was at least thoroughly familiar with Persia."[51]

Harrison notes that it is difficult to suppose that details of the Susa palace and customs would have been preserved in the west in Maccabean times. He notes that the most conservative opinion would date the author in the last half of the fifth century B.C. or possibly near the end of the Persian period (539–333).[52]

Other details favor an early date. Hatred toward Gentiles is not necessarily late or from the Maccabean period. The Elephantine Papyri show there was anti-Semitic feeling in Egypt in the fifth century B.C. In Esther the Jews were not fighting for their religion (as in the time of the Maccabees) but for their existence as a people. The fact that Ben Sira did not mention Esther or the Feast of Purim may simply mean that it originated in the East and was not yet well known in Palestine. In conclusion it is best to ascribe Esther to a date sometime in the Persian period, not later than 350 B.C.[53]

7. The Origin of Purim

The word for "lot" in Akkadian is *puru;* in Hebrew it is *gôrāl,* "stone." The word *puru* would not have been generally known among the Hebrews.[54] So how did this feast and the name Purim come together? Many scholars have doubted the explanation in Esther and try to find some other origin for the feast. In 2 Macc 15:36 it is called the "day of Mordecai." Therefore many think the Book of Esther is a later folk etymology designed to explain that the festival had a secular origin.

Hallo mentions the various "theories" that have been set forth to try to explain the origin of Purim. Speaking of the explanation in Esther, he says: "That explanation will have to do for us too, for none of the many alternatives offered during a century of the most ingenious scholarly detective work is more convincing. . . . The problem is that each of these

---

[50] The elements lacking here are commonly attributed to Persian influence when found in second-century Palestine.

[51] LaSor et al., *Old Testament Survey,* 628.

[52] Harrison, *Introduction to the Old Testament,* 1088-89.

[53] Ibid., 1090.

[54] Baldwin, *Esther,* 22.

alleged precedents rests on little more than a dubious assonance, and none of them has anything in the least to do with the casting of lots."[55] Other recent studies arrive at the same conclusion: "The view that Esther was written to give religious authority for the Feast of Purim must be challenged. The feast has no known origin in Persian, Babylonian, or other lore."[56] Keil was correct when he stated: "The names Purim and Mordechai's day are a pledge that the essential contents of this book are based upon an historical foundation."[57]

8. The Place of Esther in the Canon

Throughout history different opinions have been expressed concerning the "canonical" value of Esther. Luther was hostile to the book and said he wished it did not exist. On the other hand, the medieval Jewish scholar Maimonides (1135–1204) considered Esther the most important biblical book after the Pentateuch.[58]

We know that in regard to the Jewish canon, some rabbis questioned its inclusion. In the Cairo Genizah there are more fragments of Esther than of any other book except the Pentateuch, so it must have been widely used among the Jews. However, Esther was the only Old Testament book not found at Qumran. This suggests that the book was not popular there and that the Festival of Purim was not celebrated by the Jewish sect at Qumran. The Essenes celebrated other festivals not found in the Pentateuch, so the absence of the Feast of Purim from the Pentateuch cannot be the only reason.

Beckwith suggests that the Qumran rejection of Purim can by explained by the unique Qumran calendar. The Qumran sectarians used a calender of 364 days, divided exactly in weeks. Therefore the same date always fell on the same day of the week. The Feast of Purim always would have fallen on the Sabbath.[59] To have celebrated a high-spirited festival like Purim on the Sabbath would have been against all that is holy according to the laws of the Qumran communities. This calendar probably originated in the third century B.C.; it is found in 1 Enoch 72–82.[60]

---

[55] W. W. Hallo, "The First Purim," *BA* 46:1 [1983]: 22.

[56] LaSor et al., *Old Testament Survey,* 627.

[57] Keil, *Esther,* 304.

[58] Moore, "Archaeology," 63.

[59] R. Beckwith, *The Old Testament Canon of the New Testament Church* (Grand Rapids: Eerdmans, 1985), 292.

[60] Ibid., 293.

The Book of Esther seems to have a firm position in the canon at least by the first century A.D. The school at Jamnia used Esther similar to Scripture in A.D. 90. Josephus may have viewed it as canonical. It is included in the oldest list of the Jewish canon, *Baraitha* in *Baba Bathra* 14b-15a, a Talmudic work from the second century A.D.[61] "All in all, the canonical position of Esther seems to have been very secure in the first century A.D."[62]

However, several centuries after Jamnia the book was still disputed by some Jews. This is indicated by two passages in the Talmud and by a list of the Jewish canonical books in the east from A.D. 170. Some Jews rejected the book even as late as the third or fourth centuries A.D. (*Megilla* 7a; *Sanhedrin* II).

Why was the book rejected by some Jews? The reasons were theological, historical, and textual. The absence of religious elements is evident. The king of Persia is mentioned 190 times in 167 verses, but God is not mentioned once. No reference is made to the law or covenant, prayer, or angels. Kindness, mercy, and forgiveness are missing. However, religious concepts such as providence, prayer, and fasting are taken for granted.[63]

The other reasons for questioning the book in the Talmud can be reduced to two: (1) such a nationalistic feast would have made the Jews hated by others, and (2) the Jews were not to make additions to the Mosaic law.

In the first and second centuries, four important rabbis presented evidence to show that Esther is divinely inspired.[64] Later the Talmud's objection was based on a late interpretation of Lev 27:34 and Num 36:13: "These are the commands." The Talmudic interpretation was, "These and no other." The accepted answer to the objection was that Esther had been revealed to Moses on Sinai and was passed on orally until the time of Esther and Mordecai.[65]

Christians also have had different opinions about the canonicity of Esther. It was not included in the list of canonical books made by Bishop Melito of Sardis in A.D. 170. Various other lists of canonical books are from the church fathers, councils, and synods. Athanasius (295–373) did not include Esther in the canon but considered it edifying reading along with Judith, Tobit, and others. Clement of Alexandria, between A.D. 190

---

[61] Moore, *Esther,* XXII.

[62] Beckwith, *Old Testament Canon,* 315.

[63] Moore, *Esther,* XXXI.

[64] Beckwith, *Old Testament Canon,* 289.

[65] Ibid., 291

and 200, seems to have regarded it as inspired.[66] Origen (before 231) included Esther in the books accepted by the Jews.[67] In the West, Esther usually was included in the canon, but in the East it was often omitted.[68] The Council of Carthage, A.D. 397, included Esther in the canon.

What should be our conclusion? As Baldwin says: "The book is in the canon. So we must decide what value it has for us and what should be our response."[69] Its firm position in the Jewish canon and the consensus of Christian believers since the early church indicate that it should be considered part of the canon of Scripture. We have no choice but to recognize and treat it as part of God's message to his people.

9. The Teaching of Esther

What value does the Book of Esther have for Christians today? The commentary that follows will make suggestions to indicate its relevance. Here it will be helpful to note a few general teachings of the book. In each of the following it is important to note the cooperation of the elements of narrative as suggested by Sternberg: ideology, historiography, and aesthetics.

(1) The Providence of God

Although God is not referred to explicitly, the author presupposed divine providence. This is the ideological theme of the book. In Israel's history the prophets spoke of the constant care given its nation by God both in salvation and discipline. All things happen at God's hand. The story of Esther is to be read within this particular worldview of the Old Testament. The most pervasive teaching in the entire book is the importance and extent of God's providence—his sovereignty over nature, nations, and individuals.

Although there is no exact Hebrew synonym for the English word "providence,"[70] the concept of God's superintendence or preservation of creatures is evident throughout the Old Testament. It is taught largely by illustrations because Israel's understanding of divine providence grew out of its experiences. God's providence is seen in the stories of Abraham, the other ancestors, judges, kings, and the whole nation. Israel re-

---

[66] Ibid., 296.
[67] Ibid.
[68] Moore, *Esther,* XXV.
[69] Baldwin, *Esther,* 16.
[70] Hebrew פְּקֻדָּה is translated "providence" in Job 10:12 (NIV).

membered God's marvelous deeds in the exodus and wilderness wanderings as paradigms of God's providence in caring for and directing his people in every circumstance.

Belief in God's providence also affected the Israelite's self-understanding. God is not only interested in the concerns of the whole nation but guides and upholds each individual. "A man's steps are directed by the Lord" (Prov 20:24). The psalmist said, "I am always with you; you hold my right hand" (Ps 73:23).[71] The New Testament continues this same emphasis on God's care for each person.

The author of Esther stands in the same Hebrew tradition as all other Old Testament writers by taking for granted all these aspects of divine providence. God's providence is the driving force of the narrative. The author of Esther wanted his readers to see the mystery of God's hand in history. He chose to show how human decision and action are the instrumentation of divine purpose.

Also, the book's careful avoidance of explicit references to God suggests that application should be made in particular to those situations in which God appears to be least visible. When we are most tempted to think that God has forgotten us, that "my way is hidden from the LORD; my cause is disregarded by my God" (Isa 40:27), we can be sure that he at work. Furthermore, as the story unfolds, before the wicked Haman is even introduced and his malicious plan devised, God already had installed the instruments of deliverance: he had placed Esther in the royal court and Mordecai in the king's favor.[72] The point is that even before our problems arise, God has made provision for them. As Abraham said to Isaac, "God himself will provide" (Gen 22:8; cf. vv. 13-14).[73]

(2) The Conflict of Worldviews

In Esther the author presented two conflicting worldviews. This is in essence a clash of ideological differences. One is represented by Haman, who believed in fate and tried to use it to destroy his enemies (3:7). Haman was very proud; even though he believed in fate, he thought he

---

[71] See also passages such as Job 5:19-27; Pss 16:5-8; 37:5,18,23; 73:24-26; 139:16.

[72] See McConville, *Ezra, Nehemiah, and Esther,* 163.

[73] The verb Abraham used, רָאָה, means "to see." See W. Brueggemann, *Genesis* (Atlanta: John Knox, 1982), 191. The same might be said of Esther, Mordecai, and the Jews, that Brueggemann says of Abraham: "Abraham finds his only refuge in the divine provider whom he finds inscrutable but reliable. Abraham has turned from his own way to the way of God which lies beyond his understanding (cf. Isa. 55:8-9) but upon which he is prepared to act in concrete ways" (ibid., 188).

could control the direction of events. This belief in fate was part of the worldview that pervaded all the ancient world except Israel. It was based on a kind of pantheistic outlook that sees innate laws in the totality of the universe; even the gods were subject to these laws. Thus they used magic against each other. This worldview formed the basis of astrology, the horoscope, omens, and magic practices that the Old Testament strongly condemns.[74]

Haman's casting of lots to find the auspicious day to carry out his malevolent plans draws attention to this "pagan" worldview. New archaeological discoveries from the ancient world illustrate this use of lots. In his explanation of a cube known as "The Die of Iahali" (dated from the reign of Shalmaneser III, king of Assyria from 858 to 824 B.C.), F. J. Stephens said, "It was believed that the events of the year were predetermined on New Year's Day when the new eponym was inaugurated in office."[75] "The inscription upon this piece contained an invocation to the great gods of Assyria, Ashur, and Adad, and a prayer that the events determined on the auspicious occasion of the installation of Iahali may constantly remain in the mind of the great gods to insure good crops for the land during the year."[76]

In his conclusion the author of Esther called attention to the foolishness of such reliance on supernatural power other than the Lord's (9:24-25). The auspicious day on which Haman had depended for the destruction of the Jews turned out to be the day of his destruction and of their triumph. The author showed the biblical perspective of how people's decisions affect history—belief in a God who stands not only above history but is the force behind it (4:14). Human agents are the tools God uses to bring justice. This biblical view of history is of paramount importance throughout the whole Bible. God is the Lord of history, but he has made humans responsible for their decisions and actions. The Bible does not teach fatalism; rather, history is a dialogue between God and humans. God is in control, and history moves toward a goal that God has marked. God takes into account human decisions, weaving them into the very fabric of history.

Another important teaching from Esther is that the Jews occupy a special place in divine purpose. In spite of pogroms and attempts to destroy them throughout history, the Jews can continue to see God's providence

---

[74] Many aspects of this ancient pagan worldview are being revived in modern times. Thus the revival of the horoscope, magic arts, etc.

[75] Cited in W. Hallo, "The Die of Iahali," *BA* 46/1 (1983).

[76] Ibid., 27.

in preserving them. This must be a major factor in why the book was canonized.

(3) Obedience to God's Will

In the characters Esther and Mordecai we find examples of how to live the obedient life. Like Joseph and Daniel in foreign courts, so Esther and Mordecai were obedient to God's direction and plan. Esther was a model disciple of God we should imitate. She constantly did the right thing, made the right decision, and said the right words. Esther embodied faith.

(4) The Danger of Anti-Semitism

There is something deeper here than a natural reaction against an ethnic group. Even in Moses' time, Pharaoh tried to destroy this people. Later Merneptah, another pharaoh, said he had destroyed them.[77] "Ultimately, as brought out in the New Testament, this is not merely anti-Jewish hostility but hatred of the people of God (John 15:18). Its source is satanic: the attempt to defeat God in his redemptive purpose. Its historic outworking involves all of God's people, Christians as well as Jews."[78]

In light of this, Christians must always be conscious of new outcroppings of insidious anti-Semitism. Not only is it a manifestation of Satan's work in the world and his enmity against God, but it will result in repression of true Christian life and work. Christians are also the object of the world's hatred (John 15:18-20). Esther teaches that believers can trust God for relief and deliverance as did Mordecai.[79] Esther says to the Christian that anti-Jewish hostility is intolerable to God.

What does the book say about the modern situation of the Jews? Certainly it teaches God's faithfulness to his covenant. But one cannot find simple answers; how does one explain Masada, the expulsion from Spain in the fifteenth century, and the Nazi holocaust? The attack and murder of Jews is against all of the laws of God. Throughout history, peoples have exercised pograms against the Jews, God's chosen people (Exod 19:1-6). In Esther, to attack the Jews is to attack God. Haman found this out. That is why Haman became the paradigm by which all subsequent enemies of the Jews are judged.

How can we relate all this to the teaching of Rom 9–11? "The book of

---

[77] This is according to the inscription on the stelae of Merneptah, 1220 B.C.

[78] LaSor et al., *Old Testament Survey,* 629. See comments on Ezra 4:6 and Esth 4:14.

[79] Ibid.

Esther provides the strongest canonical warrant in the whole Old Testament for the religious significance of the Jewish people in an ethnic sense. . . . The inclusion of Esther within the Christian canon serves as a check against all attempts to spiritualize the concept of Israel—usually by misinterpreting Paul—and thus removing the ultimate scandal of biblical particularity."[80]

10. Texts and Versions of Esther

Esther is included in all complete private Bible codices and is appended to the Law in most of the rolls used in synagogues. All of these manuscripts utilize the Tiberian system of vocalization, which is used in our printed editions of Hebrew.[81] However, we have no Hebrew manuscripts of Esther earlier than the tenth century A.D. because none were found in Qumran.

The citations of Esther in the Talmud generally support our present consonantal text. In the first or second century A.D. the rabbis adopted an official standard text of the Old Testament. In addition to the manuscripts there are many *midrashim* and later Jewish commentaries of Esther. They all represent the same basic text.

Several ancient versions of the Book of Esther have been preserved. The Syriac version, possibly from the second century A.D., is a faithful translation of the Hebrew. A few words are added for clarification, but it is generally quite close to the original. The Syriac version is known as the Peshitta.

The Greek (Septuagint or LXX) version of Esther was made in the second century B.C. Some suggest 178 B.C., but Paton suggests 114 B.C.[82] However, we have only the Greek in five recensions from much later dates, so it is hard to reconstruct the original. The Septuagint edition of Esther has a number of additions that add 105 verses to the 167 in the Hebrew. We do not know when they were added. They were already there when Jerome made the Vulgate at end of the fourth century. A brief description of these additions will be given below. Josephus narrates Es-

---

[80] Childs, *Introduction*, 606.

[81] Paton, *Book of Esther*, 6. This system of vocalization was introduced by the Masoretes of Tiberias around A.D. 650. For further reading on the text tradition of Esther, see D. J. A. Clines, *The Esther Scroll: The Story of the Story* (Sheffield: JSOT, 1984); C. A. Moore, "Esther, Book of" in *ABD*, vol 2, ed. D. N. Freedman (New York: Doubleday, 1992), 640-42; M. V. Fox, *Character and Ideology in the Book of Esther* (Columbia: University of South Carolina Press, 1991), 252-73.

[82] Paton, *Esther*, 29.

ther and seems to follow the Septuagint but with some omissions and additions.

We also have two targums (Aramaic paraphrases of the Old Testament) of Esther. Targum Rishon, or the First Targum, is Palestinian Aramaic. "In its relation to the Hebrew original this translation is a curious compound of fidelity and freedom."[83] It translates faithfully but also adds new material; thus the book is twice as long as the Hebrew Esther. The First Targum is not earlier than the seventh century A.D. but must have been composed from earlier targums and the oral targum of the synagogues. The Second Targum adds more new material, so it is four times as long as our Hebrew text. It is the targum most used among the Jews. Its translation of the Hebrew is quite literal but adds much legendary material. Paton dates it around A.D. 800.[84]

We also have the Latin version of Jerome, made in Bethlehem between A.D. 390 and 405. It has numerous additions, many of which are also in the Syriac and Septuagint, so they must represent a text possessed by Jerome that differed somewhat from our Masoretic Text. There are also some omissions.

11. The Greek Additions

The Greek Septuagint has significant additions not found in the Hebrew text of Esther. Six passages with a total of 105 verses were added, probably by an Egyptian Jew sometime around 100 B.C.[85] They add the religious emphasis that appears to be lacking in the book as we have it in Hebrew. Jerome removed these passages from their context because they were not in the Hebrew text. He put them together as an appendix to the Book of Esther. That is why they are numbered from 10:4 to 16:24 in the Vulgate.

Addition A, Mordecai's dream (11:2–12:6), precedes 1:1; Addition B, the edict of Artaxerxes against the Jews (13:1-7), should be placed after 3:13; Addition C, prayers of Mordecai and Esther (13:8–14:19), and Addition D, Esther's appearance before the king (15:1-16), should be placed after 4:17; Addition E, the decree of Artaxerxes on behalf of the Jews (16:1-24), comes after 8:12; and Addition F, the interpretation of Mordecai's dream (10:4–11:1), is placed immediately after 10:3. Bibles con-

---

[83] Ibid., 18.

[84] Ibid., 22.

[85] *IDB*, vol. 2, 151. For the definitive study, see C. Moore, *Daniel, Esther, and Jeremiah: The Additions*, AB 44 (Garden City: Doubleday, 1977), 153-252.

taining the Apocryphal Books include these additions; sometimes they include a translation of the whole book (the canonical part plus the additions) as it is found in the Septuagint.[86]

─────────── *OUTLINE OF THE BOOK* ───────────

──────────────────────────────

[86] For example, *The New English Bible with the Apocrypha: Oxford Study Edition* (New York: Oxford University Press), 1976.

I. KING XERXES' GREAT BANQUET (1:1-22)

The Book of Esther begins with a banquet given by King Xerxes. The events of the banquet led to the king's disapproval of the queen. This event is vital in understanding the book as a whole. The anger Xerxes exhibits toward Vashti, and her subsequent departure, sets the stage for Esther to come forth and deliver her people.

1. Introduction (1:1-3)

[1]This is what happened during the time of Xerxes, the Xerxes who ruled over 127 provinces stretching from India to Cush: [2]At that time King Xerxes reigned from his royal throne in the citadel of Susa, [3]and in the third year of his reign he gave a banquet for all his nobles and officials. The military leaders of Persia and Media, the princes, and the nobles of the provinces were present.

1:1 "This is what happened"[1] is a conventional Hebrew way to begin a story. It often designates the continuation of a narrative that preceded but can also be used at the beginning of a narrative (Ruth 1:1).

The name "Xerxes" is a Greek derivation from Persian *khsyay'rsha*[2] and refers to Xerxes I, who reigned from 485 to 465 B.C. From his father Darius I he inherited the great Persian Empire that extended from India to Ethiopia. Xerxes himself said he was king over many tribes; among

---

[1] In Hebrew וַיְהִי.
[2] The Hebrew is אֲחַשְׁוֵרוֹשׁ, sometimes translated as Ahasuerus.

the nations he listed are "the Indus land" and "the Cushites" (Ethiopians). India here refers to the area drained by the Indus River, now Pakistan. Ethiopia was the territory south of Egypt, now the northern part of the Sudan. This was the largest empire known up to that time. The existence of large empires and the desire for (and abuse of) power have been a part of fallen humanity's life on earth during the greater part of history (Gen 11).

The "127 provinces" is thought by some to be inaccurate since Herodotus listed thirty satrapies. The term "province" (Heb. *mĕdînâ*), however, refers to a subdivision of a satrapy (Ezra 2:1), and their number varied (cf. Dan 6:1).[3]

1:2 At the beginning of King Xerxes' reign, he had put down rebellions in Egypt and Babylon.[4]

Susa had been the capital of ancient Elam. Darius I rebuilt and used it as his residence before Persepolis became his capital. Xerxes also had his main residence at Persepolis but lived in Susa in the winter.

"Citadel"[5] here means an "acropolis or fortified area" raised above the rest of the city. The citadel fortress was a rectangular platform seventy-two feet above the general level of the city. It was surrounded by a huge wall two and a half miles long.[6]

1:3 "The third year of his reign" was 483 B.C., three years before his famous expedition against the Greek mainland. Rulers used banquets to display their greatness and to help maintain the faithfulness and loyalty of their subjects. Herodotus described Persian royal banquets at which the king gave gifts to his fellow Persians. "It is said, fifteen thousand might be his guests."[7] The royal chamberlain afterwards had the duty of "putting his inebriated master to bed."[8]

"Nobles and officials" and "military leaders" indicate that the elite of the army (*hêl*) from all over the empire must have attended. Xerxes' own bodyguard included two thousand select horsemen, two thousand lancers, and ten thousand infantry.[9]

Verses 1-3 provide the setting of the story of Esther, namely, the Per-

---

[3] See also the critical evaluation of Herodotus as an authority in G. G. Cameron, "The Persian Satrapies and Related Matters," *JNES* 32 (1973): 46-56.

[4] A. T. Olmstead, *History of the Persian Empire* (Chicago: University Press, 1948), 234-37.

[5] הַבִּירָה.

[6] L. B. Paton, *The Book of Esther,* ICC (Edinburgh: T & T Clark, 1908).

[7] Olmstead, *History,* 182-83.

[8] Ibid.

[9] Herodotus, *History,* vii, 40.

sian court in Susa in the fifth century B.C. The main character, Esther, is not mentioned. A banquet is given that will function similarly to the banquet in Dan 5, where the king saw the handwriting on the wall. Xerxes would also receive a revelation but with different consequences.

2. The Splendor of the King (1:4-8)

[4]For a full 180 days he displayed the vast wealth of his kingdom and the splendor and glory of his majesty. [5]When these days were over, the king gave a banquet, lasting seven days, in the enclosed garden of the king's palace, for all the people from the least to the greatest, who were in the citadel of Susa. [6]The garden had hangings of white and blue linen, fastened with cords of white linen and purple material to silver rings on marble pillars. There were couches of gold and silver on a mosaic pavement of porphyry, marble, mother-of-pearl and other costly stones. [7]Wine was served in goblets of gold, each one different from the other, and the royal wine was abundant, in keeping with the king's liberality. [8]By the king's command each guest was allowed to drink in his own way, for the king instructed all the wine stewards to serve each man what he wished.

Wanting to show what one possesses is natural but prideful (cf. 2 Kgs 20:13). Herodotus was greatly impressed with the wealth of the affluent Persian king. Cyrus had conquered Babylon (539 B.C.) and ruled as far as the Aegean Sea. Cambyses conquered Egypt and added it to the empire. Darius I added northwest India as far as the Indus River and had organized the empire; thus Xerxes inherited an immense and powerful empire.

1:4 "For a full 180 days" does not necessarily mean the banquet lasted that long. Xerxes must have had some sort of public exposition that lasted half a year. The nobles and army officials were invited to see all this luxury. This may also have been a time of planning for the military campaign against Greece (480–479 B.C.). Herodotus says that after 180 days of showing the riches and glory of his empire, Xerxes presented his proposal to the nobles and princes. So the banquet in v. 5 may have been the same as that of v. 3, which gives an introduction while the present paragraph gives more of the setting.[10]

---

[10] Some commentators think there were two or three banquets. Some then use the (supposed) exaggeration of a 180-day banquet to show that Esther cannot be historical. See, however, C. Moore (*Esther,* AB [Garden City: Doubleday, 1971], 6), who states that the large number of days is similar to the 120 days of celebration in Jdt 1:16. Moore also states that the only problem of the number of days is a practical one: the heat in Susa in the summer is unbearable.

1:5 "The king gave a banquet" marks the narration of the actual banquet. It lasted seven days and was held in the garden inside the king's palace. At a banquet news or events are revealed or announced. Later the motif of the banquet returns with ironic consequences (5:8; 7:1-10).

1:6-7 Verse 6 emphasizes the dazzling luxury of the Persian palace. Herodotus related an incident that occurred during Xerxes' retreat from Greece when the king left his tent in one of the abandoned camps. The Greeks were astounded to find gold and silver couches in the tent. They asked one another why the rich Persian king would want to conquer their Greek "poverty." Though the world still lives for material things, such as "wine . . . in goblets of gold," Christian values are different.

Verses 6-7 function in an aesthetic sense by describing in ornamental detail the beauty of the garden and the banquet hall. Visual image is important in the mind of the reader. Writers of the Old Testament books were economical with their words. By spending time on the nature of the garden and the hall, the writer of Esther clearly displayed a sense that in the midst of such ornate beauty and false pretense, true wealth would be discovered in being loyal to God's will.

1:8 The word *dāt* ("decree," "law") is used nineteen times in the book and each time refers to royal decrees.[11] Usually the toastmaster would indicate when everyone was to drink, but here the king commanded that each could drink as he pleased. This suggests the luxurious but licentious character of the banquet. As McConville has said, the issue dealt with in vv. 1-11 is the "unacceptable face of human power," which in Xerxes is "self-serving and grotesque."[12]

3. The Queen's Banquet (1:9)

⁹Queen Vashti also gave a banquet for the women in the royal palace of King Xerxes.

1:9 The phrase "Queen Vashti also gave a banquet" indicates that the queen had liberty to make decisions and take action. Some have thought that because the queen gave a banquet for the women, the men

---

[11] Paton, *Book of Esther,* 146. Here "according to the decree" could mean "flagons," so the translation would be "drinking was by flagons without restraint." However, the NIV rendering is better (J. G. Baldwin, *Esther* [Downers Grove: InterVarsity, 1984], 59). See Ezra 7:12, where it is used for the Old Testament Books of Genesis to Deuteronomy but occurs in the Aramaic.

[12] J. G. McConville, *Ezra, Nehemiah, and Esther,* DSB (Philadelphia: Westminster, 1985), 156.

and women were segregated at banquets. However, Persian custom did not require that men and women eat separately. In fact, according to Herodotus, Persians usually had their wives with them at their feasts.[13]

Herodotus said the name of Xerxes' queen was Amestris. Many see this as an indication that this story is fictitious and not historical. However, the king may have had other queens, or perhaps she had different names. Some suggest that Vashti, which means "sweetheart," may have been an epithet. The point of v. 9 is simply that Xerxes and Vashti were not acting in accord with each other. Their actions foreshadowed their separation soon to come.

4. The King's Request Denied (1:10-12)

[10]On the seventh day, when King Xerxes was in high spirits from wine, he commanded the seven eunuchs who served him—Mehuman, Biztha, Harbona, Bigtha, Abagtha, Zethar and Carcas—[11]to bring before him Queen Vashti, wearing her royal crown, in order to display her beauty to the people and nobles, for she was lovely to look at. [12]But when the attendants delivered the king's command, Queen Vashti refused to come. Then the king became furious and burned with anger.

1:10 "When King Xerxes was in high spirits from wine" probably indicates that he was at least partly inebriated. The eunuchs are listed here for a reason. The names serve to verify the event. Because they were eunuchs, they could be trusted to go to the queen and bring her safely to the king.

1:11 "Queen Vashti" was "lovely to look at." But Esther would replace her (2:9-18). Though they were both beautiful, the main difference between them was Esther's wisdom.

1:12 "Queen Vashti refused to come." The rabbis as well as modern commentators discussed the queen's refusal. The rabbis thought the king wanted Vashti to appear naked since she was to wear (only, they said) "her royal crown." One of the Targums says the king commanded her to appear naked.[14] The author of the book did not say why she refused. We

---

[13] Herodotus, Book v.

[14] Vashti was ordered so because of three prior events not mentioned in the Book of Esther. First, the *Targum Rishon* says that Mordecai prayed for seven days. Second, when Xerxes was inebriated, the Targum says that the Lord "incited an angel against him, the angel of confusion to confound their festivities." Third, Vashti was to come in the nude because, as the Targum says, she used to make the Israelite girls work in the nude on the Sabbath. Because God is not mentioned explicitly in Esther, the Targums supply the interpretation of God's activity in these events. See B. Grossfeld, *The Two Targums of Esther, The Aramaic Bible,* vol. 18 (Collegeville: Liturgical, 1991), 34-35. The Targums are Aramaic paraphrases of the Hebrew Scripture. They are of value because they provide a glimpse at the history of the interpretation of the Bible.

do know that to display her beauty would have implied coming unveiled, which would have been a violation of custom. No doubt the queen also knew what it would be like to show her beauty before that large group of men, many of whom had drunk too much wine.

"The king became furious." Although at least some of the Persian kings tried to please their subject peoples, some were also capricious and cruel. Herodotus's description of Darius II's actions in Egypt gives an idea of how horribly cruel the king could be. He could kill anyone (even his personal servants and friends) who defied him or tried to give him advice that went against his will. Xerxes was also known to have been capricious and cruel at times. The account does not indicate whether the king was furious simply because the queen did not fulfill his whims or her decision to disobey was a serious offense. The queen refused a formal command of the king in the presence of the officers of the whole empire, so it could have been considered serious by those officers.

Vashti's courage must be acknowledged. She defied her king and her husband by refusing to shame herself in public. Whatever else may be said of her, she was brave. She was willing to give up her status and position as queen in order to do what was right. Her dignity was more important than her place in society. Her act of courage in refusing to present herself before the king is equaled by that of Esther, who entered the king's presence without permission (5:1).[15] Both Vashti and Esther made plain that the king was not in charge; rather, human dignity and all things right were in charge. The king suffered from his obsession with manipulative power while Vashti and Esther exhibited the power of rightness. Ultimately the question of authority is at stake. As McConville has expressed it, "What or who *really* controls what happens in the world?" Who should be obeyed, when, and at what cost?[16] It is not the power of humans that should be adhered to but rather the will of God. "Earthly authority, alas, leads too readily to pride; those who bear it in wisdom know it is rightly accompanied by humility."[17]

5. The King's Counsel (1:13-15)

[13]**Since it was customary for the king to consult experts in matters of law and justice, he spoke with the wise men who understood the times** [14]**and were closest to the king—Carshena, Shethar, Admatha, Tarshish, Meres,**

---

[15] McConville, *Ezra, Nehemiah, and Esther,* 157.
[16] Ibid.
[17] Ibid., 159.

Marsena and Memucan, the seven nobles of Persia and Media who had special access to the king and were highest in the kingdom.

15"According to law, what must be done to Queen Vashti?" he asked.
"She has not obeyed the command of King Xerxes that the eunuchs have
taken to her."

1:13-15   Although he was powerful, "it was customary for the king
to consult" advisors. Persian kings sometimes killed advisors, as did Darius II when they angered him. In Egypt, Cambyses killed officials who
criticized him.[18]

Ezra 7:14 also speaks of the Persian king's seven advisors. "Matters of
law and justice" in Hebrew are *dāt* and *dîn*, sounds that add an allitera-
tive touch to the narrative. Every culture has certain accepted norms.
Mesopotamia had a long tradition of laws and legal matters. Jewish law
is distinctive in that it is the revelation of the God who is near to them
and hears their prayers (Deut 4:5-8). Again, names of seemingly insignificant persons are given in order to lend credence to the story. The phrase
"highest in the kingdom" indicates that this is the best. Like the ornate
garden and the beautiful Vashti, Persia possessed nobles of renown.

6. The "Seriousness" of the Matter (1:16-18)

16Then Memucan replied in the presence of the king and the nobles,
"Queen Vashti has done wrong, not only against the king but also against all
the nobles and the peoples of all the provinces of King Xerxes. **17**For the
queen's conduct will become known to all the women, and so they will despise their husbands and say, 'King Xerxes commanded Queen Vashti to be
brought before him, but she would not come.' **18**This very day the Persian
and Median women of the nobility who have heard about the queen's conduct will respond to all the king's nobles in the same way. There will be no
end of disrespect and discord.

1:16-18   "Memucan" is one of the nobles mentioned in v. 14. His
voice and judgment, "Queen Vashti has done wrong, . . . against all the
nobles and peoples," indicate his status among the nobles. There is some
truth in Memucan's judgment (see comment on v. 12). Certainly the example of leaders affects the whole community. But apparently Memucan's
answer was intended to justify the king's decision and thereby maintain
the king's favor. Memucan gave an astute answer, for it relieved the king
of personal capriciousness and found support in the all-male gathering.

---

[18] Herodotus, *History*, iii.

7. The Queen's Punishment and the King's Decree (1:19-22)

[19]"Therefore, if it pleases the king, let him issue a royal decree and let it be written in the laws of Persia and Media, which cannot be repealed, that Vashti is never again to enter the presence of King Xerxes. Also let the king give her royal position to someone else who is better than she. [20]Then when the king's edict is proclaimed throughout all his vast realm, all the women will respect their husbands, from the least to the greatest."
[21]The king and his nobles were pleased with this advice, so the king did as Memucan proposed. [22]He sent dispatches to all parts of the kingdom, to each province in its own script and to each people in its own language, proclaiming in each people's tongue that every man should be ruler over his own household.

1:19-21 Memucan continued his pronouncement with a sentence of exile for Vashti. She would remain in Persia, but her duties as queen had been revoked. From here on the title "queen" is not used again with the name "Vashti." She was deposed, and the king was to look for another.

The author was familiar with Persian customs and the use of an efficient system of communication in the whole empire. Verse 19b opens the narrative for a new character. The line is full of implication and suspense. Memucan's decision was not just to send Vashti away but to "let the king give her royal position to someone else who is better than she." She was beautiful, and she possessed dignity. Anyone better than she would be hard to find. What Xerxes heard was quite different; he understood "better" to mean "obedient," but the narrative will tell us what was said, not heard.

Baldwin notes the subtle ironies the author communicates in this narrative. The great king of a huge empire is humiliated by his queen; in a fit of rage he is appeased by his counselors and makes a decree that makes him look like a fool.[19] The author knew the weaknesses of human kings and officials. The author had faith in a God who as King and Lord of the universe is above all forms of capriciousness.

1:22 The Hebrew phrase for "proclaiming in each people's tongue" comes at the end of the verse and appears to be part of the command to each household; it says literally, "and speaking according to the tongue of his people." The traditional interpretation (as found also in the Targums and many Jewish commentaries) is that everyone was to speak only the father's native language in his house. However, many find it difficult to think such a decree would be made by a Persian king. The NIV trans-

---

[19] Baldwin, *Esther*, 63.

poses the phrase before the command "that every man should be ruler," thus separating it from the "proclamation" clause. Other explanations have been given, but they require changes in the text.[20]

The chapter ends on a note of suspense, preparing the reader for the next episode. The narrative suddenly closes on the present scene and opens to the entire empire. Since the author was Jewish, three things need to be said. First, the reader now knows that a new character is needed to replace Vashti. The anticipated character is Esther, a Jew. Second, it will be a woman. Like Miriam, Deborah, Ruth, and others before her, the new character in this story will emerge as a heroine of her people. Third, God is present implicitly, but not explicitly. Already the reader anticipates that Xerxes as a Gentile will be superceded by God's sovereign choice of a new queen, even the Jew Esther.

The narrative is now ready to introduce us to a new character. Vashti has courageously entered and exited. She has prepared the way for one to replace her and to exceed her courage.

---

[20] וּמְדַבֵּר כִּלְשׁוֹן עַמּוֹ. See D. J. A. Clines, *Ezra, Nehemiah, Esther*, NCB (Grand Rapids: Eerdmans, 1984), 283.

II. ESTHER BECOMES QUEEN (2:1-18)

With Vashti removed from her duties, the search for a replacement commenced. This chapter is a good example of the art of the author. The story is actually quite detailed and suspenseful. The conclusion is that the Jew Esther was found to be the most beautiful of all the women who were brought before the king. What he would find out later is that she was also, perhaps, the most courageous.

1. A Proposal for a New Queen (2:1-4)

[1]Later when the anger of King Xerxes had subsided, he remembered Vashti and what she had done and what he had decreed about her. [2]Then the king's personal attendants proposed, "Let a search be made for beautiful young virgins for the king. [3]Let the king appoint commissioners in every province of his realm to bring all these beautiful girls into the harem at the citadel of Susa. Let them be placed under the care of Hegai, the king's eunuch, who is in charge of the women; and let beauty treatments be given to them. [4]Then let the girl who pleases the king be queen instead of Vashti." This advice appealed to the king, and he followed it.

2:1 "Later" does not specify how much later. Verse 16 indicates that when Esther came before the king, it was the seventh year of Xerxes' reign. That would be four years after the events of chap. 1. We do not know how much time the search for the women occupied. Xerxes' campaign against the Greeks must have taken place in this interval.

Perhaps Xerxes "remembered Vashti" because he was sorry for his former decision or at least desired to have her again. But he had made an irrevocable decree.

2:2 The "king's personal attendants" had a proposal: search for the most beautiful virgins in the kingdom and let the king choose a new queen. Though this sounds like a beauty contest, it was not a very happy assignment for most of the women. They were uprooted from their communities, which implied confinement to the king's harem, and moved to what would actually be perpetual widowhood.

2:3 "Beauty treatment" included purification and the use of precious ointments.[1] Like the gardens and the banquet hall, Xerxes had great appreciation for beautiful things. Unfortunately, "things" are exactly what Xerxes thought women were. As Vashti had shown, and as Esther would show, the women were as courageous and intelligent as the men in this story. In fact, both Vashti and Esther showed that they had much more respect for the dignity of life than did Xerxes and Haman.

2:4 The king could have had any young woman he wanted. The Oriental kings caused much suffering among many people in satisfying their personal desires. Similar oppression still occurs today, although the means of carrying it out are sometimes so indirect (e.g., economic) that few notice the injustice. The prophets of Israel raised their voices against such unjust oppression (e.g., Amos 5:7-12).

2. Esther the Jew in the King's Palace (2:5-9)

[5]Now there was in the citadel of Susa a Jew of the tribe of Benjamin, named Mordecai son of Jair, the son of Shimei, the son of Kish, [6]who had been carried into exile from Jerusalem by Nebuchadnezzar king of Babylon, among those taken captive with Jehoiachin king of Judah. [7]Mordecai had a cousin named Hadassah, whom he had brought up because she had neither father nor mother. This girl, who was also known as Esther, was lovely in form and features, and Mordecai had taken her as his own daughter when her father and mother died.

[8]When the king's order and edict had been proclaimed, many girls were brought to the citadel of Susa and put under the care of Hegai. Esther also was taken to the king's palace and entrusted to Hegai, who had charge of the harem. [9]The girl pleased him and won his favor. Immediately he provided her with her beauty treatments and special food. He assigned to her seven maids selected from the king's palace and moved her and her maids into the best place in the harem.

In this paragraph the author interrupts the narrative to introduce the two protagonists in the following incidents. The whole narrative flows swiftly without introducing more details than necessary.

---

[1] C. F. Keil, *Esther* (Grand Rapids: Eerdmans, 1980), 333. See the introduction above and comment on v. 12.

2:5-6 "A Jew . . . named Mordecai" is the author's first mention of the Jewish people. It is interesting that the Jews are spoken of in the third person.[2]

"Who had been carried into exile" can refer grammatically either to Mordecai or to Kish. However, Jehoiachin was taken captive in 597 B.C., over a century before the present narrative, making Mordecai over 120 years of age if he is the antecedent. Therefore the relative pronoun must refer to Kish.

"Mordecai" is similar to the Babylonian name Mardukaya. In a text from the last years of Darius I or early years of Xerxes, we find mention of a Marduka who was an accountant on an inspection tour from Susa.[3] This could have been the same person. The name also may come from the Mesopotamian god Marduk. It was not uncommon for Jews to take a name indigenous to the country in which they lived (e.g., Dan 1:6-7).

2:7 "Hadassah" means "myrtle."[4] The name "Esther" means "star" and is derived from the same root as the name of the goddess Ishtar.[5]

Mordecai had adopted Esther, who was his cousin. Adoption was common in the Nuzi texts.[6] It was known in Israel as is evident from its use to depict God's relation to his people (Exod 4:22; 2 Sam 7:14; Pss 2:7-8; 89:27-28; Jer 3:19; 31:9). However, there are few examples of adoption in Israel. When practiced, it usually involved adoptions within the ex-

---

[2] R. Gordis suggests that the author was a Jew but that he wrote this narrative as though it were a Persian court chronicle written by a non-Jew. He calls it a unique literary genre ("Religion, Wisdom and History in the Book of Esther—A New Solution to an Ancient Crux," *JBL* 100 [1981]: 375).

[3] C. A. Moore, "Archaeology and the Book of Esther," *BA* (1975): 74. See further on Mordecai in the Introduction, "The Historicity of Esther."

[4] Various figurative meanings have been suggested. Myrtle branches signify peace and thanksgiving when carried in the procession at the Feast of Tabernacles (J. Baldwin, *Esther*, TOTC [Downers Grove: InterVarsity, 1984], 66).

[5] Note the similarity between Esther's name and Old Persian *stara*, modern Persian *sitareh*, and Greek *huster*. R. Gordis suggests that it could be a shortened form of the "Amestris" whom Herodotus said was Xerxes' wife. However, in "Esther—A New Solution" (384) he notes that most scholars find difficulty with the name Amestris since linguistically it cannot be the same as Vashti and it seems distant from Esther. But Gordis notes the Greek tendency to shorten foreign names; for example, "Sander" for "Alexander." He says: "It is not impossible that *Esther* represented an apocopated form of the name *Amestris*. . . . The relationship between Marduk and Ishtar in Mid-Eastern mythology would also encourage shortening the name of *Amestris* to *Esther*." However, most scholars find it difficult to identify Amestris with Esther. See further in the Introduction, "The Historicity of Esther."

[6] The Nuzi texts are clay tablets written in cuneiform Akkadian found in Nuzi. They inform us about family customs in Mesopotamia around 1400 B.C.

tended family, as in this case. Esther does not speak or even appear here in the story herself but rather is merely introduced. Suspense is a key element in this narrative. Vashti was beautiful. The physical absence of Esther thus far leaves much to the imagination of the reader. "Esther was lovely in form and features." Beauty is a gift from God. In this case it was used by God for the good of his people.

2:8 Commentators speculate about how many girls were brought. Josephus said there were four hundred. Paton calculates that if the king had a different girl each night for four years, there would have been 1,460.[7]

"Esther also was taken." We are not told whether the girls were given a choice, but we may assume they were not. One Targum says she was taken forcibly. As noted above, for most of the girls it was not a happy experience.

2:9 "To 'please' ('be good') is the oil in the wheels of the Persian bureaucracy."[8] There is a strong note of irony here in that she "please him," that is, the eunuch. Esther's beauty was overpowering, even to a eunuch. The word "favor" is *hesed,* which can also refer to covenant loyalty or "kindness" (e.g., 1 Kgs 2:7; 3:6; Ezra 9:9).[9] Although God is not mentioned, the use of this word indicates that there is a religious mood to the text.

Some wonder why Esther did not protest eating the unclean food of the king as Daniel did.[10] The text gives no answer. In the following paragraph, however, we see that Esther was not to disclose her identity.

After 31 verses of narrative covering a significant period of time, Esther is finally in the harem of the king. We still have not seen her or heard from her. The narrative builds in intensity. And yet, why is she coming to the court? We anticipate that she will replace Vashti, but for what purpose? Simply to be queen is not enough. The author has cleverly

---

[7] L. B. Paton, *The Book of Esther,* ICC (Edinburgh: T & T Clark, 1908), 172-73. But this seems exaggerated. He seems to assume that this was a continual process during the four years between chaps. 1 and 2. But the text does not indicate that this process continued four years. As noted, it is more likely that the four-year period included Xerxes' Greek campaign.

[8] D. J. A. Clines, *Ezra, Nehemiah, Esther,* NCBC (Grand Rapids: Eerdmans, 1984), 288. Notice how often the concept of "pleasing" is repeated (1:21; 2:4 [twice]; 1:10,11,19; 2:2,3,7,9).

[9] The phrase is also used in 2:15 and 5:12. To "win" favor carries a more active sense than the normal "obtain favor." Esther was a "success" even prior to appearing before King Xerxes (ibid.).

[10] Daniel 1:8-21. Jehoiachin also ate the king's food without protest (2 Kgs 25:29).

disguised the purpose of Esther's slow rise to the court in "pomp and circumstance."

3. Esther's Time of Preparation and Waiting (2:10-14)

[10]Esther had not revealed her nationality and family background, because Mordecai had forbidden her to do so. [11]Every day he walked back and forth near the courtyard of the harem to find out how Esther was and what was happening to her.

[12]Before a girl's turn came to go in to King Xerxes, she had to complete twelve months of beauty treatments prescribed for the women, six months with oil of myrrh and six with perfumes and cosmetics. [13]And this is how she would go to the king: Anything she wanted was given her to take with her from the harem to the king's palace. [14]In the evening she would go there and in the morning return to another part of the harem to the care of Shaashgaz, the king's eunuch who was in charge of the concubines. She would not return to the king unless he was pleased with her and summoned her by name.

2:10 One wonders why Mordecai insisted on her concealing her identity. According to Herodotus, the king should have looked for a queen among the leading Persian families. Esther might have had no chance of becoming queen if her nationality had been disclosed. Ambition, however, does not seem to characterize Mordecai elsewhere. Did he have the foresight to think the position might prove advantageous to her people? However, Persian kings did not always stay within the accepted limits. He may have thought the knowledge of her identity might prove dangerous to her. Perhaps anti-Semitism already existed in the environment. The king's ignorance of her nationality, however, almost meant her undoing as well as that of her people (3:10-11). Even Mordecai was not able to control the plans of God.[11]

2:11 One wonders how Esther could have hidden her nationality if she had daily communication with Mordecai, who was well known as a Jew. In a country so diversified as Persia, however, such interaction would have been common.

2:12-14 Verses 12-14 indicate the process used to present the girls to the king. Apparently most of the girls spent only one night with the king. They moved on to the house of Shaashgaz, where they were concubines. There was no guarantee that the king would call them again, so many were confined to virtual widowhood. Again we see how one person, the

---

[11] McConville, *Ezra, Nehemiah, and Esther,* DSB (Philadelphia: Westminster, 1985), 163.

king, could use so many other human beings just to satisfy his personal
desires. Xerxes' abuse of power is evident in the demise of so many in-
nocent women for his physical pleasure. Even today those who have no
fear of God sometimes can satisfy their desires without limit.[12]

4. Esther Chosen as Queen (2:15-18)

[15]**When the turn came for Esther (the girl Mordecai had adopted, the
daughter of his uncle Abihail) to go to the king, she asked for nothing other
than what Hegai, the king's eunuch who was in charge of the harem, suggested. And Esther won the favor of everyone who saw her.** [16]**She was taken
to King Xerxes in the royal residence in the tenth month, the month of Te-
beth, in the seventh year of his reign.**

[17]**Now the king was attracted to Esther more than to any of the other
women, and she won his favor and approval more than any of the other virgins. So he set a royal crown on her head and made her queen instead of
Vashti.** [18]**And the king gave a great banquet, Esther's banquet, for all his nobles and officials. He proclaimed a holiday throughout the provinces and distributed gifts with royal liberality.**

2:15 Esther is finally introduced into the narrative. Apparently each
girl had certain liberty in choosing her adornment (v. 13). It is said that
some took advantage of this to deck themselves with many jewels. Esther
was content to stay with Hegai's advice. That was wise since certainly he
knew what pleased the king. Exactly what she took is unknown. We do
know she took with her a desire to remain loyal both to God and her people. This took great wisdom.

Esther's sound life, based on Hebrew (biblical) ethical principles, was
expressed in the character and poise of her person.

2:16 "The tenth month" in the Jewish religious calendar was a cold,
wet month in the middle of winter (Dec.-Jan.). "The seventh year" would
have been 479 B.C. What happened during the four years since chap. 1?
We know that Xerxes waged war against Greece in 480–479, but this fact
is of no interest in the story. The only point is that the search for a new
wife had taken a long time. Now Esther's arrival changes the entire com-
plexion of the narrative.

2:17 "So he . . . made her queen." In this key verse in the narrative,
Esther became queen instead of Vashti. The future of the story depends
on this event. The sudden decision on the part of Xerxes reveals that he

---

[12] The psalmist said we are not to fret about this (Ps 37:1); though troubled, he confessed, "I entered the sanctuary of God; then I understood their final destiny" (Ps 73:17).

was overwhelmed by the sight of Esther. Readers can only imagine. Such beauty can only be made manifest through the presence of God. Such an overwhelmed king probably reflects that as he had done with Pharaoh and Cyrus, God had influenced this foreign king as well.

2:18 Since his decision was important, the king celebrated. "He proclaimed a holiday" is literally "a causing to rest." Some interpret it as a remission of taxes, which was not impossible in the Persian Empire. Herodotus (Book iii) tells how Smerdis proclaimed a three-year remission of taxes when he became king. However, it is best to understand the event as a holiday.

Throughout the narrative of chap. 2, the hand of God is understood to be the force behind the development of the story. The author was in no way claiming that the events herein were from human hands but that the course of events was understandably at the direction of a power larger than this story. The first readers of Esther must have been amused at the reading of the text as they realized this important truth. The people were oppressed. Since there was no chance for a Jew to become king, Esther was brought into the royal court to become queen. As Joseph was introduced to the court of the Pharaoh and Daniel to the court of Nebuchadnezzar, Esther came to the court for a similar purpose. Joseph's leadership meant food for his famine-stricken family and their eventual prosperity. Daniel's leadership led to a new status of acceptance of Jews in Babylonia. Esther's leadership would yield similar results. The common element in all three is that it was God who brought about these results.

III. MORDECAI DISCOVERS A PLOT (2:19-23)
  1. Mordecai at the King's Gate (2:19-20)
  2. The Plot to Kill the King (2:21-23)

──────── **III. MORDECAI DISCOVERS A PLOT (2:19-23)** ────────

Mordecai had a place of reputation at the king's gate. When the women were gathered a second time, Mordecai overheard a plot to kill the king. Mordecai told Esther and the plot was stopped. This event would play a major role later in the narrative (ch. 6). This act of courage by both Mordecai and Esther reflects their loyalty to Xerxes, who possessed the political power either to destroy or to deliver.

1. Mordecai at the King's Gate (2:19-20)

[19]When the virgins were assembled a second time, Mordecai was sitting at the king's gate. [20]But Esther had kept secret her family background and nationality just as Mordecai had told her to do, for she continued to follow Mordecai's instructions as she had done when he was bringing her up.

2:19 Verse 19 contains two phrases that have caused much discussion. The first says "the virgins were assembled a second time." Some scholars think it is a flashback to a time before Esther was chosen queen. But Keil correctly maintains that it can only mean a second gathering of virgins after Esther was made queen.[1] Gordis agrees and says: "In view of the context which describes Esther's coronation, we suggest that the verse refers to a second procession of the unsuccessful contestants, whose undeniable charms served to set off in more striking relief Esther's beauty."[2]

Throughout the Near East, law cases and official matters were handled near the gate area. Therefore, that Mordecai was "sitting at the king's gate" suggests that he was an official of some sort (cf. Lot in Gen 19:1).

---

[1] C. F. Keil, *Esther, Commentary on the Old Testament* (Grand Rapids: Eerdmans, 1980), 341.

[2] R. Gordis, "Studies in the Esther Narrative," *JBL* 95/1 (1976): 47.

Gordis supposes that "after Esther became queen, she had Mordecai appointed a magistrate or judge, a lesser position in the elaborate hierarchy of Persian officials."[3] Thus Esther was able to show her appreciation for Mordecai's help and also make it possible to maintain communication with him.

2:20 Esther's keeping "secret her family background" is information the author already has revealed (v. 10). The use of repetition suggests that this hidden agenda is a clue to the development of the plot. In v. 20 the author again emphasized Esther's obedience and loyalty to Mordecai. Since she had learned obedience when he brought her up, she continued to respect his advice. Here mutual confidence and respect benefited an entire nation.

2. The Plot to Kill the King (2:21-23)

[21]**During the time Mordecai was sitting at the king's gate, Bigthana and Teresh, two of the king's officers who guarded the doorway, became angry and conspired to assassinate King Xerxes.** [22]**But Mordecai found out about the plot and told Queen Esther, who in turn reported it to the king, giving credit to Mordecai.** [23]**And when the report was investigated and found to be true, the two officials were hanged on a gallows. All this was recorded in the book of the annals in the presence of the king.**

2:21 The names probably meant nothing to the first readers and do not help us identify them since they are not mentioned elsewhere. But like the list of eunuchs and nobles in chap. 1, this listing lends credence to the historicity of the events. These details probably were available to the author in the court records of the period. The two officers who guarded the palace, although "minor characters," had important positions. Since conspiracies by government officials were a constant danger, Mordecai told Esther, who informed the king. She did not forget to give Mordecai credit for discovering the plot. We must give Mordecai credit for keeping alert and for maintaining contact with the queen. Both qualities—alertness and communication—made a difference that affected history.

2:22 As the Targums interpret, Mordecai's discovery of the plot was by God's design, not by Mordecai's wisdom. This verse is one of the pivotal verses in the book because it brings Mordecai into the good graces of the king and foreshadows his reward and exaltation in 6:1-14. As a

---

[3] Ibid., 48.

Jew, Mordecai could have let the plot continue and taken a chance on having a new king. Such action, however, would have proven harmful to Esther's role as queen (also cf. Jer 29:7; 1 Tim 2:2). Therefore, in the interest of his adopted Esther and the fate of the Jewish people, Mordecai foiled the plot of the would-be killers.

2:23 Mordecai's action in saving the king's life was recorded "in the book of the annals," but the king forgot the incident until he read of it on a sleepless night (6:1-14). Herodotus tells of King Xerxes, who had his secretaries record each time he saw one of his officers behaving with distinction during a battle against the Greeks.[4]

Esther has been introduced as the new queen, and Mordecai has a place of high standing in the gate. Vashti has exited almost as fast as she entered, yet she will be remembered throughout because any reference to Esther as queen will make us recall whose place she took. Xerxes is consumed with power yet powerless as sovereign events unfold.

---

[4] Herodotus, *History*, 8.90.

IV. HAMAN'S PLOT TO DESTROY THE JEWS (3:1-15)
   1. The King Honors Haman (3:1-2)
   2. Haman Plans Revenge (3:3-15)
      (1) Haman's Anger (3:3-6)
      (2) Haman Presents His Plan (3:7-11)
      (3) Haman's Edict Published (3:12-15)

—— IV. HAMAN'S PLOT TO DESTROY THE JEWS (3:1-15) ——

Here the account takes a sudden threatening turn. The story now has a villain. Haman was promoted above all "other nobles" (Esth 3:1). Power took hold of his life and led him to a decision he would soon regret. He plotted the death of all the Jews because Mordecai refused to bow down to honor him. The story is similar to Dan 3, where the three young Hebrew men refused to worship the golden image established by Nebuchadnezzar. It is perhaps more similar to the story in Dan 6, where the officials plotted against Daniel for praying to God and not praying to Darius. In each of these three accounts allegiance to God and the Jewish tradition proved to be rewarded by God with the gift of life. Here in Esth 3 the narrative plot is intensified with a detailed account of the plot to destroy the Jews unparalleled in Daniel. This chapter has an aesthetic appeal in that one can almost hear and smell death approaching.

1. The King Honors Haman (3:1-2)

¹After these events, King Xerxes honored Haman son of Hammedatha, the Agagite, elevating him and giving him a seat of honor higher than that of all the other nobles. ²All the royal officials at the king's gate knelt down and paid honor to Haman, for the king had commanded this concerning him. But Mordecai would not kneel down or pay him honor.

3:1 We are not told why Haman was honored in such a way. In any society there are degrees of authority and honor in which some will be honored above others. It is natural that the king should delegate authority and require that the people honor his chief officials. However, in this narrative the author portrays Xerxes as a king who was maneuvered too readily by others.

Haman is introduced as "the Agagite," an intentional reference to the tension between the Israelites and the Amalekites.[1] This enmity stems from the time of the exodus when Israel fought with Amalek in the wilderness. Exodus 17:15 foretells that the Lord would be at war with them from "generation to generation." Balaam's oracle (Num 24:7) predicts that the Israelite king would "be greater than Agag" (the Amalekite royal title). The ancient feud between the Israelites and the Amalekites is reported in 1 Sam 15. Agag was king of the Amalekites. Saul the Benjamite, son of Kish (1 Sam 9:1-2) was directed to destroy totally the Amalekites but failed to do so even though he won the war. He took Agag prisoner, but Samuel the prophet confronted Saul and cursed him for not completing the task. Samuel cut Agag into pieces, and Saul's downfall began. Such a military conquest of Agag and his army is part of Israel's tradition, which stands behind the scenes of the Book of Esther.

Together with the information that Mordecai was a Benjamite and a descendant of Kish (2:5), this mention of Haman as an Agagite gives the knowledgeable reader a clue that the conflict between the two was centuries old and would result in the Agagite's demise.

Thus Haman became a prototype of all anti-Semitic leaders who want to destroy the Jewish people. Though some think the story improbable and fictitious, there are both ancient and modern examples of mass genocide against specific peoples. Gordis cites an example from the Roman province of Asia Minor in 88 B.C. Mithradates VI of Pontus "ordered a general slaughter" of everyone of the Italic race, "men, women and children of every age within the newly subjugated territory." A specific day was set so that the massacre could be carried out everywhere at the same time. According to the report, eighty thousand were killed in one day.[2] Modern history cites mass genocide of six million Jews in Nazi Germany, of other peoples in Stalin's Russia, as well as other examples such as the Armenians, who suffered under the Turks.

3:2 It may seem odd to have so many people "at the king's gate." The entrance to the palace of Persian kings probably was large; at least the one excavated in Persepolis was spacious. Haman, as grand vizier, was second only to the king; so the king commanded that the officials

---

[1] On the importance of biblical epithets, see M. Sternberg, *The Poetics of Biblical Narrative: Ideological Literature and the Drama of Reading* (Bloomington: Indiana University Press, 1985), 331-37.

[2] R. Gordis, "Religion, Wisdom and History in the Book of Esther—A New Solution to an Ancient Crux," *JBL* 100 (1981): 383.

bow down to him.

The narrative does not indicate why "Mordecai would not kneel down." Since Mordecai later became the leading official in place of Haman, he must have honored the king. One of the Targums says that no self-respecting Benjamite would show reverence to a descendant of the Amalekites. In light of "court tales" like Dan 3 and 6, the explanation is that Mordecai bowed only to God (Exod 20:2-6). The text does not say this, but to the original Jewish audience what was not said was just as powerful as what was said. Keil says it was because of religious scruples. Although the Israelites used the custom of bowing down to superiors (2 Sam 14:4; 18:28; 1 Kgs 1:16), the Persians saw it as an act of reverence that bordered on recognizing the official as divine.[3] We should conclude that Mordecai had both religious and political reasons for adamantly not bowing down to Haman.

2. Haman Plans Revenge (3:3-15)

(1) Haman's Anger (3:3-6)

[3]Then the royal officials at the king's gate asked Mordecai, "Why do you disobey the king's command?" [4]Day after day they spoke to him but he refused to comply. Therefore they told Haman about it to see whether Mordecai's behavior would be tolerated, for he had told them he was a Jew.

[5]When Haman saw that Mordecai would not kneel down or pay him honor, he was enraged. [6]Yet having learned who Mordecai's people were, he scorned the idea of killing only Mordecai. Instead Haman looked for a way to destroy all Mordecai's people, the Jews, throughout the whole kingdom of Xerxes.

3:3 The rhetorical question, "Why do you disobey the king's command?" implies a righteous answer. No explicit answer is given, but the "right" answer is that only God is to be honored in such a manner.

3:4 "Day after day they spoke to him." Haman at first did not notice that Mordecai acted differently from the other officials. One wonders why the officials told Haman, but Haman probably had the officials keep a close eye out for Mordecai's actions.

"He had told them he was a Jew," which tends to support the argument that Mordecai had religious reasons for not bowing down to Haman.

"Haman . . . was enraged." People sometimes want to be revered as

---

[3] C. F. Keil, *Esther, Commentary on the Old Testament* (Grand Rapids: Eerdmans, 1980), 342-44.

gods. Haman is pictured as a proud person who constantly desired human praise. In short, he was hungry for power.

3:6 "Haman looked for a way to destroy all . . . the Jews." Here the principal plot of the book is introduced: the attempt to destroy the Jewish people. Now the story begins to fall into place. Esther had been brought to a position of power for purposes not known until now. The threat of an all-out pogrom was now a reality. Mordecai refused to honor a human being, thus keeping the commandments. He identified himself as a Jew. Identification with God's people can result in hardship. Hatred and bitterness were at the root of Haman's quest for power. For him power rested in the complete destruction of the Jews. Haman had not yet encountered the power of their God.

(2) Haman Presents His Plan (3:7-11)

[7]In the twelfth year of King Xerxes, in the first month, the month of Nisan, they cast the pur (that is, the lot) in the presence of Haman to select a day and month. And the lot fell on the twelfth month, the month of Adar.

[8]Then Haman said to King Xerxes, "There is a certain people dispersed and scattered among the peoples in all the provinces of your kingdom whose customs are different from those of all other people and who do not obey the king's laws; it is not in the king's best interest to tolerate them. [9]If it pleases the king, let a decree be issued to destroy them, and I will put ten thousand talents of silver into the royal treasury for the men who carry out this business."

[10]So the king took his signet ring from his finger and gave it to Haman son of Hammedatha, the Agagite, the enemy of the Jews. [11]"Keep the money," the king said to Haman, "and do with the people as you please."

3:7 "The twelfth year" was five years after Esther became queen. This was more than a century after the destruction of Jerusalem by Nebuchadnezzar, some sixty-four years after the first return with Zerubbabel, and sixteen years before Ezra's return to Jerusalem. Mordecai and Esther were from Jewish families that had stayed in Mesopotamia even after the first return from captivity.

The subject of the verb "to cast" is left indefinite in Hebrew ("they" in NIV), but it must refer to astrologers or magicians versed in the practice.[4] The common Hebrew term for "lot" is *gôrāl* (cf. 9:24). The word *pur* is a Hebrew form of the Babylonian *pūru*, meaning "lot." Secondarily, it meant "fate."[5] The magicians used pebbles or broken stones for

---

[4] Keil, *Esther*, 344-45.

dice, thus the relation between the root and the meaning as "lot." Both Herodotus and Xenophon spoke of the Persian custom of casting lots.[6]

Haman used the lot to select a favorable day to carry out his plot. This represents a view toward life that was part of the ancient world. Thousands of ancient Mesopotamian texts are omen texts. Kings decided whether or not to go to battle according to these omens, which were read from the livers of sacrificed animals. Astrology, magic, and a series of pagan practices were prohibited in the Old Testament. They were prohibited because the biblical viewpoint is diametrically opposed to the pagan worldview.[7]

The casting of the lots, however, displays a unique irony. The first readers of this story knew how the story ended. When this text was read, therefore, the readers quickly realized that the casting of the lots would not mean the doom of the Jews; ironically it meant that those who cast the lots would suffer the fate intended for someone else (cf. Eccl 11:1).

Many forms of a basically pagan worldview pervade our modern world and even Western culture. Thus there is an increase of spiritism, horoscopes, magic, and various forms of Oriental religions that are based on a pantheism. Some, such as Transcendental Meditation and The New Age, are a subtle mixture designed to offer guidance that is misplaced and erroneous.

So in Haman's worldview it was important to find the most opportune (or lucky) day to carry out his scheme. The discovery of ancient dice in the Assyrian Empire helps explain ancient Near Eastern usage. It is believed that in the first month of the year lots were cast to choose opportune days for important events.[8] This would explain why Haman cast lots in the first month and chose a date so much later.[9]

3:8 "In all the provinces" indicates that the Jews were quite widespread throughout the Persian Empire, although Haman no doubt was exaggerating.

Today God's people are different and must recognize their distinctive-

---

[5] C. A. Moore, "Esther, Book of," *ABD*, 2.637.

[6] See the Introduction to Esther under the heading "The Origin of Purim."

[7] The Israelites sometimes used a kind of "lot," the Urim and Thummim, to find God's will; but it is depicted as a means God used to provide guidance on specific matters. It was not based on magic. See Lev 16:8-10; Num 26:55-56; Judg 20:9; 1 Sam 14:41-42; Neh 10: 34; 11:1.

[8] See W. W. Hallo, "The First Purim," *BA* 46:1 (1983): 19-27.

[9] Other theories have been offered to explain the long lapse of time before the intended "doomsday." Keil accepted Clericus's conjecture that the motive was to induce many Jews to leave their property and flee to other countries (Keil, *Esther,* 38).

ness. "Their customs are different," or "their laws are different," explains that their emphasis on the law, God's revelation in the Mosaic Torah,[10] made them different. Our basis of authority and our priorities mold our customs. If we take seriously the authority of God's Word and allow his ethical principles to form our customs, we will be different from those who live by different authority (e.g., human reason, humanism) or ethical principles.

Haman used a mixture of truth, error, and exaggeration to convince the king. C. Moore describes it vividly: "Haman's accusation of the Jews (v. 8) was diabolically clever in its construction, proceeding as it did from the truth ('dispersed and scattered') to half-truth ('customs are different') to an outright lie ('who do not obey the king's laws')."[11] Those who oppose God's work use seemingly logical arguments to persuade official (and public) opinion. The method is similar to that found in Matt 4:1-11 (and Luke 4:1-13).

3:9 The Persian government was extremely rich, and apparently Haman also was wealthy. He probably would have expected to gain vast sums from the plundering of the Jews. Again note that opponents have no scruples against using bribes or economic advantage to hinder God's work and God's people.

3:10 "The king gave his signet ring to Haman." That was his way of giving him unlimited authority. Sometimes rulers give authority to others without realizing the consequences. That seems to have been the case here. The author of Esther depicted the king as one whose own wife disobeyed him and one who was deceived by his leading official (cf. Ps 72:2).

3:11 "Keep the money" is literally, "The silver is given to you." Was the king simply being polite, or did he not expect Haman to take the money? In 7:4 Esther assumed a payment was involved, for she said her people had "been sold." It is interesting that in this presentation Haman did not mention the Jews by name.

"Do with this people as you please." The king did not know all that was involved; but even so, he acted without a sense of human rights. The delegation of authority is impossible to avoid, but the key to doing it successfully is in knowing who you are giving power to. Whether or not Xerxes knew Haman well is not revealed. Nevertheless, the deed was done. God's great reversal of the fortunes of Haman and the Jews is signaled in 9:5 with the repetition of this phrase with the Jews as its subject:

---

[10] See Deut 4:5-8.
[11] C. Moore, *Esther,* AB (Garden City: Doubleday, 1971), 42.

"They did what they pleased to those who hated them."

(3) Haman's Edict Published (3:12-15)

¹²**Then on the thirteenth day of the first month the royal secretaries were summoned. They wrote out in the script of each province and in the language of each people all Haman's orders to the king's satraps, the governors of the various provinces and the nobles of the various peoples. These were written in the name of King Xerxes himself and sealed with his own ring. ¹³Dispatches were sent by couriers to all the king's provinces with the order to destroy, kill and annihilate all the Jews—young and old, women and little children—on a single day, the thirteenth day of the twelfth month, the month of Adar, and to plunder their goods. ¹⁴A copy of the text of the edict was to be issued as law in every province and made known to the people of every nationality so they would be ready for that day.**

¹⁵**Spurred on by the king's command, the couriers went out, and the edict was issued in the citadel of Susa. The king and Haman sat down to drink, but the city of Susa was bewildered.**

3:12 Again the author provided information that adds to the artistry of the narrative by giving a date only a Jew would know. The fourteenth day was the first day of Passover, the celebration of deliverance from Egypt. The irony is unmistakable. The day before celebrating freedom from Egyptian oppression, a decree had been made for their very destruction. In the ancient world things that were considered important were written down, so officials had their secretaries record events and transactions. This decree was a type of death document.

3:13 Throughout history many have tried to destroy the Jews, from the time of the exodus to the twentieth century.¹² Christians must be careful never to support in any way the rise of anti-Semitism, although it often has been "in the name of Christ" that such pogroms have taken place. Christians ought to be active in the fight against anti-Semitism as well as racism. Although the two are not synonymous, they are closely related. Many times anti-Semitism is based on an economic motive or excuse. In Nazi Germany, Jews were carried off to concentration camps, and their homes and possessions were confiscated, "to plunder their goods." This was an excuse, but the reason was that those in charge of Nazi Germany with many followers were guilty of pure hatred.

3:14 Laws can be bad and unjust. Christians cannot always use the

---

¹² On his stelae (dated 1220 B.C.), the Egyptian pharaoh Merneptah said Israel was defeated never to rise again. Others throughout history have said the same, but God has preserved his chosen people. This is the theme of Esther.

existing laws as justification for their action, as learned in the civil rights protests in the 1960s. Some people have found it necessary at times to break certain laws in order to correct them. Though good, law-abiding Jews in the time of Amos kept their government's laws, the prophets condemned them for oppressing their own fellow Jews indirectly by "legitimate" economical means (cf. Amos 5).

3:15 Though Persia had an efficient postal system, communication still took a long time compared to our standards. Herodotus calculated that the post would take ninety days from Sardis (in Asia Minor) to Susa.[13] The author does not call the occasion a banquet, but he wanted to show the contrast with the phrase that follows.

The most horrifying sight in the narrative so far is in this verse. The death document had been issued, and "the king and Haman sat down to drink." The text does not use the king's name, but it does mention Haman by name and thus highlights the fact that this pogrom was his idea.

Though some may have had anti-Semitic feelings, in general the people were "bewildered" by such an edict. No doubt many thought, *If it can happen to them, it could happen to others.* History has shown this to be true. Twentieth-century dictators not only tried to exterminate the Jews but massacred many others, including Christians, in the process. When Christians see the beginnings of anti-Semitism, they must realize that they must raise their voices against it for two reasons: (1) it is against the will of God, and (2) similar persecution could fall on them as well. Those who have persecuted the Jews have always come to ruin. We must still take seriously God's promise to Abraham and his descendants: "I will bless those who bless you, and whoever curses you I will curse; and all peoples on earth will be blessed through you" (Gen 12:3).

---

[13] Herodotus, *History*, 5.

V. ESTHER'S COURAGEOUS DECISION (4:1–5:14)
  1. Mordecai's Consternation (4:1-3)
  2. Esther and Mordecai Plot to Save the Jews (4:4-17)
    (1) Esther's Concern for Mordecai (4:4-5)
    (2) Mordecai Informs the Queen (4:6-8)
    (3) Esther Considers Her Options (4:9-11)
    (4) Mordecai Insists (4:12-14)
    (5) Esther Risks Her Life (4:15-17)
  3. Esther Stands before the King (5:1-14)
    (1) Esther in the King's Presence (5:1-4)
    (2) Esther's Banquet (5:5-8)
    (3) Haman's Pride and Anger (5:9-14)

V. ESTHER'S COURAGEOUS DECISION (4:1–5:14)

This is the central section in the book. With the fate of the Jews sealed in the edict of Haman, Esther was challenged to confront the king courageously and ask for help. This is what she was brought to the court to do (4:14): to deliver her people. God is not mentioned explicitly, but his providential care is evident.

1. Mordecai's Consternation (4:1-3)

¹**When Mordecai learned of all that had been done, he tore his clothes, put on sackcloth and ashes, and went out into the city, wailing loudly and bitterly. ²But he went only as far as the king's gate, because no one clothed in sackcloth was allowed to enter it. ³In every province to which the edict and order of the king came, there was great mourning among the Jews, with fasting, weeping and wailing. Many lay in sackcloth and ashes.**

4:1 "Wailing loudly and bitterly" shows Mordecai's intense grief over the edict. In the West we tend to keep our emotions to ourselves, but in Oriental society it was common to show one's grief. Mordecai was a man of strong feeling as well as strong convictions. One should not hide one's concern in crisis situations.

"He tore his clothes" is an expression of intense grief seen throughout the Old Testament (Gen 37:34; 2 Sam 1:11; Isa 3:24; Dan 9:3); it also was customary among other nations (Isa 15:3; Ezek 27:30-33). Herodotus told how the Persians under Xerxes tore their clothes because of their grief at having lost the battle at Salamis.[1]

"Sackcloth and ashes" also was a way of showing extreme grief (cf. Job 2:7-8). First, the garments were torn. Next, a hairy garment was put on and ashes spread on the head. Sackcloth, or haircloth (made of goat hair), was the apparel of mourners, especially those mourning for the dead.

There is no indication that Mordecai was sorry for his actions in refusing to bow down to Haman. This would support the idea that his action was based on religious convictions. Rather, he grieved over the signed fate that his people would perish.

4:2 "No one clothed in sackcloth was allowed to enter" because it was against Persian law, not because the king did not want to be depressed by having mourners in the palace. In the midst of grief and despair, Mordecai upheld the law of the land, but only because it did not conflict with the law of God.

4:3 The scene of Mordecai's mourning was duplicated all over the empire by Jews who heard about the edict. This verse is the low point in the narrative. Certain death was unavoidable except for the coming of a deliverer and liberator.

2. Esther and Mordecai Plot to Save the Jews (4:4-17)

Verses 4-17 present three stages in the dialogue between Esther and Mordecai, although they never spoke personally with each other.[2] First, Esther simply sent clothes to Mordecai (vv. 4-5), but he "would not accept them" (v. 4). In the second interchange (vv. 6-8), Esther sent Hathach to find out why Mordecai was grieving, who sent back a detailed explanation. The third exchange (vv. 9-17) is a longer dialogue that explains Esther's understanding that to approach the king would take planning for the urgency of her daring decision.

(1) Esther's Concern for Mordecai (4:4-5)

⁴When Esther's maids and eunuchs came and told her about Mordecai, she was in great distress. She sent clothes for him to put on instead of his

---

[1] Herodotus, *History*, 8.99.

[2] D. J. A. Clines, *Ezra, Nehemiah, Esther*, NCBC (Grand Rapids: Eerdmans, 1984), 300-303.

sackcloth, but he would not accept them. **⁵Then Esther summoned Hathach, one of the king's eunuchs assigned to attend her, and ordered him to find out what was troubling Mordecai and why.**

4:4 Esther "was in great distress" because of Mordecai's actions. She kept in touch with Mordecai and continued to be concerned about his welfare. "She sent clothes" so he could enter the palace, and to be seen with Mordecai in his present situation would imply that she was Jewish.

4:5 "Hathach, one of the king's eunuchs," apparently was assigned to Esther in her role as queen. He must have been a trusted eunuch for her to send him with this message to Mordecai. She did not go herself because her Jewish nationality was still a secret.

(2) Mordecai Informs the Queen (4:6-8)

⁶So Hathach went out to Mordecai in the open square of the city in front of the king's gate. ⁷Mordecai told him everything that had happened to him, including the exact amount of money Haman had promised to pay into the royal treasury for the destruction of the Jews. ⁸He also gave him a copy of the text of the edict for their annihilation, which had been published in Susa, to show to Esther and explain it to her, and he told him to urge her to go into the king's presence to beg for mercy and plead with him for her people.

4:6 The open area outside of the city gates was normally used as a marketplace.

4:7 Mordecai was well informed, even of details about the money Haman offered the king. He seems to have emphasized the "exact amount of money" Haman would give the king. Money is not the evil here, but rather it is the power one has with money. Money would be the instrument that made Mordecai sorry he had not honored Haman, or at least that was what Haman thought.

Mordecai even sent Esther a copy of Haman's edict so she could see for herself the seriousness of the situation; he was not exaggerating. Mordecai told Esther what to do; he urged her to go before the king and plead for her people. Now she would have to make known her Jewishness. Mordecai "urged" her to make this strategic and hard decision. In the community of faith, Christians must support one another in making difficult decisions.

(3) Esther Considers Her Options (4:9-11)

⁹Hathach went back and reported to Esther what Mordecai had said. ¹⁰Then she instructed him to say to Mordecai, ¹¹"All the king's officials and

the people of the royal provinces know that for any man or woman who approaches the king in the inner court without being summoned the king has but one law: that he be put to death. The only exception to this is for the king to extend the gold scepter to him and spare his life. But thirty days have passed since I was called to go to the king."

4:9-11 "Any man or woman who approaches the king" (v. 11) refers to a law. Herodotus confirmed that the Persian kings had such a law, but he also said that people could send a message to the king and request an audience.[3] It is not clear why Esther did not do this. Perhaps she did not because she would have had to reveal her purpose. Another possibility is that since she had not been called for thirty days, such a request for an audience of the king was not feasible. Most likely she did not ask permission because she knew what was called for (see comment on 5:11).

(4) Mordecai Insists (4:12-14)

[12]When Esther's words were reported to Mordecai, [13]he sent back this answer: "Do not think that because you are in the king's house you alone of all the Jews will escape. [14]For if you remain silent at this time, relief and deliverance for the Jews will arise from another place, but you and your father's family will perish. And who knows but that you have come to royal position for such a time as this?"

4:13 Mordecai warned Esther that she could not hide. She faced danger if she approached the king uninvited; but she also was in danger if she did nothing.

4:14 Esther could have ignored Mordecai's request and remained silent. Her decision in the paragraph that follows shows courage and faith. Again the author alluded to a principal theme of the book, that God takes care of his people Israel; he will deliver them when enemies try to destroy them.[4] The Book of Esther provides a basis for discussing anti-

---

[3] Herodotus, *History*, 3.118, 140.

[4] See J. Weibe "Esther 4:14: 'Will Relief and Deliverance Arise for the Jews from Another Place?'" *CBQ* 53 (1991): 409-15. Weibe argues that this phrase should be translated as a rhetorical question, suggesting that the implied answer is no; help would not arise from anywhere else. Thus Esther was the only hope for their deliverance. Weibe suggests that this translation fits the context of the Book of Esther much better than the traditional rendering. Such a reading would, however, limit the resources of God, who brought this about, and transplant the emphasis from God's work to Esther's work. God is capable of using anyone for his purposes. He was not limited to using just Esther, but she turned out to be the one because she answered the challenge.

Semitism, a danger even today. The charges that Jews control the press and government, hold financial power in many countries, and are leagued together in a plot to take over the world are the creation of those who would destroy the Jews. Anti-Semitism is a manifestation of demonic power, and its most violent and destructive outbreak has come in the twentieth century of the Christian Era in a country that had known the Christian message for a thousand years.[5]

At this moment Esther's life purpose was at stake. God had guided in her being chosen queen. In the biblical perspective election is for service, not just for one's own benefit. Being liberator of her people was more important than being the queen of Persia.[6] Mordecai's statement reveals a deep conviction of God's providence, a belief that God rules in the world, even in the details of the nations and in the lives of individuals. Mordecai told Esther, "If you remain silent, . . . you . . . will perish" (v. 14). In a crisis situation such as this, there was no neutral position. Failure to decide brings personal loss and misses the opportunity to fulfill God's purpose. In God's providence each person has a unique task.

(5) Esther Risks Her Life (4:15-17)

[15]Then Esther sent this reply to Mordecai: [16]"Go, gather together all the Jews who are in Susa, and fast for me. Do not eat or drink for three days, night or day. I and my maids will fast as you do. When this is done, I will go to the king, even though it is against the law. And if I perish, I perish."
[17]So Mordecai went away and carried out all of Esther's instructions.

4:15-16 Esther felt identified with her people. She now looked to them for spiritual support. "And fast for me" implies prayer and fasting. This suggests that Esther had a genuine faith in God. By her request for fasting (and certainly prayer is assumed), Esther showed that she needed the support of others and recognized the need for God's intervention. Even she and her maids would fast as well. This meant she would share her faith with these maids. Esther believed God answers prayer. Such prayer changes situations; in fact, it is one of the chief instruments God uses to change history.

"I will go" marks Esther's momentous decision that risked her own life. At first Esther apparently was more concerned about her own safety. But when she realized the influence she could have and perhaps God's purpose in putting her in her position "for such a time as this," she decid-

---

[5] B. Anderson, "Esther," IB (Nashville: Abingdon, 1954), 3:853.
[6] See J. Baldwin, Esther, TOTC (Downers Grove: InterVarsity, 1984), 80.

ed to act, committing herself to God. Many Christians are more concerned about their own security than about the desperate physical and spiritual needs of the world. If they understood that their decision could make a difference, many would make the commitment God is asking of them.

"Do not eat or drink for three days" means until the third day, when Esther planned to appear before the king (5:1). The added words "night or day" mean the fast was to be continuous (not broken by eating at night); fasting usually was practiced only during the day. The emphasis on fasting is worth noting. Throughout the Old Testament fasting seems important, although the Israelites were required to fast on only one day in the year, the Day of Atonement. However, there are many examples of fasting on special occasions or in times of special need. In Isa 58:1-12 true fasting was not just ritual; rather, it was the meeting of the needs of people. Fasting is a means by which one denies one's own needs and focuses directly on his or her relationship with God and the world.

"And if I perish, I perish." Both Vashti and Mordecai displayed courage in life-threatening situations, and now so did Esther. Vashti showed courage in her refusal to humiliate herself for the whimsical desire of her husband, and Mordecai did so in refusing to bow down to Haman. Esther proved braver still. She had decided to break the law of her husband and risk her very life for her people (cf. John 15:13). God's providential care had brought Esther to this point, but Esther accepted the challenge that might cost her life.

4:17 This verse shows that Mordecai was satisfied with Esther's decision and instructions. He proceeded to carry out her request.

3. Esther Stands before the King (5:1-14)

Chapter 5 is filled with irony and surprise. There is irony in that what was believed to have been a banquet in "honor" of Xerxes and Haman was a foreshadowing of Haman's fall. There was surprise in that the banquet was merely a delaying tactic to bring about subsequent events.

(1) Esther in the King's Presence (5:1-4)

[1]On the third day Esther put on her royal robes and stood in the inner court of the palace, in front of the king's hall. The king was sitting on his royal throne in the hall, facing the entrance. [2]When he saw Queen Esther standing in the court, he was pleased with her and held out to her the gold scepter that was in his hand. So Esther approached and touched the tip of the scepter.
[3]Then the king asked, "What is it, Queen Esther? What is your request?

Even up to half the kingdom, it will be given you."
⁴"If it pleases the king," replied Esther, "let the king, together with Ha-man, come today to a banquet I have prepared for him."

5:1 "On the third day" indicates the third day of the fast. Keil says the fast would have lasted from the afternoon of the first day until the morning of the third day, forty or forty-five hours.[7] Esther realized that she should act at once. If she believed that prayer and fasting were effective, her faith would require that she act.

"Esther put on her royal robes," which must have been beautiful and enhanced her natural beauty. The king's attire must have been even more luxurious. Olmstead describes the glittering splendor of the king's extremely costly robes, adorned with gold and precious stones. He states that when the king entered, "all must prostrate themselves in adoration, for by ancient oriental custom the king is in a very real sense a divinity."[8]

The two words "and stood" must not be overlooked. This was an act of breaking the law by standing in the king's court without having been called. Esther had come to her moment of truth. She publicly had confronted the king.

5:2 The king quickly forgave Esther because she pleased him. After thirty days he had perhaps forgotten how beautiful she was, but most importantly he had no idea why she had come.

5:3 "What is it?" is literally, "What to you?" The king knew that if Esther came like this, at risk of her life, she must have an important matter in mind. "Up to half the kingdom" apparently was a formality, but Herodotus told how another woman, Artaynte, once took advantage of Xerxes when he made the same promise and asked for the beautiful robe that Amestris, his wife, had given him. The results were disastrous and finally brought about the death of Xerxes' brother and family.[9]

5:4 "Let the king . . . come today." The initial letters of each word in this phrase spell the divine name, "Yahweh" (YHWH). A few codices even have these letters written large to call attention to this fact.[10] If this was the author's intent, then the divine name *is* used in Esther in a coded form. Such cryptic codes are not needed to find God in the text. The

---

[7] C. F. Keil, *Esther, Commentary on the Old Testament* (Grand Rapids: Eerdmans, 1980), 355.

[8] A. T. Olmstead, *History of the Persian Empire* (Chicago: University Press, 1948), 283.

[9] Herodotus, *History*, 9.109-11.

[10] L. B. Paton, *The Book of Esther*, ICC (Edinburgh: T & T Clark, 1908), 235.

course of events is the best evidence of divine guidance and all that one needs to see the presence of God.

Esther did not wish to make her request there in the court. At least two guards were present and perhaps more. The narrative artistry of this verse is that she invited Haman to his own downfall. It is apparent Haman did not suspect that Esther's petition would determine his fate.

Esther must have been confident the king would accept her presence and request. As another indication of her faith, she had prepared the banquet, which is where the plot becomes interesting (1:3,9; 2:18; 3:15; 5:4). Here in 5:4-8 the banquet leads to yet another banquet (7:1-10).

(2) Esther's Banquet (5:5-8)

5"Bring Haman at once," the king said, "so that we may do what Esther asks."

So the king and Haman went to the banquet Esther had prepared. 6As they were drinking wine, the king again asked Esther, "Now what is your petition? It will be given you. And what is your request? Even up to half the kingdom, it will be granted."

7Esther replied, "My petition and my request is this: 8If the king regards me with favor and if it pleases the king to grant my petition and fulfill my request, let the king and Haman come tomorrow to the banquet I will prepare for them. Then I will answer the king's question."

5:5 Apparently the king was quite dependent on Haman and was ready to include him immediately. Ironically, everyone but Haman and Xerxes knew about Esther's petition. The main characters knew, and we, the readers, know. Haman and Xerxes may have felt especially prideful, and yet at the first banquet (5:5-8) he would have been disappointed in that nothing important would happen.

5:6-8 Why did Esther make the king wait? The delay adds suspense to the story. It certainly was a risk, for the king's mood could have changed. Many explanations have been attempted. We must take into account Oriental custom and protocol. Conversation and preparation are essential in any important transaction. We can also see an indication of God's wisdom given to Esther. She sensed that the time was not right for her important request. In God's providence time was needed for some other details before Esther made her request. We need to be sensitive to God's timing and not be impatient with delays. McConville adds that the delay allowed time "for Haman's misguided self-confidence to mature."[11]

---

[11] J. G. McConville, *Ezra, Nehemiah, Esther*, DSB (Philadelphia: Westminster, 1985), 177.

(3) Haman's Pride and Anger (5:9-14)

[9]Haman went out that day happy and in high spirits. But when he saw
Mordecai at the king's gate and observed that he neither rose nor showed
fear in his presence, he was filled with rage against Mordecai. [10]Nevertheless,
Haman restrained himself and went home.

Calling together his friends and Zeresh, his wife, [11]Haman boasted to them
about his vast wealth, his many sons, and all the ways the king had honored
him and how he had elevated him above the other nobles and officials. [12]"And
that's not all," Haman added. "I'm the only person Queen Esther invited to
accompany the king to the banquet she gave. And she has invited me along
with the king tomorrow. [13]But all this gives me no satisfaction as long as I see
that Jew Mordecai sitting at the king's gate."

[14]His wife Zeresh and all his friends said to him, "Have a gallows built,
seventy-five feet high, and ask the king in the morning to have Mordecai
hanged on it. Then go with the king to the dinner and be happy." This suggestion delighted Haman, and he had the gallows built.

Here the author included another episode in the struggle between Haman and Mordecai. Mordecai had removed his sackcloth and was back
again in his former position.

5:9 Haman's happiness depended on circumstances—in this case on
his being honored. This type of happiness is not lasting, as the author
quickly showed. As soon as Haman saw Mordecai, who did not honor
him, his happiness evaporated. The satisfaction that depends on worldly
honor and glory can be extinguished easily.

5:10-11 Haman's boasting indicates a proud person whose priorities
consisted of riches and power. What an honor to be the only one invited
with the king to Esther's banquet! The author was bringing out the contrast between Haman's present honor and his forthcoming downfall.

5:12-13 With his place of power and all of his riches, he was still
unhappy and dissatisfied because one person refused to honor him. His
pride was the source of his sin. More importantly, v. 13 illustrates that
one person can make a difference in life. Mordecai's refusal to kneel
down to Haman reveals that as long as there is one person willing to risk
his or her life, God's will can break through the oppression of society.

5:14 The author again pointed out the world's idea of happiness. If
Haman could get rid of Mordecai first, then he would be happy at the
next day's banquet.

Many commentators think "seventy-five feet" is an exaggeration. It
may be the use of hyperbole to show the large size; it could also suggest
that the gallows were placed on a hill to be more visible to the public.

Haman wanted the people to see his victory over Mordecai. He and his advisors took for granted that the king would immediately grant his request.

Haman did not realize he was preparing his own doom, and he was not alone in preparing his own downfall. The Bible teaches that all are guilty of the same sin: "Because of your stubbornness and your unrepentant heart, you are storing up wrath against yourself for the day of God's wrath, when his righteous judgment will be revealed" (Rom 2:5).

VI. MORDECAI HONORED (6:1-14)
1. The King Reviews His Records (6:1-3)
2. Mordecai Honored; Haman Humiliated (6:4-14)

VI. MORDECAI HONORED (6:1-14)

This chapter is an example of irony in the Bible. That which is expected to happen does not, and that which is unexpected does. The king had a sleepless night, itself a reversal of the norm. Most importantly, however, the lives of Mordecai and Haman were changed dramatically. Whereas Haman is expecting to be honored by his enemy Mordecai, it is Mordecai who would be publicly honored by Haman. Haman was humiliated. Mordecai was uplifted. The intensity in the narrative is growing with the conflict between Haman and the Jews.

1. The King Reviews His Records (6:1-3)

¹That night the king could not sleep; so he ordered the book of the chronicles, the record of his reign, to be brought in and read to him. ²It was found recorded there that Mordecai had exposed Bigthana and Teresh, two of the king's officers who guarded the doorway, who had conspired to assassinate King Xerxes.

³"What honor and recognition has Mordecai received for this?" the king asked.

6:1 "Could not sleep" is literally, "The sleep of the king fled." This is the pivotal verse in the story. The reader has known all along of the injustice about to be done, but thus far only the possible victims, the Jews, and the instigator, Haman, have known about it. Now, in a dream, the king is disturbed. For the first reader as well as the present reader, there can be no doubt that God was behind the king's sleeplessness. "That night" certainly would suggest God's providence in the section of the annals that was read and in the timing of the reading.

The kings of the great ancient empires always kept annals of their reigns. Apparently the king delighted in hearing the records of his own reign.

6:2 The king was reminded of Mordecai's heroic deed (2:19-23). Historically and politically, this event seems minor. The king's disturbed state of mind, however, was eased when he heard of Mordecai's actions. Only God could have been involved in this restoration. Xerxes probably never realized that God was behind it, but like the Pharaoh and King Cyrus of Persia, Xerxes was used by God for a certain work to help the Jews.

6:3 Again we can see God's providence in the account about Mordecai, who saved the king's life. The author intended the reader to see God's hand in causing the king's sleeplessness and in reading the court records at the exact spot where Mordecai was mentioned. The Persian kings prided themselves in rewarding well those who helped them in some significant way. Xerxes realized that he had failed to honor Mordecai, so he decided to repair that error immediately.

2. Mordecai Honored; Haman Humiliated (6:4-14)

[4]The king said, "Who is in the court?" Now Haman had just entered the outer court of the palace to speak to the king about hanging Mordecai on the gallows he had erected for him.

[5]His attendants answered, "Haman is standing in the court."

"Bring him in," the king ordered.

[6]When Haman entered, the king asked him, "What should be done for the man the king delights to honor?"

Now Haman thought to himself, "Who is there that the king would rather honor than me?" [7]So he answered the king, "For the man the king delights to honor, [8]have them bring a royal robe the king has worn and a horse the king has ridden, one with a royal crest placed on its head. [9]Then let the robe and horse be entrusted to one of the king's most noble princes. Let them robe the man the king delights to honor, and lead him on the horse through the city streets, proclaiming before him, 'This is what is done for the man the king delights to honor!'"

[10]"Go at once," the king commanded Haman. "Get the robe and the horse and do just as you have suggested for Mordecai the Jew, who sits at the king's gate. Do not neglect anything you have recommended."

[11]So Haman got the robe and the horse. He robed Mordecai, and led him on horseback through the city streets, proclaiming before him, "This is what is done for the man the king delights to honor!"

[12]Afterward Mordecai returned to the king's gate. But Haman rushed home, with his head covered in grief, [13]and told Zeresh his wife and all his friends everything that had happened to him.

His advisers and his wife Zeresh said to him, "Since Mordecai, before whom your downfall has started, is of Jewish origin, you cannot stand against

him—you will surely come to ruin!" [14]**While they were still talking with him, the king's eunuchs arrived and hurried Haman away to the banquet Esther had prepared.**

6:4-5 The story is superbly written without superfluous minutia. All the details either add expectation or lead directly toward the climax. Could it just have happened that Haman was in the court at this hour (perhaps now early in the morning)? Haman came early to be sure of an audience with the king and to annihilate Mordecai as quickly as possible. The reader who is concerned about Mordecai is to understand that God turns adversity into gain. The constant emphasis is on God's providence without its mention directly.

6:6 Haman did not have a chance to tell the king why he was there. The king immediately asked, "What should be done for the man the king delights to honor?" The king was wise in asking counsel of Haman, for he expected Haman to explain how he himself would like to be honored. Haman's own pride caused his chagrin. He wanted public acclaim, and his prestige mattered above everything else.

As C. Moore notes, the verse is a masterful piece of dramatic construction. The king's question to Haman "creates instant dismay in the reader: how unfortunate that the king should consult Haman, of all people, on the way to reward Mordecai!"[1] Haman then suggested the highest honors, assuming they were for himself. The narrative is full of irony and the reversal of expected outcomes.

6:7-8 To wear a robe that the king had worn and ride a horse that the king had ridden was the highest mark of honor that could be shown to a subject.[2] The horse was to have "a royal crest placed on its head."

6:9 Haman did not realize what was about to happen. He was blinded by his own arrogance. Little did he realize that he would be the prince to lead the horse on which Mordecai was honored. Proverbs 16:18 says, "Pride goes before destruction, a haughty spirit before a fall."

6:10-11 "Go . . . do just as you have suggested for Mordecai the Jew." What a blow for Haman, who had to obey! He had prepared his own doom. Now he had to lead the horse on which the resplendent Mordecai rode, and he had to proclaim to all, "This is what is done for the man the king delights to honor." Apparently the king was not aware of the deep animosity between Haman and Mordecai, but the people knew.

---

[1] C. Moore, *Esther,* AB (Garden City: Doubleday, 1971), 67.

[2] C. F. Keil, *Esther, Commentary on the Old Testament* (Grand Rapids: Eerdmans, 1980), 360.

It must have been an enigma to them and an extremely humiliating experience for Haman.

6:12 That is why Haman "rushed home with his head covered in grief." Covering the head symbolized grief, so Haman publicly showed his distress. In the meantime, "Mordecai returned to the king's gate." The whole experience did not change his status. As Haman was beginning to learn, that kind of honor does not have lasting value.

6:13 "Since Mordecai . . . is of Jewish origin, . . . you will surely come to ruin." The author again inserted his principal theme: God will take care of the Jews; their enemies will be confounded and destroyed. Here it comes from the mouth of Zeresh, his wife, and Haman's advisors. The "advisors" in Hebrew are called "wise men." That may be ironic because they were only wise after Haman started to fall; earlier they advised him to make the gallows for Mordecai. They also must have been aware of the revival of the Jewish people since the time of Cyrus. If they were sensitive to the signs of the times, perhaps they were aware that divine providence was responsible for the Jews' protection.[3]

Zeresh stated an important truth that was observable even at that time. After the Babylonian conquest the Edomites, for example, did not survive as a distinct people, even though they were not carried captive. The words of the friends of Haman are a foreshadowing of things to come. They do not say that he might not stand; they tell him that he "cannot stand." They now realized that Mordecai had with him the God of the Jews, and Haman would not survive his attack of Mordecai. The Persians realized the power of the God of Israel and the importance of Israel's election. Once when Martin Luther was asked what argument he could use to prove the Bible was true, he answered, "The Jews."

6:14 The plot moves along at a quickening pace. Haman thought he would have a happier banquet this day if he could first destroy Mordecai. But now he must have gone to the banquet with fear; the words of his wife, "before whom your downfall has started," must have been ringing in his ears. He would go to the banquet with high but reserved expectations. He had wrongly anticipated the events recorded in chap. 6, and to hope for Mordecai's death seemed untimely at best. The banquet would reveal Esther's true desires.

---

[3] Ibid., 362.

VII. HAMAN CONDEMNED TO DEATH (7:1-10)
1. Esther's Second Banquet (7:1-2)
2. Esther's Request (7:3-7)
3. Haman Hanged (7:8-10)

VII. HAMAN CONDEMNED TO DEATH (7:1-10)

The pace of the narrative quickens as we approach the climax. The narrative exhibits a masterful job of maintaining suspense and keeping the action moving without using superfluous details. In this chapter the banquet of Esther proves to be the arena for surprise and intense activity. And yet, this is not the climax.

1. Esther's Second Banquet (7:1-2)

[1]So the king and Haman went to dine with Queen Esther, [2]and as they were drinking wine on that second day, the king again asked, "Queen Esther, what is your petition? It will be given you. What is your request? Even up to half the kingdom, it will be granted."

7:1 Haman had no idea of what was coming. Destruction and adversity can fall quickly. The banquet was planned following a previous banquet (5:3-8). This banquet would be the place where the conflict with Haman would come to a climax. Thus far Esther, Mordecai, and the reader knows that Haman's plot is going to be reversed. But only Esther has figured out how.

7:2 The narrator did not give the hour "they were drinking wine." It may have been in the afternoon since so much still was to happen that same day. [1]

The king addressed Esther as "Queen" and again asked to know her petition. He was still well disposed toward her. There is great irony in Xerxes' request. He assumed that she would ask for material possessions when in reality she was interested in what really matters: human lives. Xerxes, of course, did not know this. Another ironic element in this event

---

[1] C. Moore, *Esther,* AB (Garden City: Doubleday, 1971), 69.

is that Xerxes was sitting with his most trusted official.

2. Esther's Request (7:3-7)

[3]Then Queen Esther answered, "If I have found favor with you, O king, and if it pleases your majesty, grant me my life—this is my petition. And spare my people—this is my request. [4]For I and my people have been sold for destruction and slaughter and annihilation. If we had merely been sold as male and female slaves, I would have kept quiet, because no such distress would justify disturbing the king."

[5]King Xerxes asked Queen Esther, "Who is he? Where is the man who has dared to do such a thing?"

[6]Esther said, "The adversary and enemy is this vile Haman."

Then Haman was terrified before the king and queen. [7]The king got up in a rage, left his wine and went out into the palace garden. But Haman, realizing that the king had already decided his fate, stayed behind to beg Queen Esther for his life.

7:3 The king must have been startled and perplexed. Why was Esther's life in danger? She did not tell him in this verse who her people were. Esther realized that it was a life-and-death matter, and she risked her life to do something about it. Esther must have remembered Vashti's fate and thought of the possible severity of her own actions. This did not stop her, but rather she continued her heroic actions.

7:4 Esther identified herself with her people not by their name, the Jews, but rather by their fate. Next, she accused Haman of conspiracy. These announcements placed her in a dangerous position. She did not know how the king would react. She was probably uncertain whether Haman or she would have more influence. "Have been sold" is a phrase sometimes used for being handed over or betrayed; here Esther no doubt was also making allusion to the money Haman offered the king. "For destruction and slaughter and annihilation" are the same words that were used in Haman's decree in 3:13. By now the king must have remembered that decree and realized what Esther was talking about.

The last phrase of the verse, "No such distress would justify disturbing the king," is difficult to translate. The NIV note gives an alternate translation that emphasizes the loss the king would suffer by exterminating the Jews: "The compensation our adversary offers cannot be compared with the loss the king would suffer."

7:5 "King Xerxes asked Queen Esther" is literally, "Then King Xerxes spoke and he said to Esther the queen." Some think the repetition of the verb "spoke" or "he said"[2] is a dittography (accidental scribal repetition of the same word), but it may well have been the purpose of the narrator to heighten the suspense. First, the text says the king spoke but does not say to whom; then the text adds, "He spoke to Esther." The telling sign in this verse is that her Jewish identity is not known; for if it had been known, the king would have known that Haman was responsible.

"Dared to do" is literally "filled his heart to do." "Who" and "where" are the crucial questions. "Who is he?" is a rhetorical question. It is a question that should be asked often in order to find out who would oppose God.

7:6 Esther's answer was short and exact, "This vile Haman." She made her case as strong and clear as possible. By announcing Haman as the guilty person, she revealed her Jewishness. Haman must have felt doomed immediately because he realized he had not condemned to death just a people from another land, for that had never bothered him. What was troubling was that the king's favorite wife also was a Jew. This would be certain trouble for Haman. "Haman was terrified," and he had every right to be afraid for his life. His plots and lies had now been uncovered by the one who had more power than he, the king.

7:7 Why was the king so angry? Certainly he was angry because he had been tricked into making the decree that meant the death of his own beloved queen, Esther. The king left "his wine," which is literally "from the banquet of wine."

"Haman . . . stayed behind to beg Queen Esther." Haman knew that the real power was not with Xerxes but rather with Esther. After all this, Xerxes was willing to give her up to half of his kingdom, and therefore he certainly would not condemn his wife but rather the one who had caused this havoc, Haman.

3. Haman Hanged (7:8-10)

8Just as the king returned from the palace garden to the banquet hall, Haman was falling on the couch where Esther was reclining.

The king exclaimed, "Will he even molest the queen while she is with me in the house?"

As soon as the word left the king's mouth, they covered Haman's face. **9**Then Harbona, one of the eunuchs attending the king, said, "A gallows seventy-five feet high stands by Haman's house. He had it made for Mordecai, who spoke up to help the king."

The king said, "Hang him on it!" **10**So they hanged Haman on the gallows he had prepared for Mordecai. Then the king's fury subsided.

---

2 In Hebrew it is the same word, וַיֹּאמֶר.

7:8 "Haman was falling on the couch" just as the king returned. The heightening of the tension in the narrative is superb. The Orientals reclined on couches at their feasts (Amos 6:4-7). Haman, in typical Near Eastern form, probably grabbed the feet of Esther, kissed them, and begged for forgiveness.[3] Such action would explain why the king interprets Haman as about to "molest" Esther. The irony here is that Haman, who had demanded that Mordecai bow before him, was at the feet of the Jew Esther.

In this verse the character of the three protagonists is brought out. Haman was a prideful man with a cowardly heart. The king was easily influenced and weak in spite of his appearance of power. Esther was courageous and steadfast. She is not to be considered hard and calloused because she would not listen to Haman's pleas. She could not have helped even if she had wished to do so.

"The word left the king's mouth" does not refer to the question just quoted. Hebrew *haddābār* refers to a judicial sentence. The narrative is concise; the king pronounced the decree to execute Haman.

In Greek and Roman cultures criminals' faces were covered before taking them away to be executed. This may indicate the same practice, but we have no other evidence that it was customary in Persia (cf. 6:12).

7:9 The "Harbona" here probably is the same one as in 1:10. Apparently Haman had no friends there. What Harbona said was in essence another accusation that confirmed the king's decision to execute Haman. The ultimate irony is that the death instrument built for Mordecai would now be the method of death for its creator, Haman.

7:10 The evil that Haman planned for his enemy fell on him. A number of proverbs express the truth of what happened here. According to Prov 11:6: "The righteousness of the upright delivers them, but the unfaithful are trapped by evil desires" (cf. Prov 29:16; 26:27).

These proverbs teach by expressing contrasts, which the author of Esther frequently used: Haman celebrated, but the people were bewildered (3:15); Esther and Mordecai fasted, but then Esther invited the king and Haman to a banquet (4:15; 5:4); Haman expected honor, but Mordecai received that honor, and Haman was humiliated (6:11-12); Haman schemed to execute Mordecai, but he himself was condemned.

The story is not over. The narrative has shown the rise and fall of Haman, but the edict of annihilation is still intact. More is at stake here than just Mordecai's life; also at stake are the lives of all of the Jews in the Persian Empire.

---

[3] Moore, *Esther*, 72. See also Esth 8:3; 2 Kgs 4:27; Matt 28:9.

VIII. KING XERXES HELPS THE JEWS (8:1-17)

With Haman out of the way, Esther requested that the Jews be spared of the approaching massacre. Since the king was unable to overturn an official edict, he made another edict authorizing the Jews to defend themselves against anyone who would attack them. Because of Esther, the Jews now had hope for deliverance.

1. Esther Rewarded and Mordecai Promoted (8:1-2)

¹That same day King Xerxes gave Queen Esther the estate of Haman, the enemy of the Jews. And Mordecai came into the presence of the king, for Esther had told how he was related to her. ²The king took off his signet ring, which he had reclaimed from Haman, and presented it to Mordecai. And Esther appointed him over Haman's estate.

8:1 "King Xerxes gave" the whole estate of Haman to Esther, and it must have included great riches. This is the next step in the turning of the tables in this story. We have indication that in the Persian Empire the goods and property of condemned criminals were taken over by the king.[1]

"Esther had told" of her relation to Mordecai. We do not know how much time elapsed between these details. There were two months and ten days between the edict Haman made (3:7) and the new edict (8:9). The

---

[1] Herodotus, *History*, 3.128-29; cf. the story of Naboth's vineyard in 1 Kgs 21:7-16. C. Moore, *Esther*, AB (Garden City: Doubleday, 1971), 77.

fact is that Esther finally revealed her nationality and relationship to Mordecai. This actually helped Mordecai's position before the king.

8:2 "The king took off his signet ring . . . and presented it to Mordecai." Thus he placed Mordecai in the position of grand vizier, the position that Haman had held previously. If this were a story only about the conflict between Haman and Esther and Mordecai, this scene would be the anticlimactic point where the righteous people are rewarded for their courage and loyalty. The story, however, has almost lulled the reader to forget one very important aspect.

2. Esther's Request to Save the Jews (8:3-6)

³Esther again pleaded with the king, falling at his feet and weeping. She begged him to put an end to the evil plan of Haman the Agagite, which he had devised against the Jews. ⁴Then the king extended the gold scepter to Esther and she arose and stood before him.

⁵"If it pleases the king," she said, "and if he regards me with favor and thinks it the right thing to do, and if he is pleased with me, let an order be written overruling the dispatches that Haman son of Hammedatha, the Agagite, devised and wrote to destroy the Jews in all the king's provinces. ⁶For how can I bear to see disaster fall on my people? How can I bear to see the destruction of my family?"

8:3 Not just the fate of Esther and Mordecai was at stake but that of the entire Jewish population of the Persian Empire. Esther had saved the Jews from Haman, but not from his handiwork: the death document. Still in force was Haman's original edict, approved by the king and sent to all the provinces for the destruction of the Jews on the thirteenth day of the twelfth month. Esther did not stop with her personal deliverance; she was concerned about her people—the whole Jewish community throughout the empire. Her "falling at his feet and weeping" indicates her strong emotions as she collapsed. She could only plead the king's mercy.

8:4 "The king extended the gold scepter." This happened before in 5:2. This time the scepter was not raised to save Esther's life but rather to show that she is more than welcome in the king's presence. Some understand that Esther again risked her life by going into the king's presence without being called. However, others[2] suggest that v. 3 does not introduce a new scene; it is a continuation of the scene described in vv. 1-2. Thus the king's act of extending the scepter was simply an encouragement to Esther to rise and speak.

---

[2] For example, Moore, *Esther*, 82.

8:5 Esther was extremely diplomatic in presenting this request. It was of utmost importance that the king accept her request.[3] He already was upset because Haman had tricked him into making the edict to destroy the Jews, but reversing an edict the king had signed was a delicate matter.

Esther did not use the word "law," for she knew that Persian laws could not be repealed. She put all the blame on Haman and avoided blaming the king.

8:6 "How can I bear to see" is repeated in the parallel, almost poetic form of Esther's request. She adroitly used her own feelings and the king's favorable disposition toward her ("if he is pleased with me") to secure his permission for her request.

3. A New Edict Published (8:7-17)

(1) The King Commands the Edict (8:7-8)

7King Xerxes replied to Queen Esther and to Mordecai the Jew, "Because Haman attacked the Jews, I have given his estate to Esther, and they have hanged him on the gallows. 8Now write another decree in the king's name in behalf of the Jews as seems best to you, and seal it with the king's signet ring—for no document written in the king's name and sealed with his ring can be revoked."

8:7 Because Haman attacked the Jews, the king had him hanged and gave his estate to Esther. The author was making clear that he who attacks the Jews will fall. The king reminded Esther and Mordecai of all he had already done, to show that he was favorably disposed toward the Jews. However, it was Esther, not the king, who took the initiative in counteracting Haman's destructive decree.

8:8 "Now write" is literally "you write." The "you" is emphatic and includes both Esther and Mordecai. Verses 8-17 are parallel in language to 3:9–4:3, but here the whole situation is reversed. Another decree was necessary to counter the initial one. Now the Jews would destroy their enemies rather than be destroyed.

The fact that laws sealed by the king were irrevocable calls our attention to the many inhuman laws in our day and the number of lives that are sacrificed to them. God's law of justice must always be above kings and human laws. "Remove the wicked from the king's presence, and his

---

[3] "The right thing to do" is the translation of כָּשֵׁר, which is the same root later used for legitimate foods (כֹּשֶׁר).

throne will be established through righteousness" (Prov 25:5).

(2) The Edict Prepared (8:9-10)

⁹At once the royal secretaries were summoned—on the twenty-third day of the third month, the month of Sivan. They wrote out all Mordecai's orders to the Jews, and to the satraps, governors and nobles of the 127 provinces stretching from India to Cush. These orders were written in the script of each province and the language of each people and also to the Jews in their own script and language. ¹⁰Mordecai wrote in the name of King Xerxes, sealed the dispatches with the king's signet ring, and sent them by mounted couriers, who rode fast horses especially bred for the king.

8:9 This verse sets the story in a particular historical context and reveals the procedure for writing an edict. "Secretaries" had prepared Haman's edict, but this time more were needed to send the edict in the Jews' language. The Persian Empire was well organized. Now that Mordecai was the grand vizier, or prime minister, he was ready to act when the opportunity came.

"On the twenty-third day" was two months and ten days after Haman's edict had been proclaimed (3:12). This indicates that the story is condensed. Verse 9 is the longest verse in the Hagiographa;[4] it contains forty-three words and 192 letters.

8:10 In yet another reversal motif, Mordecai wrote an edict of life for the Jews whereas Haman had written an edict of death for the Jews.

(3) The Contents of the Edict (8:11-13)

¹¹The king's edict granted the Jews in every city the right to assemble and protect themselves; to destroy, kill and annihilate any armed force of any nationality or province that might attack them and their women and children; and to plunder the property of their enemies. ¹²The day appointed for the Jews to do this in all the provinces of King Xerxes was the thirteenth day of the twelfth month, the month of Adar. ¹³A copy of the text of the edict was to be issued as law in every province and made known to the people of every nationality so that the Jews would be ready on that day to avenge themselves on their enemies.

8:11 "The Jews" were scattered in many countries and cities. "The right to assemble" perhaps had been denied to them, or that denial might

---

⁴ That is, the Writings of the OT which include Job, Psalms, Proverbs, and all other books that are not in Gen to Deut, Josh to 2 Kgs, and Isa to Mal.

have been implicit in Haman's decree. "Destroy, kill and annihilate" is the same wording as the other decree (3:13), but this time the Jews were allowed to defend themselves.[5]

To whom were they to do this? The object of the verbs is "any armed force . . . that might attack them." But the end of the sentence appears to give the Jews the right to plunder any of their enemies. Many ask why the decree was so harsh. Moore says it was the wisdom doctrine of retributive justice that the author was showing here, for that was what the edict of Haman proclaimed against the Jews.[6] Haman's followers were to reap what they had sown. Crucial at this point, however, is the fact that the Jews would act in self-defense.

8:12-13   "The day appointed" was the same day Haman's edict had set for plundering the Jews (3:13). The obvious reason was so that the Jews could defend themselves. The edict sounds harsh; however, the people knew that the Jews had permission to defend themselves, but only against people who attacked them first. The purpose of the edict was to ward off anyone who might try to attack the Jews. All this seems impossible. Many consider it fiction; but if we remember what happened under Hitler, it does not appear so impossible.

(4) The Jews Rejoice (8:14-17)

14The couriers, riding the royal horses, raced out, spurred on by the king's command. And the edict was also issued in the citadel of Susa.

15Mordecai left the king's presence wearing royal garments of blue and white, a large crown of gold and a purple robe of fine linen. And the city of Susa held a joyous celebration. **16**For the Jews it was a time of happiness and joy, gladness and honor. **17**In every province and in every city, wherever the edict of the king went, there was joy and gladness among the Jews, with feasting and celebrating. And many people of other nationalities became Jews because fear of the Jews had seized them.

8:14   The verbs "riding," "raced out," and "spurred" heighten the urgency of the narrative. The edict also was issued in the area of the palace, no doubt to confirm Mordecai's position before the king.

8:15   The description encourages the reader to imagine how the king looked. The word "crown" here is different from that of 1:11; 2:17; and 6:8. Mordecai was vindicated and promoted, and "the city of Susa held a

---

[5] See W. Kaiser, Jr., *Hard Sayings of the Old Testament* (Downers Grove: InterVarsity, 1988), 144-46.

[6] Moore, *Esther*, 81.

joyous celebration." As indicated in 3:15 by Susa's bewilderment with the original decree, Mordecai may have been popular with the people. Another possibility is that Susa was not anti-Semitic, but its leaders were. Regardless, the text does not specify who in Susa was anti-semitic. The author wanted to show that the welfare of the Jews meant the good of the whole society.

8:16   The Jews realized the importance of this deliverance. This is in contrast with 4:3, where there was mourning, fasting, weeping, and wailing.

8:17   "Many people became Jews" is often taken to show the fictitious nature of the narrative since Jewish proselytizing only appears in the intertestamental period. In some parts of the Old Testament, however, there are indications that others became part of the Jewish nation (cf. Isa 42:6). In the exodus there was a "mixed multitude" that went out of Egypt. Some non-Jews joined the Jews in the exodus. A careful study of genealogical lists suggests that later in Canaan some local clans (of Canaanites or other peoples) were assimilated into the various Jewish tribes. Keil says that most of those who became Jews must have done it out of conviction of the truth of the Jewish religion. The Jews' trust in God "contrasted with the vanity and misery of polytheism," and the evident providential turn of events confirmed this conviction.[7] We know this was the case several centuries later when Paul was preaching the gospel throughout the Hellenistic world. Many of the converts to Christ were "God-fearing Greeks" (Acts 17:4) who had become disillusioned with the pagan religions and were attracted by the Jews' faith in one God and their high ethical principles. The joyous celebration is a prelude to Purim, but at that time it may have been because they assumed that no one would attack the Jews. This, however, would not be the case.

---

[7] Keil, *Esther,* 371.

IX. THE TRIUMPH OF THE JEWS (9:1-17)
1. The Jews United and Strengthened (9:1-4)
2. The Jews' Destruction of Their Enemies (9:5-17)
   (1) The Jews in Susa (9:5-15)
   (2) The Jews in the Provinces (9:16-17)

IX. THE TRIUMPH OF THE JEWS (9:1-17)

Esther was brought to the king's court "for such a time as this" (4:14). The purpose in all that had taken place to this point was so that the Jews would not be destroyed by Haman's evil plot. Even with Haman dead, however, the edict was still in effect. Esther's plan worked. The Jews defended themselves against their enemies and preserved their communities. The result was the celebration of Purim, a feast commemorating their deliverance from Haman.

1. The Jews United and Strengthened (9:1-4)

^{1}On the thirteenth day of the twelfth month, the month of Adar, the edict commanded by the king was to be carried out. On this day the enemies of the Jews had hoped to overpower them, but now the tables were turned and the Jews got the upper hand over those who hated them. ^{2}The Jews assembled in their cities in all the provinces of King Xerxes to attack those seeking their destruction. No one could stand against them, because the people of all the other nationalities were afraid of them. ^{3}And all the nobles of the provinces, the satraps, the governors and the king's administrators helped the Jews, because fear of Mordecai had seized them. ^{4}Mordecai was prominent in the palace; his reputation spread throughout the provinces, and he became more and more powerful.

9:1 The day finally came. Haman had cast lots to choose this day. The edict he had issued to destroy the Jews was still in effect. But now the tables were turned (cf. v. 22) because of the edict Mordecai had made. The author has been leading up to this point. Proverbs 16:33 must express his feelings: "The lot is cast in the lap, but its every decision is from the LORD." The teaching that those who try to destroy the Jews will be destroyed appears repeatedly in the Scriptures. "Those who plunder you will be plundered; all who make spoil of you I will despoil" (Jer 30:16). The Jews' enemies had hoped to destroy them and take their riches, but their plans failed. Although the situation is expressed with the passive "the tables were turned," the sense is clearly that God had caused them to turn. As McConville has noted, "In a world from which God *appears* to be absent he is nonetheless present."[1]

9:2 The Jews had time to prepare since the edict of Mordecai was published months before this date. "No one could stand" does not mean that the enemies failed to attack; however, they could not prevail against the Jews. In the Bible many times God caused fear to fall on the enemies of the Israelites. Here he used the circumstances, the change of power, and the authority given to the Jews to defend themselves.

9:3 "And all the nobles . . . helped the Jews." Since Mordecai was now the grand vizier, the rulers wanted to please him. It is amazing how rapidly political winds can change. Many times it is because of God's work behind the scenes. The author here was careful not to mention God, but certainly he wanted his readers to see God's hand in the matter.

9:4 "Mordecai . . . became more and more powerful." He had gone through difficult days and had been in danger of death. But his crisis became in God's providence a stepping stone to greater influence. This fact is repeated often in the lives of God's servants.

2. The Jews' Destruction of Their Enemies (9:5-17)

(1) The Jews in Susa (9:5-15)

⁵The Jews struck down all their enemies with the sword, killing and destroying them, and they did what they pleased to those who hated them. ⁶In the citadel of Susa, the Jews killed and destroyed five hundred men. ⁷They also killed Parshandatha, Dalphon, Aspatha, ⁸Poratha, Adalia, Aridatha, ⁹Parmashta, Arisai, Aridai and Vaizatha, ¹⁰the ten sons of Haman son of Hammedatha, the enemy of the Jews. But they did not lay their hands on the plunder.

¹¹The number of those slain in the citadel of Susa was reported to the king that same day. ¹²The king said to Queen Esther, "The Jews have killed and destroyed five hundred men and the ten sons of Haman in the citadel of Susa. What have they done in the rest of the king's provinces? Now what is your petition? It will be given you. What is your request? It will also be granted."

¹³"If it pleases the king," Esther answered, "give the Jews in Susa permis-

---

[1] J. G. McConville, *Ezra, Nehemiah, and Esther*, DSB (Philadelphia: Westminster, 1985), 193.

sion to carry out this day's edict tomorrow also, and let Haman's ten sons be hanged on gallows."

[14]So the king commanded that this be done. An edict was issued in Susa, and they hanged the ten sons of Haman. [15]The Jews in Susa came together on the fourteenth day of the month of Adar, and they put to death in Susa three hundred men, but they did not lay their hands on the plunder.

9:5 This passage is the climax of the narrative. The primary theme of the story is the survival of the Jews. This passage presents the details of their survival. A people in a foreign land like the Jews in Persia could never have survived without the grace and power of God, and yet God is still not mentioned explicitly. The deliverance of the Jews, however, is a theme throughout the Bible because God was their deliverer, and this incident is no different.

This emphasis on killing and destruction seems very harsh.[2] The expression "they did what they pleased," however, should not be understood as a reference to cruelty but to the reversal of Haman's plans. The king had given him authority to "do with the people as you please" (3:11). That royal authorization, however, had been overturned by a higher authority.

Verses 2-4 indicate that the majority of Persians refused to fight the Jews. This can lead to two assumptions. First, it might be assumed that professional soldiers, that is, mercenaries, attacked in loyalty to Haman. Second, if they were not mercenaries, they were people who hated Jews and stood to gain at their losses. The retribution was limited to the enemies of the Jews and to those who hated them. It also was limited to men. Again, many suppose that this is fiction; however, some events of modern history are strikingly parallel. In 1907-1908, P. Haupt wrote: "If the authorities had allowed the Jews to organize armed resistance, the numerous massacres in Russia during the past few years would have been nipped in the bud. . . . But, as a rule, the assailants of the Russian Jews were supported by the governors, military commanders, officers of the police."[3]

As Christians and part of the new covenant, we are under the ethical teachings of Jesus. The Old Testament is God's Word and contains a

---

[2] Clines notes that chaps. 9–10 portray an inferior narrative style in comparison to chaps. 1–8. He suggests that they were added by a different author (D. J. A. Clines, *Ezra, Nehemiah, Esther*, NCBC [Grand Rapids: Eerdmans, 1984], 319-20). Such an argument, in the absence of more concrete evidence, is too nebulous to be employed in exegesis and overlooks the versatility of an author's narrative skill.

[3] Quoted in J. Baldwin, *Esther*, TOTC (Downers Grove: InterVarsity, 1984), 104.

wealth of teaching that is needed by all Christians. But our application of it must always be within the framework of the whole Bible. We cannot apply anything in a way that would contradict the teachings of Jesus.

9:6 "In the citadel of Susa" the Jews must have had many enemies. Perhaps Haman had influenced them. Although five hundred sounds excessive, it was not a high percentage of the population. This indicates that most people in Susa were in support of the Jews.

9:7-10 "They also killed . . . the ten sons of Haman," no doubt to avoid their taking revenge on Mordecai and the Jews. In the Hebrew text the names of the ten sons are written in two parallel columns. Later the rabbis speculated over the reasons for this.[4]

9:10 The author considered it important that they "did not lay their hands on the plunder," for he said it three times (vv. 10,15-16). The Jews were careful not to use material gain as the reason for their action. They simply defended their right to live. The author may also have had in mind the incident recorded in 1 Sam 15:17-23, when Saul disobeyed God by taking plunder from the Amalekites. This time the Jews were careful not to make the same mistake.

9:11-12 Apparently the king was indifferent to the results. If the Jews killed so many in Susa, how many must they have killed in all the empire? The king still asked Esther what further request she had, but this time he did not add "up to half the kingdom."

Since the numbers seem large, some suggest they were exaggerated. Sometimes large numbers apparently were used in a hyperbolic way to show the importance of an event. At any rate this constituted a loss for the king; it is also true that the loss would have been greater if Haman's edict alone had been obeyed.

9:13-15 "Tomorrow also" makes Esther appear hard and cruel for wanting to continue the massacre. Apparently the Jews wanted to clear the palace area of all their enemies. Some suggest that the second day of massacre was introduced here to explain why Purim was celebrated on two successive days. The king's permission was needed to hang publicly Haman's sons, just as Haman had sought the king's permission to hang Mordecai (5:14). Since they were already dead, this act must have been for the purpose of displaying their bodies (vv. 7-10).

---

[4] Some said they were written that way because that was the way the ten sons were hanged. Also it was said that the ten names should all be uttered in one breath (L. B. Paton, *The Book of Esther*, ICC [Edinburgh: T & T Clark, 1908], 284).

(2) The Jews in the Provinces (9:16-17)

¹⁶**Meanwhile, the remainder of the Jews who were in the king's provinces also assembled to protect themselves and get relief from their enemies. They killed seventy-five thousand of them but did not lay their hands on the plunder.** ¹⁷**This happened on the thirteenth day of the month of Adar, and on the fourteenth they rested and made it a day of feasting and joy.**

9:16   The number "seventy-five thousand" seems quite large; the Septuagint quotes fifteen thousand, and the Targums read 10,107 men. One possibility is that the word for "thousand" may have meant families or clans. If this was the case, the number would be reduced drastically, for example, seventy-five families, but this would be extended families including cousins, in-laws, and others. There could have been anywhere from ten to fifty people in a clan. The author wanted to emphasize the great victory of the Jews.[5]

9:17   "A day of feasting and joy" was the first Purim celebration. The author was leading up to the institution of the Feast of Purim described in the following sections. The only other Jewish festivals known in the last five months of the Jewish calendar (October-November to March) are the Feast of Dedication (Hanukkah) and Nicanor's Day. Both of these were instituted in the second century B.C., in the time of the Maccabees. Nicanor's Day fell on the thirteenth of Adar and was the commemoration of a great victory by Judas Maccabee over Nicanor, a Syrian general who hated the Jews and vowed to destroy them. After the Hasmonian period it declined in popularity. Some think that it helps explain the origin of Purim. It is more likely that it was supplanted by the Feast of Purim because this latter feast (which originated among Jews in Persia) came to be observed among the Jews of Palestine.

---

[5] See further "The Historicity of Esther" in the Introduction.

——X. THE FEAST OF PURIM INAUGURATED (9:18-32)——

While the main theme of the Book of Esther is the deliverance of the people from destruction, the end result is the celebration of the feast of Purim. This chapter gives instruction on when and in what ways to celebrate this most joyful occasion.

1. Mordecai's Letter of Instructions (9:18-22)

[18]**The Jews in Susa, however, had assembled on the thirteenth and fourteenth, and then on the fifteenth they rested and made it a day of feasting and joy.**
[19]**That is why rural Jews—those living in villages—observe the fourteenth of the month of Adar as a day of joy and feasting, a day for giving presents to each other.**
[20]**Mordecai recorded these events, and he sent letters to all the Jews throughout the provinces of King Xerxes, near and far,** [21]**to have them celebrate annually the fourteenth and fifteenth days of the month of Adar** [22]**as the time when the Jews got relief from their enemies, and as the month when their sorrow was turned into joy and their mourning into a day of celebration. He wrote them to observe the days as days of feasting and joy and giving presents of food to one another and gifts to the poor.**

9:18-19 This entire narrative has the sense of being an etiological story, that is, a story that explains the origin of an event (see 9:26). In this case the narrative recounts the origins of the celebration of Purim. This does not imply that the story is in any way false, and actually the contrary is the most likely. In the provinces they feasted on the fourteenth day, but in Susa they feasted on the fifteenth because they had taken another day of vengeance. Verse 19 is a kind of parenthetical explanation. These summaries may appear to be contradictory (cf. v. 19 with vv. 21-22), but as summaries they *telescope* the events.[1] In other words, they are too brief to give all the details that would show that they are not contradictory.

9:20   The text does not say where Mordecai recorded the events; perhaps in the court annals or in the letters he sent. Mordecai has a key role in founding this festival. His great authority and the efficient postal system made good communication possible.

9:21   The date was established; they were to "celebrate annually." The Talmudic Tractate *Meghilla* gives instructions for observing the Feast of Purim; the roll of Esther was to be read in unwalled towns on the eleventh, twelfth, and thirteenth or fourteenth of Adar and in walled towns on the fifteenth.

9:22   "Giving presents of food to one another and gifts" emphasizes community. As a group the Jews form a major character in the story although they have no specific speaking role. It was for their survival that Esther was brought to the court—"for such a time as this" (4:14). They were to celebrate by giving portions of food to each other and by giving gifts to the poor. The responsibility to help the poor is repeated throughout the Bible.

2. The Feast Established by the Jews (9:23-28)

[23]So the Jews agreed to continue the celebration they had begun, doing what Mordecai had written to them. [24]For Haman son of Hammedatha, the Agagite, the enemy of all the Jews, had plotted against the Jews to destroy them and had cast the *pur* (that is, the lot) for their ruin and destruction. [25]But when the plot came to the king's attention, he issued written orders that the evil scheme Haman had devised against the Jews should come back onto his own head, and that he and his sons should be hanged on the gallows. [26](Therefore these days were called Purim, from the word *pur*.) Because of everything written in this letter and because of what they had seen and what had happened to them, [27]the Jews took it upon themselves to establish the custom that they and their descendants and all who join them should without fail observe these two days every year, in the way prescribed and at the time appointed. [28]These days should be remembered and observed in every generation by every family, and in every province and in every city. And these days of Purim should never cease to be celebrated by the Jews, nor should the memory of them die out among their descendants.

---

[1] The suggestion that vv. 20-32 or all of chaps. 9–10 were later additions to the original Book of Esther, which would have ended with 8:17, distracts from the holistic symmetry of the book. In this case the narrative makes perfect sense in its entirety.

9:23 Some see vv. 23-28 as a third account of the institution of the feast, but these verses give a summary of the events that lay behind the Feast of Purim.

9:24 "Haman . . . had cast the pur." This links the name "Purim" with *pur,* the Babylonian word for "lot."[2] The use of lots is found in many ancient cultures.[3]

Many scholars have been sceptical about the validity of Esther as a historical explanation for the origin of the Feast of Purim, and numerous theories of its origin have been set forth. However, none of them is convincing. It seems better to accept the explanation given in Esther. Hallo says, "That explanation will have to do for us too, for none of the many alternatives offered during a century of the most ingenious scholarly detective work is more convincing."[4]

9:25 The word "plot" is not in the Hebrew. The Hebrew verb "came" has a feminine pronoun which could be translated either as "she" (Esther) or "it" (plot).[5] Thus some translate as in the NIV note, "When Esther came before the king." On contextual grounds it is preferable to consider the pronoun to refer to "plot," which is understood in the previous verse, and maintain the NIV translation.

The narrative gives the king credit for condemning Haman. Since this is a brief summary, it does not mention the time difference between his death and that of his sons.

9:26 The author recapitulated and reviewed what had been said throughout the book and showed why the Feast of Purim was established.

9:27-28 This verse indicates that the Jewish community accepted Mordecai's letter; "And all who join them" again speaks of others who joined the Jewish faith and the Jewish community.[6] Purim is still celebrated by the Jews on the fourteenth day of Adar, which in our calendar varies from February 25 to March 25. In some places the fifteenth day of Adar, called Shushan Purim, is also celebrated. The thirteenth day of Adar is the Fast of Esther.

---

[2] *See* 3:7 and comments there.

[3] Hallo mentions Assyrian and Hittite texts. He says the cube as a device for playing games of chance can be traced back to the Indus Valley and was known in Mesopotamia before 2000 B.C. (W. W. Hallo, "The First Purim," *BA* 46:1 [1983]: 19-27).

[4] Ibid., 22. See further on "The Origin of Purim" in the Introduction.

[5] וּבְמָאָה.

[6] See the comments on Esth 8:17.

3. The Custom Confirmed by Queen Esther (9:29-32)

²⁹So Queen Esther, daughter of Abihail, along with Mordecai the Jew, wrote with full authority to confirm this second letter concerning Purim. ³⁰And Mordecai sent letters to all the Jews in the 127 provinces of the kingdom of Xerxes—words of goodwill and assurance— ³¹to establish these days of Purim at their designated times, as Mordecai the Jew and Queen Esther had decreed for them, and as they had established for themselves and their descendants in regard to their times of fasting and lamentation. ³²Esther's decree confirmed these regulations about Purim, and it was written down in the records.

The purpose of this section is to reinforce the official authority for the institution of the Feast of Purim.[7] At this point in the story conflicts have been resolved, and the characters are out of danger. Here the meaning of the events are being summarized in a form seen throughout the Bible. All the events of this story have led up to the point of understanding why Purim is celebrated and why is it such a joyous occasion.

9:29 "Full authority," Hebrew *tōqep* , means "power" in 10:2 and Dan 11:17. The paragraph emphasizes that Queen Esther used her authority to help establish Purim.

9:30 "Words of goodwill and assurance" is literally "words of peace and truth," and the construction at the end of v. 31 is similar, "times of fasting and lamentation," literally, "words of fasting and lamentation."

9:31 In Jewish history there had been a time of fasting related to the joyous celebration of Purim. In the time of the Talmud it was known as a three-day fast and observed after the Feast of Purim. From the ninth century A.D., the day before the Feast of Purim (thirteenth of Adar) has been observed as a day of fasting.[8]

9:32 The importance of a written document cannot be overlooked. Although we no longer have Esther's decree, we have the book by her name in which are recorded the events and occasions that brought about the decree. Keil says this cannot refer to her writing in v. 29; he suggests that it was a document about Purim that has not been preserved.[9] There is

---

[7] Some consider this section (vv. 29-32) a later addition to the book. They find it superfluous that this brief retelling of the story should be added at the end of such a brilliantly written narrative. However, Hebrew and Near Eastern literature in general is known for its repetitive style. Repetition is an intentional tool in educating people. This simple repetition enables the readers of Esther to remember the story, and it enhances the narrative through emphasis.

[8] C. F. Keil, *Esther, Commentary on the Old Testament* (Grand Rapids: Eerdmans, 1980), 378.

emphasis both on written records (vv. 26,32) and on remembering these events for the benefit of future generations (v. 28). Again there is a didactic, that is, educational, function to the narrative centered around the celebration of Purim.

---

[9] Ibid.

XI. THE GREATNESS OF MORDECAI (10:1-3)
   1. Mordecai Remembered in the Annals (10:1-2)
   2. Mordecai's Work for the People (10:3)

XI. THE GREATNESS OF MORDECAI (10:1-3)

This final section emphasizes Mordecai's rise to greatness (v. 2). Mordecai represents the rise of the Jewish people in the society and culture of Persia. Esther is not mentioned, although she was both the heroine and deliverer of the people.

1. Mordecai Remembered in the Annals (10:1-2)

¹King Xerxes imposed tribute throughout the empire, to its distant shores. ²And all his acts of power and might, together with a full account of the greatness of Mordecai to which the king had raised him, are they not written in the book of the annals of the kings of Media and Persia?

10:1 The book ends on a note similar to that of its beginning—the greatness, wealth, and splendor of King Xerxes. This example of inclusio is common in Hebrew literature. The author emphasized the great extent of the empire, "to its distant shores." This must refer to the coastlands of the Mediterranean area under the Persian Empire.

Taxation, "imposed tribute," was not a pleasant subject, but the author mentioned it here. Perhaps in keeping with one of the themes of the book he wanted to show that King Xerxes, who saved the Jews from extinction, later prospered. Although he did not receive the great gift Haman had promised, King Xerxes prospered by receiving all this tribute.

10:2 "The greatness of Mordecai" brings us to the real purpose of this section. The author wanted to praise Mordecai as an example of one who put the welfare of his people before his own personal interests.

What was this "book of the annals of the kings of Media and Persia?" It is not likely that a Jewish prime minister would have received much space in official Persian records. The phrase is similar to references in Kings and Chronicles to other written sources (1 Kgs 14:19; 15:7,23,31; 1 Chr 27:24). Thus it is suggested that these were not official royal archives but some popular account of the Persian kings, most likely written by a Jew.[1]

2. Mordecai's Work for the People (10:3)

[3]Mordecai the Jew was second in rank to King Xerxes, preeminent among the Jews, and held in high esteem by his many fellow Jews, because he worked for the good of his people and spoke up for the welfare of all the Jews.

10:3 Why was Mordecai so highly esteemed? Two reasons are mentioned. First, "he worked for the good of his people." He did not think only of his own advancement or even of his own family. Second, he "spoke up for the welfare of all the Jews." Many times it is dangerous to "speak up" in the midst of a hostile environment. God needs servants today who will speak up when his people are in danger or when injustice and corruption are rampant in society.

The book closes with a picture of peace and prosperity for the Jews. The author did not mention God even one time in the book. But it is evident that he wanted his readers to see God's hand in preserving the Jews. The Feast of Purim celebrates a historical event and has been repeated many times over two thousand years. Over that time period, the Jews have often been in danger of annihilation by their enemies, but God has "miraculously" preserved them. In many cases, for example the Holocaust, many Jews died while others were saved from such an end. God is still faithful to his promise to Abraham and his descendants: "I will bless those who bless you, and whoever curses you I will curse; and all peoples on earth will be blessed through you" (Gen 12:3). The challenge the Book of Esther presents is that we must recognize when our "time" has come to act (Esth 4:14). Upon such recognition we must immediately proceed in doing God's will, trusting in God's presence and favor.

There are few books of the Old Testament more relevant to life in a society hostile to the gospel. Believers are scattered throughout the world, awaiting the Lord's return. Although he is present and active now as much as ever, he is usually "hidden" behind the events of life that he is directing for his own glory and the benefit of his children. Although unbelievers can refuse to acknowledge him, those "who have eyes to see" are able to recognize his hand at work in the affairs of life. "In a world in which hostility to the household of faith seems to flourish naturally, and indeed in which atheistic explanations of the universe grow more strident, 'scientific' and apparently convincing, it belongs to faith to 'hold fast' *nevertheless* to our hope–now specifically in Christ–'for he who promised is faithful' (Heb. 10:23)."[2]

---

[1] C. Moore, *Esther,* AB (Garden City: Doubleday, 1971), 99.

[2] J. G. McConville, *Ezra, Nehemiah, and Esther,* DSB (Philadelphia: Westminster, 1985), 194.

Subject Index

Person Index

Selected Scripture Index